PLACE-NAME CHANGES SINCE 1900

A World Gazetteer

Compiled by

ADRIAN ROOM

The Scarecrow Press, Inc.
Metuchen, N.J. & London
1979

Library of Congress Cataloging in Publication Data

Room, Adrian.
  Place-name changes since 1900.

  Bibliography: p.
  1. Gazetteers.   I.   Title.
G103.5.R66   910'.3   79-4300
ISBN 0-8108-1210-X

CONTENTS

iii

INTRODUCTION

For many countries of the world, the first three-quarters of the 20th century have brought an era of change unparalleled in history. Hardly a single state has escaped the consequences of either a global war or a more limited conflict. In Russia and China two age-old imperial dynasties have been overthrown, and in Africa, more recently, colonial ties have been broken and new democratic or dictatorial regimes established.

A frequent result of an old order yielding, painfully or painlessly, to a new is a change of another kind. It is this change--the renaming of places in a particular country--that is the concern of the present Gazetteer, which aims to record many of the name changes that have taken place in the world since the beginning of the present century. Since the broad principle holds, that the more turbulent the history of a country, the more numerous are its renamings, it is self-evident that the name changes of some countries will be more fully represented than of others. There have simply been more to record.

The highest proportion of renamings will be found to be those of China and the USSR.

Since the last of the Chinese emperors abdicated in 1912, the history of the country has been both troubled and complex. First torn by civil wars, then split between Nationalists and Communists, China was eventually proclaimed a People's Republic in 1949. Political unrest during these nearly forty years was further aggravated by an open war with Japan. Even since 1949 the road to a "true" communism has been anything but smooth. Of the thousands of place-name changes during this period, only a small number can necessarily be represented here, and these are chiefly of the pre-

1949 era.   Chinese place names are, moreover, complex by nature:
county seats, for example, take their name with them when they are
transferred from one region to another.   Again, hundreds of places
have the same name, and very many have more than one name
simultaneously.

In spite of such a toponymic deterrent, a sizeable selection
of Chinese renamings have been included.

In the Soviet Union, where the swing of the political pendu-
lum from right to left has been even more dramatic, place-name
changes since the 1917 Revolution have been legion.   It has been es-
timated that of the total number of about 709,000 populated places in
the USSR probably as many as half have had their names changed in
some way since the revolution [see Peterson, p. 15, in the Bibli-
ography].   As a general policy, all religious, monarchical and eth-
nically undesirable names are out, although in some places a name
derived from a church or monastery has survived, as Arkhangelsk
(after the monastery of St. Michael the Archangel) and Blagoveshchensk (after the church of the Annunciation).

But specific reasons have increased the Soviet renamings con-
siderably.   One of these was the redistribution of territories and
frontiers in European Russia at the end of the Second World War.
As a result of the Potsdam Conference, for example, the northern
half of East Prussia was annexed by the USSR and reorganized as
the Kaliningrad Oblast of the RSFSR, with the consequent renaming
of over a thousand places.   Another major feature of Soviet topo-
nymics--the naming of places for party leaders and national heroes
--has resulted more than once in a vast rechristening program when
a particular individual has fallen from grace and has had to have
his name expunged from the map.   When Molotov, Malenkov and
Kaganovich were expelled from high office as members of an "anti-
party group" in July 1957, for instance, the many places named
after them all had to be found another appellation.   A few years
later, the same fate, in a more spectacular way, befell Stalin, so
that the thousands of places named for him, from the largest city
to the smallest street, had to be renamed.   Many of them were re-

named for Lenin in or around 1961 as the result of a decree by the
Supreme Soviet of the USSR, although one of the most famous places,
the city of Stalingrad, was renamed Volgograd (for the river), as of
course a Leningrad already existed. (Renamings of this kind are
not retrospective, so that Russians still talk of the Battle of Stalingrad.)

Thus Russian and Chinese renamings predominate in the Gazetteer.

In Algeria, meanwhile, the old French colonial names were
replaced by Arabic ones in or soon after 1962, and since then Portuguese names in Angola and Mozambique have mostly been replaced
by African ones.

It must not be thought, however, that political or military
motives are the only ones for a place-name change. In the United
States, for instance, many place-name changes have been made
quite peaceably as the result of territorial expansion and growth and
the "promotion" of various settlements. A good many American renamings occurred before 1900, in fact, so will not have been included in the Gazetteer. From one point of view this is a pity, as
there have been some record-breakers. Glen Ellen, for example,
now a residential suburb of Chicago, has been renamed no less than
seven times: initially Babcock's Grove (1833), after the first set-
tlers, it subsequently became DuPage Center (1834), Stacy's Corn-
ers (1835), Newton's Station (1849), Danby (1851) and Prospect Park
(1882) before finally acquiring its present name in 1889. Portland,
Maine, an older place, can claim a similar rollcall. Since its orig-
inal settling in 1632 it has been known as Machigonne, Indigreat,
Elbow, The Neck, Casco and Falmouth before eventually establishing
itself as Portland in 1786.

With such renamings the aim was usually quite simply to find
a better name, one that was more suitable or dignified or meaningful
or memorable.

There are many countries where names that have existed for
years, even centuries, have suddenly come to be regarded as un-
suitable on what might be termed esthetic grounds, and so have been

changed. France, for instance, renamed five of her departments
between 1941 and 1970. Three of the names contained the com-
ponent "Inférieure" and two had "Basses. " Although these simply
denoted the geographical location of the region--"lower, " by com-
parison with a department that was more northerly or elevated and
so "higher"--the names, it was felt, had another connotation, that
of "inferior" or "low. " But how base, how shameful! They were
therefore renamed with a more appropriate word, "Maritime" or
"Atlantique, " a purely seaside designation that can upset nobody.

     Where names can be translated like this, the motivation for
a renaming will frequently be found to be an esthetic, social or
linguistic undesirability. Many of the Russian renamings, in fact,
will be seen to be of this kind, and not politically motivated at all.
Thus in Belorussia Zagryazye ("dirty place") was renamed Bereznyanka ("birch trees"), Pyany Les ("drunken forest") was rechristened
Sosnovaya ("pine tree"), and Yazvy ("ulcers") became Vostochnaya
("eastern"). Away with the old and decadent, in with the new and
decent!

     By contrast, there are many countries in the world that have
had few or no renamings in the present century. Iceland, for example, has not had one place-name change since 1900. Even the
United Kingdom has had very few, in spite of the recent (1974) reorganization of local government in England and Wales and the re-
arrangement of many administrative areas. But the British are by
nature conservative, and if there are places in Britain called Swines-
head, Ugley, Nasty, Foul Hole, Greedy Gut and Boils--why, we're
proud of 'em, dammit!

DEFINITION
OF A NAME CHANGE

The renamings in the Gazetteer are, for the most part, those that have been officially decided. "For the most part" since certain renamings, although widely recognized and in general use, have not actually had governmental sanction. In Ireland, for instance, the five towns (strictly speaking, urban districts) Navan, Queenstown, Kells, Naas and Kingstown were all officially renamed, by local government act, prior to 1946 (see these places). King's County and Queen's County, however, were respectively renamed Offaly and Laoighis in 1920 without legal authority--yet who now calls these counties by their old names? The vast majority of renamings included here are, however, official ones, even if the naming authority is that of an occupying or invading power, as happened in Poland, for example, in the Second World War. (Ironically, many of the German names were reverting to ones that had existed some two centuries earlier. But that is another story.)

As has been mentioned, there are several motives for a place-name change. One frequent cause of a renaming is that of an official change of status of a place, usually an upgrading. When, for example, a village becomes a town or a town is promoted to a city, it acquires a new standing and the event may well be marked by the conferment of a new name of some kind. This new name may be a completely different one or simply a modification of the old one. Sometimes the name may <u>have</u> to change simply because of the country's native language structure. In the USSR, again, a village frequently acquires a different suffix when upgraded to an urban settlement, if only because of a change in grammatical gender--villages are feminine or neuter, while urban settlements and towns are masculine. Thus in 1941 the village of <u>Konstantinovskaya</u> (feminine) was upgraded to an urban settlement and renamed <u>Konstantinovsky</u> (masculine), and in 1967 it was further promoted to town status as <u>Konstantinovsk</u>. Such a renaming is not, therefore, merely a respelling or orthographical improvement but a necessary and meaningful alteration--indeed, a linguistically obligatory one.

Changes that are in fact purely alterations in spelling, as such, are on the whole not included in the Gazetteer, unless such a respelling is a radical one. Many of the renamings in India, for instance, that occurred after 1947 with the rise in nationalism, cannot be regarded as anything more than reformed spelling changes. For this reason changes of the type Adirampatnam to Adirampattinam and Kanauj to Kannauj are mostly excluded from the book.

Certain other categories of name change, real and apparent, do not figure in the Gazetteer. Among them are the following:

1 Alternative spellings, as Berkhamstead/Berkhamsted in England.

2 Alternative names in different languages, as French Trèves for German Trier, or the parallel names in Finnish and Swedish in Finland or in Flemish and French in Belgium.

3 New names arising as the result of administrative reorganization when the new territory does not correspond to the old, as the Welsh county of Gwynedd formed from the whole of Caernarvonshire and Anglesey, most of Merionethshire, and a small part of Denbighshire.

4 New names resulting from a simple amalgamation or merger, even where there is no change in territory area, as the new English county of Hereford and Worcester formed from he exact territory of the two former counties of Herefordshire and Worcestershire.

5 Temporary renamings, as those in Poland at the end of the Second World War, when, for instance, the German-named Wartenburg was temporarily Wartembork before becoming Barczewo, while Wartha became Warta for a while before settling as Bardo, and Berlinchen progressed to Barlinek via Berlinek. (Such language changes, for the purposes of the Gazetteer, count as genu-

ine renamings, not simply as respellings.   Many East European
renamings are along these lines).

6 Specialist or restricted renamings, as the renaming of a
town for the purposes of a military exercise, or the cant or jar-
gon renaming of a place by thieves or the "underworld. "   These
are not real renamings anyway, since they do not replace the
true name, which continues in normal use.

In the main, too, changes in the full official name or title
of a country, usually as the result of a political turnabout or possibly a coup are likewise not included.   Some exceptions are de-
liberately made for recent official renamings (post-1970), especially where an earlier change had occurred, as in Madagascar, or
where such a change also involved a change in the standard name of
the country, as in Kampuchea, formerly Cambodia.   Throughout the
Gazetteer, countries are thus normally referred to by their ordinary
names, as China, Egypt (not the People's Republic of China or the
Arab Republic of Egypt).   Here again certain exceptions are made
where ambiguity might arise, as with the People's Republic of the
Congo--formerly the Congo (Brazzaville)--which must be distinguished
from the former Congo (Kinshasa), now Zaïre.

Since, however, the full names of countries are used inter-
nationally as "standardized" names, as well as internally in official
documents, a list of the full names and titles of many countries in
the world is given in Appendix 1.

The fact that a place has been officially or by common con-
sensus renamed in a particular year does not necessarily mean, of
course, that the new name will instantly or even quickly gain general acceptance.   There are thus many people who still think of Sri
Lanka as Ceylon.   There are those, indeed, who will argue that
since Sri is simply a title meaning blessed or holy, and that Lanka
is not a new name but one that has long been in local use anyway,
Ceylon has not in effect been renamed at all!   The same argument
can be made for Iran (alias Persia) and Thailand (otherwise Siam).
But many sources do regard such name changes as official, and
they therefore find their place in the book.

Habit dies hard, though, and not everyone is willing or interested enough to call a renamed place by its new name. Even today, thirty years and more after the end of the Second World War, the British Post Office Guide (August 1978, p. 299) still feels it necessary, in the section dealing with mailings to Poland, to include the reminder, "The place name DANZIG should not be used; the correct form of address for this place is GDANSK."

Many former names, in fact, officially live on, however paradoxically, since in some very large countries, such as the United States, Canada and the Soviet Union, the old names still apply to the objects to which they were originally given: post offices and railway stations. It was the setting up of such important communications centers that in many cases led to the expansion of a nearby settlement, which was often subsequently renamed. That is to say, the post office or station, when constructed, took the name of a nearby settlement and retained it, even after the populated place had assumed a new name. (This in turn, of course, could often result in the assumption by the post office or station of the new name of the flourishing community, if only to avoid confusion. Having indirectly caused the name change, by improving the place's communications, it must now follow suit!)

ARRANGEMENT
OF THE ENTRIES

The main entries and the cross-references run continuously in alphabetical order.

Of any given place, each main entry will normally give five pieces of information, viz., ① present name, ② identification, ③ location, ④ former name or names, ⑤ year or years of renaming. Thus, in the entry

  ①   ②   ③   ④   ⑤

Daniels. Village, Maryland, USA : Alberton (-1940)

the information given is that a village called Daniels in the state of Maryland, in the United States, was until 1940 called Alberton. To take each point separately:

① PRESENT NAME

The normal or conventional name of the place in English or relevant foreign language is given, with diacritics (accents) as necessary for names in European languages. The spelling of the name is either that as given in Webster's New Geographical Dictionary or, if not entered there, as given in the Columbia-Lippincott World Gazetteer. Places in neither volume are spelled as given in the source where found, which in most cases is one of the works listed in the Bibliography. For many Chinese names alternative spellings are given in square brackets: there are the ones given in the Columbia-Lippincott work. Russian names present a special problem, since there are different ways of transliterating them. The town entered in this Gazetteer as Gorky, for example, can elsewhere be found as Gor'kiy, Gorkiy, Gor'kij or Gorkij. The most appropriate thing here seems to be a transliteration system that is both simple,

xiii

widely used and reasonably accurate. A simplified system is therefore employed, details of which are given in Appendix 3. The system is based closely on that used, in fact, by the <u>Encyclopaedia
Britannica.</u>

Places with exactly identical spelling are numbered (1), (2),
etc. in the alphabetical order of their former name, or earliest
former name, if there are more than one.

A place having part of its name in parentheses, as Krosno
(Ordzanskie), means that the parenthesized part is a defining or
mainly optional element. The alphabetical order for such names
ignores the brackets, so that (Ilirska) Bistrica will be found under
I, not B.

② IDENTIFICATION[1]

Each place is followed by a describer which states whether it
is a natural geographical object, as a mountain, river, island, etc.,
or a "manmade" one, as a village, town, province and the like.
The vast majority of places in the Gazetteer are populated places of
this latter kind, and here the describer indicates the status, as far
as it can be established, of the place concerned, that is, "township," "urban settlement," "city," and the like. This status is the
one accorded the place by the relevant authority and the current
one. Allowances must be made here for official administrative
terminology: what may be a "city" in one country may be only a
"village" in another. This accounts for the high proportion of
"cities" in Brazil, for example--and the complete absence of them
in the USSR.

In populated places in the Soviet Union, a common status is
that of an "urban settlement." Such a place, more accurately a

---

[1]It is the very nature of things that geographical information dates
rapidly; it is not only possible but certain that the status of a place
as given in the Gazetteer will in some cases be outdated. This is
particularly true of rapidly expanding places in East Europe, China
and Africa. Though such unavoidably obsolete information is of
course regretted, the name change of the place will be accurate
enough, and that is, after all, the prime objective of the book.

"settlement of town type," is in size and standing midway between
a village and a town, with at least 2000 inhabitants. Russian
"towns" are generally larger and more important than urban settlements, many meriting what in other countries would be the status
of a city. Thus a typical Soviet promotion pattern for an inhabited
place is village to urban settlement to town.

Where the identity of a place is quite clear from its name
alone, as Acadia National Park, there will be no need for a describer, although in a few cases of possible ambiguity--is Coos Bay
a bay or a city?--the nature of the place will be given.

③ LOCATION

The location of a place is fixed in one of two ways: either
by a point of the compass, using additionally the word "central"--
as "northern," "southwestern," "east-central" and the like--or by
naming the administrative region in which the place is situated.
Geographical (i.e., compass-point) locations are used mainly for
non-English-speaking countries, whereas administrative regions are
used for English-speaking ones, since on the whole they will be well
enough known. One notable exception to this is for the USSR,
where the sheer size of the country--it is the largest in the world
--dictates a more precise location than an approximate compass
bearing. For places in the Soviet Union, therefore, the basic administrative region is given in the relevant Soviet socialist republic.[1] In many cases this is an oblast. In some republics, however, there are no oblasts, while in others there are both oblasts
and other kinds of administrative region. To assist the user of the
Gazetteer in finding his way around the USSR, therefore, a break-
down of the various territorial and administrative units of the country is given, with all their names, in Appendix 2.

For English-speaking countries, the location of places is
given by administrative regions as follows: by state in the United

[1]Throughout the Gazetteer, the abbreviation "SSR" is used for Soviet Socialist Republic; also used is "RSFSR" for Russian Soviet
Federated Socialist Republic.

States, by province or territory in Canada, by county in the United
Kingdom and Ireland, by state or territory in Australia, and by
province in South Africa. Places in New Zealand are located as
being in North Island, South Island, or on one of the lesser
islands.

Where a country has a large number of islands as an integral
part of its territory, as Greece or Japan, a place will be located
on a particular island in a particular island group. Further, if the
island is sizeable or important, as Honshu, Hokkaido, Shikoku and
Kyushu (Japan) or Sicily (Italy), a compass-point location will additionally be given. In the Philippines location is given by province
rather than individual island.

Places in India and China are fixed by geographical location
rather than by state or province, in spite of the size of these countries, as it is felt this will be sufficient for the purposes of most
users of the Gazetteer. India, after all, has 21 states and eight
union territories and China 22 provinces and four autonomous regions: would it be more meaningful to locate a place in Manipur or
Mizoram, or Shansi or Shensi? For all except experts and geographical wizards, probably not! The exact location of such places can
always, of course, be determined by means of a detailed gazetteer
or large-scale atlas.

Sometimes a place may extend over the territory of two ad-
joining regions, or be shared by them. In such cases--where the
location is being fixed administratively--the names of both regions,
countries, etc. will be given divided by a virgule (/), such as
"Arkansas/Oklahoma" or "Uganda/Zaïre. "

④ FORMER NAME(S)

The former name of a place is given, as is the present one,
in the accepted standard English or foreign spelling, with the same
provisions for the transliteration of Russian names. In a few cases,
a non-English version of a name may be given if it is virtually as
familiar as the English one, so that Moyen Congo is given, for example, as well as Middle Congo for the former (French) name of

the People's Republic of the Congo.   If there has been more than one naming since 1900, the former names are given in chronological order.   Where a place formerly belonged, with a different name, to another country, this country will be given at the very end of the entry, after the year of renaming.   For examples of this, see the names of places now in the Kaliningrad Oblast of the RSFSR, where after the year of renaming (mostly 1945 or 1946) comes "Germany." (Strictly speaking, the places were in Prussia, but Germany, of which Prussia was a state, is given since it denotes both the nationality and language of the former name.)   Indications of former nationality are not normally given when the occupying or possessing country was acting in a colonial capacity, as France was, say, with regard to Algeria, or Italy with regard to Ethiopia.

Alternative former names appear in square brackets as they do for present names.

⑤ YEAR(S) OF RENAMING

Where the year of renaming has been established, it is given following the former name.   Since the Gazetteer deals only with name changes that have occurred since 1900 (inclusive), no indication will normally be given of any name change before then or of how long a former name was in use before 1900.   Thus the common form "(-1938)" means that the former name was in use at least from 1900 to 1938 and possibly for some time before 1900.   In some cases, however, a year before 1900 is given.   Such a year--which will in turn never be earlier than 1800--applies when a new name reverted to one used in the 19th century.   See, for example, Bethpage, which name was in use both from 1936 and earlier, until 1841. [1]

In several cases it has not been possible to determine precisely the year of renaming.   In such cases either an approximation

---

[1]Many places reverted to names used longer ago than 1800; one example is Wrocław, in Poland, which in 1741 fell to Prussia and was renamed Breslau, a name it was to keep until 1945 when it reverted to Wrocław.   The history of many other Polish place names is similar.   Chinese names, too, have reverted and re-reverted over the centuries.

is given, as "(-early 1920s), " or the abbreviation "c. " (Latin circa, "about"). With a small number of places it has not been possible to fix the renaming year at all, and in such cases a question mark is given in place of the year.

If a year is not preceded by a hyphen, as "(1924), " the name before it was in use only for the one year, or at some time during that year.

A year given at the end of an entry after the name of a country means that the year of acquisition or annexation of the place by that country was different from the year of renaming. For example, in the entry "Chekhov (2). Town, Sakhalin Oblast, RSFSR : Noda (1905-47), Japan (-1945), " the years indicate that Chekhov was called Noda from 1905 to 1947 but that the place passed back to the USSR from Japan two years before this, in 1945--that is, the place bore its Japanese name for two years as a Russian town.

SYMBOLS

The two symbols, asterisk (*) and dagger (†), need an explanation.

An asterisk before a year indicates that the name then came into use for the first time. This may have been because the place was newly settled or built, first discovered then, or administratively reorganized in this year, perhaps by an amalgamation. Thus the town of Ayaguz first arose in 1931, as a settlement for workers on a new railway, with the name Sergiopol.

Where a place is now no longer in existence, its name is followed by a dagger to indicate its demise. In some such cases the year when a place ceased to exist administratively is also given, as: Izmail Oblast (1954†).

CROSS-REFERENCES

Every former name is cross-referenced to its present or

last existing name with the notation "see"; for example, "Kribi <u>see</u> Ocean. " Former variant spellings are similarly cross-referenced. [1] Present variant spellings cross-refer to a more common or conventional spelling of the name by means of an equal sign (=), such as "Hsi-chi = Sichi. " This means that all alternative names in square brackets will cross-refer to the name that heads an entry. Many of these alternatives are of Chinese names, and here it should be noted that where the letters, but not the punctuation marks used conventionally (apostrophe and hyphen), correspond exactly in both names, there will be no cross-reference. Thus alongside Changshun appears the alternative rendering Ch'ang-shun, but this second version of the name will not separately cross-refer to the first since both are spelled identically.

Where the former name is identical for more than one present name, the cross-reference enumerates the new names in alphabetical order, such as "Hochow <u>see</u> (1) Hochwan [Ho-ch'uan]; (2) Hohsien; (3) Linsia [Lin-hsia]. "

A former name cross-referring to a present name followed by a number means that the present name is shared by more than one place, such as "Kruglyakov <u>see</u> Oktyabrsky (5)"--that is, see the Oktyabrsky entry numbered (5). [2]

---

[1]In a very few instances an alternative spelling of a former name will cross-refer to a new name where it will not be repeated. This applies notably to spellings sometimes used by English speakers for six well-known Russian towns. According to the transliteration system used in the Gazetteer (and elsewhere) the names of these towns more correctly begin with Ye-. Some people, however, know them better with an initial E-. The towns cross-referenced with this spelling are Ekaterinburg, Ekaterinenstadt, Ekaterinodar, Ekaterinoslav, Elizavetgrad and Elizavetpol. They are of course normally cross-referenced also under Yekaterinburg, etc.

[2]Thus numbers need distinguishing both before and after a name. Occasionally extra care is needed, as in the cross-reference "Kirova, imeni <u>see</u> (1) Bank; (2) Kirovo (1), (2); (3) Kirovsk (2), " which means that a place now called Bank, two places called Kirovo and another place--number 2 of that name in the present Gazetteer--called Kirovsk were all once called imeni Kirova. (The Russian word <u>imeni</u> means "named after" and, in the Gazetteer headings, is preceded by the name element.)

ACKNOWLEDGMENTS

Much of the material for this Gazetteer was obtained from books such as those listed in the Bibliography. There were many individuals, however, who were helpful in many ways, and to such persons I here and now express my considerable gratitude. Without their assistance the Gazetteer would be a far poorer and thinner book.

An initial task when planning the work was to approach virtually every embassy, consulate and high commission in London for information regarding place-name changes in the relevant country, and to request sources. Many such bodies replied, although few were able to offer much practical help. A number offered an address, usually a government office, in their own country. All such contacts were taken up, but again, not every approach met with success. Some simply failed to reply at all.

In the face of a decidedly mixed response, therefore, it does not seem in the least invidious to single out those bodies and their representatives who were not merely useful but positively and generously helpful, both in London and overseas. Such were Miss L. Compton of the Australian High Commission; Miss Thelma Archer-McKenzie of the Barbados Board of Tourism; Mr. Alan Rayburn, Executive Secretary of the Geographical Names Secretariat, Canada, and Mr. W. B. Yeo, Head of Toponymy Research there; Mme. Perrine Ramin-Canavaggio of the Mission des Archives Nationales, Ministère de l'Intérieur, Paris; Mr. G. Papapavlou of the Greek Embassy; Ms. Jennifer Gill of the Ministry of Information, Guyana; Miss L. Travis of the High Commission of India; Mr. Art Ó Maolfabhail, Assistant Director of the Ordnance Survey Office, Dublin, and Miss D. Coughlan of the Irish Embassy; Dr. P. E. Raper,

President of the South Africa Centre of Onomastics, Human Sciences
Research Council, Pretoria, who was constantly of assistance; Sr.
Francisco Vázquez-Maure of the Comisión Española de Nombres
Geográficos, Madrid; and Donald J. Orth, Executive Secretary,
Domestic Geographic Names, United States Board on Geographic
Names, Washington, D. C.

I also express my personal thanks to my aunt, Mrs. Margaret Millar, of Bandar Seri Begawan, Brunei, for researching and
dispatching important facts and figures relating to place-name changes
in Indonesia.

Apart from diplomatic and government staff, one person in
particular has been especially helpful throughout the compilation of
the Gazetteer, and has contributed significantly towards the end
product. This is Mr. P. J. M. Geelan, of the Permanent Commit-
tee on Geographical Names at the Royal Geographical Society, London. Together, he and his colleague P. J. Woodman have generously devoted time and energy on my behalf to the tracking down of
names and dates in the enviably numerous sources at their disposal.
They were particularly helpful with name changes in Algeria, Angola,
Hungary and Mozambique. I am very grateful to them, and hope
that this present Gazetteer, although modest in scope, may in some
way repay them for their services and prove an acceptable addition
to their reference shelves.

Help was obviously welcome for the translation of material in
foreign languages and here I owe thanks to Mr. A. H. Tomlin of
Stamford, England, for translating a large section of a register of
names in Greek, and for similar assistance over a work in Hungarian to Mrs. F. A. Benton of Melton Mowbray, England.

Several good ladies helped in the mechanics of compiling the
Gazetteer. Lesley Brooks (now Mrs. Bennett) typed out all the
record cards, Nicola Village sorted, alphabetized and cross-checked
them, and Mrs. Joyce Watson typed out the final manuscript. In
addition Mrs. Hazel Nichols stepped in at a time when I was especially busy to help hunt for name changes in the 2148 pages of the
Columbia-Lippincott World Gazetteer. In London, meantime, Linda

Dalling cheerfully put up with a number of frustrations and no small amount of red tape to obtain up-to-date material from embassies and public bodies. My sincere thanks to them all.

      The Gazetteer is something of a pioneer venture, and as such can obviously be improved upon. It is intended that a subsequent edition will not only be more comprehensive but that a number of the date queries in the present edition will have been eliminated. New name changes between now and then will of course also be entered. Meanwhile the author will be grateful if any errors or inaccuracies in the book could be reported to him, quoting the appropriate source. In the United States and Canada comments can be sent him care of the publisher; in the United Kingdom they can be sent direct to him at his home address: 5, Sunny Bank, East Street, Stamford, Lincolnshire PE9 1QG.

Adrian Room
December, 1978

Abakan. Capital of Khakass
Autonomous Oblast, Kras-
noyarsk Kray, RSFSR : Ust-
Abakanskoye (-1931)
Abakanskoye see Krasnoturansk
Abakumova see Dzhansugurov
Abay (1). Village, Chimkent
Oblast, Kazakh SSR : Abay-
Bazar (-c. 1960)
Abay (2). Town, Karaganda
Oblast, Kazakh SSR :
Churubay-Nura (-1961)
Abay see Karaaul
Abay-Bazar see Abay (1)
Abbazia see Opatija
Åbenrå. City, southeastern
Denmark : Apenrade (-1920),
Germany
Abercorn see Mbala
Ablan. Barrio, Ilocos Norte,
Philippines : Barat (-1969)
Ableman see Rock Springs
Abolição. Town, southern
Brazil, South America :
Patrocínio
Abovyan. Town, Armenian
SSR : Elar (-1963)
Acadia National Park. Maine,
USA : Sieur de Monts Na-
tional Monument (*1916-19),
Lafayette National Park
(1919-29)
Achalpur. Town, central In-
dia : Dadra (-1966)
Acheng [A-ch'eng]. Town,
northeastern China : Ashihho
(-1909)
Achkoy-Martan. Village,
Checheno-Ingush Autonomous
SSR, RSFSR : Novoselskoye
(1944-c. 1965)
Acul see Vidin

Adelphi see Westwold
Ademi see Adimi
Adernò see Adrano
Adimi. Urban settlement, Pri-
morsky Kray, RSFSR : Ademi
(-c. 1940)
Adrano. Town, eastern Sicily,
Italy : Adernò (-1929)
Adygey Autonomous Oblast.
Krasnodar Kray, RSFSR :
Cherkess (Adygey) Autonomous
Oblast (*1922), Adygey (Cher-
kess) Autonomous Oblast
(1922-36)
Adygey (Cherkess) Autonomous
Oblast see Adygey Auton-
omous Oblast
Adygeysk see Teuchezhsk
Adyk. Settlement, Kalmyk Au-
tonomous SSR, RSFSR :
Yuzhny (-c. 1960)
Adzhibakul see Kazi-Magomed
Afars and Issas see Djibouti
Affreville see Khemis Miliana
Afonso Pena see Conceição do
Almeida
Agbulakh see Tetri-Tskaro
Aggelóna. Village, southern
Greece : Agkylóna (-1960s)
Agkylona see Aggelona
Agnessa see Shokalsky
Agnew. Railway point, Manitoba,
Canada : Monda (-1905)
Agram see Zagreb
Agrigento. Province and its cap-
ital, southern Sicily, Italy :
Grigenti (-1927)
Aichow [Yaichow] see Aihsien
Aiga. Town, southern Honshu,
Japan : Oka (-1934)
Aigrefeuille see Aigrefeuille-
sur-Maine

1

Aigrefeuille-sur-Maine. Village, western France :
Aigrefeuille (-1934)

Aihsien. Town, southeastern China: Aichow [Yaichow] (-1912)

Aïn Benian. Town, northern Algeria, northern Africa : Guyotville (-c. 1962)

Aïn Berda. Village, northeastern Algeria, northern Africa : Penthièvre (-c. 1962)

Aïn Defla. Village, northern Algeria, northern Africa : Duperré (-c. 1962)

Aïn el Hammam. Village, northern Algeria, northern Africa : Michelet (-c. 1962)

Aïn el Kebira. Village, northeastern Algeria, northern Africa : Perigotville (-c. 1962)

Aïn Mokra see Berrahal

Aïn Oulmene. Village, northeastern Algeria, northern Africa : Colbert (-c. 1962)

Aïntab see Gaziantep

Aïn Touta. Town, northeastern Algeria, northern Africa : MacMahon (-c. 1962)

Aiud. Town, west-central Romania : Strassburg (-c. 1939), Germany

Akchi-Karasu see Toktogul

Akhali-Afoni see Novy Afon

Akhalkhevi. Village, Georgian SSR : Itum-Kale (-1944)

Akhangaran. River, Tashkent Oblast, Uzbek SSR : Angren (-c. 1960)

Akhigria see Icaria

Akhouria Vavouríou see Platános

Akhta see Razdan (1)

Akhtala. Urban settlement, Armenian SSR : Nizhnyaya Akhtala (-1939)

Akhunbabayev. Town, Andizhan Oblast, Uzbek SSR : Sufikishlak (-1975)

Akhuryan. Village, Armenian SSR : Duzkend (-1945)

Akkerman see Belgorod-Dnestrovsky

Akkerman Oblast see Izmail Oblast

Akmal-Abad see Gizhduvan

Akmangit see Belolesye

Ak-Mechet see (1) Chernomorskoye, (2) Kzyl-Orda

Akmolinsk see Tselinograd

Akmolinsk Oblast see Tselinograd Oblast

Akow see Pingtung [P'ing-tung]

Akrolímne. Village, northern Greece : Gymná (-1960s)

Aksay. Town, Uralsk Oblast, Kazakh SSR : Kazakhstan (-1967)

Ak-Sheikh see Razdolnoye

Aktam. Village, Osh Oblast, Kirgiz SSR : Chanach (-c. 1960)

Aktau see Shevchenko

Alagoa de Baixo see Sertânia

Alagoa Nova. City, northeastern Brazil, South America : Laranjeiras (1939-43)

Alagoas see Marechal Deodoro

Alagyoz see Aragats

Alaid see Atlasova

Alais see Alès

Al-Anbar. Province, western Iraq : Al-Dilame (-1971)

Alanskoye. Village, North Ossetian Autonomous SSR, RSFSR : Psedakh (-1944)

Alawiya see Latakia

Alba Iulia. City, west-central Romania : Weissenburg (-?) Germany, Karlsburg (?-c. 1918), Germany

Albalat de Segart see Albalat de Taronchers

Albalat de Taronchers. Village, eastern Spain : Albalat de Segart (-1949)

Albany. City, California, USA : Ocean View (1908-09)

Albat see Kuybyshevo (1)

Albert, Lake see Mobutu Sese Seko, Lake

Albert-Edward, Lake see Idi Amin Dada, Lake

Albertinia. Town, Cape of Good Hope, South Africa : Riversdale (-1904)

Albert National Park see Vir-

unga National Park
Alberton. Town, Transvaal,
South Africa : Elandsfontein
(-1904)
Alberton see Daniels
Albertville see Kalemi
Albor see Libyo
Alchevsk see Kommunarsk
Alcobaça see Tucuruí
Aldan. Town, Yakutsk Au-
tonomous SSR, RSFSR :
Nezametny (-1939)
Aldea del Rey see Aldea
Real
Aldea Real. Village, north-
central Spain : Aldea del
Rey (-c. 1920)
Al-Dilame see Al-Anbar
Alejandro Selkirk. Island, Juan
Fernandez group, Chile,
South America : Más Afuera
(-1962), Piloto Juan Fernan-
dez (1962-66)
Aleksandropol see Leninakan
Aleksandrov Dar see Rakh-
manovka
Aleksandrovka see (1) Loz-
no-Aleksandrovka; (2) Ord-
zhonikidze (1)
Aleksandrovsk. Town, Perm
Oblast, RSFSR : Aleksan-
drovsky (-1951)
Aleksandrovsk see (1) Belo-
gorsk (1); (2) Polyarny;
(3) Zaporozhye
Aleksandrovsk-Grushevsky see
Shakhty
Aleksandrovsk Guberniya =
Zaporozhye Guberniya
Aleksandrovskoye see Kirov-
skoye (1)
Aleksandrovsk-Sakhalinsky.
Town, Sakhalin Oblast,
RSFSR : Aleksandrovsky
Post (-1926)
Aleksandrovsky see Alek-
sandrovsk
Aleksandrovsky Post see
Aleksandrovsk-Sakhalinsky
Alekseyevsk see Svobodny
Alekseyevskoye see Lenin-
skoye (1)
Alès. Town, southeastern

France : Alais (-1926)
Alexandria see Arlington
Alexandroúpolis. City, north-
eastern Greece : Dedeagaç
(-1919), Turkey
Alfredo Chaves see Veranopolis
Al-Hawtah see Lahij
Al-Hoceima. Town and province,
northern Morocco, northwest-
ern Africa : Villa Sanjurjo
(*1926-c. 1958)
Aliabad see Shahi
Ali Butus see Slavjanka
Alice Springs. Town, Northern
Territory, Australia : Stuart
(-1933)
Alija del Infantado. Village,
northwestern Spain : Alija de
los Melones (c. -1960)
Alija de los Melones see Alija
del Infantado
Al-Ittihad see Madinal ash-
Sha'b
Alkatvaam. Village, Magadan
Oblast, RSFSR : Valkatlen
(-c. 1960)
Al-Khalil see Hebron
Allenburg see Druzhba (1)
Allenstein see Olsztyn
Alleroi see Shuragat
Alma. City, Quebec, Can-
ada : Saint-Joseph-d'Alma
(-1954)
Alma-Ata. Capital of Kazakh
SSR : Verny (-1921)
Almalii see Yabalkovo
Al-Marj. Town, northern Libya,
northern Africa : Barce (-?)
Almazar. Urban settlement,
Tashkent Oblast, Uzbek SSR :
Vrevsky (-1963)
Almenara. City, southeastern
Brazil, South America :
Vigia (-1944)
Almeria see Kawayan
Al-Muntafak see Dhi Qar
Alouette Lake. Lake, British
Columbia, Canada : Lillooet
Lake (-1914)
Alpargatal see Vicente Noble
Alpes-de-Haute-Provence. De-
partment, southeastern France
: Basses-Alpes (-1970)

Alpicat. Village, northeastern Spain : Villanueva de Alpicat (-c. 1950)

Al-Qadisiya. Province, south-central Iraq : Diwaniya (-1971)

Alsoközpont see Mórahalom

Alsoszentgyörgy see Jászal-sószentgyörgy

Al-Tamin. Province, north-eastern Iraq : Kirkuk (-1971)

Altamirano. City, southwestern Mexico, North America : Pungarabato (-1936)

Altdamm see Dabie

Altentreptow. Town, northern West Germany : Treptow (an der Tollense) (-1940s)

Alt Gaarz see Rerik

Altofonte. Village, northern Sicily, Italy : Parco (-1931)

Alto Parnaíba. City, north-eastern Brazil, South America : Vitória do Alto Parnaíba (-1944)

Altsohl see Zvolen

Alvarães. Town, northwestern Brazil, South America : Caiçara (-1944)

Alyoshki see Tsyurupinsk

Amamlu see Spitak

Amangeldy. Village, Kustanay Oblast, Kazakh SSR : Batbak-kara (-1936)

Amapari see Ferreira Gomes

Amara see Maysan

Amarração see Luís Correia

Amasiya. Village, Armenian SSR : Gukasyan (-c. 1960)

Amatitlán. Town, southeastern Mexico, North America : Amatlán (-1938)

Amatlán see Amatitlán

Ambarica see Levski

Ambleside see Hahndorf

Ambridge. Town, Pennsylvania, USA : Economy (-1906)

Ambrolauri. Town, Georgian SSR : Yenukidze (-mid-1930s)

Americana. City, southeastern Brazil, South America : Villa Americana (-1938)

Amerika see (1) Nakhodka; (2) Sovetskaya (1)

Amherst see Kyaikkami

Ami see Kaiyüan [K'ai-yüan]

Amlan. Municipality, Negros Oriental, Philippines : New Ayuquitan (-1950)

Amu-Darya. Urban settlement, Chardzhou Oblast, Turkmen SSR : Samsonovo (-1962)

Amursk. Urban settlement, Khabarovsk Kray, RSFSR : Padali (-1958)

Amvrosiyevka. Town, Donetsk Oblast, Ukrainian SSR : Donetsko-Amvrosiyevka (-c. 1955)

Anacetaba. City, northeastern Brazil, South America : São Gonçalo (-1944)

Anadyr. Capital of Chukot Auto-nomous Okrug, Magadan Oblast, RSFSR : Novo-Mariinsk (-1920)

Analândia. City, southeastern Brazil, South America : Aná-polis (-1944)

Analostan Island see Theodore Roosevelt Island

Ananyevo. Village, Issyk-Kul Oblast, Kirgiz SSR : Sazanovka (-1942)

Anao-aon see San Francisco (1)

Anapolis see (1) Analândia; (2) Simão Dias

Anchieta see Piatã

An-ch'ing = Anking

Andirá. City, southern Brazil, South America : Ingá (-1944)

Andreyev see Jędrzejów

Andreyevsk see Tezebazar

Andreyevskoye see Dneprovskoye

Anfu see Linli

Angaco Norte. Town, western Argentina, South America : Kilómetro 924 (-?)

An Geata Mór. Town, County Mayo, Ireland : Binghamstown (-?)

Angel Albino Corzo see Jalte-nango

Angerapp see Ozyorsk

Angerburg see Węgorzewo

Anglo-Egyptian Sudan see Sudan

Angoche. City, eastern Mozam-bique, southeastern Africa : Vila António Enes (-1970),

António Enes (1970-76)
Angola. Republic, southwestern
Africa : Portuguese West
Africa (-1951)
Angora see Ankara
Angren see Akhangaran
Angshui see Sansui
Angus (1975†). County, eastern
Scotland, UK : Forfarshire
(-1928)
Anhwa see (1) Ipeh [Ipei],
(2) Tehkiang [Te-chiang]
Aniva. Town, Sakhalin Oblast,
RSFSR : Rudaka (1905-46),
Japan (-1945)
Anjen see Yükiang [Yü-chiang]
Ankang [An-k'ang]. Town, cen-
tral China : Hingan (-1913)
Ankara. Capital of Turkey :
Angora (-1930)
Ankhialo see Pomoriye
Anking [An-ch'ing]. City, eastern
China : Hwaining [Huai-ning]
(1911-49)
An-kuo = Ankwo
Ankwo [An-kuo]. Town, north-
eastern China : Chichow
(-1914)
Anlu. Town, northeastern
China : Teian (-1912)
Anlu see Chungsiang [Chung-
hsiang]
Anlung. Town, southern China :
Hingi (-1913) : Nanlung (1913-
31)
Annaba. Port, northeastern
Algeria, northern Africa :
Bône (-c. 1962)
Annenfeld see Shamkhor
Annino see Shamkhor
Annobón see Pagalu
Ano Exántheia see Exántheia
Ano Leukímme. Village, Corfu,
Greece : Riggládes (-1960s)
Anpeh [Anpei]. Town, northern
China : Tashetai (-1925)
Anpei = Anpeh
Anping see Makwan [Makuan]
Ansu see Süshui [Hsü-shui]
Antananarivu. Capital of Demo-
cratic Republic of Madagascar,
southeastern Africa : Tanana-
rive (1895-1976)

Antarctic Peninsula. Region of
Antarctica : Graham Land,
Palmer Peninsula, O'Higgins
Land, San Martín Land (-1961)
Antatet see Luna (1)
Anting see (1) Changtze [Ch'ang-
tzu]; (2) Tingsi [Ting-hsi]
Antipolo. Barrio, Marinduque,
Philippines : Hinubuan (-1957)
António Enes see Angoche
Antono-Kodintsevo see Komin-
ternovskoye
Antratsit. Town, Voroshilovgrad
Oblast, Ukrainian SSR : Bokovo-
Antratsit (-1962)
Antrea see Kamennogorsk
An-tse = Antseh
Antseh [An-tse]. Town, central
China : Yoyang (-1914)
Antung see Lienshui
Antze [An-tz'u]. Town, north-
eastern China : Tungan (-1914)
An-tz'u = Antze
An Uaimh see Navan
Anyang. City, north-central
China : Ch'ang-te (-1913)
Anzaldo. Town, central Bolivia,
South America : Paredón (-1900s)
Anzeba see Chekanovsky
Aparados da Serra. City, southern
Brazil, South America : Bom
Jesus (-1944)
Aparecida see Bertolínia
Apeírathos. Village, Naxos,
Cyclades Islands, Greece :
Apýranthos (-1960s)
Apenrade see Åbenrå
Appila. Town, South Australia,
Australia : Yarowie (-1941)
Aprelsk. Urban settlement,
Irkutsk Oblast, RSFSR :
Nadezhdinsky Priisk (-1925)
Apsheronsk. Town, Krasnodar
Kray, RSFSR : Apsheronskaya
(-1947)
Apsheronskaya see Apsheronsk
Apuania see Massa-Carrara
Apýranthos see Apeírathos
Arabistan see Khuzestan
Arab Republic of Egypt [Egypt].
Republic, northeastern Africa :
Egypt (-1958), United Arab
Republic (1958-71) [jointly with

Syria 1958-61]
Araçá see Mari
Araceli. Municipality, Palawan, Philippines : Dumaran (-1954)
Araçoiaba da Serra. City, southeastern Brazil, South America : Campo Largo (-1944)
Aracruz. City, southeastern Brazil, South America : Santa Cruz (-1944)
Aragats. Urban settlement, Armenian SSR : Alagyoz (-c. 1955)
Araguacema. City, north-central Brazil, South America : Santa Maria do Araguaia (-1944)
Araguaçu see Paraguaçu Paulista
Araguatins. City, north-central Brazil, South America : São Vicente (-1944)
Araíporanga. City, northeastern Brazil, South America : São Jerônimo (-1944)
Arak. City, west-central Iran : Sultanabad (-mid-1930s)
Aral see Kuybyshevsky (1)
Aranyosmarót see Zlaté Moravce
Araquari. City, southern Brazil, South America : Parati (-1944)
Araripina. City, northeastern Brazil, South America : São Gonçalo (-1944)
Arariúna. City, northern Brazil, South America : Cachoeira (-1944)
Araticu. City, northern Brazil, South America : Oeiras (-1944)
Arborea. Village, western Sardinia, Italy : Villaggio Mussolini (-c. 1935), Mussolinia di Sardegna (c. 1935-c. 1944)
Arcangel. Barrio, Ilocos Norte, Philippines : Santo Tomas (-1971)
Arcoverde. City, northeastern Brazil, South America : Rio Branco (-1944)

Ardino. Village, southern Bulgaria : Yegri-Dere (-1934)
Area see Mundelein
Areia see Ubaíra
Arensburg see Kingisepp (1)
Argenta see North Little Rock
Arkansas National Forest see Ouachita National Forest
Arkhaíai Kleonaí. Village, southern Greece : Kontóstablos (-1960s)
Arkhangelo-Pashisky Zavod see Pashiya
Arkhangelskoye. Village, Bashkir Autonomous SSR, RSFSR : Arkhangelsky Zavod (-c. 1930)
Arkhangelsky Zavod see Arkhangelskoye
Arktichesky. Cape, Komsomolets Island, Severnaya Zemlya, Krasnoyarsk Kray, RSFSR : Molotov (?-c. 1957)
Arlington. County, Virginia, USA : Alexandria (-1920)
Arnswalde see Choszczno
Arroyo de la Luz. Village, western Spain : Arroyo del Puerco (-c. 1940)
Arroyo del Puerco see Arroyo de la Luz
Arsenyev. Town, Primorsky Kray, RSFSR : Semyonovka (-1953)
Artashat. Town, Armenian SSR : Kamarlu (-c. 1955)
Artesia. City, New Mexico, USA : Stegman (-1905)
Arti. Urban settlement, Sverdlovsk Oblast, RSFSR : Artinsky Zavod (-1929)
Artigas. City, northwestern Uruguay, South America : San Eugenio (-1930s)
Artigas see Río Branco
Artinsky Zavod see Arti
Artsiz. Town, Odessa Oblast, Ukrainian SSR : Artsyz (1940-44)
Artsyz see Artsiz
Artyoma, imeni. Suburb of Krivoy Rog, Dnepropetrovsk Oblast, Ukrainian SSR : Galkovsky Rudnik (-c. 1926), Artyomovsky Rudnik (c. 1926-?)

Artyomovsk (1). Town, Donetsk
Oblast, Ukrainian SSR :
Bakhmut (-1924)
Artyomovsk (2). Town, Kras-
noyarsk Kray, RSFSR :
Olkhovsky (*1911-39)
Artyomovsky. Town, Sverd-
lovsk Oblast, RSFSR :
Yegorshino (-1938)
Artyomovsky Rudnik see
Artyoma, imeni
Aruaña. Town, central Brazil,
South America : Leopoldina
(-1944)
Arumeru. District, northern
Tanzania, eastern Africa :
Arusha (-1974)
Arunachal. Town, northeastern
India : Masimpur (-1950s)
Arunachal Pradesh. Union
territory, northeastern
India : North East Frontier
Agency (-1972)
Arusha see Arumeru
Arys see Orzysz
Asaka. City, central Honshu,
Japan : Hizaori (-1932)
Asba Littoria see Asba Tafari
Asba Tafari. Town, east-
central Ethiopia, northeastern
Africa : Asba Littoria (1936-
41)
Asbest. Town, Sverdlovsk
Oblast, RSFSR : Asbestovyye
Rudniki (-1928), Kudelka
(1928-33)
Asbestovyye Rudniki see Asbest
Asé Goniá. Village, western
Crete, Greece : Asigonía
(-1960s)
Asenovgrad. Town, southern
Bulgaria : Stanimaka (-1934)
Asha. Town, Chelyabinsk
Oblast, RSFSR : Asha-
Balashevsky Zavod (-c. 1928)
Asha-Balashevsky Zavod see
Asha
Ashihho see Acheng
Ashkhabad. Capital of Turk-
men SSR : Askhabad
(-1919), Poltoratsk (1919-27)
Ashraf see Behshahr
Asht. Village, Leninabad Oblast,

Tadzhik SSR : Shaydan (-c. 1960)
Asigonía see Asé Goniá
Askhabad see Ashkhabad
Askraía. Village, central
Greece : Panagía (-1960s)
Asnières see Asnières-sur-
Seine
Asnières-sur-Seine. Town,
northern France : Asnières
(-1968)
Assab. Town, northern Ethiopia,
northeastern Africa : Dancalia
Meridionale (-1941)
Assake see Leninsk (2)
Assuruá see Santo Inácio
Astapovo see Lev Tolstoy
Astarabad see Gorgan
Astrabad see Gorgan
Astrakhan-Bazar see Dzhalilabad
Atella di Caserta. Town, southern
Italy : Atella di Napoli (1927-
45)
Atella di Napoli see Atella di
Caserta
Atentze see Tehtsin [Te-ch'in]
Atig. Urban settlement, Sverd-
lovsk Oblast, RSFSR : Atigsky
Zavod (-1929)
Atigsky Zavod see Atig
Atkinson Field see Timerhi
Atlasova. Island, Sakhalin Oblast,
RSFSR : Alaid (-c. 1955)
Attock see Campbellpore
Auerbakhovsky Rudnik see
Rudnichny
Auezov. Urban settlement,
Semipalatinsk Oblast, Kazakh
SSR : Bakyrchik (-1967)
Augusto Cardosa. Town, north-
western Mozambique, south-
eastern Africa : Matangala
(-1963)
Aulenbach see Kalinovka (1)
Auliye-Ata see Dzhambul
Aulowönen see Kalinovka (1)
Aulus see Aulus-les-Bains
Aulus-les-Bains. Village,
southern France : Aulus (-1938)
Aumale see Sour el-Ghozlane
Aumont see Aumont-Aubrac
Aumont-Aubrac. Village, southern
France : Aumont (-1937)
Aurisina. Village, northeastern

Italy : Nabresina (-c. 1920)
Aurora. City, Colorado, USA :
Fletcher (-1907)
Aurora see San Francisco (2)
Auschwitz see Oświęcim
Auspitz see Hustopeče
Aussig see Ústí nad Labem
Aust-Agder. County, southern
Norway : Nedenes (-1918)
Austerlitz see Slavkov
Australian Capital Territory.
Territory, southeastern Au-
stralia : Yass-Canberra
(-1911), Federal Capital Ter-
ritory (1911-38)
Avelavo Bay see Vaila Voe Bay
Avellaneda. City, eastern Ar-
gentina, South America :
Barracas al Sur (-1904)
Avesta see Erickson
Avli-Koi see Zhivkovo
Avlona see Vlorë
Avraamovskaya see (1) Khvoy-
naya Polyana; (2) Partizan-
skaya (1)
Avşar see Türkeh
Ayaguz. Town, Semipalatinsk
Oblast, Kazakh SSR : Sergiopol
(*1931-39)
Ayat. Urban settlement, Sverd-
lovsk Oblast, RSFSR : Ayats-
koye (-1944)
Ayatskoye see Ayat
Ayni. Village, Tadzhik SSR :
Zakhmatabad (-c. 1960)
Ayni see Zafarabad
Ayuquitan. Barrio, Negros
Occidental, Philippines : Old
Ayuquitan (-1950)
Ayutinsky. Urban settlement,
Rostov Oblast, RSFSR :
Vlasova-Ayuta (-c. 1960)
Azaña see Numancia de la
Sagra
Azetfoun. Village, north-central
Algeria, northern Africa :
Port-Gueydon (-c. 1962)
Azizbekov. Urban settlement,
Armenian SSR : Pashalu
(-c. 1935), Soylan (c. 1935-
1956)
Azizbekov see Zaritap
Azovskoye. Urban settle-

ment, Crimean Oblast, Ukrain-
ian SSR : Kolai (-1944)
Azuma see Ninomiya
Azurduy. Town, south-central
Bolivia, South America :
Pomabamba (-1900s)

Babelsberg†. Suburb of Potsdam,
southwestern East Germany :
Nowawes (-1938)
Babil. Province, central Iraq :
Hilla (-1971)
Babimost. Town, western Poland
: Bomst (-1945), Germany
Babol [Babul]. Town, northern
Iraq : Barfurush (-1930)
Babolser. Town, northern Iraq :
Meshkhede-Ser (-1930)
Baborów. Town, southern Poland :
Bauerwitz (-1945), Germany
Babul = Babol
Babushkin (1). Suburb of Moscow,
Moscow Oblast, RSFSR :
Losino-Ostrovskaya (-1939)
Babushkin (2). Town, Buryat
Autonomous SSR, RSFSR :
Mysovsk (-1941)
Babushkina, imeni. Village,
Vologda Oblast, RSFSR :
Ledengskoye (-c. 1940)
Bachaty see Starobachaty
Bachinsky see Solzavod
Bacuit see El Nido
Bad Altheide see Polanica
Zdrój
Bad Düben. Town, central East
Germany : Düben (-1948)
Bad Flinsberg see Swieradów
Zdrój
Bad Hofgastein. Town, west-
central Austria : Hofgastein
(-1936)
Bad Kudowa see Kudowa Zdrój
Bad Landeck see Lądek Zdrój
Bad Polzin see Połczyn Zdrój
Bad Radein see Slatina Radenci
Bad Reinerz see Duszniki Zdrój
Bad Salzbrunn see Szczawno
Zdrój
Bad Sankt Leonhard im Lavant-

tale. Village, southern Austria : Sankt Leonhard (-1935)
Bad Schönfliess in Neumark see Trzcińsko Zdrój
Bad Segeberg. Town, northwestern West Germany : Segeberg (-1924)
Bad Warmbrunn see Cieplice Śląskie Zdrój
Badyaly see Krinichnaya
Bagara see Kirovskoye (2)
Bagdadi see Mayakovsky
Bagenalstown see Muine Bheag
Bagni della Porretta see Porrette Terme
Bagni San Giuliano see San Giuliano Terme
Bagnorea see Bagnoregio
Bagnoregio. Town, central Italy : Bagnorea (-1922)
Bagrationovsk. Town, Kaliningrad Oblast, RSFSR : Preussisch-Eylau (-1946), Germany (-1945)
Bailen see General Emilio Aguinaldo
Bailundo see Luau
Bairak see Kalininsk (1)
Baixo Mearim see Vitória do Mearim
Bajabonico see Imbert
Bakal. Town, Chelyabinsk Oblast, RSFSR : Bakalsky Zavod (-1928)
Bakalsky Zavod see Bakal
Baker. City, Montana, USA : Lorraine (-1908)
Bakhmut see Artyomovsk
Bakht. Urban settlement, Syrdarya Oblast, Uzbek SSR : Velikoalekseyevsky (-1963)
Baki see Krasnyye Baki
Baktalórántháza. Town, northeastern Hungary : Nyírbakta (*1932-33)
Bakwanga see Mbuji-Mayi
Bakyrchik see Auezov
Balagtas. Municipality, Bulacan, Philippines : Bigaa (-1966)
Balanda see Kalininsk (2)
Balatonkiliti. Town, west-central Hungary : Kiliti (-1922)

Balatonmária see Balatonmáriafürdő
Balatonmáriafürdő. Town, west-central Hungary : Balatonmária (-1927)
Balbunar see Kurbat
Baldenburg see Biały Bór
Baldzhuan see Boldzhuan
Baley. Town, Chita Oblast, RSFSR : Novo-Troitskoye (-1938)
Balfour. Town, Transvaal, South Africa : McHattiesburg (*c. 1900-05)
Balindong. Municipality, Lanao, Philippines : Water (-1956)
Balkansky Priisk see Balkany
Balkany. Settlement, Chelyabinsk Oblast, RSFSR : Balkansky Priisk (-1929)
Balkhash. Town, Dzhezkazgan Oblast, Kazakh SSR : Bertys (*1929-?), Pribalkhash (?-1937)
Ballescas. Barrio, Antique, Philippines : Barasanan (-1957)
Ballydesmond. Town, County Cork, Ireland : Kingwilliamstown (-c. 1950)
Balsas. City, northeastern Brazil, South America : Santo Antônio de Balsas (-1944)
Baltiysk. Town, Kaliningrad Oblast, RSFSR : Pillau (-1946), Germany (-1945)
Baltiysky Port see Paldiski
Baltser see Krasnoarmeysk (2)
Bancroft see Chililabombwe
Banda Atjeh. Town, Sumatra, Indonesia : Kutaradja (-c. 1966)
Bandar see Masulipat(n)am
Bandar Penggarem see Batu Pahat
Bandar Seri Begawan. Capital of Brunei, Kalimantan, southeastern Asia : Brunei (Town) (-1970)
Bandundu. Town, western Zaïre, central Africa : Banningville (-1966)
Bangladesh. Republic, southern Asia : East Pakistan (*1947-71)
Banjul. Capital of Gambia, western Africa : Bathurst (-1973)

Bank. Urban settlement, Azerbaijan SSR : Narimanova, imeni (-1939), Kirova, imeni (1939-c. 1940)

Banki see Krasnogorsk (1)

Banningville see Bandundu

Bannovsky see Slavyanogorsk

Bannu. City, northwestern Pakistan : Edwardesabad (-1903)

Banská Bystrica. Town, central Czechoslovakia : Neusohl (-1918, 1939-45), Germany

Banská Stiavnica. Town, southeastern Czechoslovakia : Schemnitz (-1918, 1939-45), Germany

Banto-Anin see Bukal

Banza Congo. Town, northwestern Angola, southwestern Africa : São Salvador do Congo (-c. 1976)

Banzyville see Mobayembongo

Baquba see Diyala

Baran. Urban settlement, Vitebsk Oblast, Belorussian SSR : Krasny Oktyabr (c. 1918-1920s)

Baranchinsky. Urban settlement, Sverdlovsk Oblast, RSFSR : Baranchinsky Zavod (-1928)

Baranchinsky Zavod see Baranchinsky

Barangay see Hilario Valdez (1)

Baranovichi. Town, Brest Oblast, Belorussian SSR : Baranowicze (1921-39), Poland

Baranowicze see Baranovichi

Barão de Cocais. City, southeastern Brazil, South America : Morro Grande (-1944)

Barasanan see Ballescas

Barat see Ablan

Barba de Puerco see Puerto-Seguro

Barbará see Santa María de Barbará

Barce see Al-Marj

Barczewo. Town, northeastern Poland : Wartenburg (-1945), Germany

Bardejov. Town, northeastern Czechoslovakia : Bartfeld (-1918, 1939-45), Germany

Bardily see Zaleshany

Bardo. Town, southwestern Poland : Wartha (-1945), Germany

Barfurush see Babol

Bar Harbor. Town, Maine, USA : Eden (-1918)

Baria see Dewgard Baria

Barlinek. Town, northwestern Poland : Berlinchen (-1945), Germany

Bärn see Moravský Beroun

Barnegat City see Barnegat Light

Barnegat Light. Borough, New Jersey, USA : Barnegat City (-1948)

Barnsdall. City, Oklahoma, USA : Bigheart (-1921)

Baronsk see Marks

Barotse see Western

Barra Bonita see Ibaiti

Barracas al Sur see Avellaneda

Barrit-Luluno see Luba

Barshatas. Village, Semipalatinsk Oblast, Kazakh SSR : Chubartau (-c. 1960)

Bartang. Village, Gorno-Badakhshan Autonomous Oblast, Tadzhik SSR : Sipon(d)zh (-c. 1935)

Bartenstein see Bartoszyce

Bartfeld see Bardejov

Bartolo see Betanzos

Bartoszyce. Town, northeastern Poland : Bartenstein (-1945), Germany

Bärwalde (in Neumark) see Barwice (1)

Bärwalde (in Pommern) see Barwice (2)

Barwice (1). Town, northwestern Poland : Bärwalde (in Neumark) (-1945), Germany

Barwice (2). Town, northwestern Poland : Bärwalde (in Pommern) (-1945), Germany

Baryshnikovo see Krasnogorskoye (1)

Basargechar see Vardenis

Bashanta see Gorodovikovsk

Bashkicheti see Dmanisi

Bashtanka. Urban settlement,
Nikolayev Oblast, Ukrainian
SSR : Poltavka (-c. 1930)
Basses-Alpes see Alpes-de-
Haute-Provence
Basses-Pyrénées see Pyrénées-
Atlantiques
Bassopiano Orientale see Mas-
sawa [Mitsiwa]
Basutoland see Lesotho
Batalha. City, northeastern
Brazil, South America :
Belo Monte (-1949)
Batalhão see Taperoá
Batalpashinsk see Cherkessk
Batalpashinskaya see Cherkessk
Batamshinsky. Urban settlement,
Aktyubinsk Oblast, Kazakh
SSR : Kimpersaysky (-1945)
Batang see Paan
Bata-Siala. Town, western
Zaïre, central Africa : Kai-
Mbaku (-1972)
Batavia see Jakarta
Batbakkara see Amangeldy
Bathurst see Banjul
Batingan see Narra (1)
Batken. Village, Osh Oblast,
Kirgiz SSR : Batken-Buzhum
(-1945)
Batken-Buzhum see Batken
Batovany see Partizánske
Batuli see San Isidro
Bat Yam. City, west-central
Israel : Ir Gannim (*1925-36)
Batz see Batz-sur-Mer
Batz-sur-Mer. Village, western
France : Batz (-1931)
Baudens see Belarbi
Baudouinville see Virungu
Bauerwitz see Baborów
Bauguen see Salcedo
Bauman see Shafirkan
Baumanabad see Pyandzh
Bay see Bay Village
Bayag see Calanasan
Bayan-Tumen see Choybalsan
Baymak. Town, Bashkir Auton-
omous SSR, RSFSR : Baymak-
Tanalykovo (-1944)
Baymak-Tanalykovo see Baymak
Bay Village. Suburb of Cleve-
land, Ohio, USA : Bay (*1903-
50)

Bayville see Kirkwood
Bazargic see Tolbukhin
Bazarjik see Tolbukhin
Bazar-Yaypan. Urban settlement,
Fergana Oblast, Uzbek SSR :
Yaypan (-c. 1940)
Beauaraba see Pittsworth
Bečej. Village, northeastern
Yugoslavia : Stari Bečej (-c.
1947)
Béchar. Town, western Algeria,
northern Africa : Colomb-
Béchar (-c. 1962)
Bechuanaland see Botswana
Becsehely. Town, western Hun-
gary : Beksénypólya (*1941-42)
Beda see Noviki (1)
Bedeau see Ras el Ma
Bedeyeva Polyana. Village,
Bashkir Autonomous SSR,
RSFSR : Bedeyevo (-c. 1940)
Bedeyevo see Bedeyeva Polyana
Bedford see North Bedfordshire
Bedloe's Island see Liberty
Island
Bednodemyanovsk. Town, Penza
Oblast, RSFSR : Spassk (-1925)
Będzin. City, southern Poland :
Bendin (-1919), Russia; Bends-
burg (1939-45), Germany
Begovat see Bekabad
Behshahr. Town, northern Iran :
Ashraf (-mid-1930s)
Beilau see Pilawa
Beira see Sofala
Beitsch see Biecz
Béjaïa. Town, northern Algeria,
northern Africa : Bougie
(-c. 1962)
Bekabad. Town, Tashkent Oblast,
Uzbek SSR : Begovat (-1964)
Bek-Budi see Karshi
Beksénypólya see Becsehely
Bela Aliança see Rio do Sul
Belá pod Bezdězem. Town,
northwestern Czechoslovakia :
Weisswasser (-1918, 1939-45),
Germany
Belarbi. Village, northwestern
Algeria, northern Africa :
Baudens (-c. 1962)
Bela Slatina see Byala Slatina
Bela Vista see (1) Echaporã;
(2) Suçuapara

Belaya Kalitva. Town, Rostov
Oblast, RSFSR : Ust-Belokalit-
venskaya (-c. 1935), Belokalit-
venskaya (late 1930s)
Belém see (1) Jatinã; (2) Pal-
meirais
Belgard see Białogard
Belgian Congo see Zaire
Belgorod-Dnestrovsky. Town,
Odessa Oblast, Ukrainian
SSR : Akkerman (-1918),
Cetatea-Albă (1918-40, 1941-
44), Romania
Belinsky. Town, Penza Oblast,
RSFSR : Chembar (-1948)
Belize. British crown colony,
Central America : British
Honduras (1840-1973)
Bella Unión. Town, northwest-
ern Uruguay, South America :
Santa Rosa (-1930s)
Bella Vista. Town, southern
Mexico, North America :
San Pedro Remate (-1934)
Belle Glade. City, Florida,
USA : Hillsborough Land
settlement (-1921)
Bellin. Town, Quebec, Canada :
Payne Bay (-1965)
Bellingham. City, Washington,
USA : Whatcom (-1903)
Bellville. Railway station of
town of Bellville, Cape of
Good Hope, South Africa :
Durban Road (-1906)
Belmeken see Kolarov
Belmont see Belmont-de-la-
Loire
Belmont-de-la-Loire. Village,
southeastern France : Bel-
mont (-1936)
Belmonte see Manissobal
Belogorsk (1). Town, Amur
Oblast, RSFSR : Bochkarevo
(-1926), Aleksandrovsk (1926-
35), Kuybyshevka-Vostochnaya
(1935-57)
Belogorsk (2). Town, Crimean
Oblast, Ukrainian SSR : Kara-
subazar (-1944)
Belogorsk (3). Urban settle-
ment, Kemerovo Oblast,
RSFSR : Kiya-Shaltyr (-c. 1960)

Belogorye. Urban settlement,
Khmelnitsky Oblast, Ukrainian
SSR : Lyakhovtsy (-1946)
Belo Horizonte. City, southeast-
ern Brazil, South America :
Cidade de Minas (-1901)
Belokalitvenskaya see Belaya
Kalitva
Belolesye. Village, Odessa Ob-
last, Ukrainian SSR : Akmangit
(-c. 1960)
Belolutsk. Urban settlement,
Voroshilovgrad Oblast, Ukrain-
ian SSR : Belolutskaya (-1937)
Belolutskaya see Belolutsk
Belo Monte see Batalha
Belomorsk. Town, Karelian Au-
tonomous SSR, RSFSR : Soroka
(-1938)
Belorechensk. Town, Krasnodar
Kray, RSFSR : Belorechenskaya
(-1958)
Belorechenskaya see Belorech-
ensk
Beloretsk. Town, Bashkir Au-
tonomous SSR, RSFSR : Bel-
oretsky Zavod (-1923)
Beloretsky Zavod see Beloretsk
Beloshchelye see Naryan-Mar
Belotsarsk see Kyzyl
Belovo see Zemen
Belovodsk. Urban settlement,
Voroshilovgrad Oblast, Ukrain-
ian SSR : Belovodskoye (-1937)
Belovodskoye. Village, Kirgiz
SSR : Stalinskoye (1937-61)
Belovodskoye see Belovodsk
Bely Bychek see Chagoda
Bely Klyuch see Krasny Klyuch
Belyye Kresty see Sazonovo
Bendery. Town, Moldavian SSR :
Tighina (1918-40, 1941-44),
Romania
Bendin see Będzin
Bendix see Teterboro
Bendsburg see Będzin
Beneditinos. City, northeastern
Brazil, South America : São
Benedito (-1944)
Benefactor see San Juan
Bengal. State, northeastern
India : West Bengal (*1947-72)
Benin. Republic, western Africa :

Dahomey (-1975)
Benjamin Constant <u>see</u> Remate de Males
Berane <u>see</u> Ivangrad
Berdyansk. Town, Zaporozhye Oblast, Ukrainian SSR : Osipenko (1939-58)
Beregovoy. Urban settlement, Omsk Oblast, RSFSR : Kharino (-c. 1960)
Berestovitsa <u>see</u> Pogranichny (1)
Berezanka. Urban settlement, Nikolayev Oblast, Ukrainian SSR : Tiligulo-Berezanka (-c. 1960)
Bereznik. Urban settlement, Arkhangelsk Oblast, RSFSR : Semyonovskoye (-c. 1960)
Berezniki. Town, Perm Oblast, RSFSR : Usolye-Solikamskoye (-1932)
Bereznitsa (1). Village, Vitebsk Oblast, Belorussian SSR : Lezhni (-1964)
Bereznitsa (2). Village, Grodno Oblast, Belorussian SSR : Treputikha (-1964)
Bereznyaki. Village, Vitebsk Oblast, Belorussian SSR : Sinebryukhi (-1964)
Bereznyanka. Village, Vitebsk Oblast, Belorussian SSR : Zagryazye (-1964)
Berezovichi. Village, Brest Oblast, Belorussian SSR : Parshevichi (-1964)
Bergreichenstein <u>see</u> Kašperské Hory
Bergstadt <u>see</u> Leśnica
Beringovsky. Urban settlement, Chukot Autonomous Okrug, Magadan Oblast, RSFSR : Ugolny (-1957)
Berkovets <u>see</u> Kotsyubinskoye
Berlengas <u>see</u> Valença do Piauli
Berlin <u>see</u> Kitchener
Berlinchen <u>see</u> Barlinek
Bernstadt (in Schlesien) <u>see</u> Bierutów
Bernstein <u>see</u> Pełczyce
Berrahal. Town, northeastern

Algeria, northern Africa : Aïn Mokra (-c. 1962)
Bertolínia. City, northeastern Brazil, South America : Aparecida (-1944)
Bertys <u>see</u> Balkhash
Berwyn <u>see</u> Gene Autry
Beryoza. Town, Brest Oblast, Belorussian SSR : Beryoza-Kartuzskaya (-1939)
Beryoza-Kartuzskaya <u>see</u> Beryoza
Beryozov <u>see</u> Beryozovo
Beryozovo. Urban settlement, Khanty-Mansi Autonomous Okrug, Tyumen Oblast, RSFSR : Beryozov (-1926)
Beryozovshchina. Village, Grodno Oblast, Belorussian SSR : Bozhedary (-1964)
Beryozy. Village, Grodno Oblast, Belorussian SSR : Martyshki (-1964)
Berzence. Town, southwestern Hungary : Berzencze (-1918)
Berzencze <u>see</u> Berzence
Besh-Aryk <u>see</u> Kirovo (1)
Beskhlebichi <u>see</u> Sosnovichi
Bessarabka. Urban settlement, Moldavian SSR : Romanovka (-c. 1960)
Betanzos. Town, southeastern Bolivia, South America : Bartolo (-1900s)
Bethel <u>see</u> Bethel Park
Bethel Park. Suburb of Pittsburgh, Pennsylvania, USA : Bethel (-1960)
Bethpage. Village, New York, USA : Central Park (1841-1936)
Bettioua. Village, northwestern Algeria, northern Africa : Saint-Leu (-c. 1962)
Beuthen <u>see</u> Bytom
Beuthen an der Oder <u>see</u> Bytom Odrzański
Beverly <u>see</u> Beverly Hills
Beverly Hills. Suburb of Los Angeles, California, USA : Beverly (*1907-11)
Beyuk-Vedi <u>see</u> Vedi
Bezdelichi <u>see</u> Razdolnaya
Bezdružice. Town, western Czechoslovakia : Weseritz

Bezhitsa

14

(-1918, 1939-45), Germany
Bezhitsa (1956†, when amal-
gamated with Bryansk).
Town, Bryansk Oblast, RSFSR
: Ordzhonikidzegrad (1941-44)
Bezwada see Vijayayada
Biafra, Bight of see Bonny,
Bight of.
Biała. Town, southwestern
Poland : Zülz (-1945), Ger-
many
Biała (Piska). Town, northeast-
ern Poland : Gehlenburg
(-1938), Germany, Bialla
(1938-45), Germany
Bialla see Biała (Piska)
Białogard. Town, northwestern
Poland : Belgard (-1945),
Germany
Biały Bor. Town, northwestern
Poland : Baldenburg (-1945),
Germany
Biały Kamień. Town, south-
western Poland : Weiss-
stein (-1945), Germany
Bié. Town, central Angola,
southwestern Africa : Silva
Porto (c. 1900-c. 1976)
Bielawa. Town, southwestern
Poland : Langenbielau
(-1945), Germany
Bielitz see Bielsko
Bielsko. City, southern Poland
: Bielitz (-1919), Germany
Bierutów. Town, southwestern
Poland : Bernstadt (in
Schlesien) (-1945), Germany
Biga see El Rio
Bigaa see Balagtas
Bigheart see Barnsdall
Bilimbay. Urban settlement,
Sverdlovsk Oblast, RSFSR :
Bilimbayevsky Zavod (-1929)
Bilimbayevsky Zavod see
Bilimbay
Bílovec. Town, north-central
Czechoslovakia : Wagstadt
(-1919, 1939-45), Germany
Binangoan de Lampon see
Infanta
Bingerau see Węgrów
Binghamstown see An Geata
Mór

Binokor see Pakhtakor
Bircao see Bur Gao
Birdville see Halton City
Bir Mogreïn. Town, northwestern
Mauritania, western Africa :
Fort-Trinquet (-c. 1958)
Birobidzhan. Capital of Jewish
Autonomous Oblast, Khabarovsk
Kray, RSFSR : Tikhonkaya
(-1928)
Biruni. Town, Karakalpak Au-
tonomous SSR, Uzbek SSR :
Shabbaz (-1957)
Biryuch see Krasnogvardeyskoye
(1)
Biryusinsk. Town, Irkutsk
Oblast, RSFSR : Suyetikha
(-1967)
Birzhi see Madona
Birzula see Kotoysk (1)
Bischoflack see Skofja Loka
Bischofsburg see Biskupiec (1)
Bischofstal see Ujazd
Bischofstein see Bisztynek
Bischofswerder see Biskupiec
(2)
Bisert. Urban settlement, Sverd-
lovsk Oblast, RSFSR : Bisertsky
Zavod (-1942)
Bisertsky Zavod see Bisert
Biskupiec (1). Town, northeastern
Poland : Bischofsburg (-1945),
Germany
Biskupiec (2). Town, northeastern
Poland : Bischofswerder (-1945),
Germany
Bismarckburg see Kasanga
Bistrica see (1) (Ilirska) Bis-
trica; (2) (Slovenska) Bistrica
Bisztynek. Town, northeastern
Poland : Bischofstein (-1945),
Germany
Bitola [Bitolj]. City, southeastern
Yugoslavia : Monastir (-1913),
Turkey
Bitolj = Bitola
Bitschwiller see Bitschwiller-
lès-Thann
Bitschwiller-lès-Thann. Village,
eastern France : Bitschwiller
(-1938)
Bitulok see Gabaldon
Biyuk-Onlar see Oktyabrskoye (1)

Björkö see Krasnoostrovsky
Blachownia (Śląska). Town,
southern Poland : Blechham-
mer (-1945), Germany
Black Diamond see Pittsburg
Blackwell's Island see Frank-
lin D. Roosevelt Island
Blagoevgrad. Town, southwest-
ern Bulgaria : Gorna Djumaya
(-1950)
Blagoveshchensk. Town, Bash-
kir Autonomous SSR, RSFSR
: Blagoveshchensky Zavod
(-1942)
Blagoveshchensky Zavod see
Blagoveshchensk
Blanco see Luperón
Blechhammer see Blachownia
Śląska
Bliznetsy see Bliznyuki
Bliznyuki. Urban settlement,
Kharkov Oblast, Ukrainian
SSR : Bliznetsy (-c. 1960)
Bloom see Chicago Heights
Bloshniki see Kalinovaya (1)
Bloshno see Podgornaya (1)
Bluden see Pervomayskoye (1)
Bluefield. City, Virginia, USA
: Graham (-1921)
Bluefields see Zelaya
Bluff. Town, South Island, New
Zealand : Campbelltown
(-1917)
Blumenau see Stettler
Blyukherovo see Leninskoye
(6)
Blyukherovsk see Srednyaya
Nyukzha
Boa Esperança. City, southeast-
ern Brazil, South America :
Dores da Boa Esperança
(-1940)
Boa Esperança see (1) Boa
Esperança do Sul; (2) Es-
perantina
Boa Esperança do Sul. City,
southeastern Brazil, South
America : Boa Esperança
(-1944)
Boa Vista see (1) Coripós;
(2) Tocantinópolis
Boa Vista (de Erechim) see
Erechim

Bobovozovshchina see Urozhay-
naya (1)
Bobriki see Novomoskovsk
Bocâina. City, southeastern
Brazil, South America : São
João da Bocâina (-1938)
Bocaiúva see (1) Bocaiúva do
Sul; (2) Macatuba
Bocaiuva do Sul. City, southern
Brazil, South America : Bo-
caiúva (-1944), Imbuial (1944-
48)
Bochkarevo see Belogorsk (1)
Bocsarlapujtő see Karancslapujtő
Bodenbach see Podmokly
Bogatoye. Village, Kuybyshev
Oblast, RSFSR : Pavlovka
(-c. 1960)
Bogatynia. Town, southwestern
Poland : Reichenau (-1945),
Germany
Bogatyye Saby. Village, Tatar
Autonomous SSR, RSFSR :
Saby (late 1930s)
Boghari see Ksar el Boukhari
Bogodukhovka see Chkalovo (1)
Bogomdarovanny see Kommunar
Bogor. City, western Java,
Indonesia : Buitenzorg (-1945)
Bogorodsk see Noginsk
Bogorodskoye see (1) Kamskoye
Ustye; (2) Leninskoye (2)
Bogoslovsk see Karpinsk
Bogoslovsky see Karpinsk
Bogoyavlensk see Zhovtnevoye
(1)
Bogoyavlenskoye see Pervomaysky
(1)
Boguszów. City, southwestern
Poland : Gottesberg (-1945),
Germany
Böhmisch-Brod see Český Brod
Böhmisch-Kamnitz see Česká
Kamenice
Böhmisch-Leipa see Česká Lípa
Böhmisch-Skalitz see Česká
Skalice
Böhmisch-Trübau see Česká
Třebová
Bokovo-Antratsit see Antratsit
Boldyuki see Zarechnaya (1)
Boldzhuan. Village, Kulyab Ob-
last, Tadzhik SSR : Baldzhuan

(-c. 1940)
Bolesławice. Village, southwestern Poland : Bunzelwitz (-1945), Germany
Bolesławiec. Town, southwestern Poland : Bunzlau (-1945), Germany
Boleszkowice. Town, northwestern Poland : Fürstenfelde (-1945), Germany
Bolívar. Town, northwestern Peru, South America : Cajamarquilla (-1925)
Bolívar see (Cerro) Bolívar
Bolnisi. Town, Georgian SSR : Yekaterinofeld (-?), Lyuksemburg (?-1936), Lyuksemburgi (1936-43)
Bologhine. Suburb of Algiers, Algeria, northern Africa : Saint-Eugèn (-c. 1962)
Bolshakovo. Village, Kaliningrad Oblast, RSFSR : Gross Skaisgirren (-1938), Germany, Kreuzingen (1938-45), Germany
Bolshaya Garmanda see Evensk
Bolshaya Martynovka. Village, Rostov Oblast, RSFSR : Martynovka [Martynovskoye] (-c. 1944)
Bolshaya Novosyolka see Velikaya Novosyolka
Bolshaya Promyshlenka see Promyshlennovsky
Bolshaya Tsaryovshchina see Volzhsky
Bolshaya Ussurka. River, Primorsky Kray, RSFSR : Iman (-1974)
Bolshevo. Village, Moscow Oblast, RSFSR : Stalinsky (1928-61)
Bolshiye Arabuzy see Pervomayskoye (2)
Bolshiye Soli see Nekrasovskoye
Bolshoy Beryozovy. Island, Gulf of Finland, Leningrad Oblast, RSFSR : Koivisto (-1949), Finland (-1940)
Bolshoye Ignatovo. Village, Mordovian Autonomous SSR,

RSFSR : Ignatovo (-c. 1940)
Bolshoy Kosheley see Komsomolskoye (1)
Bolshoy Tokmak see Tokmak (1), (2)
Bolshoy Yanisol see Velikaya Novosyolka
Bolton see Stonefort
Bolvan see Zagornaya
Bolvanovka see Noviki (2)
Bolvany see Borovaya (1)
Boly. Town, southern Hungary : Németbóly (-1950)
Bom Jardim. City, southeastern Brazil, South America : Vergel (1944-48)
Bom Jardim see (1) Bom Jardim de Minas; (2) Catuiçara
Bom Jardim de Minas. City, southeastern Brazil, South America : Bom Jardim (-1944)
Bom Jesus see Aparados da Serra
Bom Jesus do Triunfo. City, southern Brazil, South America : Triunfo [Triumpho] (-1944)
Bom Retiro see Inhandava
Bomst see Babimost
Bondyuzhsky see Mendeleyevsk
Bondyuzhsky Zavod see Mendeleyevsk
Bône see Annaba
Bonfim see (1) Senhor do Bonfim; (2) Silvânia
Bonito see Bonito de Santa Fé
Bonito de Santa Fé. City, northeastern Brazil, South America : Bonito (-1944)
Bonny, Bight of [name used by Nigeria]. Bay, Gulf of Guinea, western Africa : Biafra, Bight of (-1975)
Borchalo see Marneuli
Borden. Town, Prince Edward Island, Canada : Carleton Point (-1916)
Bordj Bounaama. Village, northern Algeria, northern Africa : Molière (-c. 1962)
Bordj el Bahri. Village, northern Algeria, northern Africa : Cap-Matifou (-c. 1962)
Bordj el Kiffan. Town, northern

Algeria, northern Africa :
Fort-de-l'Eau (-c. 1962)
Borgo San Donnino see Fidenza
Borgotaro see Borgo Val di
Taro
Borgo Val di Taro. Town,
north-central Italy : Borgotaro
(-c. 1930)
Borisoglebskiye Slobody see
Borisoglebsky
Borisoglebsky. Urban settle-
ment, Yaroslavl Oblast,
RSFSR : Borisoglebskiye
Slobody (-c. 1960)
Borisovgrad see Pârvomaj
Borja see Sagbayan
Borki Wielkie see Velikiye
Borki
Borovaya (1). Village, Vitebsk
Oblast, Belorussian SSR :
Bolvany (-1964)
Borovaya (2). Village, Brest
Oblast, Belorussian SSR :
Korostovka (-1964)
Borovichi. Village, Gomel
Oblast, Belorussian SSR :
Gryazliv (-1964)
Borovshchina (1). Village,
Vitebsk Oblast, Belorussian
SSR : Peredelki (-1964)
Borovshchina (2). Village, Minsk
Oblast, Belorussian SSR :
Puziki (-1964)
Borovsk (†now merged with
Solikamsk). Town, Perm
Oblast, RSFSR : Ust-Borovaya
(-1949)
Bor u Ceske Lipy see Nový
Bor
Borzhom see Borzhomi
Borzhomi. Town, Georgian
SSR : Borzhom (-1936)
Boshnyakovo. Urban settlement,
Sakhalin Oblast, RSFSR :
Nishi-shakutan (1905-45),
Japan
Bosquet see Hadjadj
Botev. Mountain, central Bul-
garia : Ferdinandov-vrach
(?-?), Yamrukchal (?-1950)
Botevgrad. City, western Bul-
garia : Orkhaniye (-1934)
Botswana. Republic, southern

Africa : Bechuanaland (-1966)
Boufatis. Village, northwestern
Algeria, northern Africa :
Saint-Louis (-c. 1962)
Bougaâ. Village, northeastern
Algeria, northern Africa :
Lafayette (-c. 1962)
Bougie see Béjaïa
Bou Hanifia el Hamamat. Village,
northwestern Algeria, northern
Africa : Bou Hanifia les
Thermes (-c. 1962)
Bou Hanifia les Thermes see
Bou Hanifia el Hamamat
Bou Ismaïl. Village, northern
Algeria, northern Africa :
Castiglione (-c. 1962)
Bou Kadir. Village, northern
Algeria, northern Africa :
Charon (-c. 1962)
Boulder Dam see Hoover Dam
Boulogne-Billancourt. Suburb of
Paris, north-central France :
Boulogne-sur-Seine (-1924)
Boulogne-sur-Seine see Boulogne-
Billancourt
Bourbourg. Town, northern
France : Bourbourg-Ville
(-1945)
Bourbourg-Ville see Bourbourg
Bous. Town, western West Ger-
many : Buss (1936-45)
Bovdilovtsy see Slobozhany
Boykovo. Village, Kuril Islands,
Sakhalin Oblast, RSFSR :
Kataoka (1905-45), Japan
Boynton see Boynton Beach
Boynton Beach. City, Florida,
USA : Boynton (-1926)
Boynton Beach see Ocean Ridge
Boyoma Falls. Cataracts, river
Congo, Zaïre, central Africa :
Stanley Falls (-1972)
Bozhedarovka see Shchorsk
Bozhedary see Beryozovshchina
Boži Dar. Town, western
Czechoslovakia : Gottesgab
(-1918, 1939-45), Germany
Bragança see Bragança Paulista
Bragança Paulista. City, south-
eastern Brazil, South America
: Bragança (-1944)
Bragg's Spur see West Memphis

Brahestad see Raahe
Brandenburg see Old Glory
Braniewo. Town, northeastern
Poland : Braunsberg (-1945),
Germany
Brantovka see Oktyabrsky (1)
Braşov. Town, central Ro-
mania : Kronstadt (-1918),
Germany; Oraşul Stalin
(1950-60)
Bratislava. City, south-central
Czechoslovakia : Pressburg
(1939-45), Germany
Bratsberg see Telemark
Bratsk see Porozhsky
Brätz see Brójce
Braunsberg see Braniewo
Brazil. Federal republic,
east-central South America :
United States of Brazil (1891-
1967)
Brea. City, California, USA :
Randolph (1908-11)
Břeclav. Town, southern
Czechoslovakia : Lundenburg
(-1918, 1939-45), Germany
Breitenstein see Ulyanovo (1)
Brejo da Madre de Deus. City,
northeastern Brazil, South
America : Madre de Deus
(1939-48)
Bremerhaven. City, northern
West Germany : Wesermünde
(1938-47)
Bremersdorp see Manzini
Breslau see Wrocław
Brest. Capital of Brest Oblast,
Belorussian SSR : Brest-
Litovsk (-1921), Brzesč nad
Bugiem (1921-39), Poland
Brest-Litovsk see Brest
Brieg see Brzeg
Briesen see Wąbrzeźno
British Central Africa (Protec-
torate) see Malawi
British East Africa see Kenya
British Guiana see Guyana
British Honduras see Belize
British Solomon Islands (Pro-
tectorate) see Solomon
Islands
Brno. City, southern Czecho-
slovakia : Brünn (-1918,

1939-45), Germany
Brochów. Town, southwestern
Poland : Brockau (-1945),
Germany
Brockau see Brochów
Brod (Makedonskie). Town,
southeastern Yugoslavia :
Juzni Brod (-c. 1945)
Broderick Falls see Webuye
Brodnica. Town, north-central
Poland : Buddenbrock (-1945),
Germany
Brójce. Town, western Poland :
Brätz (-1945), Germany
Broken Hill see Kabwe
Bromberg see Bydgoszcz
Bronkhorstspruit. Town, Trans-
vaal, South Africa : Erasmus
(*1904-29)
Brookfield. Village, Illinois,
USA : Grossdale (-1905)
Brooklyn see Keystone Heights
Brotas see Brotas de Macaúbas
Brotas de Macaúbas. City,
eastern Brazil, South America
: Brotas (-1944)
Bruckmühl. Village, southern
West Germany : Kirchdorf am
Haunpold (-1948)
Brunei (Town) see Bandar Seri
Begawan
Brünn see Brno
Brunshaupten see Kühlungsborn
Bruntál. Town, north-central
Czechoslovakia : Freudenthal
(1919, 1939-45), Germany
Brzeg. City, southwestern
Poland : Brieg (-1945), Ger-
many
Brzeg Dolny. Town, southwestern
Poland : Dyhernfurth (-1945),
Germany
Brzesč-nad-Bugiem see Brest
Brzeziny. Town, central Poland
: Löwenstadt (1939-45), Ger-
many
Buayan see General Santos
Bucana see Suhaile Arabi
Budarinskaya see Cherkesovsky
Budatétény. Suburb of Budapest,
Hungary : Kistétény (-1915)
Buddenbrock see Brodnica
Búdszentmihály see Tiszavasvári

Budweis see České Budějovice
Budyonnovka see Novoazovsk
Budyonnovsk. Town, Stavropol
Kray, RSFSR : Svyatoy Krest
(-1922), Prikumsk (1922-35,
1957-73)
Budyonnoye see Krasnogvardey-
skoye (1)
Budyonny see Chatbazar
Buenavista. Barrio, Sorsogon,
Philippines : Gibigaan (-1914)
Bugaz see Zatoka
Bugho see Javier
Buitenzorg see Bogor
Bujumbura. Capital of Burundi,
central Africa : Usumbura
(-1962)
Bukal. Barrio, Marinduque,
Philippines : Banto-Anin
(-1957)
Bukavu. Town, eastern Zaïre,
central Africa : Costermans-
ville (-1966)
Bukhara. Capital of Bukhara
Oblast, Uzbek SSR : Staraya
Bukhara (-1935)
Bukharino see Dolgintsevo
Bukittinggi. Town, western
Sumatra, Indonesia : Fort
de Kock (-c.1966)
Bulbugan see Santa Maria
Bulembu. Town, northwestern
Swaziland, southern Africa :
Havelock (-1976)
Bunclody. Town, County Wex-
ford, Ireland : Newtownbarry
(-1950)
Bunge Rudnik see Yunokom-
munarovsk
Bunker Hill Air Force Base
see Grissom Air Force
Base
Bunzelwitz see Bolesławice
Bunzlau see Bolesławiec
Bureya-Pristan see Novo-
bureysky
Bur Gao [Bircao]. Town,
southern Somalia, eastern
Africa : Port Durnford
(-c.1926)
Burgos (1). Municipality, Ilocos
Norte, Philippines : Nagpart-
ian (-1914)

Burgos (2). Municipality, Pan-
gasinan, Philippines : San
Isidro de Potot (-1914)
Burhave see Butjadingen
Buribay. Urban settlement,
Bashkir Autonomous SSR,
RSFSR : Buryubay (-1938)
Burkatów. Village, southwestern
Poland : Burkersdorf (-1945),
Germany
Burkersdorf see Burkatów
Burnas see Lebedevka
Bursa. Province, northwestern
Turkey : Khodavendikyar
(-1920s)
Burundi. Republic, east-central
Africa : Urundi (1918-66)
Burunny see Tsagan-Aman
Buryat Autonomous SSR. RSFSR
: Buryat-Mongol Autonomous
SSR (*1923-58)
Buryat-Mongol Autonomous SSR
see Buryat Autonomous SSR
Buryubay see Buribay
Buss see Bous
Buston. Urban settlement, Lenin-
abad Oblast, Tadzhik SSR :
Yantak (-c.1960)
Butjadingen. Village, northern
West Germany : Burhave (-1936)
Butler. Village, Wisconsin, USA
: New Butler (-1930)
Bütow see Bytów
Butterworth see Gcuwa
Butuka-Luba. Town, Macias
Nguema Biyoga, Equatorial
Guinea, western Africa : San
Carlos (-1973)
Butysh see Kama
Buynaksk. Town, Dagestan Au-
tonomous SSR, RSFSR : Temir-
Khan-Shura (-1922)
Büyükada. Island, Sea of Mar-
mara, western Turkey :
Prinkipo (-?)
Buyun-Uzun see Moskovsk
Buzuldza see Hadzi Dimitar
Byala Slatina. City, northern
Bulgaria : Bela Slatina (-c.1945)
Byczyna. Town, southern Poland
: Pitschen (-1945), Germany
Bydgoszcz. City, north-central
Poland : Bromberg (-1919,

1939-45), Germany
Byorksky see Krasnoostrovsky
Byorkyo see Krasnoostrovsky
Byrd Land. Region, Antarc-
tica : Marie Byrd Land
(*1929-67)
Bystrzyca. River, southwest-
ern Poland : Weistritz
(-1945), Germany
Bystrzyca Kłodzka. Town,
southwestern Poland : Habel-
schwerdt (-1945), Germany
Bytom. City, southwestern
Poland : Beuthen (1939-45),
Germany
Bytom Odrzánski. Town,
western Poland : Beuthen
an der Oder (-1945), Ger-
many
Bytów. Town, northwestern
Poland : Bütow (-1945),
Germany

Cabagan. Municipality, Isabela,
Philippines : Cabagan Nuevo
(-1914)
Cabagan Nuevo see Cabagan
Cabaret see Duvalier-Ville
Cabo Yubi see Tarfaya
Cabrália see Cabrália
Paulista
Cabrália Paulista. Town,
southeastern Brazil, South
America : Cabrália (-1944),
Pirajaí (1944-48)
Cabrera de Mar. Village,
northeastern Spain : Cabrera
de Mataró (-c. 1970)
Cabrera de Mataró see
Cabrera de Mar
Cacadu. Town, western Tran-
skei, southern Africa :
Glen Grey (-1976)
Cacaguatique see Ciudad
Barrios
Caçapava see Caçapava do Sul
Caçapava do Sul. City, south-
ern Brazil, South America :
Caçapava (-1944)
Cáceres. City, western

Brazil, South America : São
Luiz de Cáceres (-1939)
Cachoeira see (1) Arariúna;
(2) Cachoeira do Sul; (3)
Cachoeira Paulista; (4)
Solonópole
Cachoeira do Sul. City, southern
Brazil, South America :
Cachoeira (-1944)
Cachoeira Paulista. City, south-
eastern Brazil, South America
: Cachoeira (-1944), Valparaíba
(1944-48)
Cachoeiras see Cachoeiras de
Macacu
Cachoeiras de Macacu. City,
southeastern Brazil, South
America : Cachoeiras (-1943)
Cachuela Esperanza. Town,
northern Bolivia, South Amer-
ica : Esperanza (-1900s)
Caddoa Reservoir see John
Martin Reservoir
Caí. City, southern Brazil,
South America : São Sebastião
do Caí (-c. 1938)
Caiapônia. City, central Brazil,
South America : Rio Bonito
(-1944)
Caiçara see Alvarães
Caiuás see Rio Brilhante
Caja see Čepelarska
Cajamarquilla see Bolívar
Calabar. Town, southeastern
Nigeria, western Africa : Old
Calabar (-1904)
Calamba. Town, Mindanao,
Philippines : Plaridel (-1940s)
Calamunding see Lucio Laurel
Calanasan. Municipality, Mountain
Province, Philippines : Bayag
(-1967)
Calandagan. Barrio, Palawan,
Philippines : Tudela (-1957)
Calanutan see Don Felix Coloma
Caldas. City, southeastern Bra-
zil, South America : Parreiras
(1940-48)
Callang see San Manuel
Calumet. Village, Michigan,
USA : Red Jacket (-1929)
Calumet City. City, Illinois,
USA : West Hammond (-1924)

Camaquã. City, southern Brazil, South America : São João de Camaquã (-1938)

Camaratuba see São Joaquim do Monte

Camarazal see Mulungu

Camassari. City, eastern Brazil, South America : Montenegro (-1939)

Camataquí see Villa Abecia

Cambé. City, southern Brazil, South America : Nova Dantzig (-1944)

Cambirela see Santo Amaro da Imperatriz

Cambodia see Kampuchea

Cammin see Kamień (Pomorski)

Campbell. City, Ohio, USA : East Youngstown (-1926)

Campbellpore [Campbellpur]. District and its capital, north central Pakistan : Attock (-?)

Campbellpur = Campbellpore

Campbelltown see Bluff

Camp Cooke see Vandenberg Air Force Base

Camp Coulter see Powell

Camp David. Country estate, Maryland, USA : Shangri-La (-?)

Campestre see São José do Campestre

Camp Hughes. Locality, Manitoba, Canada : Sewell (-c. 1914)

Camp Morton. Settlement, Manitoba, Canada : Faxa (-?), Haas (?-1925)

Campo Belo see Itatiaia

Campo Florido. City, southeastern Brazil, South America : Campo Formoso (-1944)

Campo Formoso see (1) Campo Florido; (2) Orizana

Campo Grande see Inhuça

Campo Largo see Araçoiaba da Serra

Campo Lugar. Village, western Spain : El Campo (-c. 1960)

Campo Quijano. Town, northwestern Argentina, South

America : Kilómetro 1172 (-1930s)

Campos see Tobias Barreto

Camrose. City, Alberta, Canada : Sparling (*1905-1907)

Canal Dover see Dover

Canarias see (1) Las Palmas; (2) Santa Cruz de Tenerife

Canaveral, Cape. Florida, USA : Kennedy, Cape (1963-73)

Canchungo see Teixeira Pinto

Cangas de Narcea. Village, northwestern Spain : Cangas de Tineo (-c. 1930)

Cangas de Tineo see Cangas de Narcea

Caniçado see Vila Alferes Chamusca

Cañizar de Argano. Village, northern Spain : Cañizar de los Ajos (-c. 1970)

Cañizar de los Ajos see Cañizar de Argano

Canterbury see Invermere

Cantin, Cap see Meddouza

Canton. City, southern China : Punyü (1913-35)

Caoyan see Hilario Valdez (2)

Cape Colony see Cape of Good Hope (Province)

Capela. City, northeastern Brazil, South America : Conçeicão do Paraíba (1944-48)

Cape of Good Hope (Province) [Cape Province]. Southern South Africa : Cape Colony (-1910)

Cape Province = Cape of Good Hope (Province)

Capim. City, northern Brazil, South America : São Domingos da Boa Vista (-1939), São Domingos do Capim (1939-43)

Capivari see Silva Jardim

Capiz see Roxas

Cap-Matifou see Bordj el Bahri

Caporetto see Kobarid

Carabao Island see San Jose (1)

Caraguatay see La Cordillera

Caraza see Santiváñez

Caribrod see Dimitrovgrad (1)

Caririaçu. City, northeastern Brazil, South America : São

Pedro (do Cariry) (-1944)
Carleton Point see Borden
Carlingville see Crandall
Carlos Reyles. Town, central
    Uruguay, South America :
    Molles (-c. 1945)
Carmo see Carmópolis
Carmópolis. City, northeastern
    Brazil, South America :
    Carmo (-1944)
Caronno Milanese see Caronno
    Pertusella
Caronno Pertusella. Village,
    northern Italy : Caronno
    Milanese (-c. 1940)
Carstensz Top see Jaya,
    Puncak
Carteret. Borough, New Jersey,
    USA : Roosevelt (-1906)
Casar del Puerto see Casas
    de Miravete
Casas del Puerto de Tornavacas
    see Puerto de Castilla
Casas de Miravete. Village,
    western Spain : Casas del
    Puerto (-c. 1920)
Casim see General Toshevo
Čáslav. Town, east-central
    Czechoslovakia : Czaslau
    (-1918, 1939-45), Germany
Cassaigne see Sidi Ali
Castelo see (1) Castelo do
    Piauí; (2) Manuel Urbano
Castelo do Piauí. City, north-
    eastern Brazil, South Amer-
    ica : Castelo (-1944), Marvão
    (1944-48)
Castelrosso see Kastellorizon
Castiglione see Bou Ismaïl
Castillo de San Marcos National
    Monument. St. Augustine,
    Florida, USA : Fort Marion
    National Monument (*1924-42)
Castle Mountain see Eisenhower,
    Mount
Castrogiovanni see Enna
Catambia. Town, west-central
    Mozambique, southeastern
    Africa : Catandica (-1915),
    Vila Gouvera (1915-76)
Catandica see Catambia
Catigbian. Municipality, Bohol,
    Philippines : San Jacinto (-1954)

Cattaro see Kotor
Catuiçara. Town, eastern Bra-
    zil, South America : Bom
    Jardim (-1944)
Caucaia. City, northeastern
    Brazil, South America : Soure
    (-1944)
Caurel see Folgoso de Caurel
Cavazuccherina see Iesolo
Caviúna see Rolândia
Cawayanon see Vintar
Cawnpore see Kanpur
Caxias see Caxias do Sul
Caxias do Sul. City, southern
    Brazil, South America : Caxias
    (-1944)
Ceannanus Mór. Town, County
    Meath, Ireland : Kells (-c. 1930)
Cebolla de Trabancas see San
    Cristobal de Trabancos
Cedar Grove. Township, New
    Jersey, USA : Verona (1907-08)
Cedro see Darcilena
Ceduna. Town, South Australia,
    Australia : Murat Bay (-1915)
Cedynia. Town, northwestern
    Poland : Zehden (-1945),
    Germany
Celebes see Sulawesi
Centane. Town, southern Tran-
    skei, southern Africa : Kentani
    (-1976)
Central African Empire. Mon-
    archy, central Africa : Ubanghi
    Shari (*1920-58), Central Afri-
    can Republic (1958-76)
Central African Protectorate see
    Malawi
Central African Republic see
    Central African Empire
Central Industrial Oblast see
    Moscow Oblast
Central Park see Bethpage
Central Provinces see Madhya
    Pradesh
Čepelarska. River, southern
    Bulgaria : Caja (-1967)
Čepinska. River, south-central
    Bulgaria : Elidere (-1967)
Cerknica. Village, northwestern
    Yugoslavia : Zirknitz (-1918),
    Germany
Cernăuţi see Chernovtsy

(Cerro) Bolívar. Mountain, eastern Venezuela, South America : La Parida (-1948)

Česká Kamenice. Town, northwestern Czechoslovakia : Böhmisch-Kamnitz (-1918, 1939-45), Germany

Česká Lípa. Town, northwestern Czechoslovakia : Böhmisch-Leipa (-1918, 1939-45), Germany

Česká Skalice. Town, northwestern Czechoslovakia : Böhmisch-Skalitz (-1918, 1939-45), Germany

Česká Třebová. Town, east-central Czechoslovakia : Böhmisch-Trübau (-1918, 1939-45), Germany

České Budějovice. City, southwestern Czechoslovakia : Budweis (-1918, 1939-45), Germany

Český Brod. Town, east-central Czechoslovakia : Böhmisch-Brod (-1918, 1939-45), Germany

Český Krumlov. Town, southwestern Czechoslovakia : Krummau (-1918, 1939-45), Germany

Český Těšín. Town, north-central Czechoslovakia : Teschen (-1919, 1939-45), Germany

Cetatea-Albă see Belgorod Dnestrovsky

Ceylanpinar. Village, southeastern Turkey : Resulayn (-c. 1945)

Ceylon see Sri Lanka

Chaco. Province, northern Argentina, South America : Presidente Juán Perón (1950-55)

Chad see Oktyabrsky (2)

Chagoda. Urban settlement, Vologda Oblast, RSFSR : Bely Bychek (-1939)

Chaikang see Linnam

Chalakazaki see Kyzylasker

Chalantun see Yalu

Chalchicomula see (Ciudad) Serdán

Chanach see Aktam

Chancay see Chancaybaños

Chancaybaños. Village, northwestern Peru, South America : Chancay (-1942)

Chan-chiang. City, southeastern China : Fort Bayard (1898-1945)

Changan [Ch'ang-an]. Town, central China : Wangkü (-1942)

Changan see Sian [Hsi-an] (1)

Changchai see Changshun [Ch'ang-shun]

Chang-chia-k'ou. City, northeastern China : Wan-ch'üan (1911-29)

Changchih [Ch'ang-chih]. Town, northeastern China : Luan (-1912)

Chang-chiu = Changkiu

Ch'ang-chou = Changchow

Changchow [Ch'ang-chou]. City, eastern China : Wutsin (1912-49)

Changchow see Lungki [Lung-ch'i]

Changhwa see Cheongkong

Changkiu [Chang-chiu]. Town, eastern China : Mingshui (-1949)

Changku see Luho

Changlo see Wufeng

Changning [Ch'ang-ning]. Town, southwestern China : Yutien (-1935)

Changpeh. Town, northeastern China : Sinho (-1918)

Changshan see Yaonan

Changshow see Yenshow

Changshun [Ch'ang-shun]. Town, southern China : Changchai (-1942)

Ch'ang-te see Anyang

Changting [Ch'ang-t'ing]. Town, southeastern China : Tingchow (-1913)

Changtze [Ch'ang-tzu]. Town, central China : Wayaopu (-c. 1940), Anting (1940-49)

Ch'ang-tzu = Changtze

Changwucheng see Chaotung

Changyeh. Town, north-central China : Kanchow (-1913)

Chan-hua = Chanhwa

Chanhwa [Chan-hua]. Town,

southern China : Chantui
(-1912), Hwaiju (1912-16)
Chanta see Lienshan
Chantui see Chanhwa [Chan-
hua]
Chanyü. Town, southwestern
China : Kaihwachen (-1915)
Chaoan [Ch'ao-an]. Town, south-
eastern China : Chaochow
(-1914)
Chaochow see (1) Chaoan
[Ch'ao-an]; (2) Chaohsien;
(3) Fengyi [Feng-i]
Chaohsien. Town, northeastern
China : Chaochow (-1913)
Chaotung. Town, northeastern
China : Changwucheng (-1913)
Chaoyangchwan see Shulan
Chapayev. Town, Uralsk Ob-
last, Kazakh SSR : Lbish-
chensk (-1939)
Chapayevka. Left tributary of
river Volga, Kuybyshev Ob-
last, RSFSR : Mocha (-c. 1930)
Chapayevsk. Town, Kuybyshev
Oblast, RSFSR : Ivashchen-
kovo (-1919), Trotsk (1919-
27)
Chapin see Edinburg
Chaplygin. Town, Lipetsk
Oblast, RSFSR : Ranenburg
(-1948)
Chapopotla. Town, southeastern
Mexico, North America :
Ixhuatlán (-1938)
Chara. Village, Irkutsk Ob-
last, RSFSR : Ust-Zhuya
(-c. 1960)
Charazani see Villa (General)
Pérez
Chardzhou. Capital of Chard-
zhou Oblast, Turkmen SSR :
Chardzhuy (-1924, 1927-37),
Leninsk (-Turkmensky)
(1924-27)
Chardzhuy see Chardzhou
Charente-Inférieure see
Charente-Maritime
Charente-Maritime. Depart-
ment, western France :
Charente-Inférieure (-1941)
Charentsavan. Town, Armenian
SSR : Lusavan (-1967)

Charlesville see Djokupunda
Charleville see Rathluirc
Charlotte Amalie. Capital of
United States Virgin Islands,
West Indies : St. Thomas
(1921-36)
Charon see Bou Kadir
Charsk. Town, Semipalatinsk
Oblast, Kazakh SSR : Charsky
(-1963)
Charsky see Charsk
Chasseloup-Laudat see Râs el
Ma
Chatbazar. Village, Kirgiz SSR :
Budyonny (c. 1937-c. 1965)
Châteaudun-du-Rhumel see
Chelghoum-el-Aïd
Château-Salins. Village, north-
eastern France : Salzburgen
(1940-44), Germany
Chatham see East Hampton
Chaykovsky. Town, Perm Ob-
last, RSFSR : Kamskoy GES,
stroiteley (-1962)
Cheb. Town, western Czecho-
slovakia : Eger (-1918, 1939-
45), Germany
Chehalis see Grays Harbor
Chejung. Town, southeastern
China : Cheyang (-1945)
Chekalin. Town, Tula Oblast,
RSFSR : Likhvin (-1944)
Chekanovsky. Urban settlement,
Irkutsk Oblast, RSFSR :
Anzeba (-1963)
Chekhov (1). Town, Moscow
Oblast, RSFSR : Lopasnya
(-1954)
Chekhov (2). Town, Sakhalin
Oblast, RSFSR : Noda (1905-
47), Japan (-1945)
Chekmagush. Village, Bashkir
Autonomous SSR, RSFSR :
Chekmagushi (-1945)
Chekmagushi see Chekmagush
Chelghoum-el-Aïd. Town, north-
eastern Algeria, northern
Africa : Châteaudun-du-Rhumel
(-c. 1962)
Chelmsko Śląskie. Town, south-
western Poland : Schömberg
(-1945), Germany
Chelny see Naberezhniye Chelny

Chelyabkopi see Kopeysk
Chembar see Belinsky
Chemnitz see Karl-Marx-
Stadt
Chenan see (1) Heishan;
(2) Tienpao [T'ien-pao]
Chen-chiang. City, eastern
China : Tan-t'u (1912-18)
Chenchow see (1) Chenhsien
[Ch'en-hsien]; (2) Hwaiyang
[Huai-yang]
Chenfan see Mintsin [Min-
ch'in]
Cheng-chou = Chengchow
Chengchow [Cheng-chou].
City, east-central China :
Chenghsien (1913-49)
Chenghsien see Chengchow
[Cheng-chou]
Chenhsien [Ch'en-hsien]. Town,
south-central China : Chen-
chow (-1913)
Chen-hua = Chenhwa
Chenhwa [Chen-hua]. Town,
eastern China : Ningtsing
(-1949)
Chenlai. Town, northeastern
China : Chentung (-1949)
Chenpa. Town, central China :
Tingyüan (-1913)
Chenpien see Lantsang [Lan-
ts'ang]
Chenping see Chiuling
Chentung see Chenlai
Chenyüeh. Town, southwestern
China : Yiwu (-1929)
Cheongkong. Town, southeast-
ern China : Changhwa (-1914)
Cheremshany. Urban settle-
ment, Primorsky Kray,
RSFSR : Sinancha (-1972)
Cherente see Miracema do
Norte
Cherepni see Vishnyovaya (1)
Cherkasskoye see Zimogorye
Cherkesovsky. Village, Volgo-
grad Oblast, RSFSR :
Budarinskaya (-c. 1940)
Cherkess (Adygey) Autonomous
Oblast see Adygey Autono-
mous Oblast
Cherkessk. Capital of Kara-
chaevo-Cherkess Autonomous

Oblast, Stavropol Kray, RSFSR
: Batalpashinskaya (-1931),
Batalpashinsk (1931-36),
Sulimov (1936-37), Yezhovo-
Cherkessk (1938-39)
Chernomorka. Spa, Odessa
Oblast, Ukrainian SSR :
Lyustdorf (-?)
Chernomorskoye. Urban settle-
ment, Crimean Oblast, Ukrain-
ian SSR : Ak-Mechet (-1944)
Chernorechye. Suburb of Grozny,
Checheno-Ingush Autonomous
SSR, RSFSR : Novyye Aldy
(-1940)
Chernorechye see Dzerzhinsk
(1)
Chernovitsy see Chernovtsy
Chernovtsy. Capital of Chernovtsy
Oblast, Ukrainian SSR :
Czernowitz (-1918), Germany,
Cernăuţi (1918-40), Romania,
Chernovitsy (1940-44)
Chernyakhovsk. Town, Kalinin-
grad Oblast, RSFSR : Inster-
burg (-1946), Germany (-1945)
Chernyayevo see Yangiyer
Chernyshevskaya see Sovetskaya
(2)
Chernyshevskoye. Village, Ka-
liningrad Oblast, RSFSR :
Eydtkuhnen (-1938), Germany,
Eydtkau (1938-45), Germany
Cherry Hill. Township, New
Jersey, USA : Delaware (-?)
Chersky. Urban settlement,
Yakutsk Autonomous SSR,
RSFSR : Nizhniye Kresty
(-c. 1960)
Chertkov see Chortkov
Chertovshchina see Rassvet
Cherven. Town, Minsk Oblast,
Belorussian SSR : Igumen
(-1925)
Chervonoarmeysk (1). Urban
settlement, Zhitomir Oblast,
Ukrainian SSR : Pulin (-c. 1935)
Chervonoarmeysk (2). Town,
Rovno Oblast, Ukrainian SSR :
Radzivilov (-1940)
Chervonoarmeyskoye see
Volnyansk
Chervonograd. Town, Lvov

Oblast, Ukrainian SSR :
Kristinopol (-1953)
Chervonogrigorovka. Urban
settlement, Dnepropetrovsk
Oblast, Ukrainian SSR :
Krasnogrigoryevka (-1939)
Chervonoye (1). Urban settle-
ment, Zhitomir Oblast,
Ukrainian SSR : Krasnoye
(-c. 1935)
Chervonoye (2). Village,
Sumy Oblast, Ukrainian
SSR : Luzhki (-c. 1960)
Cheryomukha. Village, Minsk
Oblast, Belorussian SSR :
Zatychino (-1964)
Cheryomushki (1). Village,
Grodno Oblast, Belorussian
SSR : Mondino (-1964)
Cheryomushki (2). Village,
Vitebsk Oblast, Belorussian
SSR : Poddannyye (-1964)
Chesnokovka see Novoaltaysk
Chetumal. City, southeastern
Mexico, North America :
Payo Obispo (-1935)
Cheyang see Chejung
Chia-hsien = Kiahsien
Chi-an = Kian
Chiang-ch'eng = Kiangcheng
Chiang-k'ou = Kiangkow
Chiang-ling = Kiangling
Chiang-ning (1) = Kiangning;
(2) see Nanking
Chiang Saen. Village, northern
Thailand : King Chiang Saen
(1930s)
Chiao-hsien = Kiaohsien
Chia-shan = Kiashan
Chibizovka see Zherdevka
Chibyu see Ukhta
Chicacole see Srikakulam
Chicago Drainage Canal see
Sanitary and Ship Canal
Chicago Heights. Suburb of
Chicago, Illinois, USA :
Bloom (-1901)
Chichka see Oktyabrsk (1)
Chichow see Ankwo
Ch'i-ch'un = Kichun
Chiehchow see Chiehsien
[Chieh-hsien]
Chieh-hsien = Chiehsien

Chiehsien [Chieh-hsien]. Town,
northeastern China : Chiehchow
(-1912)
Ch'ien-ch'ang = Kienchang
Ch'ien-ch'eng = Kiencheng
Chien-ho = Kienho
Ch'ien-hsien = Kienhsien
Chien-ko = Kienko
Ch'ien-ning = Kienning
Chien-ou = Kienow
Chien-te = Kienteh
Chien-yang = Kienyang
Chiesa see Chiesa in Valmalenco
Chiesa in Valmalenco. Village,
northern Italy : Chiesa (-c. 1940)
Chih-chiang = Chihkiang
Chih-chin = Chihkin
Chihchow see Kweichih [Kuei-
ch'ih]
Chihkiang [Chih-chiang]. Town,
south-central China : Yüanchow
(-1913)
Chihkin [Chih-chin]. Town, south-
ern China : Pingyüan (-1914)
Chihli see Hopeh
Chi-hsien = Kihsien
Chihtan. Town, central China :
Paoan (-1949)
Chih-te = Chihteh
Chihteh [Chih-te]. Town, eastern
China : Kiupu (-1932)
Chike see Sünko [Hsün-k'o]
Chikhachyov Bay. Tatar Strait,
Khabarovsk Kray, RSFSR :
De-Kastri Bay (-1952)
Chilalin see Shihwei
Ch'i-lien = Kilien
Chililabombwe. Town, north-
central Zambia, central Africa
: Bancroft (-late 1960s)
Chililaya see Puerto Pérez
Chilumba. Town, northern
Malawi, southeastern Africa :
Deep Bay (-?)
Chimkent Oblast. Kazakh SSR :
South Kazakhstan Oblast
(*1932-62)
Chin-chai = Kinchai
Chin-ch'eng = Tsincheng
Chin-chiang = Tsinkiang
Ch'in-chou see T'ien-shui
Ch'ing-chiang(-pu) = Tsingkiang
(pu)

Ching-ch'uan = Kingchwan
Ching-hsi = Tsingsi
Ching-hsien = Tsinghsien
Ching-ku = Kingku
Ch'ing-lung = Tsinglung
Ch'ing-p'ing = Tsingping
Ching-t'ai = Kingtai
Ching-te-chien = Kingtehchen
Ching-yü = Tsingyü
Kingyüan
Ching-yüan =
Ch'ing-yüan (1) see Pao-ting;
(2) = Tsingyüan
Chinhsien. Town, northeastern
China : Kinchow (-1945)
Chin-hsien = Tsinhsien (1)
Ch'in-hsien = Tsinhsien (2)
Chini see Kalpa
Chi-ning = Tsining
Chinnai see Krasnogorsk (2)
Chinnamp'o see Namp'o
Chinomiji see Tyatino
Chin-p'ing = Kinping
Chin-sha = Kinsha
Chin-t'ang = Kintang
Ch'in-yang = Tsinyang
Chinyüan. Town, northeastern
China : Taiyüan (-1947)
Chios. Island, Aegean Sea,
Greece : Sakiz-Adasi
(-c. 1913), Turkey
Chipata. Town, eastern Zam-
bia, south-central Africa :
Fort Jameson (-c. 1965)
Chirchik. Town, Tashkent
Oblast, Uzbek SSR : Kirgiz-
Kulak (-1932), Komsomolsky
(1932-34)
Chirie see Kotikovo
Chişinău see Kishinyov
Chistyakovo see Torez
Chitaldrug see Chitradurga
Chitipa. Town, northern
Malawi, southeastern Africa
: Fort Hill (-?)
Chitradurga. Town, southern
India : Chitaldrug (-1966)
Chittaranjan. Village, north-
eastern India : Mihidjan
(-1966)
Chitung [Ch'i-tung]. Town,
eastern China : Hweilungchen
(-1929)
Chiu-chüan = Kiuchüan

Chiuling. Town, southeastern
China : Chenping (-1914)
Ch'iung-lai = Kiunglai
Ch'iung-shan = Kiungshan
Ch'iung-tung = Kiungtung
Chiu-t'ai = Kiutai
Chkalov. Island, Okhotsk Sea,
Khabarovsk Kray, RSFSR :
Udd (-c. 1939)
Chkalov see Orenburg
Chkalovo (1). Village, Kokchetav
Oblast, Kazakh SSR : Bogoduk-
hovka (-1939)
Chkalovo (2). Village, Sakhalin
Oblast, RSFSR : Kitose
(1905-45), Japan
Chkalovo (3). Village, Dnepropet-
trovsk Oblast, Ukrainian SSR :
Novo-Nikolayevka (-1939)
Chkalovo see Kurchaloy
Chkalov Oblast see Orenburg
Oblast
Chkalovsk. Town, Gorky Oblast,
RSFSR : Vasilyova Sloboda
(-1927), Vasilyovo (1927-37)
Chkalovskoye (1). Village,
Chuvash Autonomous SSR,
RSFSR : Shikhirdany (-1939)
Chkalovskoye (2). Village,
Primorsky Kray, RSFSR :
Zenkovka (-1939)
Chkalovsky see Kayrakkum
Chobienia. Town, southwestern
Poland : Köben (an der Oder)
(-1945), Germany
Choca see Praia da Condúcia
Chochow see Chohsien
Chocianów. Town, southwestern
Poland : Kotzenau (-1945),
Germany
Chociwel. Town, northwestern
Poland : Freienwalde (-1945),
Germany
Choerhcheng see Talai
Chohsien. Town, northeastern
China : Chochow (-1913)
Chojna. Town, northwestern
Poland : Königsberg (-1945),
Germany
Chojnów. City, southwestern
Poland : Haynau [Hainau]
(-1945), Germany
Choloma. Town, northwestern

Honduras, Central America : El Paraiso (-early 1930s)

Chomutov. City, northwestern Czechoslovakia : Komotau (-1918, 1939-45), Germany

Chon-Ak-Dzhol see Dzhangy-Dzhol

Chongning see Sunfung

Choque. City, southern Mozambique, southeastern Africa : Guija (-1960), Vila Alferes Chamusca (1960-64), Vila Trigo de Morais (1964-71), Trigo de Morais (1971-76)

Chortkov. Town, Ternopol Oblast, Ukrainian SSR : Czortków (1919-39), Poland; Chertkov (1939-44)

Chorzów. Suburb of Katowice, southern Poland : Königshütte (-1921), Germany; Królewska Huta (1921-1930s)

Choszczno. Town, northwestern Poland : Arnswalde (-1945), Germany

Chotzeshan see Lungsheng

Chou-ning = Chowning

Chowning [Chou-ning]. Town, southeastern China : Chowtun (-1945)

Chowtun see Chowning [Chou-ning]

Choybalsan. Town, eastern Mongolian People's Republic : San-Beyse (-1921), Bayan-Tumen (1921-41)

Chozas de la Sierra see Soto del Real

Christburg see Dzierzgoń

Christiania see Oslo

Chrzanów. Town, southern Poland : Krenau (1939-45), Germany

Chtimba. Town, northeastern Malawi, southeastern Africa : Florence Bay (-c. 1964)

Chüanchow see Tsinkiang

Chubarovka see Pologi

Chubartau see Barshatas

Chubek see Moskovsky

Chuchow see (1) Chuhsien [Ch'u-hsien]; (2) Lishui

Chüchow see Chühsien [Ch'ü-hsien]

Chuho see Shangchih

Chuhsien [Ch'u-hsien]. Town, eastern China : Chuchow (-1912)

Chühsien [Ch'ü-hsien]. City, eastern China : Chüchow (-1913)

Chukotskaya Kultbaza see Lavrentiya

Chulaktau see Karatau

Chungchow see Chunghsien

Chung-hsiang = Chungsiang

Chunghsien. Town, central China : Chungchow (-1913)

Ch'ungmu. City, southeastern South Korea : Tongyŏng (-1955)

Chungpu see Hwangling (Huangling]

Chungshan see Tangkiakwan [T'ang-chia-kuan]

Ch'ung-shan = Tsungshan

Chungsiang [Chung-hsiang]. Town, east-central China : Anlu (-1912)

Ch'ung-te = Tsungteh

Chungyang. Town, northeastern China : Niangsiang (-1914)

Chün-hsien = Künhsien

Churchill. Statistical region, North Island, New Zealand : South Auckland (-1963)

Churchill Falls. Waterfall, Churchill River, Newfoundland, Canada : Grand Falls (-1965)

Churchill River. River, Newfoundland, Canada : Hamilton River (-1965)

Churubay-Nura see Abay (2)

Chusovoy. Town, Perm Oblast, RSFSR : Chusovskoy Zavod (-1933)

Chusovskoy Zavod see Chusovoy

Chust see Khust

Chutzeshan see Weichang [Wei-ch'ang]

Chwankow see Minho

Chwanping see Lankao

Chyormoz. Town, Perm Oblast, RSFSR : Chyormozsky Zavod (-1943)

Chyormozsky Zavod see Chyormoz

Chyorny Rynok see Kochubey

Cidade de Minas see Belo

Horizonte
Ciechocinek. Town, north-
central Poland : Hermannsbad
(1939-45), Germany
Cieplice Śląskie Zdrój. Town,
southwestern Poland : Bad
Warmbrunn (-1945), Germany
Cinzas. City, southern Brazil,
South America : Jundiaí
(-1944)
City of The Dalles. City, Ore-
gon, USA : The Dalles
[Dalles City] (-1966)
Ciudad Arce. Town, west-cen-
tral Salvador, Central Amer-
ica : El Chilamatal (*1921-
c. 1948)
Ciudad Barrios. City, eastern
Salvador, Central America :
Cacaguatique (-1913)
Ciudad González see Doctor
Hernández Alvarez
Ciudad Madero. City, eastern
Mexico, North America :
Villa Cecilia (*1924-30)
Ciudad Porfirio Díaz see
Piedras Negras
(Ciudad) Serdán. Puebla, cen-
tral Mexico, North America
: Chalchicomula (-1934)
Ciudad Trujillo see Santo
Domingo
Clairfontaine see El Aouinet
Claviere. Village, northwestern
Italy : Clavières (-c. 1936),
France
Clavières see Claviere
Clinch-Powell Reservoir see
Norris Lake
Clinton see Galena Park
Cloyes see Cloyes-sur-le-Loir
Cloyes-sur-le-Loir. Village,
northwestern France : Cloyes
(-1938)
Cluj. Town, northwestern
Romania : Klausenburg
(-1920), Germany
Coal Creek see Lake City
Coast see Pwani
Coatzacoalcos. Town, south-
central Mexico, North Amer-
ica : Puerto México (-?)
Cóbh. Town, County Cork,

Ireland : Queenstown (1849-
1922)
Coelho Neto. City, northeastern
Brazil, South America : Cur-
ralhinho (-1939)
Cofimvaba. Town, southwestern
Transkei, southern Africa :
St. Marks (-1976)
Cogon-Bingkay see Salvacion (1)
Colbert see Aïn Oulmene
Colinas. City, northeastern Bra-
zil, South America : Picos
(-1944)
College Park see East Lansing
Colleville-Montgomery. Village,
northwestern France : Colle-
ville-sur-Orne (-1946)
Colleville-sur-Orne see Colle-
ville-Montgomery
Colomb-Béchar see Béchar
Colonia see Libertad (1)
Colônia Leopoldina. City, north-
eastern Brazil, South America
: Leopoldina (-1944)
Colonia Mineira see Sisqueira
Campos
Colony Province see Ikeja
Province
Comandante Arbues see Miran-
dópolis
Comendador see Elías Piña
Communism Peak. Mountain,
Pamirs Range, Tadzhik SSR :
Garmo Peak [name subsequently
transferred to present Garmo
Peak, south of this] (-1933),
Stalin Peak (1933-62)
Comunanza. Village, central
Italy : Comunanza del Littorio
(c. 1937-45)
Comunanza del Littorio see
Comunanza
Conceição do Almeida. City,
eastern Brazil, South America
: Afonso Pena (-1944)
Conceição do Paraíba see Capela
Concepcion. Barrio, Masbate,
Philippines : Sawmill (-1957)
Concepcion see Gregorio del
Pilar
Condé-Smendou see Zighout
Youcef
Coney. Island, off northeastern

Singapore : Serangoon
(-c. 1970)
Congo see (1) People's Repub-
lic of the Congo; (2) Zaïre
Congo Belge see Zaïre
Congo (Brazzaville) see
People's Republic of the
Congo
Congo Free State see Zaïre
Congo (Kinshasa) see Zaïre
Congonhas. City, southeastern
Brazil, South America :
Congonhas do Campo (-1948)
Congonhas do Campo see
Congonhas
Conquista see Vitória da
Conquista
Constantinople see Istanbul
Coos Bay. City, Oregon, USA
: Marshfield (-1944)
Copperbelt. Province, western
Zambia, south-central
Africa : Western (-1971)
Copper City see Invermere
Coquilhatville see (1) Équateur;
(2) Mbandaka
Cordeiro see Cordeirópolis
Cordeirópolis. City, south-
eastern Brazil, South
America : Cordeiro (-1944)
Cordillera Capetónica see
Sistema Central
Cordillera Mariánica see
Sierra Morena
Cordillera Oretana see
Montes de Toledo
Coreaú. City, northeastern
Brazil, South America :
Palma (-1944)
Coripós. City, northeastern
Brazil, South America :
Boa Vista (-1944)
Corneille see Merouana
Corneto (Tarquinia) see
Tarquinia
Corregidora. Town, central
Mexico, North America :
El Pueblito (-1946)
Corumbá see Corumbá de
Goiás
Corumbá de Goiás. City,
central Brazil, South Amer-
ica : Corumbá (-1944)

Corupá. Town, southern Brazil,
South America : Hansa (-1944)
Cosel see Koźle
Cossette see Inwood
Costa Mesa. City, California,
USA : Harper (*1906-21)
Costermansville see (1) Bukavu;
(2) Kivu
Cotillas see Las Torres de
Cotillas
Cotinguiba. City, northeastern
Brazil, South America :
Socorro (-1944)
Cotopaxi. Province, north-central
Ecuador, South America :
León (-1939)
Cotrone see Crotone
Cottage City see Oak Bluffs
Country Club Estates see
Miami Springs
Coxim. City, western Brazil,
South America : Herculânia
(1939-48)
Crandall. Village, Manitoba,
Canada : Carlingville (-1901)
Cristina see Cristinápolis
Cristinápolis. City, northeastern
Brazil, South America :
Cristina (-1944)
Crosby. Town, Mississippi,
USA : Stephenson (-1934)
Crossen see Krosno (Odrzań-
skie)
Crotone. Town, southern Italy :
Cotrone (-1928)
Cruz do Espírito Santo. City,
northeastern Brazil, South
America : Espírito Santo
(-1944), Maguari (1944-48)
Cruzeiro see Joaçaba
Cruzeiro do Sul see Joaçaba
Csév see Pilicsév
Cuamba see Nova-Freixo
Cuatro de Junio. Town, west-
central Argentina, South Amer-
ica : La Toma (-c. 1945)
Cuevas de Almanzora. Village,
southern Spain : Cuevas de
Vera (-c. 1930)
Cuevas de Vera see Cuevas de
Almanzora
Cuiabá see Mestre Caetano
Culebra see Dewey

Culebra Cut see Gaillard Cut
Cumbe see Euclides da
   Cunha
Cummings' Island see Vanier
   (1)
Curador see Presidente Dutra
Curba see San Roque
Curralinho see Coelho Neto
Curt-Bunar see Tervel
Curuzu. Town, northeastern
   Brazil, South America :
   São Benedito (-1944)
Cybinka. Town, western Po-
   land : Ziebingen (-1945),
   Germany
Cypress. City, California,
   USA : Waterville (-1956),
   Dairy City (1956)
Czaplinek. Town, northwestern
   Poland : Tempelburg (-1945),
   Germany
Czarne. Town, northwestern
   Poland : Hammerstein
   (-1945), Germany
Czaslau see Čáslav
Czernina. Town, western
   Poland : Tschirnau (-1937),
   Germany, Lesten (1937-45),
   Germany
Czernowitz see Chernovtsy
Człopa. Town, northwestern
   Poland : Schloppe (-1945),
   Germany
Człuchów. Town, northwestern
   Poland : Schlochau (-1945),
   Germany
Czortków see Chortkov

Daber see Dobra
Dabie. Town, northwestern
   Poland : Altdamm (-1945),
   Germany
Dąbromierz. Town, southwest-
   ern Poland : Hohenfriedeberg
   (-1945), Germany
Dąbrowa Górnicza. Town, south-
   western Poland : Dombrova
   (-1919), Russia
Dąbrowno. Town, northeastern
   Poland : Gilgenburg (-1945),

Germany
Dachnoye. Village, Sakhalin
   Oblast, RSFSR : Shimba
   (1905-45), Japan
Dacudao see General Roxas
Dadra see Achalpur
Dahomey see Benin
Daingean. Village, County Offaly,
   Ireland : Philipstown (-?)
Dairen. City, northeastern
   China : Dalny (-1905), Russia
Dairy City see Cypress
Dajabón. Province, northwestern
   Dominican Republic, West
   Indies : Libertador (*1938-61)
Dakhla. Town, western Spanish
   Sahara, northwestern Africa :
   Villa Cisneros (-1976)
Dalagan see San Antonio
Dalatando. Town, northwestern
   Angola, southwestern Africa :
   Vila Salazar (1930s-c. 1976)
Dalence see Teniente Bullaín
Dalle see Yirga-Alam
Dalles City see City of The
   Dalles
Dalnegorsk. Urban settlement,
   Primorsky Kray, RSFSR :
   Tetyukhe (-1972)
Dalnerechensk. Town, Primorsky
   Kray, RSFSR : Iman (-1972)
Dalny see Dairen
Dambrowica see Dubrovitsa
Da Nang. City, northeastern
   Vietnam : Tourane (-?)
Dancalia Meridionale see Assab
Daniels. Village, Maryland,
   USA : Alberton (-1940)
Danish West Indies see Virgin
   Islands (of the United States)
Dansalan see Marawi
Danzig see Gdańsk
Dáphne. Village, southern Greece
   : Koutroumpoúkhion (-1960s)
Daphnokhórion see Glypháda
Dara Dere see Zlatograd
Daraga. Municipality, Albay,
   Philippines : Locsin (-1967)
Darasun see Vershino-Dara-
   sunsky
Darcilena. City, northeastern
   Brazil, South America : Cedro
   (-1944)

Dar el Beïda. Village, north-
ern Algeria, northern Africa
: Maison-Blanche (-c. 1962)
Dar es Salaam. District,
eastern Tanzania, eastern
Africa : Mzizima (-1974)
Darkehmen see Ozyorsk
Darwin. Capital of Northern
Territory, Australia : Pal-
merston (-1911)
Dashev. Urban settlement,
Vinnitsa Oblast, Ukrainian
SSR : Stary Dashev (-c. 1930)
Dashkesan. Town, Azerbaijan
SSR : Verkhny Dashkesan
(*c. 1945-48)
Dasokhórion. Village, eastern
Greece : Zarkhanádes
(-1960s)
Datu Piang. Municipality,
Cotabato, Philippines : Dula-
wan (-1954)
Daugavgriva. Fortified port,
Riga, Latvian SSR : Ust-
Dvinsk (-1917), Russia
Daugavpils. Town, Latvian
SSR : Dvinsk (-1920), Russia,
Latgale (1920-40), Latvia,
Dünaburg (1941-44), Germany
Davydkovo see Tolbukhino
Dawley see Telford
Deberai. Peninsula, northwest-
ern Irian Jaya, Indonesia :
Vogelkop (-1963)
Dębica. Town, southeastern
Poland : Dembica (1939-45),
Germany
Dęblin. Village, eastern Poland
: Ivangorod (-1915), Russia
Debrzno. Town, northwestern
Poland : Preussisch Friedland
(-1945), Germany
Decemvrie 30, 1947. Suburb of
Bucharest, Romania : Prin-
cipele-Nicolae (-1948)
Děčín. City, western Czech-
oslovakia : Tetschen (-1918,
1939-45), Germany
Dedeağaç see Alexandroúpolis
Dedovsk. Town, Moscow Ob-
last, RSFSR : Guchkovo
(-1925), Dedovsky (1925-40)
Dedovsky see Dedovsk

Deep Bay see Chilumba
Deep River. Town, Connecticut,
USA : Saybrook (-1947)
Deerfield see Deerfield Beach
Deerfield Beach. City, Florida,
USA : Hillsboro (-1907),
Deerfield (1907-39)
Degtyarka see Degtyarsk
Degtyarsk. Town, Sverdlovsk
Oblast, RSFSR : Degtyarka
(-1954)
Deichow see Dychów
De-Kastri Bay see Chikhachyov
Bay
Dekhkanabad. Village, Kashka-
darya Oblast, Uzbek SSR :
Tengi-Kharam (-c. 1935)
Delaware see Cherry Hill
del Carmen. Municipality,
Surigao del Norte, Philippines
: Numancin (-1966)
Delmiro. Town, northeastern
Brazil, South America : Pedra
(-1944)
Delray see Delray Beach
Delray Beach. City, Florida,
USA : Linton (-c. 1901), Delray
(c. 1901-27)
Demárion. Village, western
Greece : Dimarión (-1960s)
Dembica see Dębica
Demidov. Town, Smolensk Ob-
last, RSFSR : Porechye (-1918)
Democratic Kampuchea =
Kampuchea
Democratic Republic of Madagas-
car. Southeastern Africa :
Madagascar (-1958), Malagasy
Republic (1958-75)
Democratic Republic of the Congo
see Zaïre
Demyanovka see Leninskoye (3)
Denezhkin Kamen. Nature re-
serve, Sverdlovsk Oblast,
RSFSR : Ivdel (-c. 1960)
Denisovka see Ordzhonikidze (2)
Denwood see Wainwright
Deodoro see Piraquara
Deorha see Jubbal
Derbeshka see Derbeshkinsky
Derbeshkinsky. Urban settlement,
Tatar Autonomous SSR, RSFSR
: Derbeshka (-1940)

Derbinskoye see Tymovskoye
Derby. City, Kansas, USA :
  El Paso (-1957)
Deryaki see Gornaya (1)
Derzhavinsk. Town, Turgay
  Oblast, Kazakh SSR :
  Derzhavinsky (-1966)
Derzhavinsky see Derzhavinsk
Deschnaer Kuppe see Velká
  Destná
Desenzano del Garda. Town,
  northern Italy : Desenzano
  sul Lago (-1926)
Desenzano sul Lago see
  Desenzano del Garda
Detskoye Selo see Pushkin
Deutsch Brod see Havlíčkův
  Brod.
Deutsch-Eylau see Iława
Deutsch Gabel see Jablonné
  v Podještědí
Deutsch Krone see Wałcz
Deutsch Przemysl see
  Przemysl
Devin. City, southwestern
  Bulgaria : Dovlen (-1934)
Dewey. Town, Culebra island,
  Puerto Rico, West Indies :
  Culebra (-c. 1940)
Dewgard Baria. Town, western
  India : Baria (-1950s)
Dhi Qar. Province, southeast-
  ern Iraq : Al Muntafak
  (-1971)
Diciosânmartin see Târnǎveni
Diedenhofen see Thionville
Dievenow see Dziwnów
Diez y Ocho de Julio. Village,
  southeastern Uruguay, South
  America : San Miguel (-1909)
Dilman see Shahpur
Dimarión see Demárion
Dimitrovgrad (1). Town, south-
  eastern Yugoslavia : Caribrod
  [Tsaribrod] (-1950)
Dimitrovgrad (2). Town,
  Ulyanovsk Oblast, RSFSR :
  Melekess (-1972)
Dimitrovo. Village, west-cen-
  tral Bulgaria : Kostenets
  (-1950)
Dimitrovo see Pernik
Dinokot see Macias

Díon. Village, northern Greece
  : Malathriá (-1960s)
Díon see Karítsa
Dirizhablstroy see Dolgoprudny
Dirrákhion see Dyrrákhion
Dirschau see Tczew
Divnogorsk. Town, Krasnoyarsk
  Kray, RSFSR : Skit (-1963)
Diwaniya see Al-Qadisiya
Diyala. Province, eastern Iraq :
  Baquba (-1971)
Djajapura = Jayapura
Djakarta = Jakarta
Djakova see Djakovica
Djakovica. Town, southwestern
  Yugoslavia : Djakova (-1913),
  Turkey
Djalma Dutra see (1) Miguel
  Calmon; (2) Poções
Djaya, Puntjak = Jaya, Puncak
Djerba. Town, Djerba island,
  eastern Tunisia, northern
  Africa : Houmt Souk (-?)
Djibouti. Republic, northeastern
  Africa : French Somaliland
  (-1967), Afars and Issas
  (1967-77)
Djokupunda. Town, south-central
  Zaïre, central Africa :
  Charlesville (-1972)
Dmanisi. Urban settlement,
  Georgian SSR : Bashkicheti
  (-1947)
Dmitriyevsk see Makeyevka
Dmitriyevskoye see Talas
Dmitriyevsky see Makeyevsk
Dneprodzerzhinsk. Town, Dnepro-
  petrovsk Oblast, Ukrainian
  SSR : Kamenskoye (-1936)
Dnepropetrovsk. Capital of
  Dnepropetrovsk Oblast, Ukrain-
  ian SSR : Yekaterinoslav (-1926)
Dneprovskoye. Village, Smolensk
  Oblast, RSFSR : Andreyevskoye
  (-c. 1960)
Doberlug. Town, eastern East
  Germany : Dobrilugk (-1937)
Dobiegniew. Town, western
  Poland : Woldenberg (-1945),
  Germany
Dobra. Town, northwestern
  Poland : Daber (-1945), Ger-
  many

Dobřany. Town, western Czechoslovakia : Wiesengrund (-1918,
1939-45), Germany

Dobre Miasto. Town, northeastern Poland : Guttstadt
(-1945), Germany

Dobric see Tolbukhin

Dobrilugk see Doberlug

Dobrinka. Village, Volgograd
Oblast, RSFSR : Nizhnyaya
Dobrinka (-c. 1940)

Dobrna. Village, northwestern
Yugoslavia : Neuhaus (-1918),
Germany

Dobrodzień. Town, southern
Poland : Guttentag (-1945),
Germany

Dobropolye. Town, Donetsk
Oblast, Ukrainian SSR :
Svyatogorovsky Rudnik (-c.
1918), Valdgeym (c. 1918-
c. 1935), Rot-Front (c. 1935-
41), Krasnoarmeysky Rud-
nik (1941-53)

Dobrovolsk. Village, Kaliningrad Oblast, RSFSR : Pillkallen (-1938), Germany,
Schlossberg (1938-46), Germany (-1945)

Dobroye. Village, Sakhalin
Oblast, RSFSR : Naibo (1905-
45), Japan

Dobrzany. Town, northwestern
Poland : Jacobshagen (-1945),
Germany

Doctor Hernández Alvarez. City,
central Mexico, North America : Ciudad González (-1938)

Dodecanese. Island group,
Aegean Sea, Greece : Pos-
sedimenti Italiani dell' Egeo
(1912-45)

Dogo see Dogoyuno-machi

Dogoyuno-machi. Town, northwestern Shikoku, Japan :
Dogo (-1923)

Dokshukino see Nartkala

Dokuchayevsk. Town, Donetsk
Oblast, Ukrainian SSR :
Yelenovskiye Karyery (-1954)

Dolban see Liman

Dolgintsevo. Suburb of Krivoy
Rog, Dnepropetrovsk Oblast,

Ukrainian SSR : Bukharino
(1920s-c. 1935)

Dolgoprudny. Town, Moscow
Oblast, RSFSR : Dirizhablstroy
(-1938)

Dolinovskoye. Urban settlement,
Voroshilovgrad Oblast, Ukrainian SSR : Petro-Golenishchevo
(-c. 1960)

Dolinsk. Town, Sakhalin Oblast,
RSFSR : Otiai (1905-46),
Japan (-1945)

Dolinskaya. Town, Kirovograd
Oblast, Ukrainian SSR :
Shevchenkovo (mid-1920s,
c. 1940-44)

Dolinskoye. Village, Odessa
Oblast, Ukrainian SSR :
Valegotsulovo (-1945)

Doma see Gombe

Domažlice. Town, southwestern
Czechoslovakia : Taus (-1918,
1939-45), Germany

Dombarovka see Dombarovsky

Dombarovsky. Urban settlement,
Orenburg Oblast, RSFSR :
Dombarovka (-1939)

Dombasle see El Hachem

Dombrau see Dąbrowa Górnicza

Dombrovitsa see Dubrovitsa

Domman-Asfaltovy Zavod see
Leninsky (1)

Domnau see Domnovo

Domnovo. Village, Kaliningrad
Oblast, RSFSR : Domnau
(-1945), Germany

Doña Alicia see Mabini

Doña Rosario. Barrio, Agusan,
Philippines : Victory (-1952)

Donetsk (1). Town, Rostov
Oblast, RSFSR : Gundorovka
(-1955)

Donetsk (2). Capital of Donetsk
Oblast, Ukrainian SSR :
Yuzovka (-1924), Stalin (1924-
c. 1935), Stalino (c. 1935-61)

Donetsko-Amvrosiyevka see
Amvrosiyevka

Donetsk Oblast. Ukrainian SSR :
Stalino Oblast (*1938-61)

Don Felix Coloma. Barrio,
Pangasinan, Philippines :
Calanutan (-1972)

Don Mariano. Barrio, Ilocos
Norte, Philippines : Sitio
Rawrawang (-1972)
Donskoye (1). Village, Kalinin-
grad Oblast, RSFSR : Gross
Dirschkeim (-1945), Germany
Donskoye (2). Village, Lipetsk
Oblast, RSFSR : Patriarsheye
(-1930s), Vodopyanovo (1930s-
c. 1965)
Dor. Settlement, northwestern
Israel : Tantura (-1949)
Dores da Boa Esperança see
Boa Esperança
Doristhal see Razino
Dorokawa see Ulyanovskoye (1)
Döryzomba see Zomba
Dostluk. Urban settlement,
Chardzhou Oblast, Turkmen
SSR : Yuzhny (-c. 1960)
Dothan. City, Alabama, USA :
Poplar Head (-1911)
Douchy see Douchy-les-Mines
Douchy-les-Mines. Town,
northern France : Douchy
(-1938)
Doué see Doué-la-Fontaine
Doué-la-Fontaine. Town, west-
ern France : Doué (-1933)
Dovbysh. Urban settlement,
Zhitomir Oblast, Ukrainian
SSR : Markhlevsk (-1944)
Dover. City, Ohio, USA :
Canal Dover (-1920)
Dover see Westlake
Dovlen see Devin
Dozdab see Zakhedan
Draâ Ben Khedda. Village,
northern Algeria, northern
Africa : Mirabeau (-c. 1962)
Draâ Esmar. Village, northern
Algeria, northern Africa :
Lodi (-c. 1962)
Drable see (José Enrique)
Rodó
Dragomirovo see Proletarsk
(1)
Dramburg see Drawsko
Dravograd. Village, northwest-
ern Yugoslavia : Unterdrau-
burg (-1918), Germany
Drawno. Town, northwestern
Poland : Neuwedell (-1945),

Germany
Drawsko. Town, northwestern
Poland : Dramburg (-1945),
Germany
Drayton Valley. Town, Alberta,
Canada : Power House (*c.
1907-c. 1918)
Drekhcha Panenskaya see
Kutuzovka
Dresser. Village, Wisconsin,
USA : Dresser Junction (-1940)
Dresser Junction see Dresser
Drezdenko. Town, western
Poland : Driesen (-1945),
Germany
Driesen see Drezdenko
Drissa see Verkhnedvinsk
Drochilovo see Gagarino
Droichead Nua. Town, County
Kildare, Ireland : Newbridge
(-?)
Drosiá. Village, central Greece
: Khalía (-1960s)
Drosokhórion. Village, eastern
Greece : Typhloséllion (-1960s)
Drosopege. Village, southern
Greece : Mpásion (-1960s)
Drossen see Ośno
Drozhzhanoye see (Staroye)
Drozhzhanoye
Druskeniki see Druskininkay
Druskininkay. Town, Lithuanian
SSR : Druskeniki (1921-39)
Druzhba (1). Village, Kaliningrad
Oblast, RSFSR : Allenburg
(-1946), Germany (-1945)
Druzhba (2). Town, Sumy Oblast,
Ukrainian SSR : Khutor-Mikhay-
lovsky (-1962)
Druzhba (3). Town, Khorezm
Oblast, Uzbek SSR : Sharlak
(-1976)
Druzhkovka. Town, Donetsk
Oblast, Ukrainian SSR :
Gavrilovsky Zavod (-1930s)
Dryazgi see Oktyabrskoye (2)
Drymón. Village, Levkás,
Ionian Islands, Greece : Káto
Exántheia (-1960s)
Duarte, Pico. Mountain, central
Dominican Republic, West
Indies : Monte Trujillo (1936-
61)

Düben see Bad Düben
Dubovsky. Urban settlement,
Voroshilovgrad Oblast,
Ukrainian SSR : Gromovsky
(-c. 1960)
Dubrovitsa. Town, Rovno Ob-
last, Ukrainian SSR : Dam-
browica (-1939), Poland;
Dombrovitsa (1939-45)
Dubrovnik. Town, southwest-
ern Yugoslavia : Ragusa
(-1919), Germany
Dudergof see Mozhaysky
Duders Beach see Umupuia
Dufault see Genthon
Duisburg. City, western West
Germany : Duisburg-Hamborn
(1929-34)
Duisburg-Hamborn see Duisburg
Dulawan see Datu Piang
Dumaran see Araceli
Dünaburg see Daugavpils
Dunaújváros. Town, west-
central Hungary : Sztálinváros
(*1950-1962)
Dun Laoghaire. Town, County
Dublin, Ireland : Kingstown
(1821-1921)
Duperré see Aïn Defla
Dupnitsa see Stanke Dimitrov
Durasovka see Ozyornoye
Durazzo see Durrës
Durban Road see Bellville
Durichi see Znamenka (1)
Durnevichi see Lugovaya (1)
Durrës. City, western Albania
: Durazzo (1939-43), Italy
Dushanbe. Capital of Tadzhik
SSR : Dyushambe (-1929),
Stalinabad (1929-61)
Dushet see Dusheti
Dusheti. Town, Georgian SSR :
Dushet (-1936)
Dusti. Urban settlement, Tad-
zhik SSR : Pyandzh (-c. 1960)
Duszniki Zdrój. Town, south-
western Poland : Bad Reinerz
(-1945), Germany
Dutch Borneo see Kalimantan
Dutch East Indies see Indonesia
Dutch Guiana see Surinam
Duvalier-Ville. Town, Haïti,
West Indies : Cabaret (-1963)

Duvno. Town, west-central
Yugoslavia : Tomislavgrad
(1930s-c. 1945)
Duzkend see Akhuryan
Dvadtsati Shesti Bakinskikh
Komissarov, imeni. Urban
settlement, Azerbaijan SSR :
Neftechala (-c. 1960)
Dvigatelstroy see Kaspiysk
Dvinsk see Daugavpils
Dvoryanskaya Tereshka see
Radishchevo (1)
Dvurechensk. Urban settlement,
Sverdlovsk Oblast, RSFSR :
Khrompik (-c. 1960)
Dvůr Králové (nad Labem). Town,
northeastern Czechoslovakia :
Königinhof (an der Elbe) (-1918,
1939-45), Germany
Dychów. Village, western Po-
land : Deichow (-1945), Ger-
many
Dyhernfurth see Brzeg Dolny
Dyrrákhion. Village, southern
Greece : Dirrákhion (-1960s)
Dyushambe see Dushanbe
Dzagidzor see Tumanyan
Dzaudzhikau see Ordzhonikidze
(5)
Dzerzhinsk (1). Town, Gorky
Oblast, RSFSR : Chernorechye
(-?), Rastyapino (?-1929)
Dzerzhinsk (2). Town, Minsk
Oblast, Belorussian SSR :
Kaydanovo (-1932)
Dzerzhinsk (3). Village, Gomel
Oblast, Belorussian SSR :
Radzivilovichi (-1925)
Dzerzhinsk (4). Urban settle-
ment, Zhitomir Oblast,
Ukrainian SSR : Romanov
(-1931)
Dzerzhinsk (5). Town, Donetsk
Oblast, Ukrainian SSR :
Shcherbinovka (-1938)
Dzerzhinskogo, imeni see
Naryan-Mar
Dzerzhinskoye (1). Village,
Taldy-Kurgan Oblast, Kazakh
SSR : Kolpakovskoye (-?)
Dzerzhinskoye (2). Village,
Krasnoyarsk Kray, RSFSR :
Rozhdestvenskoye (-?)

Dzerzhinsky. Urban settlement, Moscow Oblast, RSFSR : Trudovaya Kommuna imeni Dzerzhinskogo (*1921-38)

Dzerzhinsky see Sorsk

Dzhalal-Ogly see Stepanavan

Dzhalilabad. Town, Azerbaijan SSR : Astrakhan-Bazar (-1967)

Dzhambay. Town, Samarkand Oblast, Uzbek SSR : Khoshdala (-1977)

Dzhambul. Capital of Dzhambul Oblast, Kazakh SSR : Auliye-Ata (-1936), Mirzoyan (1936-38)

Dzhandar see Sverdlovsk (1)

Dzhangala. Urban settlement, Uralsk Oblast, Kazakh SSR : Kisykkamys (-1975)

Dzhangy-Dzhol. Village, Osh Oblast, Kirgiz SSR : Chon-Ak-Dzhol (-1942)

Dzhansugurov. Urban settlement, Taldy-Kurgan Oblast, Kazakh SSR : Abakumova (-c. 1960)

Dzharkent see Panfilov

Dzhetysuy Guberniya (1928†). USSR : Semirechensk Guberniya (-1922)

Dzhezdy. Urban settlement, Dzhezkazgan Oblast, Kazakh SSR : Kotabaru (-?), Marganets (?-1962)

Dzhuma. Urban settlement, Samarkand Oblast, Uzbek SSR : Ikramovo (1930s)

Dzierzgoń. Town, northern Poland : Christburg (-1945), Germany

Dzierzoniów. Town, southwestern Poland : Reichenbach (-1945), Germany

Dziwnów. Town, northwestern Poland : Dievenow (-1945), Germany

Dzoraget. Urban settlement, Armenian SSR : Kolageran (-1978)

Dzurchi see Pervomayskoye (3)

Eagle Nest. Village, New Mexico, USA : Therma (-1935)

Earl Gray see Harding

East Buganda. District, southeastern Uganda, eastern Africa : East Mongo (-?)

East Detroit. Suburb of Detroit, Michigan, USA : Halfway Village (1924-29)

Eastern Province. Province, northeastern Zaïre, central Africa : Stanleyville (1935-47)

East Hamburg see Orchard Park

East Hampton. Town, Connecticut, USA : Chatham (-1915)

East Lansing. City, Michigan, USA : College Park (-1907)

East Livermore see Livermore Falls

East-Main. Town, Quebec, Canada : Eastmain (-1975)

Eastmain see East-Main

East Milwaukee see Shorewood

East Mongo see East Buganda

East Pakistan see Bangladesh

Eastview see Vanier (1)

East Windsor. Suburb of Windsor, Ontario, Canada : Ford (*1913-29)

East Youngstown see Campbell

Ebenrode see Nesterov (1)

Ebn Ziad. Village, northeastern Algeria, northern Africa : Rouffach (-c. 1962)

Ebor. Settlement, Manitoba, Canada : Sproule (-1907), Ebor Station (1907-09)

Ebor Station see Ebor

Echapora. City, southeastern Brazil, South America : Bela Vista (-1944)

Echmiadzin. Town, Armenian SSR : Vagarshapat (-1945)

Echuca. City, Victoria, Australia : Hopwood's Ferry (-?)

Economy see Ambridge

Eden. Town, North Carolina, USA : Leaksville (-c. 1970)

Eden see Bar Harbor

Edenburg see Knox

Edgewood see Homewood

Edgeworthstown see Meathas Truim

Edinburg. City, Texas, USA :
Edinburgh (-1908), Chapin
(1908-11)
Edinburgh see Edinburg
Edison. Township, New Jersey,
USA : Raritan (-1954)
Edith Ronne Land see Ronne
Land
Edson. Town, Alberta, Canada
: Heatherwood (-1911)
Edward, Lake see Idi Amin
Dada, Lake
Edwardesabad see Bannu
Eger see Cheb
Egypt see Arab Republic of
Egypt
Ehrenforst see Sławięcice
Eibenschitz see Ivančice
Eire see Ireland
Eirunepé. City, northwestern
Brazil, South America : São
Felippe (-1939), João Pessoa
(1939-43)
Eisenbrod see Železný Brod
Eisenhower, Mount. Mountain,
Banff National Park, Alberta,
Canada : Castle Mountain
(-1946)
Eisenstein see Železná Ruda
Ekaterinburg see Sverdlovsk
(3)
Ekaterinenstadt see Marks
Ekaterinodar see Krasnodar
Ekaterinoslav see Dnepropetrovsk
Ekeli see Zahirabad
Ekklesioúla see Néa Ekklesioúla
Elaión see Kamisianá
Elandsfontein see Alberton
Elandsfontein Junction see
Germiston
El Aouinet. Village, northeastern Algeria, northern
Africa : Clairfontaine (-c.
1962)
Elar see Abovyan
El-Asnam. Town, northern
Algeria, northern Africa :
Orléansville (-1964)
El Bayadh. Town, northwestern
Algeria, northern Africa :
Géryville (-c. 1962)

Elbing see Elbląg
Elbląg. Town, northern Poland :
Elbing (1939-45), Germany
El Braya. Village, northwestern
Algeria, northern Africa :
Mangin (-c. 1962)
Elbrus. Urban settlement,
Kabardino-Balkar Autonomous
SSR, RSFSR : Ialbuzi (-c. 1960)
El Campo see Campo Lugar
El Cerrito. City, California,
USA : Rust (-1917)
El Chilamatal see Ciudad Arce
Eldorado. City, southeastern
Brazil, South America :
Xiririca (-1948)
Eldorado see Port Radium
Elektrogorsk. Town, Moscow
Oblast, RSFSR : Elektroperedacha (-1946)
Elektroperedacha see Elektrogorsk
Elektrostal. Town, Moscow
Oblast, RSFSR : Zatishye
(-1938)
Elektrougli. Town, Moscow
Oblast, RSFSR : Kudinovo
(-1935)
Elektrovoz see Stupino
El Eulma. Town, northeastern
Algeria, northern Africa :
Saint-Arnaud (-c. 1962)
El Ferrol see El Ferrol del
Caudillo
El Ferrol del Caudillo. City,
northwestern Spain : El Ferrol
(-1939)
El Hachem. Village, northwestern
Algeria, northern Africa :
Dombasle (-c. 1962)
El-Harrach. Suburb of Algiers,
Algeria, northern Africa :
Maison-Carrée (-c. 1962)
Elías Piña. Town, western
Dominican Republic, West
Indies : Comendador (-1930)
Elidere see Čepinska
Élisabethville see (1) Lubumbashi; (2) Shaba
Elista. Capital of Kalmyk Autonomous SSR, RSFSR :
Stepnoy (1944-57)
Elizabeth Hall see Melanie

Damishana
Elizavetgrad see Kirovograd
Elizavetpol see Kirovabad
El-Jadida. City, western
Morocco, northwestern
Africa : Mazagan (-c. 1960)
El Jovero see Miches
Ełk. City, northeastern Poland
: Lyck (-1945), Germany
El-Kala. Town, northeastern
Algeria, northern Africa :
La Calle (-c. 1962)
Ellesmere see Scottsdale
Ellice Islands see Tuvalu
Elliotdale see Xhora
Ellore see Eluru
Ellsworth Highland see Ells-
worth Land
Ellsworth Land. Region, Ant-
arctica : Ellsworth Highland
(*1935- ?)
El Nido. Municipality, Palawan,
Philippines : Bacuit (-1954)
El Paraíso see Choloma
El Paso see Derby
El Poyo see Poyo del Cid
El Progreso. City, east-central
Guatemala, Central America :
Guastatoya (-c. 1920)
El Pueblito see Corregidora
El Rio. Barrio, Butuan, Philip-
pines : Biga (-1967)
Eluru. Town, eastern India :
Ellore (-1949)
El Vado see La Vereda
Elvershagen see Lagiewniki
Emilia see Emilia-Romagna
Emilia-Romagna. Region, north-
central Italy : Emilia (-1948)
Emílio Meyer. Town, southern
Brazil, South America :
Palmares (-1944)
Emmahaven see Telukbajur
Empingham Reservoir see
Rutland Water
Encinal see Sunnyvale
Encruzilhada see Encruzilhada
do Sul
Encruzilhada do Sul. City,
southern Brazil, South Amer-
ica : Encruzilhada (-1944)
En Gannim see Ramat Gan
Engels. Town, Saratov Oblast,

RSFSR : Pokrovsk (-1931)
Engelsburg see Kalbar
Engelsovo. Urban settlement,
Voroshilovgrad Oblast, Ukrain-
ian SSR : Shakhty imeni Engel-
sa (-c. 1960)
Enham Alamein. Village, Hamp-
shire, England, UK : Knight's
Enham (-1945)
Enlung see Tientung [T'ien-tung]
Enna. City, central Sicily, Italy
: Castrogiovanni (-1927)
Enrique B. Magalona. Municipal-
ity, Negro Occidental, Philip-
pines : Saravia (-1967)
Enshih. Town, east-central
China : Shihnan (-1912)
Enso see Svetogorsk
Entre Ríos. Town, southern
Bolivia, South America : San
Luis (-1906)
Entre Rios see (1) Joâo Ribeiro;
(2) Rio Brilhante; (3) Três
Rios
Entre-Rios. Town, north-central
Mozambique, southeastern
Africa : Malema (-1921)
Enzeli see Pahlevi
Epitácio Pessoa see Pedro
Avelino
Équateur. Province, northwestern
Zaïre, central Africa : Coquil-
hatville (1935-47)
Equatoria (1956†). Province,
southern Sudan : Mongalla
(-1936)
Equatorial Guinea. Republic,
western Africa : Spanish Guinea
(-1968)
Erasmus see Bronkhorstspruit
Erastovka see Vishnyovoye (1)
Erdély see Transylvania
Erechim. City, southern Brazil,
South America : Boa Vista
(do Erechim) (*1909-39),
José Bonifácio (1939-44)
Erechim see Getúlio Vargas
Ergfisk see Torfelt
Erhyüan. Town, southwestern
China : Langkiung (-1913)
Erice. Town, northwestern
Sicily, Italy : Monte San
Giuliano (-1934)

Erickson. Village, Manitoba,
Canada : Avesta (-1908)
Erivan see Yerevan
Ersekújvár see Nové Zámky
Erzsébetfalva see Pestszen-
terzsébet
Escarabajosa see Santa María
del Tiétar
Eschenbach see Wolframs-
Eschenbach
Eskije see Xanthe
Esparragosa de Lares see
Esparragosa del Caudillo
Esparragosa del Caudillo. Vil-
lage, southwestern Spain :
Esparragosa de Lares (-c.
1960)
Esperantina. City, northeastern
Brazil, South America :
Boa Esperança (-1944)
Esperanza see Cachuela
Esperanza
Espírito Santo see (1) Cruz
do Espírito Santo; (2)
Indiaroba
Essaouira. City, southwestern
Morocco, northwestern
Africa : Mogador (-1959)
Esto-Khaginka see Yashalta
Esutoru see Uglegorsk (1)
Eucaliptus see Tomás Barrón
Euclides da Cunha. City, east-
ern Brazil, South America :
Cumbe (-1939)
Eugenópolis. City, southeastern
Brazil, South America : São
Manuel (-1944)
Eva Perón see (1) La Pampa;
(2) La Plata
Evaton see Residensia
Evensk. Village, Khabarovsk
Kray, RSFSR : Bolshaya
Garmanda (-1951)
Exántheia. Village, Levkás,
Ionian Islands, Greece : Áno
Exántheia (-1960s)
Exokhé. Village, northern
Greece : Kalývia Kharádras
(-1960s)
Eydtkau see Chernyshevskoye
Eydtkuhnen see Chernyshevskoye
Ezaki. Town, southwestern
Honshu, Japan : Tamasaki
(-1943)

Ezhva. Urban settlement, Komi
Autonomous SSR, RSFSR :
Sloboda (-c. 1960)

Fabian Marcos. Barrio, Ilocos
Norte, Philippines : Lacub
(-1968)
Fabrika imeni Krasnoy Armii i
Flota see Krasnoarmeysk (5)
Fachow see Fahsien
Fahsien. Town, southeastern
China : Fachow (-1912)
Faire see Santo Niño (1)
Faizully Khodzhayeva, imeni see
Sverdlovsk (1)
Fakel. Urban settlement, Udmurt
Autonomous SSR, RSFSR :
Sergiyevsky (-c. 1960)
Falkenberg see Niemodlin
Falknov see Sokolov
Fangcheng [Fang-ch'eng]. Town,
east-central China : Yuchow
(-1913)
Farroupilha. City, southern
Brazil, South America : Nova
Vicenza (-1934)
Fashoda see Kodok
Fatshan see Namhoi
Faxa see Camp Morton
Faya see Largeau
Fdérik. Town, north-central
Mauritania, western Africa :
Fort-Gourand [Idjil] (-c. 1960)
Februarie 16, 1933. Suburb of
Bucharest, southern Romania :
Marele-Voevod-Mihai (-1948)
Fédala see Mohammédia
Federal Capital Territory see
Australian Capital Territory
Felipe Camarão. Town, north-
eastern Brazil, South Amer-
ica : São Gonçalo (-1944)
Felipe Carrillo Puerto. Town,
southeastern Mexico, North
America : Santa Cruz de
Bravo (-1935)
Felshtin see Gvardeyskoye
Felsőireg see Iregszemcse
Felsőszentgyörgy see Jászfel-
sőszentgyörgy
Fencheng [Fen-ch'eng]. Town,

northeastern China : Taiping
(-1914)
Fenchow see Fenyang
Fengcheng [Feng-ch'eng]. Town,
 eastern China : Fenghwang
 (-1914)
Feng-chieh = Fengkieh
Fengchüan see Fengkang
Fenghsien = Fengsien
Fenghwang see Fengcheng
 [Feng-ch'eng]
Feng-i = Fengyi
Fengkang. Town, southern
 China : Fengchüan (-1930)
Fengkieh [Feng-chieh]. Town,
 central China : Kweichow
 (-1913)
Fengsien [Fenghsien]. Town,
 eastern China : Nankiao
 (-1912)
Fengtien see Mukden (1)
Feng-t'ien see Liaoning
Fengyi [Feng-i]. Town,
 southwestern China : Chao-
 chow (-1914)
Fenyang. Town, northeastern
 China : Fenchow (-1912)
Ferdinand see Mikhailovgrad
Ferdinandov-vrach see Botev
Fergana. Capital of Fergana
 Oblast, Uzbek SSR : Novy
 Margelan (-1910), Skobelev
 (1910-24)
Fernando Po see Macias
 Nguema Bijogo
Ferreira Gomes. Town,
 northern Brazil, South
 America : Amapari (1939-43)
Ferryville see Menzel Bour-
 guiba
Festenberg see Twardogora
Fidenza. Town, north-central
 Italy : Borgo San Donnino
 (-1927)
Figueira see Governador
 Valadares
Filehne see Wieleń
Finale Ligure. Town, north-
 western Italy : Finalmarina
 (-c. 1940)
Finalmarina see Finale Ligure
Findley Point see Kaninihi
 Point
Firdaus. Town, northeastern

Iran : Tun (-1920s)
Fischhausen see Primorsk (1)
Fishing Lake see Rossman
 Lake
Fiume see Rijeka
Fizuli. Town, Azerbaijan SSR :
 Karyagino (-1959)
Flagstaff see Siphaqeni
Flatow see Złotów
Flers see Flers-en-Escrebieux
Flers-en-Escrebieux. Suburb
 of Douai, northern France :
 Flers (-1938)
Fletcher see Aurora
Florânia. City, northeastern
 Brazil, South America :
 Flores (-1944)
Florence Bay see Chtimba
Flores see (1) Florânia; (2)
 Timon
Florissant. City, Missouri,
 USA : St. Ferdinand (-1939)
Fohai. Town, southwestern
 China : Menghai (-1929)
Fokino. Town, Bryansk Oblast,
 RSFSR : Tsementny (-1964)
Folgoso de Caurel. Village,
 northwestern Spain : Caurel
 (-c. 1950)
Fondouk see Khemis el Khechna
Fontaine-de-Vaucluse. Village,
 southeastern France : Vaucluse
 (-1946)
Foochow [Fuchow, Fu-chou].
 City, southeastern China :
 Minhow (1934-43)
Ford see East Windsor
Forest Park. Village, Illinois,
 USA : Harlem (-1907)
Forfarshire see Angus
Formosa see Ilhabela
Fort-Aleksandrovsky see Fort-
 Shevchenko
Fortaleza see Pedra Azul
Fort Andres Bonifacio. Munici-
 pality, Rizal, Philippines :
 Fort William McKinley (-1905)
Fort Archambault see Sarh
Fort Bayard see Chan-chiang
Fort-Bayard see Siying (Hsi-
 ying]
Fort Carcenera see Fort Jose
 Abad Santos
Fort Crook see Offutt Air

42

Force Base
Fort de Kock see Bukittinggi
Fort-de-l'Eau see Bordj el
  Kiffan
Fort de Polignac see Illizi
Fort Flatters see Zaouiet
  El-Kahla
Fort-Foureau see Kousseri
Fort George see Prince
  George
Fort-Gouraud see Fdérik
Fort Hall see Muranga
Fort Hertz see Putao
Fort Hill see Chitipa
Fort Jameson see Chipata
Fort Johnston see Mangoche
Fort Jose Abad Santos. Barrio,
  Lanao, Philippines : Fort
  Carcenera (-1957)
Fort Lamy see Ndjamena
Fort-Laperrine see Tamanras-
  set
Fort MacLeod. Town, Alberta,
  Canada : MacLeod (-1952)
Fort Manning see Mchinji
Fort Marion National Monument
  see Castillo de San Marcos
  National Monument
Fort-National see L'Arbaa
  Naït Irathen
Fort Rosebery see Mansa
Fort-Rousset see Owando
Fort-Rupert see Rupert House
Fort Sandeman see Zhob
Fort-Shevchenko. Town,
  Mangyshlak Oblast, Kazakh
  SSR : Fort-Aleksandrovsky
  (-1939), Fort Uritskogo
  (1920s)
Fort Thomas. City, Kentucky,
  USA : Highlands (-1914)
Fort Trinquet see Bir Mogreïn
Fort Uritskogo see Fort-
  Shevchenko
Fort Walton see Fort Walton
  Beach
Fort Walton Beach. City,
  Florida, USA : Fort Walton
  (-1953)
Fort William McKinley see
  Fort Andres Bonifacio
Fou-liang = Fowliang
Fou-ling = Fowling

Fouras see Fouras-les-Bains
Fouras-les-Bains. Town, western
  France : Fouras (-1948)
Fou-yang = Fowyang
Fowchow see Fowling [Fou-ling]
Fowliang [Fou-liang]. Town,
  southeastern China : Kingteh-
  chen [Ching-te-chen] (-1931)
Fowling [Fou-ling]. Town, cen-
  tral China : Fowchow (-1913)
Fowyang [Fou-yang]. Town,
  eastern China : Yingchow
  (-1912)
Fraidorf see Novosyolovskoye
Francisco Morazán. Department,
  south-central Honduras, Cen-
  tral America : Tegucigalpa
  (-1943)
Franco. Barrio, Ilocos Norte,
  Philippines : Palpalicong
  (-1969)
Frankenstein (in Schlesien) see
  Ząbkowice Śląskie
Franklin see Nutley
Franklin D. Roosevelt Island.
  Island, East River, New York
  City, USA : Blackwell's Island
  (-1921), Welfare Island (1921-
  73)
Fraserburg Road see Leeu-
  Gamka
Fraserpet see Kushalnagar
Fraserville see Rivière-du-Loup
Fraserwood. Hamlet, Manitoba,
  Canada : Kreuzberg (-1918)
Frauenstadt see Wadowice
Fraustadt see Wschowa
Fredrikshald see Halden
Fredriksvern see Stavern
Freeport see Wayne
Freiberg see Příbor
Freiburg (in Schlesien) see
  Świebodzice
Freienwalde see Chociwel
Frei Paulo. City, northeastern
  Brazil, South America : São
  Paulo (-1944)
Freiwaldau see Jesenik
French Guinea see Guinea
French Rocks see Pandrapura
French Somaliland see Djibouti
French Sudan see Mali
French Togoland see Togo

Fresnes see Fresnes-sur-
Escaut
Fresnes-sur-Escaut. Town,
northern France : Fresnes
(-1941)
Freudenthal see Bruntál
Freystadt see (1) Kisielice;
(2) Kożuchów
Fridenfeld see Komsomol-
skoye (2)
Friedau see Ormož
Friedeberg see Mirsk
Friedeberg in Neumark see
Strzelce Krajénskie
Friedland see (1) Mieroszów;
(2) Pravdinsk
Friedrichshain. District of
East Berlin, East Germany :
Horst Wessel Stadt (?-1945)
Frignano see Villa di Briano
Frisches Haff see Vistula
Lagoon
Friuli see Udine
Frohenbruck see Veselí nad
Lužnicí
Fronteiras. City, northeastern
Brazil, South America :
Socorro (-1944)
Frunze (1). Urban settlement,
Osh Oblast, Kirgiz SSR :
Kadamdzhay (-1937)
Frunze (2). Capital of Kirgiz
SSR : Pishpek (-1926)
Frunzenskoye. Village, Osh
Oblast, Kirgiz SSR : Pulgan
(-1940)
Frunzensky. Suburb of Dnepro-
petrovsk, Dnepropetrovsk
Oblast, Ukrainian SSR :
Kamenka (-c. 1935)
Frunzovka. Urban settlement,
Odessa Oblast, Ukrainian
SSR : Zakharovka (-c. 1935)
Fu-chou = Foochow
Fuchow (1) = Foochow; (2)
see Funing
Fuhsien. Town, northeastern
China : Wafangtien (-1931)
Fuhsih see Yenan
Fukiang see Kanku
Fukung. Village, southwestern
China : Shangpo (-1935)
Fulford see North Miami Beach

Fulgencio. Barrio, Capiz,
Philippines : Northon (-1957)
Funan. Town, southern China :
Sinning (-1914)
Funing. Town, southwestern
China : Fuchow (-1927)
Funing see Siapu [Hsia-p'u]
Furmanov. Town, Ivanovo Ob-
last, RSFSR : Sereda (-1941)
Furmanovo. Village, Uralsk
Oblast, Kazakh SSR : Slomik-
hino (-1935)
Fürstenfelde see Boleszkowice
Furukamappu see Yuzhno-
Kurilsk
Fu-shun. City, northeastern
China : Hsing-jen (1902-08)
Fuyi see Lintseh [Lin-tse]
Fuyü. Town, northeastern
China : Petuna (-1914)
Fuyüan. Town, northeastern
China : Suiyüan (-1929)

Gabaldon. Municipality, Nueva
Ecija, Philippines : Bitulok
(-1953), Sabani (1953-55)
Gaberones see Gaborone
Gablonz see Jablonec (nad
Nisou)
Gaborone. Capital of Botswana,
southern Africa : Gaberones
(-1969)
Gabú (Sara) see Nova Lamego
Gaden see Zelyony Bor
Gafurov. Town, Leninabad Ob-
last, Tadzhik SSR : Stantsiya-
Leninabad (?-c. 1960), Sovetabad
(c. 1960-78)
Gagarin (1). Town, Smolensk
Oblast, RSFSR : Gzhatsk
(-1968)
Gagarin (2). Town, Dzhizak
Oblast, Uzbek SSR : Yerzhar
(-1974)
Gagarino. Village, Grodno Ob-
last, Belorussian SSR :
Drochilovo (-1969)
Gaillard Cut. Section of Panama
Canal, Canal Zone, Panama,
Central America : Culebra

Cut (-1913)

Galane. Village, northeastern
Greece : Kromníkos (-1960s)

Galena Park. City, Texas,
USA : Clinton (-1928)

Galkovsky Rudnik see Artyoma,
imeni

Gamelleira do Assuruá see
Santo Inácio

Gancheshty see Kotovsk (2)

Gandizhan Guberniya (1920†).
Russia : Yelizavetpol
Guberniya (1868-1918)

Gandzha see Kirovabad

Garampang see San Jose (2)

Gardabani. Town, Georgian
SSR : Karayazy (-1947)

Garfield Heights. Suburb of
Cleveland, Ohio, USA :
South Newburgh (*1907-19)

Garmo Peak see Communism
Peak

Garson. Village, Manitoba,
Canada : Lyall (*1915-27)

Gasan-Kuli Nature Reserve
see Krasnovodsk Nature
Reserve

Gaspar Strait see Kelasa
Strait

Gassen see Jasień

Gassino see Gassino Torinese

Gassino Torinese. Village,
northwestern Italy : Gassino
(-c. 1936)

Gastello. Urban settlement,
Sakhalin Oblast, RSFSR :
Nairo (1905-45), Japan

Gata see Poona Bayabao

Gatchina. Town, Leningrad
Oblast, RSFSR : Trotsk
(1923-29), Krasnogvardeysk
(1929-44)

Gatyana. Town, southern
Transkei, southern Africa :
Willowvale (-1976)

Gaudencio Antonio (1). Barrio,
Davao del Norte, Philippines
: Pangi (-1969)

Gaudencio Antonio (2). Barrio,
Oriental Mindoro, Philippines
: Tinalunan (-1969)

Gavinovichi see Podgornaya (2)

Gavrilovsky Zavod see

Druzhkovka

Gaziantep. City, southern Turkey : Aintab (-1922)

Gcuwa. Town, southern Transkei,
southern Africa : Butterworth
(-1976)

Gdańsk. City, northern Poland :
Danzig (-1945), Germany

Gdingen see Gdynia

Gdyel. Village, northwestern
Algeria, northern Africa :
Saint-Cloud (-c. 1962)

Gdynia. City, northern Poland :
Gdingen (-1939), Germany;
Gotenhafen (1939-45), Germany

Geelvink Bay see Sarera Bay

Gehlenburg see Biała (Piska)

Geiranger. Village, western
Norway : Maraak [Meraak,
Merok] (-1940)

Geistingen see Hennef

Gela. Town, southern Sicily,
Italy : Terranova di Sicilia
(-1928)

Geliniátika. Village, southern
Greece : Spartináiika (-1960s)

Gemswick. Village, eastern
Barbados, West Indies : Penny
Hole (-?)

Gene Autry. Town, Oklahoma,
USA : Berwyn (-1942)

General Artemio Ricarte. Barrio,
Ilocos Norte, Philippines :
Nalasin (-1968)

General Câmara. City, southern
Brazil, South America : Santo
Amaro (-1938)

General Emilio Aguinaldo. Municipality, Cavite, Philippines
: Bailen (-1905)

General Enrique Martínez. Town,
east-central Uruguay, South
America : La Charqueada
(-early 1930s)

General Machado see General
Peraza

General Peraza. Town, western
Cuba : Lutgardita (-?),
General Machado (?-1934)

General Roxas. Barrio, Davao,
Philippines : Dacudao (-1957)

General Santos. Municipality,
Cotabato, Philippines : Buayan

(-1954)
General Tinio. Municipality,
Nueva Ecija, Philippines :
Payapa (-1957)
General Toshevo. Village,
northeastern Bulgaria : Casim
(1913-40), Romania
General Trias. Municipality,
Cavite, Philippines : San
Francisco de Malabon
(-1914), Malabon (1914-?)
General Uriburu see Zárate
General Vargas. City, southern
Brazil, South America : São
Vicente (-1944)
Generoso Ponce see Jaci-
Paraná
Genthon. Suburb of St. Vital,
Manitoba, Canada : Dufault
(-1915)
Georgenswalde see Otradnoye
George River see Port
Nouveau-Québec
Georges Clemenceau see
Stidia
Georgiu-Dezh. Town, Voronezh
Oblast, RSFSR : Liski (-1928,
1943-65), Svoboda (1928-43)
Georgiye-Osetinskoye see
Nazran
Georgoulaíika. Village, central
Greece : Várnakas (-1960s)
Georgsmarienhütte. Village,
northwestern West Germany :
Georgs Marien Hütte (-1937)
Georgs Marien Hütte see
Georgsmarienhütte
Geraldton see Innisfail
Gerdauen see Zheleznodorozhny
(1)
Gerlachovka. Mountain, north-
eastern Czechoslovakia :
Stalin Peak (1949-61)
German East Africa see
Tanganyika
German New Guinea see New
Guinea
German Southwest Africa see
Namibia
Germantown see Holbrook
Germiston. Town, Transvaal,
South Africa : Elandsfontein
Junction (-1903)

Geroyskoye. Village, Kalinin-
grad Oblast, RSFSR : Gert-
lanken (-1946), Germany
(-1945)
Gertlauken see Geroyskoye
Géryville see El Bayadh
Getúlio Vargas. City, southern
Brazil, South America :
Erechim (-1934)
Gevaram. Settlement, south-
western Israel : Kibbutz
Mahar (-1942)
Ghaghara. River, northern
India : Gogra (-1966)
Ghana. Republic, western Africa
: Gold Coast (-1957)
Ghazaouet. Town, northwestern
Algeria, northern Africa :
Nemours (-c. 1962)
Gheorghe Gheorghiu-Dej. Town,
east-central Romania : Oneşti
(-c. 1965)
Ghriss. Village, northwestern
Algeria, northern Africa :
Thiersville (-c. 1962)
Giannitsa. City, northern Greece
: Yenije-i-Vardar (-?), Turkey
Gibigaan see Buenavista
Gilgenburg see Dąbrowno
Gindlicsalád see Tengelic
Ginsburg see Kaakhka
Girard see Woodland Hills
Gissar. Urban settlement,
Tadzhik SSR : Khanaka (-c. 1960)
Gitschin see Jičín
Gizhduvan. Urban settlement,
Bukhara Oblast, Uzbek SSR :
Akmal-Abad (c. 1935-37)
Giżycko. Town, northeastern
Poland : Lötzen (-1945), Ger-
many
Gladeville see Wise
Gladstone. City, Missouri, USA
: Linden (-1952)
Glasgow Junction see Park City
Glatz see Kłodzko
Gleiwitz see Gliwice
Glen Grey see Cacadu
Glistenets see Zalesino
Gliwice. City, southwestern
Poland : Gleiwitz (-1945),
Germany
Glod see Mirnaya (1)

Glogau see Głogów

Głogów. City, southwestern
Poland : Glogau (-1945),
Germany

Głogówek. Town, southern
Poland : Oberglogau (-1945),
Germany

Głubczyce. Town, southern
Poland : Leobschütz (-1945),
Germany

Glubokaya. Urban settlement,
Sverdlovsk Oblast, RSFSR :
Malomalsk (1933-c. 1965)

Głuchołazy. Town, southern
Poland : Ziegenhals (-1945),
Germany

Glupiki see Mirnaya (2)

Glypháda. Village, central
Greece : Daphnokhórion
(-1960s)

Gnadenburg see Vinogradnoye

Gnadenflyur see Pervomayskoye
(4)

Gnesen see Gniezno

Gniezno. Town, west-central
Poland : Gnesen (-1919,
1939-45), Germany

Gnilyaki see Roshcha

Gnoyev see Vit

Gnoynitsa see Vishnevets (1)

Goedgegun see Nhlangano

Gogra see Ghaghara

Gökçe. Urban settlement,
Gökceada island, Turkey :
Imroz (-1973)

Gökçe see Sevan (1)

Gökçeada. Island, Aegean Sea,
Turkey : Imroz Adasi (-1973)

Golaya Snova see Golosnovka

Goldberg see Złotoryja

Gold Coast see (1) Ghana;
(2) Southport

Goldingen see Kuldiga

Goleniów. City, northwestern
Poland : Gollnow (-1945),
Germany

Goljam Bratan see Morozov

Gollel see Lavumisa

Gollnow see Goleniów

Golodayevka see (1) Kuybyshevo
(2); (2) Pervomayskoye (5)

Golosnovka. Village, Voronezh
Oblast, RSFSR : Golaya
Snova (-c. 1938)

Golovnino. Village, Kuril Islands,
Sakhalin Oblast, RSFSR :
Tomari (1905-45), Japan

Golyashi see Sosnovy Bor

Goly Karamysh see Krasnoarmeysk (1)

Golyshi see Vetluzhsky

Golyshmanovo. Urban settlement,
Tyumen Oblast, RSFSR :
Katyshka (-1948)

Gombe. Town, northeastern
Nigeria, western Africa :
Doma (-1913)

Gonobitz see Konjice

Góra. Town, western Poland :
Guhrau (-1945), Germany

Góra Sowia. Mountain, southwestern Poland : Hohe Eule
(-1945), Germany

Goreloye see Shumikhinsky

Gorevatka see Sovetskaya (3)

Gorgan [Gurgan]. City, northern
Iran : Astarabad [Astrabad]
(-1930)

Göritz see Górzyca

Görkau see Jirkov

Gorky. Capital of Gorky Oblast,
RSFSR : Nizhny Novgorod
(-1932)

Gorky Kray see Gorky Oblast

Gorky Oblast. RSFSR : Nizhegorod Oblast (*1929), Nizhegorod Kray (1929-32), Gorky
Kray (1932-36)

Gorky-Pavlovy see Kaminsky

Gorna Djumaya see Blagoevgrad

Gornaya (1). Village, Minsk
Oblast, Belorussian SSR :
Deryaki (-1964)

Gornaya (2). Village, Gomel
Oblast, Belorussian SSR :
Kaplitsa (-1964)

Gornji Grad. Village, northwestern Yugoslavia : Oberburg
(-1918), Germany

Gorno-Altay Autonomous Oblast.
Altay Kray, RSFSR : Oyrat Autonomous Oblast (*1922-32), Oyrot Autonomous Oblast (1932-48)

Gorno-Altaysk. Capital of Gorno-
Altay Autonomous Oblast,
Altay Kray, RSFSR : Ulala

(-1932), Oyrot-Tura (1932-48)

Gornoye see Krasny Karachay

Gornozavodsk (1). Town, Sakhalin Oblast, RSFSR : Naihoro (1905-47), Japan (-1945)

Gornozavodsk (2). Town, Perm Oblast, RSFSR : Novopashiysky (-1965)

Gorny. Urban settlement, Khabarovsk Kray, RSFSR : Solnechny (-1965)

Gornyak (1). Town, Donetsk Oblast, Ukrainian SSR : Sotsgorodok (-1958)

Gornyak (2). Town, Altay Kray, RSFSR : Zolotushino (-1946)

Gorodishche. Town, Cherkassy Oblast, Ukrainian SSR : Petrovskogo G. I. , imeni (c. 1935-44)

Gorodishche see Marganets

Gorodok. Town, Lvov Oblast, Ukrainian SSR : Gródek Jagielloński (1919-45), Poland

Gorodok see Zakamensk

Gorodovikovsk. Town, Kalmyk Autonomous SSR, RSFSR : Bashanta (-1971)

Gorovakha see Pervomay (1)

Górowo Iławeckie. Town, northeastern Poland : Landsberg (-1945), Germany

Gorsko-Ivanovskoye see Gorskoye

Gorskoye. Town, Voroshilovgrad Oblast, Ukrainian SSR : Gorsko-Ivanovskoye (-c. 1940)

Goryacheistochnenskaya see Goryachevodsky

Goryachevodsky. Urban settlement, Stavropol Kray, RSFSR : Goryacheistochnenskaya (c. 1940-c. 1957)

Gorzów (Śląski). Town, southern Poland : Landsberg in Oberschlesien (-1945), Germany

Gorzów Wielkopolski. Town, western Poland : Landsberg (an der Warthe) (-1945),

Germany

Górzyca. Town, western Poland : Göritz (-1945), Germany

Goskopi see Kopeysk

Gostingen see Gostyń

Gostinopolye see Volkhov

Gostyń. Town, western Poland : Gostingen (1939-45), Germany

Gotenhafen see Gdynia

Gotnya see Proletarsky (1)

Gottesberg see Boguszów

Gottesgab see Boži Dar

Gottschee see Kočevje

Gottwaldov. Town, east-central Czechoslovakia : Zlín (-1948)

Gotwald. Town, Kharkov Oblast, Ukrainian SSR : Zmiyov (-1976)

Governador Valadares. City, southeastern Brazil, South America : Figueira (-1939)

Grace McKinley, Mount see McKinley, Mount

Gracias see Lempira

Graham see Bluefield

Graham Land see Antarctic Peninsula

Grajos see San Juan del Olmo

Grama see São Sebastião da Grama

Grande Prairie see Westwold

Grand Falls see Churchill Falls

Grand Rapids see Wisconsin Rapids

Grantley Adams Airport = (Sir) Grantley Adams Airport

Grassy Mountain see Oglethorpe, Mount

Graudenz see Grudziądz

Grays Harbor. County, Washington, USA : Chehalis (-1915)

Great Whale River see Poste de la Baleine

Grebyonka. Town, Poltava Oblast, Ukrainian SSR : Grebyonkovsky (-1959)

Grebyonkovsky see Grebyonka

Greenwich Island. Island, South Shetland Islands, British Antartic Territory : President Gonzáles Videla (-1947)

Gregorio del Pilar. Municipality, Ilocos Sur, Philippines : Concepcion (-1955)

Greifenberg see Gryfice
Greifenhagen see Gryfino
Greiffenberg see Gryfów
Śląski
Grenfell Rapids see Zongo
Rapids
Gretna. City, Louisiana, USA :
Mechanicsham (-?)
Greylingstad. Township, Transvaal, South Africa : Willemsdal (*1913-c. 1914)
Gribnoye. Village, Minsk
Oblast, Belorussian SSR :
Khrenovoye (-1964)
Grigenti see Agrigento
Grimm see Kamensky
Grishino see Krasnoarmeysk
(2)
Grissom Air Force Base. Indiana, USA : Bunker Hill Air
Force Base (*1954-68)
Gródek Jagielloński see
Gorodok
Grodekovo see Pogranichny (2)
Grodków. Town, southwestern
Poland : Grottkau (-1945),
Germany
Gromovsky see Dubovsky
Gross-Bitesch see Velká
Bíteš
Grossdale see Brookfield
Gross Dirschkeim see Donskoye
(1)
Grosse Pointe Woods. Village,
Michigan, USA : Lochmoor
(*1926-39)
Grossheidekrug see Vzmorye
(1)
Gross Lindenau see Ozyorki
Gross-Meseritsch see Velké
Meziříčí
Gross Skaisgirren see
Bolshakovo
Gross Strehlitz see Strzelce
(Opolskie)
Gross Wartenberg see Syców
Grosulovo see Velikaya
Mikhaylovka
Grottau see Hrádek nad Nisou
Grottkau see Grodków
Grover see Tiltonsville
Grudziądz. City, north-central
Poland : Graudenz (-1919),

Germany
Grukhi see Novovyatsk
Grumbkowfelde see Pravdino
Grumbkowkeiten see Pravdino
Grünberg see Zielona Góra
Grünheide see Kaluzhskoye
Gryazliv see Borovichi
Gryaznoye see Novoye (1)
Gryaznukha see Sovetskoye (1)
Gryfice. Town, northwestern
Poland : Greifenberg (-1945),
Germany
Gryfino. Town, northwestern
Poland : Greifenhagen (-1945),
Germany
Gryfów Śląski. Town, southwestern Poland : Greiffenberg
(-1945), Germany
Guachalla. Town, western Bolivia, South America : Ilabaya
(-c. 1945)
Guaçuí. City, southeastern
Brazil, South America :
Siqueira Campos (-1944)
Guadalupe. City, northeastern
Brazil, South America : Pôrto
Seguro (-1944)
Guaíba. City, southern Brazil,
South America : Pedras
Brancas (-c. 1925)
Guamá. City, western Brazil,
South America : São Miguel
do Guamá (-1944)
Guapó. City, east-central Brazil,
South America : Ribeirão
(-1944)
Guaporé see Rondônia
Guarani see Pacajús
Guaraúna. Town, southern Brazil, South America : Valinhos
(-1944)
Guardafui, Cape see Ras Asir
Guarulhos see Guarus
Guarus. Town, southeastern
Brazil, South America :
Guarulhos (-1943)
Guastatoya see El Progreso
Guben see Wilhelm-Pieck-Stadt
Guben
Gubkin. Town, Belgorod Oblast,
RSFSR : Korobkovo (-1939)
Guchkovo see Dedovsk
Guhrau see Góra

Guijá see Trigo de Morais
Guimba. Municipality, Nueva
Ecija, Philippines : San
Juan de Guimba (-1914)
Guinea. Republic, western
Africa : French Guinea
(-1958)
Guinea-Bissau. Republic,
western Africa : Portuguese
Guinea (-1974)
Guiratinga. City, western Bra-
zil, South America : Santa
Rita do Araguaia (-1939),
Lajeado (1939-43)
Gukasyan see Amasiya
Gulbakhor. Urban settlement,
Tashkent Oblast, Uzbek
SSR : Kirda (-1977)
Gulcha. Village, Osh Oblast,
Kirgiz SSR : Gulcha-Guzar
(-1938)
Gulcha-Guzar see Gulcha
Gulistan. Capital of Syrdarya
Oblast, Uzbek SSR : Mirzachul
(-1961)
Gumbinnen see Gusev
Gumuljina see Komotine
Gundorovka see Donetsk (1)
Gunji see Rishabhatirtha
Gurgan = Gorgan
Gurkfeld see Krško
Gurskoye. Town, Khabarovsk
Kray, RSFSR : Khungari
(-1972)
Guryevsk. Town, Kaliningrad
Oblast, RSFSR : Neuhausen
(-1946), Germany (-1945)
Gusakyan. Village, Armenian
SSR : Verin-Gusakyan
(-c. 1960)
Gusev. Town, Kaliningrad
Oblast, RSFSR : Gumbinnen
(-1946), Germany (-1945)
Gusevka see Novosibirsk
Gusinoozersk. Town, Buryat
Autonomous SSR, RSFSR :
Shakhty (-1953)
Gussenbakh see Linyovo
Gustanj. Village, northwestern
Yugoslavia : Gutenstein
(-1918), Germany
Gutenstein see Gustanj

Guttentag see Dobrodzień
Guttstadt see Dobre Miasto
Guyana. Republic, northern
South America : British
Guiana (-1966)
Guyman. City, Texas, USA :
Sanford (-1901)
Guyotville see Aïn Benian
Guzitsino see Krasny Profintern
(1)
Gvardeysk. Town, Kaliningrad
Oblast, RSFSR : Tapiau (-1946),
Germany (-1945)
Gvardeyskaya. Village, Vitebsk
Oblast, Belorussian SSR :
Kukishi (-1964)
Gvardeyskoye. Village, Khmel-
nitsky Oblast, Ukrainian SSR :
Felshtin (-1946)
Gymná see Akrolímne
Győrszentmárton see Pannon-
halma
Gýtheion. Town, southern
Greece : Marathonisi (-?),
Turkey
Gzhatsk see Gagarin (1)

Haas see Camp Morton
Habelschwerdt see Bystrzyca
Kłodzka
Hackensack. City, New Jersey,
USA : New Barbadoes (-1921)
Haclagan see Santo Niño (2)
Hadersleben see Haderslev
Haderslev. City, southern Den-
mark : Hadersleben (1864-
1920), Germany
Hadjadj. Village, northwestern
Algeria, northern Africa :
Bosquet (-c. 1962)
Hadjout. Town, northern Algeria,
northern Africa : Marengo
(-c. 1962)
Hadzi Dimitar. Mountain, central
Bulgaria : Buzuldza (-1967)
Hagía Ánna. Village, central
Greece : Koúkoura (-1960s)
Hagía Kyriaké. Village, northern
Greece : Skoúliare (-1960s)

Hagía Varvára. Village, southern Greece : Káto Kollínnai (-1960s)

Hágion Pneúma. Village, northern Greece : Veznikon (-?), Monoikon (?-1930s)

Hágios Antónios see Hágios Márkos

Hágios Márkos. Village, northern Greece : Hágios Antónios (-1960s)

Hágios Nikólaos. Village, eastern Greece : Psykhé (-1960s)

Hágios Nikólaos see Kastríon

Hahndorf. Town, South Australia, Australia : Ambleside (c. 1914-35)

Haicheng see Haiyüan

Haichow see Sinhai [Hsin-hai]

Haifeng see Wuti

Hailar. City, northeastern China : Hulun (1910-47)

Hainau see Chojnów

Haindorf see Hejnice

Haiyang see Linyü

Haiyen. Town, northwestern China : Sankiocheng (-1943)

Haiyüan. Town, north-central China : Haicheng (-1914)

Halden. City, southeastern Norway : Fredrikshald (-1928)

Half-Moon Bay see Oban

Halfway Village see East Detroit

Hall see Solbad Hall in Tirol

Halq-el-Oued. Town, northern Tunisia, northern Africa : La Goulette (-c. 1958)

Halton City. City, Texas, USA : Birdville (-1949)

Hamadia. Town, northern Algeria, northern Africa : Victor Hugo (-c. 1962)

Hamanaka see Shimotsu

Hamilton see Trompsburg

Hamilton Falls see Kapachira Falls

Hamilton River see Churchill River

Hammerstein see Czarne

Hamônia see Ibirama

Hampton see Ruth

Hanchow see Kwanghan [Kuanghan]

Hanchung see Nancheng (1)

Hansa see Corupá

Han-shou = Hanshow

Hanshow [Han-shou]. Town, south-central China : Lungyang (-1912)

Hanspach see Lipová

Hantsun see Hwanghwa [Huanghua]

Hanyüan. Town, southern China : Tsingki (-1914)

Harbin. City, northeastern China : Pinkiang (1932-45), Japan

Hardenberg see Neviges

Harding. Hamlet, Manitoba, Canada : Parr Siding (-1904), Earl Gray (1904-05)

Hardteck see Krasnolesye

Harlem see Forest Park

Harmanlijska. River, southern Bulgaria : Oludere (-1967)

Harper see Costa Mesa

Harris see Westminster

Hartingsburg see Warmbad

Hasei Nameche. Village, northwestern Algeria, northern Africa : Rivoli (-c. 1962)

Haselberg see Krasnoznamensk

Haussonvillers see Naciria

Havelock see Bulembu

Havlíčkuv Brod. Town, east-central Czechoslovakia : Německý Brod [Deutsch Brod] (-1945)

Havre-Saint-Pierre. Village, Quebec, Canada : Saint-Pierre-de-la-Pointe-aux-Esquimaux (-1930)

Haynau see Chojnów

Hazendal see Sybrand Park

Hazorim see Sergunia [Szirguni]

Heatherwood see Edson

Hebron. City, western Jordan : Al-Khalil (-1950)

Heerwegen see Polkowice

Heiligenbeil see Mamonovo

Heilsberg see Lidzbark Warmiński

Heinrichswalde see Slavsk

Heishan. Town, northeastern

China : Chenan (-1914)
Hejnice. Village, northwestern
Czechoslovakia : Haindorf
(-1918, 1939-45), Germany
Hellenikón. Village, southern
Greece : Koúmares (-1960s)
Hengchow see (1) Henghsien;
(2) Hengyang
Hengfeng. Town, southeastern
China : Hingan (-1914)
Henghsien. Town, southern
China : Hengchow (-1912)
Hengshan. Town, central China
: Hwaiyüan (-1914)
Hengyang. City, south-central
China : Hengchow (-1912)
Hénin-Beaumont. Town,
northern France : Hénin-
Liétard (-1974)
Hénin-Liétard see Hénin-
Beaumont
Hennef. Village, western West
Germany : Geistingen (-1934)
Hennenman. Town, Orange
Free State, South Africa :
Ventersburgweg (-1927)
Hercegfalva see Mezőfalva
Herculândia. City, southeastern
Brazil, South America :
Herculânia (-1944)
Herculânia see (1) Coxim;
(2) Herculândia
Herguijuela de la Sierpe see
Herguijuela del Campo
Herguijuela del Campo. Village,
western Spain : Herguijuela
de la Sierpe (-c. 1930)
Hermannsbad see Ciechocinek
Hermannstadt see Sibiu
Hermsdorf see Sobięcin
Herrnstadt see Wąsosz
Hesse-Kassel†. Province,
western Germany : Kurhessen
(1944-45)
Hexamília. Village, southern
Greece : Hexamília (-1960s)
Hexamília see Hexamília
Heydebreck see Kędzierzyn
Higashi-kata see Koniya
Higashi-naibuchi see Ugle-
zavodsk
Higashitsuge see Tsuge
Higashi-uji. Town, southern

Honshu, Japan : Uji (-early
1940s)
Highland Park. Borough, New
Jersey, USA : Raritan (-1905)
Highlands see Fort Thomas
Hilario Valdez (1). Barrio,
Ilocos Norte, Philippines :
Barangay (-1971)
Hilario Valdez (2). Barrio,
Ilocos Norte, Philippines :
Caoyan (-1968)
Hilla see Babil
Hillsboro see Deerfield Beach
Hillsborough Land Settlement
see Belle Glade
Hindenburg see Zabrze
Hingan see (1) Ankang; (2)
Hengfeng
Hingcheng [Hsing-ch'eng]. Town,
northeastern China : Ningyüan
(-1914)
Hinghai [Hsing-hai]. Town,
northwestern China : Tahopa
(-1939)
Hinghwa see Putien [P'u-t'ien]
Hingi see Anlung
Hingjen [Hsing-jen]. Town,
southern China : Sincheng
(-1914)
Hingking see Sinpin [Hsin-pin]
Hingkwo see Yangsin
Hinglungchen see Mingshui
Hingning see Tzehing [Tsu-hsing]
Hinuban see Antipolo
Hirochi see Pravda
Hirschberg see Jelenia Góra
Hizaori see Asaka
Hłuboczek Wielki see Veliky
Glubochek
Hlucín. Town, north-central
Czechoslovakia : Hultschin
(-1919, 1939-45), Germany
Ho Chi Minh (City). City,
southern Vietnam : Saigon
(-1976)
Hochow see (1) Hochwan
[Ho-ch'uan]; (2) Hohsien;
(3) Linsia [Lin-hsia]
Hochstadt see Vysoké nad
Jizerou
Ho-ch'uan = Hochwan
Hochwan [Ho-ch'uan]. Town,
central China : Hochow (-1913)

Hockley see Levelland
Hoey's Bridge see Moi's
Bridge
Hofei. City, eastern China :
Lüchow (-1912)
Hofgastein see Bad Hofgastein
Hofmeyr. Town, Cape of Good
Hope, South Africa : Marais-
burg (-1912)
Hog Island see Paradise
Island
Hohe Eule see Góra Sowia
Hohenbruck see Třebechovice
pod Orebem
Hohenelbe see Vrchlabí
Hohenfriedeberg see Dąbro-
mierz
Hohenfurth see Vyšší Brod
Hohenmauth see Vysoké Mýto
Hohensalza see Inowrocław
Hohensalzburg see Lunino
Hohenstadt see Zábřeh
Hohenstein see Olsztynek
Hohsien. Town, eastern China
: Hochow (-1912)
Hoihong. Town, southeastern
China : Luichow (-1912)
Hokow see Yakiang
Holan. Town, northwestern
China : Siehkangpao (-1942)
Holbrook. Town, New South
Wales, Australia : German-
town (-c. 1918)
Hollandia see Jayapura
Holy Cross, Mount of the.
Mountain, Colorado, USA :
Holy Cross National Monument
(1929-50)
Holy Cross National Monument
see Holy Cross, Mount of the
Homewood. City, Alaska, USA
: Edgewood (*1921-26)
Honan see Loyang
Honto see Nevelsk
Hoover Dam. Dam, Colorado
River, Arizona/Nevada, USA
: Boulder Dam (*1936-47)
Hopeh. Province, northeastern
China : Chihli (-1928)
Hoppo. Town, southeastern
China : Limchow (-1912)
Hopwood's Ferry see Echuca
Hordaland. County, southwest-

ern Norway : Sondre Bergenhus
(-1918)
Horst Wessel Stadt see Fried-
richshain
Hot Springs see Truth or Con-
sequences
Houa Khong. Province, north-
western Laos : Nam Tha
(-1966)
Houmt Souk see Djerba
Hradec Králové. City, west-
ern Czechoslovakia : König-
grätz (-1918, 1939-45), Ger-
many
Hrádek nad Nisou. Village,
northwestern Czechoslovakia :
Grottau (-1918, 1939-45),
Germany
Hranice. Town, east-central
Czechoslovakia : Mährisch-
Weisskirchen (-1918, 1939-45),
Germany
Hsia-ho = Siaho
Hsi-an = Sian
Hsiang-ch'ou see Sianghsien
[Hsiang-hsien]
Hsiang-hsien = Sianghsien
Hsiang-yün = Siangyün
Hsia-p'u = Siapu
Hsi-chang = Sichang
Hsi-chi = Sichi
Hsi-ch'ou = Sichow
Hsi-hsien = Sihsien
Hsin-chin = Sinkin
Hsing-ch'eng = Hingcheng
Hsing-hai = Hinghai
Hsing-jen (1) see Fu-shun; (2)
= Hingjen
Hsing-t'ai = Singtai
Hsing-tzu = Singtze
Hsin-hai = Sinhai
Hsin-hsien = Sinhsien
Hsin-pin = Sinpin
Hsin-yang. City, east-central
China : San-chou (-1913)
Hsi-shui = Sishui
Hsiu-shui = Siushui
Hsi-ying = Siying
Hsüan-ch'eng = Süancheng
Hsüan-han = Süanhan
Hsüchang [Hsü-ch'ang]. City,
east-central China : Hsüchow
(-1913)

Hsü-chou = Süchow
Hsüchow see Hsüchang [Hsü-
ch'ang]
Hsün-i = Sünyi
Hsün-k'o = Sünko
Hsü-shui = Süshui
Hsü-yung = Süyung
Hua-an = Hwaan
Hua-hsien = Hwahsien
Huai-an. City, eastern China :
Shan-yang (1912-14)
Huaicho see Puerto Acosta
Huai-ning see Anking [An-
ch'ing]
Huai-yang = Hwaiyang
Huai-yin see Tsingkiang(pu)
[Ch'ing-chiang(-pu)]
Hua-lung = Hwalung
Huambo. City, west-central
Angola, southwestern Africa
: Nova Lisboa (1928-c. 1976)
Huang-hua = Hwanghwa
Huang-kang = Hwangkang
Huang-ling = Hwangling
Huang-lung = Hwanglung
Hua-ning = Hwaning
Huan-jen = Hwanjen
Huan-t'ai = Hwantai
Hua-t'ing see Sung-chiang
Huauco see Sucre
Hu-chou see Wu-hsing
Huchu. Town, northwestern
China : Weiyüanpu (-1931)
Hueneme see Port Hueneme
Hui-chou see She-ksien
Hui-chuan = Hweichwan
Hui-min = Hweimin
Hui-nung = Hweinung
Hui-shui = Hweishui
Hui-tse = Hweitseh
Hultschin see Hlucín
Hulun see Hailar
Huma. Town, northeastern
China : Kuchan (-1914)
Humaitá see Porto Valter
Humboldt Bay see Kayo Bay
Hummelstadt see Lewin
Hummock Hill see Whyalla
Hungshankiao see Linsen
Hungshui see Minlo
Huns Valley see Polonia
Huntington see Shelton
Huntington Beach. City, Cali-

fornia, USA : Shell Beach
(-1901), Pacific City (1901-?)
Huntington Park. City, California,
USA : La Park (*1900-04)
Hurbanovo. Town, southeastern
Czechoslovakia : Stará Ďala
(-1948)
Hustopeče. Town, southern
Czechoslovakia : Auspitz
(-1918, 1939-45), Germany
Huszt see Khust
Hutchinson. Village, Cape of
Good Hope, South Africa :
Victoria, West Road (-1901)
Hwaan [Hua-an]. Town, south-
eastern China : Hwafeng
(-1928)
Hwachow see Hwahsien [Hua-
hsien]
Hwafeng see Hwaan [Hua-an]
Hwahsien [Hua-hsien]. Town,
central China : Hwachow (-1913)
Hwaijen see Hwanjen [Huan-jen]
Hwaiju see Chanhwa [Chan-hua]
Hwaiking see Tsinyang [Ch'in-
yang]
Hwaining see Anking [An-ch'ing]
Hwaiyang [Huai-yang]. Town,
east-central China : Chenchow
(-1913)
Hwaiyin see Tsingkiang (pu)
Hwaiyüan see Hengshan
Hwalung [Hua-lung]. Town,
northwestern China : Payen-
yungko (-1912), Payung (1912-
28), Payen (1928-31)
Hwangchow see Hwangkang
[Huang-kang]
Hwanghwa [Huang-hua]. Town,
northeastern China : Hantsun
(-1937), Sinhai (1937-49)
Hwangkang [Huang-kang]. Town,
east-central China : Hwangchow
(-1912)
Hwangling [Huang-ling]. Town,
central China : Chungpu (-1944)
Hwanglung [Huang-lung]. Town,
central China : Shihpu (-1941)
Hwangtsun see Tahing [Ta-hsing]
Hwangyüan [Hwang-yüan]. Town,
northwestern China : Tangar
(-1912)
Hwaning [Hua-ning]. Town, south-

western China : Ningchow
(-1913), Ninghsien (1913-14),
Lihsien (1914-31)
Hwanjen [Huan-jen]. Town,
northeastern China : Hwaijen
(-1914)
Hwantai [Huan-t'ai]. Town,
eastern China : Sincheng
(-1914)
Hweichow see Sihsien [Hsi-
hsien] (1)
Hweichwan [Hui-chuan]. Town,
north-central China :
Kwanpao (-1944)
Hweilungchen see Chitung
[Ch'i-tung]
Hweimin [Hui-min]. Town,
eastern China : Wuting (-1913)
Hweinung [Hui-nung]. Town,
northwestern China : Paofeng
(-1942)
Hweishui [Hui-shui]. Town,
southern China : Tingfan
(-1940s)
Hweitseh [Hui-tse]. Town,
southwestern China : Tungchwan (-1929)
Hweitung see Kiungtung [Ch'-
iung-tung]
Hydrómuloi see Lydía

Ialbuzi see Elbrus
Ian. Town, northeastern China
: Lungchüanchen (-1929)
Ibaiti. City, southern Brazil,
South America : Barra Bonita
(-1944)
Ibatuba see Soledade de Minas
Ibiapinópolis see Soledade
Ibipetuba. City, eastern Brazil,
South America : Rio Prêto
(-1944)
Ibiraçu. City, southeastern
Brazil, South America :
Pau Gigante (-1944)
Ibirama. City, southeastern
Brazil, South America :
Hamônia (-1944)
Ibirarema. City, southeastern
Brazil, South America : Pau

d'Alho (-1944)
Ibiúna. City, southeastern Bra-
zil, South America : Una
(-1944)
Iboti see Neves Paulista
Içana. Town, northwestern Bra-
zil, South America : São
Felipe (-1944)
Icaria. Island, Aegean Sea,
Greece : Akhigria (-1913),
Turkey
Icaturama see Santa Rose de
Viterbo
Icheng [I-cheng]. Town, east-
central China : Tzechung
(1944-49)
Ichijo. Town, eastern Shikoku,
Japan : Shichijo (-1923)
Ichiki. Town, southern Kyushu,
Japan : Nishi-ichiki (-1932)
Ichki (-Grammatikovo) see
Sovetsky (1)
I-chou see Lini
Ichow see Lini
I-ch'uan = Ichwan
Ichun [I-ch'un]. Town, south-
eastern China : Yüanchow
(-1912)
Ichwan [I-ch'uan]. Town, east-
central China : Nantitien (-1933)
Icoraci. Town, northern Brazil,
South America : Pinheiro
(-1944)
Idenburg Top see Pilimsit,
Puncak
Idi Amin Dada, Lake. Uganda/
Zaïre, central Africa :
Albert Edward, Lake (-c. 1901),
Edward, Lake (c. 1901-73)
Idjil see Fdérik
Idlewild see Kennedy
Idlewood see University Heights
Iesolo. Village, northern Italy :
Cavazuccherina (-c. 1930)
Ifeng. Town, southeastern China
: Sinchang (-1914)
Ighil Izane. Town, northwestern
Algeria, northern Africa :
Relizane (-c. 1962)
Iglau see Jihlava
Ignatovo see Bolshoye Ignatovo
Iguaçu see (1) Itaetê; (2) Lar-
anjeiras do Sul

Iguaratinga see São Francisco do Maranhão
Iguatama. City, southeastern Brazil, South America : Pôrto Real (-1944)
Igumen see Cherven
Ihsien = Yihsien
Ikawai. Town, South Island, New Zealand : Redcliff (-1935)
Ikeja Province. Southwestern Nigeria, western Africa : Colony Province (*1954-67)
Ikramovo see Dzhuma
Ilabaya see Guachalla
Iława. Town, northern Poland : Deutsch-Eylau (-1945), Germany
Ilebo. Town, south-central Zaïre, central Africa : Port Francqui (-1972)
Ilek. Village, Orenburg Oblast, RSFSR : Iletsky Gorodok (-1914)
Ilet see Krasnogorsky
Iletskaya Zashchita see Sol-Iletsk
Iletsky Gorodok see Ilek
Ilhabela. City, southeastern Brazil, South America : Formosa (-1944)
Ili see Kapchagay
Ilim see Shestakovo
(Ilirska) Bistrica. Village, northwestern Yugoslavia : Villa del Nevoso (-1947), Italy
Iliysk see Kapchagay
Ilkenau see Olkusz
Illizi. Town, eastern Algeria, northern Africa : Fort de Polignac (-c. 1962)
Ilmenau see (1) Jordanów; (2) Limanowa
Ilovaysk. Town, Donetsk Oblast, Ukrainian SSR : Ilovayskaya (-1938)
Ilovayskaya see Ilovaysk
Ilyichyovsk. Urban settlement, Nakhichevan Autonomous SSR, Azerbaijan SSR : Norashen (-1964)
Ilyinsky. Urban settlement,

Sakhalin Oblast, RSFSR : Kushunnai (1905-45), Japan
Iman see (1) Bolshaya Ussurka; (2) Dalnerechensk
Imbert. Town, northern Dominican Republic, West Indies : Bajabonico (-1925)
Imbuial see Bocaiúva do Sul
imeni. For places in USSR beginning thus, see under next word
Imperatorskaya Gavan see Sovetskaya Gavan
Imperia. Province, northwestern Italy : Porto Maurizio (1860-1923)
Imroz see Gökçe
Imroz Adasi see Gökçeada
Inabu. Town, central Honshu, Japan : Inatake (*1930s-early 1940s)
Inatake see Inabu
Independência see Pendência
Indiaroba. City, northeastern Brazil, South America : Espírito Santo (-1944)
Indonesia. Republic, southeastern Asia : Netherlands Indies [Netherlands East Indies, Dutch East Indies] (1816-1945), United States of Indonesia (1949-50)
Indrapura see Kerintji
Industrial Acres see Jacinto City
Infanta. Municipality, Tayabas, Philippines : Binangonan de Lampon (-1902)
Infantes see Villanueva de los Infantes
Ingá see Andirá
Inghok see Yungtai
Ingichka. Urban settlement, Samarkand Oblast, Uzbek SSR : Rudnik Ingichka (-1959)
Inhandava. Town, southern Brazil, South America : Bom Retiro (-1944)
Inhuçu. City, northeastern Brazil, South America : Campo Grande (-1944)
Ining see Siushui [Hsiu-shui]
Inkermann see Oued Rhion

Innisfail. Town, Queensland,
Australia : Geraldton (-1911)
Innokentyevskaya see Lenino
(1)
Inoucdjouac. Town, Quebec,
Canada : Port Harrison
(-1965)
Inowrocław. City, north-
central Poland : Hohensalza
(-1919), Germany
Insterburg see Chernyakhovsk
Interior see Interior and
Labuan
Interior and Labuan. Residency,
northern Borneo : Interior
(-1946)
Invermere. City, British Co-
lumbia, Canada : Copper
City (-1900), Canterbury
(1900-?)
Inwood. Village, Manitoba,
Canada : Cossette (-1906)
Ionio see Taranto
Ipatovo. Village, Stavropol
Kray, RSFSR : Vinodelnoye
(-1930s)
Ipeh [Ipei]. Town, southern
China : Anhwa (-1914)
Ipei = Ipeh
Ipek see Péc
Ipiaú. City, eastern Brazil,
South America : Rio Novo
(-1944)
Ipin. City, south-central
China : Süchow [Suifu] (-1912)
Ipixuna. City, northeastern
Brazil, South America : São
Luís Gonzaga (-1944)
Iran. Kingdom, southwestern
Asia : Persia (-1935)
Irapiranga see Itaporanga
d'Ajuda
Irbitsky Zavod see Krasno-
gvardeysky
Iregszemcse. Town, west-cen-
tral Hungary : Felsőireg
(*1938-39)
Ireland. Republic, western
British Isles : Irish Free
State (*1921-37), Eire (1937-
49)
Ir Gannim see Bat Yam
Irian Barat see Irian Jaya

Irian Jaya. West part of New
Guinea, Indonesia : Irian
Barat [West Irian] (1963-76)
Irish Free State see Ireland
Irish Republic = Ireland
Iriston†. Village [now joined to
Beslan], North Ossetian Au-
tonomous SSR, RSFSR :
Tulatovo (-1941)
Is. Urban settlement, Sverdlovsk
Oblast, RSFSR : Sverdlovsky
Priisk (-1933)
Isady see Semibratovo
Isayevo-Dedovo see Oktyabrskoye
(3)
Ise. Town, southern Honshu,
Japan : Ujiyamada (-1955)
Ishan. Town, southern China :
Kingyüan (-1913)
Ishanovo see Pioner
Ishley. Village, Chuvash Au-
tonomous SSR, RSFSR :
Ishley-Pokrovskoye (-c. 1960)
Ishley-Pokrovskoye see Ishley
Isiro. Town, northeastern
Zaïre, central Africa : Paulis
(-1972)
Islam-Terek see Kirovskoye (3)
Isle of Pines see Isle of Youth
Isle of Youth. South of western
Cuba : Isle of Pines (-1978)
Ismeli see Oktyabrskoye (4)
Ispica. Town, southeastern
Sicily, Italy : Spaccaforno
(-1935)
Ispisar see Sovetabad (1)
Istanbul. City, northwestern
Turkey (of which capital to
1923) : Constantinople (-1930)
Istra. Town, Moscow Oblast,
RSFSR : Voskresensk (-1930)
Istria. Peninsula, northwestern
Yugoslavia : Pola (1919-37),
Italy
Itabaiana. City, northeastern
Brazil, South America :
Tabaiana (1944-48)
Itabira. City, southeastern Bra-
zil, South America : Itabira
(de Matto Dentro) (-1944),
Presidente Vargas (1944-48)
Itabira (de Matto Dentro) see
Itabira

Itacê. Town, east-central Brazil, South America : Pilar (-1944)

Itaetê. Town, eastern Brazil, South America : Iguaçu (-1944)

Itaguatins. City, north-central Brazil, South America : Santo Antônio da Cachoeira (-1944)

Itajahy do Sul see Rio do Sul

Itamorotinga see Serra Branca

Itapagé. City, northeastern Brazil, South America : São Francisco (-1944)

Itaparica see Petrolândia

Itapecerica see Itapecerica da Serra

Itapecerica da Serra. City, southeastern Brazil, South America : Itapecerica (-1944)

Itapira see Ubaitaba

Itapoama. City, southeastern Brazil, South America : Rio Novo (-1944)

Itaporanga. City, northeastern Brazil, South America : Misericordia (-1939, 1944-48)

Itaporanga see Itaporanga d'Ajuda

Itaporanga d'Ajuda. City, northeastern Brazil, South America : Itaporanga (-1944), Irapiranga (1944-48)

Itaretama. City, northeastern Brazil, South America : Lajes (-1944)

Itatiaia. Town, southeastern Brazil, South America : Campo Belo (-1943)

Itatupã. Town, northern Brazil, South America : Sacramento (-1943)

Itaverá. City, southeastern Brazil, South America : Rio Claro (-1943)

Itebej. Village, northeastern Yugoslavia : Srpski Itebej (-1947)

Itu = Yitu

Ituberá. City, eastern Brazil, South America : Santarém (-1944)

Itumbiara. City, east-central Brazil, South America : Santa Rita (do Paranaíba) (-1944)

Itum Kale see Akhalkhevi

Iúna. City, southeastern Brazil, South America : Rio Pardo (-1944)

Ivailovgrad. City, southeastern Bulgaria : Orta-koi (-1934)

Ivančice. Town, southern Czechoslovakia : Eibenschitz (-1918, 1939-45), Germany

Ivangorod see Dęblin

Ivangrad. Town, southwestern Yugoslavia : Berane (-1948)

Ivanishchi. Urban settlement, Vladimir Oblast, RSFSR : Ukrepleniye Kommunizma (*early 1920s-1942)

Ivano-Frankovo. Urban settlement, Lvov Oblast, Ukrainian SSR : Yanov (-1941)

Ivano-Frankovsk. Capital of Ivano-Frankovsk Oblast, Ukrainian SSR : Stanislau (-1919), Stanisɫawow (1919-45), Poland, Stanislav (1945-62)

Ivano-Frankovsk Oblast. Ukrainian SSR : Stanislav Oblast (*1939-62)

Ivanopol. Urban settlement, Zhitomir Oblast, Ukrainian SSR : Yanushpol (-1946)

Ivanovka. Urban settlement, Odessa Oblast, Ukrainian SSR : Yanovka (-1945)

Ivanovo (1). Capital of Ivanovo Oblast, RSFSR : Ivanovo-Voznesensk (-1932)

Ivanovo (2). Town, Brest Oblast, Belorussian SSR : Yanov (-1945)

Ivanovo-Voznesensk see Ivanovo (1)

Ivanovskoye see Smychka

Ivanski. Village, eastern Bulgaria : Kopryu-koi (-?), Zlokuchen (?-1950)

Ivanteyevka. Town, Moscow Oblast, RSFSR : Ivanteyevsky (1928-38)

Ivanteyevsky see Ivanteyevka

Ivashchenkovo see Chapayevsk

Ivdel see Denezhkin Kamen

IvGRES see Komsomolsk (1)
Ivugivic. Town, Quebec, Ca-
nada : Notre-Dame-d'Ivugivic
(-1975)
Ixhuatlán see Chapopotla
Izhevsk. Capital of Udmurt
Autonomous SSR, RSFSR :
Izhevsky Zavod (-1917)
Izhevsky Zavod see Izhevsk
Izhma see Sosnogorsk
Izluchistaya see Zhovtnevoye
(2)
Izmail Oblast (1954†). Ukrain-
ian SSR : Akkerman Oblast
(*1940)
Izobilno-Tishchenskoye see
Izobilny
Izobilnoye see (1) Izobilny;
(2) Staro-Izobilnoye
Izobilny. Town, Stavropol Kray,
RSFSR : Izobilno-Tishchen-
skoye (-mid-1930s), Izobilnoye
(mid-1930s-1965)
Izumi-otsu. City, southern
Honshu, Japan : Otsu (-early
1940s)
Izyaslavl see Zaslavl
Izylbash see Pristanskoye

Jääski see Lesogorsky
Jablonec (nad Nisou). City,
northwestern Czechoslovakia :
Gablonz (-1918, 1939-45),
Germany
Jablonné v Podještědí Town,
northwestern Czechoslovakia :
Deutsch Gabel (-1918, 1939-
45), Germany
Jaboatão see Japoatã
Jáchymov. Town, western
Czechoslovakia : Joachimsthal
(-1918, 1939-45), Germany
Jacinto City. City, Texas, USA
: Industrial Acres (-1946)
Jaci-Paraná. Town, western
Brazil, South America :
Generoso Ponce (-1944)
Jacksonville see Old Hickory
Jacksonville Beach. City, Flor-
ida, USA : Ruby Beach (-1925)

Jacobabad. District, south-cen-
tral Pakistan : Upper Sind
Frontier (-?)
Jacobshagen see Dobrzany
Jacuí see Sobradinho
Jadotville see Likasi
Jagodina see Svetozarevo
Jaguari see Jaguariúna
Jaguariúna. Town, southeastern
Brazil, South America :
Jaguari (-1944)
Jaguaruna. City, northeastern
Brazil, South America : União
(-1944)
Jakarta. Capital of Indonesia :
Batavia (-1949)
Jakobstadt see Jekabpils
Jákóhalma see Jászjákóhalma
Jaltenango. Town, southern
Mexico, North America :
Angel Albino Gorzo (-1934)
Jamaica Square see South Floral
Park
Jambi see Telanaipura
Jamburg see Kingisepp (2)
Jamestown see Wawa
Jamnagar. Town, western India :
Navangar (-1950s)
Janichen see Svoboda
Janików. Village, southwestern
Poland : Jankau (-1945), Ger-
many
Jankau see Janików
Janské Lázně. Village, north-
eastern Czechoslovakia :
Johannisbad (-1918, 1939-45),
Germany
Jaochow see Poyang [P'o-yang]
Japoatã. City, northeastern Bra-
zil, South America : Jaboatão
(-1944)
Jaraguá see Jaraguá do Sol
Jaraguá do Sol. City, southern
Brazil, South America :
Jaraguá (-1944)
Jarboesville see Lexington Park
Jarlsberg see Vestfold
Jaryczów Nowy see Novy
Yarychev
Jasień. Town, western Poland :
Gassen (-1945), Germany
Jasło. Town, southeastern Po-
land : Jessel (1939-45), Germany

Jastrow see Jastrowie
Jastrowie. Town, northwestern
Poland : Jastrow (-1945),
Germany
Jászalsószentgyörgy. Town,
east-central Hungary :
Alsószentgyörgy (-1907)
Jászfelsőszentgyörgy. Town,
central Hungary : Felsős-
zentgyörgy (-1911)
Jászjákóhalma. Town, central
Hungary : Jákóhalma (-1928)
Jászkarajenő. Town, central
Hungary : Karajenő (-1901)
Jatinã. City, northeastern Bra-
zil, South America : Belém
(-1944)
Jatobá see Petrolândia
Jauer see Jawor
Javhlant see Ulyasufay
Javier. Municipality, Leyte,
Philippines : Bugho (-1905)
Jawor. Town, southwestern
Poland : Jauer (-1945),
Germany
Jaya, Puncak. Mountain, Irian
Jaya, Indonesia : Carstenz
Top (-1963), Sukarno, Puntjak
(1963-69)
Jayapura. Capital of Irian Jaya,
Indonesia : Hollandia (-1963),
Sukarnapura (1963-69)
Jayawijaya, Puncak. Mountain,
Irian Jaya, Indonesia :
Oranje Top (-1963)
Jdiouia. Village, northern Al-
geria, northern Africa : Saint-
Aimé (-c. 1962)
Jędrzejów. Town, south-central
Poland : Andreyev (-1919),
Russia
Jekabpils. Town, Latvian SSR :
Jakobstadt (-?)
Jelenia Góra. City, southwestern
Poland : Hirschberg (-1945),
Germany
Jelgava [Yelgava]. Town, Latvian
SSR : Mitava (-1917), Russia,
Zemgale (1920-40), Latvia
Jema'a Mallam see Kafanchan
Jersey Homesteads see Roose-
velt
Jesenik. Town, north-central

Czechoslovakia : Freiwaldau
(-1919, 1939-45), Germany
Jessel see Jasło
Jesselton see Kota Kinabalu
Jeziorany. Town, northeastern
Poland : Seeburg (-1945),
Germany
Jičín. Town, northwestern
Czechoslovakia : Gitschin
(1918, 1939-45), Germany
Jihlava. City, west-central
Czechoslovakia : Iglau (-1918,
1939-45), Germany
Jindrichův Hradec. Town, south-
western Czechoslovakia :
Neuhaus (-1918, 1939-54),
Germany
Jirkov. Town, northwestern
Czechoslovakia : Görkau
(-1918, 1939-45), Germany
Joaçaba. City, southern Brazil,
South America : Limeira
(-1928), Cruzeiro do Sul
(1928-38), Cruzeiro (1939-43)
Joachimsthal see Jáchymov
João Belo see Xai-Xai
João Coelho. City, northern
Brazil, South America : Santa
Isabel (-1944)
João Pessoa. City, northeastern
Brazil, South America :
Paraíba (-1930)
João Pessoa see (1) Eirunepé;
(2) Mimoso do Sul; (3) Pôrto
João Ribeiro. City, southeastern
Brazil, South America : Entre
Rios (-1940)
Joaquín V. González. Town,
northwestern Argentina, South
America : Kilómetro 1082 (-?)
Johannes see Sovetsky (2)
Johannisbad see Janské Lázne
Johannisburg see Pisz
John F. Kennedy International
Airport = Kennedy
John Martin Reservoir. Colorado,
USA : Caddoa Reservoir (-1940)
Johnson City. Village, New York,
USA : Lestershire (-1910)
Johnston Falls see Mambiliama
Falls
Jordan (1). Municipality, Iloilo,
Philippines : Nagaba (-1902)

Jordan (2). Kingdom, south-western Asia : Transjordan [Transjordania] (-1946) [in general use to 1949]

Jordânia. City, southeastern Brazil, South America : Palestina (-1944)

Jordanów. Town, southern Poland : Ilmenau (1939-45), Germany

Jose Abad Santos. Municipality, Davao, Philippines : Trinidad (-1954)

José Batlle y Ordóñez. Town, southeastern Uruguay, South America : Nico Pérez (-1907)

José Bonifácio see Erechim

José de Freitas. City, northeastern Brazil, South America : Livramento (-1939)

(José Enrique) Rodó. Town, southwestern Uruguay, South America : Drable (-1924)

Jose Panganiban see Payo

Juan Lacaze. Town, southwestern Uruguay, South America : Sauce (-1909)

Juàzeiro see Juàzeira do Norte

Juàzeiro do Norte. City, northeastern Brazil, South America : Juàzeiro (-1944)

Jubbal. Town, northern India : Deorha (-1950s)

Jucás. City, northeastern Brazil, South America : São Mateus (-1944)

Jucheng [Ju-ch'eng]. Town, south-central China : Kweiyang (-1913)

Juchow see Linju

Jugohama see Okachi

Juicheng [Jui-ch'eng]. Town, northeastern China : Kiang-chow (-1912)

Juichow see Kaoan

Juliana Top see Mandala, Puncak

Junan. Town, east-central China : Juning (-1913)

Jundiaí see Cinzas

Jungbunzlau see Mladá Boleslav

Jung-chiang = Jungkiang

Jungkiang [Jung-chiang]. Town, southern China : Kuchow (-1913)

Jungwoschitz see Mladá Vožice

Junikabura see Tsuchizawa

Juning see Junan

Juqueri see Mairiporã

Juripiranga. Town, northeastern Brazil, South America : Serrinha (-1944)

Juventino Rosas. City, central Mexico, North America : Santa Cruz (de Galeana) (-1938)

Južni Brod see Brod (Makedonskie)

Kaakhka. Urban settlement, Mary Oblast, Turkmen SSR : Ginsburg (c. 1920-27)

Kabachishche see Zelenodolsk

Kabadian see Tartki

Kabakovsk see Serov

Kabany see Krasnoarmeyskaya (1)

Kabanye see Krasnorechenskoye

Kabardin Autonomous Oblast see Kabardino-Balkar Autonomous SSR

Kabardino-Balkar Autonomous Oblast see Kabardino-Balkar Autonomous SSR

Kabardino-Balkar Autonomous SSR. RSFSR : Kabardin Autonomous Oblast (*1921-22), Kabardino-Balkar Autonomous Oblast (1922-36)

Kabarega Falls. Lake Mobutu Sese Seko, Uganda, central Africa : Murchison Falls (-1972)

Kabarega National Park. Western Uganda, central Africa : Murchison Falls National Park (*1952-c. 1972)

Kabwe. Town, central Zambia, south-central Africa : Broken Hill (*1904-65)

Kadamdzhay see Frunze (1)

Kademlija see Triglav

Kadiak see Kodiak

Kadiyevka see Stakhanov

Kadnitsy see Leninskaya Sloboda

Kafanchan. Town, central Nigeria, western Africa : Jema'a Mallam (-c. 1927)

Kafiristan see Nuristan

Kagan. Town, Bukhara Oblast, Uzbek SSR : Novaya Bukhara (-1935)

Kaganovich see (1) Novokashirsk; (2) Polesskoye; (3) Sokuluk; (4) Tovarkovsky

Kaganovichabad see Kolkhozabad

Kaganovicha L. M. , imeni see Popasnaya

Kaganovichevsk see Komsomolsk (3)

Kaganovichi Pervyye see Polesskoye

Kahukura see Tikitki

Kaiaua. Town, North Island, New Zealand : New Brighton (-1927)

Kaiba-to see Moneron

K'ai-chiang = Kaikiang

Kaichow see (1) Kaiyang [K'aiyang]; (2) Puyang [P'u-yang]

Kaihwa see Wenshan

Kaihwachen see Chanyü

Kaikiang [K'ai-chiang]. Town, central China : Sinning (-1914)

Kai-Mbaku see Bata-Siala

Kainda. Urban settlement, Kirgiz SSR : Molotovsk (c. 1945-57)

Kainsk see Kuybyshev (1)

Kaiser-Wilhelm Kanal see Kiel Canal

Kaiser Wilhelmsland see North-East New Guinea

Kaiyang [K'ai-yang]. Town, southern China : Kaichow (-1914), Tzekiang (1914-30)

Kaiyüan [K'ai-yüan]. Town, southwestern China : Ami (-1931)

Käkisalmi see Priozyorsk

Kakumabetsu see Shelekhovo

Kalabak see Radomir

Kalachevsky Rudnik see Lenina, imeni

Kalai-Mirzabai see Kalininabad

Kalai-Vamar see Rushan

Kalata see Kirovgrad

Kalatinsky Zavod see Kirovgrad

Kalayaan. Municipality, Laguna, Philippines : Longos (-1956)

Kalay-Lyabiob see Tadzhikabad

Kalbar. Town, Queensland, Australia : Engelsburg (-c. 1914)

Kalemi. City, eastern Zaïre, central Africa : Albertville (1915-66)

Kalevala. Urban settlement, Karelian Autonomous SSR, RSFSR : Ukhta (-c. 1960)

Kalimantan. Southern part of Borneo, Indonesia : Dutch Borneo (-1945)

Kalinin (1). Urban settlement, Tashauz Oblast, Turkmen SSR : Porsy (-1935)

Kalinin (2). Capital of Kalinin Oblast, RSFSR : Tver (-1931)

Kalininabad. Village, Leninabad Oblast, Tadzhik SSR : Kalai-Mirzabai (-c. 1935)

Kalinina M. I. , imeni. Urban settlement, Gorky Oblast, RSFSR : Kartonnaya Fabrika (-1938)

Kalinindorf see Kalininskoye

Kaliningrad (1). Capital of Kaliningrad Oblast, RSFSR : Königsberg (-1946), Germany (-1945)

Kaliningrad (2). Town, Moscow Oblast, RSFSR : Podlipki (-1928), Kalininsky (1928-38)

Kaliningrad Oblast. RSFSR : Königsberg Oblast (*1946)

Kalinino (1). Village, Chuvash Autonomous SSR, RSFSR : Norusovo (-1939)

Kalinino (2). Urban settlement, Armenian SSR : Vorontsovka (-1935)

Kalininsk (1). Town, Donetsk Oblast, Ukrainian SSR : Bairak (-c. 1935)

Kalininsk (2). Town, Saratov Oblast, RSFSR : Balanda (-1962)

Kalininsk see Petrozavodsk

Kalininskaya. Village, Krasnodar

Kray, RSFSR : Popovichskaya
(-c. 1960)
Kalininskoye (1). Village, Kir-
giz SSR : Karabalty (-1937)
Kalininskoye (2). Urban settle-
ment, Kherson Oblast, Ukrain-
ian SSR : Seidemenukha (-c.
1928), Kalinindorf (c. 1928-44)
Kalininsky see Kaliningrad (2)
Kalinovaya (1). Village, Vitebsk
Oblast, Belorussian SSR :
Bloshniki (-1964)
Kalinovaya (2). Village, Mogil-
yov Oblast, Belorussian
SSR : Trebukhi (-1964)
Kalinovka (1). Village, Kalinin-
grad Oblast, RSFSR : Aulo-
wönen (-1938), Germany,
Aulenbach (1938-45), Germany
Kalinovka (2). Urban settle-
ment, Kiev Oblast, Ukrainian
SSR : Vasilkov pervy (-c. 1960)
Kalipetrovo. Town, northeastern
Bulgaria : Starčevo (-c. 1967)
Kalisz Pomorski. Town, north-
western Poland : Kallies
(-1945), Germany
Kallies see Kalisz Pomorski
Kallithéa (1). Village, eastern
Greece : Kalývia (-1960s)
Kallithéa (2). Village, northern
Greece : Kataphýgion (-1960s)
Kalmytsky Bazar see Privol-
zhsky
Kalpa. Village, northern India
: Chini (-1966)
Kalpákion see Orkhomenós
Kaluzhskoye. Village, Kalinin-
grad Oblast, RSFSR : Grün-
heide (-1945), Germany
Kalyvákia. Village, southern
Greece : Xenía (-1960s)
Kalývia see Kallithéa (1)
Kalývia Kharádras see Exokhé
Kama. Urban settlement, Ud-
murt Autonomous SSR, RSFSR
: Butysh (-1966)
Kamarína see Záloggon
Kamen see Kamen-na-Obi
Kamenets-Podolsk see
Kamenets-Podolsky
Kamenets-Podolsky. Town,
Khmelnitsky Oblast, Ukrainian

SSR : Kamenets-Podolsk (-1944)
Kamenets-Podolsky Oblast see
Khmelnitsky Oblast
Kamenický Šenov. Town, north-
western Czechoslovakia :
Steinschönau (-1918, 1939-45),
Germany
Kamenka. Town, Cherkassy
Oblast, Ukrainian SSR :
Kamenka-Shevchenkovskaya
(1930-44)
Kamenka see Frunzensky
Kamenka-Bugskaya. Town, Lvov
Oblast, Ukrainian SSR :
Kamenka-Strumilovskaya (-1944)
Kamenka-Shevchenkovskaya see
Kamenka
Kamenka-Strumilovskaya see
Kamenka-Bugskaya
Kamen-na-Obi. Town, Altay
Kray, RSFSR : Kamen (-?)
Kamennogorsk. Town, Leningrad
Oblast, RSFSR : Antrea (-1948),
Finland (-1940)
Kamensk see Kamensk-Uralsky
Kamenskaya see Kamensk-
Shakhtinsky
Kamenskoye see Dneprodzer-
zhinsk
Kamensk-Shakhtinsky. Town,
Rostov Oblast, RSFSR :
Kamenskaya (-1927)
Kamensk-Uralsky. Town, Sverd-
lovsk Oblast, RSFSR : Kamensk
(-1935)
Kamensky. Urban settlement,
Saratov Oblast, RSFSR : Grimm
(-1941)
Kamenz see Kamienec
Kamien (Pomorski). Town, north-
western Poland : Cammin
(-1945), Germany
Kamienec. Town, southwestern
Poland : Kamenz (-1945),
Germany
Kamienna Góra. Town, south-
western Poland : Landeshut
(-1945), Germany
Kaminsky. Urban settlement,
Ivanovo Oblast, RSFSR :
Gorky-Pavlovy (-1947)
Kami-shikuka see Leonidovo
Kamisianá. Village, western

Crete, Greece : Elaión (-1960s)
Kamnik. Village, northwestern
Yugoslavia : Stein (-1918),
Germany
Kamo. Town, Armenian SSR :
Nor-Bayazet (-1959)
Kampuchea. Republic, southern
Indochina : Cambodia (-1970),
Khmer Republic (1970-75)
Kamskoye Ustye. Urban settle-
ment, Tatar Autonomous SSR,
RSFSR : Bogorodskoye (-1939)
Kamskoy GES, stroiteley see
Chaykovsky
Kanai see Yingkiang
Kananga. City, south-central
Zaïre, central Africa :
Luluabourg (-1966)
Kanash. Town, Chuvash Au-
tonomous SSR, RSFSR :
Shikhrany (-1920)
Kan-chou = Kanchow
Kanchow [Kan-chou]. City,
southeastern China : Kanhsien
(1911-49)
Kanchow see Changyeh
Kandagach see Oktyabrsk (2)
Kanghsien [K'ang-hsien]. Town,
north-central China : Paimawan
(-1928)
Kanglo [K'ang-lo]. Town, north-
central China : Sintsi (-1930)
Kangting [K'ang-ting]. Town,
southwestern China : Tatsienlu
(-1913)
Kangwane. Homeland, Transvaal,
South Africa : Swazi (-1977)
Kanhsien see Kanchow [Kan-
chou]
Kanin. Urban settlement, Komi
Autonomous SSR, RSFSR :
Kanin Nos (-1942)
Kaniniti Point. Cape, Stewart
Island, New Zealand : Findley
Point (-1965)
Kanin Nos see Kanin
Kanku. Town, north-central
China : Fukiang (-1928)
Kannan. Town, northeastern
China : Kantsingtze (-1926)
Kanpur. City, northern India :
Cawnpore (-1948)
Kanth see Katy (Wrocławskie)

Kantsingtze see Kannan
Kantyshevo see Nartovskoye
Kanukov see Privolzhsky
Kaoan. Town, southeastern
China : Juichow (-1912)
Kaochow = Kochow
Kaohiung [Kaohsiung]. City,
southern Taiwan : Takow
(1920-45), Japan
Kaohsiung = Kaohiung
Kapachira Falls. Shire River,
Malawi, southeastern Africa :
Hamilton Falls (-c. 1972)
Kapchagay. Town, Alma-Ata
Oblast, Kazakh SSR : Iliysk
(-c. 1969), Ili (c. 1969-c. 1971)
Kaplitsa see Gornaya (2)
Kapsukas. Town, Lithuanian
SSR : Mariyampole (-1955)
Kapuskasing. Town, Ontario,
Canada : MacPherson (*1914-
17)
Karaaul. Village, Semipalatinsk
Oblast, Kazakh SSR : Abay
(-c. 1960)
Karabagish see Sovetabad
Kara-Balty. Urban settlement,
Kirgiz SSR : Mikoyana, imeni
(?-1937)
Karabalty see Kalininskoye (1)
Karabunar see Sredets
Karachayevsk. Town, Karachayevo-
Cherkess Autonomous Oblast,
Stavropol Kray, RSFSR :
Mikoyan-Shakhar (-1944),
Klukhori (1944-57)
Karachukhur see Serebrovsky
Kara-Darya see Payshanba
Karajenö see Jaszkarajenö
Kara-Kirgiz Autonomous Oblast
see Kirgiz SSR
Karaklis see Kirovakan
Karakol see Przhevalsk
Karakubstroy see Komsomolskoye
(3)
Karancslapujtö. Town, northern
Hungary : Bocsárlapujtö
(*1928-56)
Karasu see Voroshilovo
Karasubazar see Belogorsk (2)
Karatau. Town, Dzhambul Oblast,
Kazakh SSR : Chulaktau (-1963)
Karavómylos. Village, Cephalonia,

Karayazy

Ionian Islands, Greece :
Vlakháta (-1960s)
Karayazy see Gardabani
Kardeljevo. Town, western
Yugoslavia : Ploče (-1949)
Karelian Autonomous SSR
(*1923). RSFSR : Karelo-
Finnish SSR (1940-56)
Karelo-Finnish SSR see
Karelian Autonomous SSR
Karen see Kawthule
Karenni see Kayah
Kargalinskoye. Village, Aktyu-
binsk Oblast, Kazakh SSR :
Zhilyanka (-1977)
Kargowa. Town, western Po-
land : Unruhstadt (-1945),
Germany
Karítsa. Village, northern
Greece : Díon (-1960s)
Karkeln see Mysovka
Karla Libknekhta, imeni (1).
Urban settlement, Kursk
Oblast, RSFSR : Peny (-?),
Pensky Sakharny Zavod (?-
1930)
Karla Libknekhta, imeni (2).
Suburb of Krivoy Rog,
Dnepropetrovsk Oblast,
Ukrainian SSR : Shmakovsky
Rudnik (-c. 1926)
Karla Libknekhta, imeni see
Shirokolanovka
Karla Marksa, imeni. Suburb
of Dnepropetrovsk, Dneprope-
trovsk Oblast, Ukrainian SSR
: Rybalskaya (-1920s)
Karl-Marx-Stadt. City, south-
eastern East Germany :
Chemnitz (-1953)
Karlo-Marksovo. Urban settle-
ment, Donetsk Oblast, Ukrain-
ian SSR : Sofiyevsky Rudnik
(-c. 1926)
Karlomarksovsky No 7/8 Rudnik
see Shakhta No 7/8
Karlovac. City, northwestern
Yugoslavia : Karlstadt (-?)
Karlovac see Rankovićevo
Karlovo. City, southern Bul-
garia : Levskigrad (1953-62)
Karlovy Vary. Town, western
Czechoslovakia : Karlsbad

(-1918, 1939-45), Germany
Karlowitz see (1) Sremski
Karlovci; (2) Velké Karlovice
Karlsbad see Karlovy Vary
Karlsburg see Alba-Iulia
Karlstadt see Karlovac
Karnataka. State, western
India : Mysore (-1973)
Karoro see Wharemoa
Karpacz. Town, southwestern
Poland : Krummhübel (-1945),
Germany
Karpathos. Island, Dodecanese,
Greece : Scarpanto (1912-47),
Italy
Karpilovka see Oktyabrsky (3)
Karpinsk*. Town, Sverdlovsk
Oblast, RSFSR : Bogoslovsk
(-c. 1914), Bogoslovsky (c. 1914-
41), Ugolny (c. 1935-41)
*town formed from two settle-
ments Bogoslovsky and Ugolny
Karsakuwigamak see Rutten
Karsava. Town, Latvian SSR :
Korsovka (-1917), Russia
Karshi. Capital of Kashkadarya
Oblast, Uzbek SSR : Bek-Budi
(1926-37)
Kartonnaya Fabrika see Kalinina
M. I. , imeni
Kartsa see Oktyabrskoye (6)
Karudéa. Village, western
Greece : Skoúpa (-1960s)
Karyagino see Fizuli
Kasai (1962†). Province, south-
central Zaïre, central Africa :
Lusambo (1935-47)
Kasanga. Town, southwestern
Tanzania, eastern Africa :
Bismarckburg (-?)
Kaschau see Košice
Kasevo see Neftekamsk
Kashirinskoye see Oktyabrskoye
(3)
Kashirskoye. Village, Kaliningrad
Oblast, RSFSR : Schaaksvitte
(-1945), Germany
Kashiwabara see Severo-Kurilsk
Kashkatau see Sovetskoye (2)
Kashla-Koi see Zimnitsa
Kasperské Hory. Town, south-
western Czechoslovakia : Ber-
greichenstein (-1918, 1939-45),

Germany
Kaspiysk. Town, Dagestan
Autonomous SSR, RSFSR :
Dvigatelstroy (*1936-47)
Kaspiysky. Town, Kalmyk
Autonomous SSR, RSFSR :
Lagan (-1944)
Kassa see Kosice
Kassándra see Kassándreia
Kassándreia. Town, northern
Greece : Kassándra (-1960s)
Kastéllion see Kíssamos
Kastellorizon. Island, Dode-
canese, Greece : Castelrosso
(1923-47), Italy
Kastríon. Village, southern
Greece : Hágios Nikólaos
(-1960s)
Katanga see Shaba
Kataoka see Boykovo
Kataphýgion see Kallithéa (2)
Katavóthra see Metamórphosis
Káto Exántheia see Drymón
Káto Kleitoría see Kleitoría
Káto Kollínnai see Hagía
Varvára
Káto Meléa. Village, northern
Greece : Meléa (-1960s)
Káto Potamiá see Platána
Káto Vardátai see Néon
Kríkellon
Katowice. City, southern Po-
land : Kattowitz (-1922, 1939-
45), Germany, Stalinogród
(1953-56)
Katscher see Kietrz
Kattowitz see Katowice
Katy (Wrocławskie). Town,
southwestern Poland : Kanth
(-1945), Germany
Katyk see Shakhtyorsk (2)
Katyshka see Golushmanovo
Kaufman Peak see Lenin Peak
Kaukehmen see Yasnoye
Kaunas. Town, Lithuanian
SSR : Kovno (-1917), Russia
Kaunchu see Yangiyul
Kavaklii see Topolovgrad
Kavirondo Gulf see Winam
Kawakami see Sinegorsk
Kawayan. Municipality, Leyte,
Philippines : Almeria (-1907)
Kawende see Oakville

Kawthoolei = Kawthule
Kawthule [Kawthoolei]. State,
south-central Burma : Karen
(*1954-64)
Kayah. State, east-central Burma
: Karenni (*1947-52)
Kaydanono see Dzerzhinsk (2)
Kaying see Meihsien
Kayo Bay. Bay, Irian Jaya,
Indonesia : Humboldt Bay
(-1963)
Kayrakkum. Town, Leninabad
Oblast, Tadzhik SSR : Kostakoz
(-1944), Chkalovsky (1944-?),
Khodzhent (?-1963)
Kazakh Autonomous SSR see
Kazakh SSR
Kazakh SSR. USSR : Kirgiz
Autonomous SSR (*1920-25),
Kazakh Autonomous SSR (1925-
36)
Kazakhstan see Aksay
Kazbegi. Urban settlement,
Georgian SSR : Stepantsminda
(-1921)
Kazgorodok see Kurgaldzhinsky
Kazi-Magomed. Town, Azerbai-
jan SSR : Adzhibakul (-1939)
Kazincbarcika. Town, northeastern
Hungary : Sajókazinc (*1947-48)
Kazinka. Urban settlement,
Lipetsk Oblast, RSFSR :
Novaya Zhizn (-c. 1960)
Kędzierzyn. Town, southern
Poland : Heydebreck (-1945),
Germany
Kegulta see Sadovoye
Keihchow see Wutu
Keksgolm see Priozyorsk
Kelasa Strait. Channel between
Bangka and Belitung islands,
Indonesia : Gaspar Strait (-?)
Kellomäki see Komarovo
Kells see Ceannanus Mór
Kelomyakki see Komarovo
Kemerovo*. Capital of Kemerovo
Oblast, RSFSR : Shcheglovsk
(*1918-32) *town formed out of
villages Shcheglovo and Keme-
rovo
Kempen see Kepno
Kenitra. City, northwestern
Morocco, northwestern Africa :

Port-Lyautey (*1913-c. 1958)
Kennedy, Cape see Canaveral,
Cape
Kennedy [John F. Kennedy].
International airport, New
York City, USA : Idlewild
(-1963)
Kentani see Centane
Kenya. Republic, eastern Africa
: British East Africa (-1920)
Kephalokhórion. Village, western
Greece : Plagiá (-1960s)
Kephalóvryson see Leukothéa
Kepno. Town, southwestern
Poland : Kempen (-1945),
Germany
Keppel Harbour. Southern
Singapore mainland, Singa-
pore : New Harbour (-1900)
Kerbi see Poliny Osipenko,
imeni
Kerensk see Vadinsk
Kerintji. Volcano, west-central
Sumatra, Indonesia : Indra-
pura (-1963)
Kermine see Navoi
Kerr Point see Surville Cliffs
Keshishkend see Yekhegnadzor
Kętrzyn. Town, northeastern
Poland : Rastenburg (-1946),
Germany (-1945)
Kettering. City, Ohio, USA :
Van Buren (-1952)
Kexholm see Priozyorsk
Keystone Heights. Town, Flor-
ida, USA : Brooklyn (-1922)
Khabno(ye) see Polesskoye
Khakulabad see Naryn
Khakurate see Oktyabrsky (4)
Khakurinokhabl see Shovgenov-
sky
Khalía see Drosía
Khalmer-Sede. Village, Yamalo-
Nenets Autonomous Okrug,
Tyumen Oblast, RSFSR :
Tazovskoye (-c. 1930)
Khalturin. Town, Kirov Oblast,
RSFSR : Orlov (-1923)
Khamza. Town, Fergana Ob-
last, Uzbek SSR : Shakhimar-
dan (-c. 1929), Vannovsky
(c. 1929-63), Khamzy Khakim-
zade, imeni (1953-74)

Khamzy Khakimzade, imeni see
Khamza
Khanaka see Gissar
Khankendy see Stepanakert
Khanlar. Town, Azerbaijan
SSR : Yelenendorf (-1938)
Khanty-Mansi Autonomous Okrug.
Tyumen Oblast, RSFSR :
Ostyak-Vogul National Okrug
(*1930-40)
Khanty-Mansiysk. Capital of
Khanty-Mansi Autonomous
Okrug, Tyumen Oblast, RSFSR
: Ostyako-Vogulsk (*1931-40)
Kharagouli see Ordzhonikidze
(3)
Khargone. District, northern
India : West Nimar (-1973)
Kharino see Beregovoy
Khatsapetrovka see Uglegorsk
(2)
Khavast. Urban settlement,
Syrdarya Oblast, Uzbek SSR :
Ursatyevskaya (-1963)
Khebda see Sovetskoye (3)
Khem-Beldyr see Kyzyl
Khemis el Khechna. Village,
northern Algeria, northern
Africa : Fondouk (-c. 1962)
Khemis Miliana. Town, northern
Algeria, northern Africa :
Affreville (-c. 1962)
Khibinogorsk see Kirovsk (1)
Khlevishche see Orekhovichi
Khmelnitsky. Capital of Khmel-
nitsky Oblast, Ukrainian SSR
: Proskurov (-1954)
Khmelnitsky Oblast. Ukrainian
SSR : Kamenets-Podolsky
Oblast (*1937-54)
Khmer Republic see Kampuchea
Khodavendikyar see Bursa
Khodzhaakhrar see Ulugbek
Khodzha-Arif see Shafirkan
Khodzhent see (1) Kayrakkum;
(2) Leninabad
Khokhulki see Zelyony Log
Kholmsk. Town, Sakhalin Oblast,
RSFSR : Maoka (1905-46),
Japan (-1945)
Kholopkovichi see Kolosovo (1)
Khoni see Tsulukidze
Khorixas. Town, northeastern

Namibia, southwestern Africa
: Welwitschia (-1974)
Khorly. Village, Kherson
Oblast, Ukrainian SSR : Port-
Khorly (-c. 1960)
Khorramshahr. City, southwest-
ern Iran : Mohammerah
(-1924)
Khortitsa see Verkhnyaya
Khortitsa
Khósepse see Kypséle (1)
Khoshdala see Dzhambay
Khovrino see Krasnook-
tyabrsky (1)
Khrapunovo see Vorovskogo,
imeni
Khrenovoye see Eribnoye
Khrompik see Dvurechensk
Khrushchyov see Svetlovodsk
Khrysikós. Village, southern
Greece : Lykoudésion (-1960s)
Khudeni see Mirnaya (3)
Khulkhuta. Settlement, Kalmyk
Autonomous SSR, RSFSR :
Pridorozhnoye (-c. 1960)
Khungari see Gurskoye
Khust. Town, Transcarpathian
Oblast, Ukrainian SSR :
Chust (1920-39), Czechoslo-
vakia; Huszt (1939-45), Hun-
gary
Khutor-Mikhaylovsky see
Druzhba (2)
Khuzestan. Province, southwest-
ern Iran : Arabistan (-1938)
Khvoynaya Polyana. Settlement,
Gomel Oblast, Belorussian
SSR : Avraamovskaya (-1964)
Kiachow see Kiahsien [Chia-
hsien]
Kiahsien [Chia-hsien]. Town,
central China : Kiachow (-1913)
Kian [Chi-an]. City, southeast-
ern China : Luling (-1914)
Kiangcheng [Chiang-ch'eng].
Town, southwestern China :
Mangli (-1929)
Kiangchow see Juicheng [Jui-
ch'eng]
Kiangkow [Chiang-k'ou]. Town,
southern China : Tungjen
(-1913)
Kiangkow see Pingchang

[P'ing-ch'ang]
Kiangling [Chiang-ling]. Town,
east-central China : Kingchow
(-1912)
Kiangna see Yenshan
Kiangning [Chiang-ning]. Town,
eastern China : Tungshan
(-1934)
Kiangning see Nanking
Kiangtu see Yang-chou
Kianly (Tarta) see Tarta
Kiaochow see Kiaohsien [Chiao-
hsien]
Kiaohsien [Chiao-hsien]. Town,
eastern China : Kiaochow
(-1913)
Kiashan [Chia-shan]. Town,
eastern China : Sankieh (-1932)
Kiating see Loshan
Kibbutz Mahar see Gevaram
Kibra see Kuratovo
Kichow see (1) Kichun [Ch'i-
ch'un]; (2) Kihsien [Chi-hsien]
Kichun [Ch'i-ch'un]. Town, east-
central China : Kichow (-1912)
Kiechow see Wutu
Kiel Canal. Linking Baltic Sea
and North Sea, northern West
Germany : Kaiser Wilhelm
Kanal (-c. 1919)
Kienchang [Ch'ien-ch'ang]. Town,
northeastern China : Kienchangy-
ing (-1949)
Kienchang see (1) Lingyüan;
(2) Nancheng [Nan-ch'eng] (2)
Kienchangying see Kienchang
[Ch'ien-ch'ang]
Kiencheng [Ch'ien-ch'eng]. Town,
south-central China : Kienchow
(-1913), Kienhsien (1913-14)
Kienchow see (1) Kiencheng
[Ch'ien-ch'eng]; (2) Kienhsien
[Ch'ien-hsien]; (3) Kienko
[Chien-ko]; (4) Kienyang
[Chien-yang]
Kienho [Chien-ho]. Town, southern
China : Tsingkiang (-1914)
Kienhsien [Ch'ien-hsien]. Town,
central China : Kienchow
(-1913)
Kienhsien see Kiencheng [Ch'-
ien-ch'eng]
Kienko [Chien-ko]. Town, central

China : Kienchow (-1913)
Kienkünchen see Yungshow
[Yung-shou]
Kienning [Ch'ien-ning]. Town,
southern China : Taining
(-1945)
Kienning see Kienow [Chien-
ou]
Kienow [Chien-ou]. Town,
southeastern China : Kienning
(-1913)
Kienping see Langki [Lang-
ch'i]
Kienteh [Chien-te]. Town,
eastern China : Yenchow
(-1914)
Kienyang [Chien-yang]. Town,
central China : Kienchow
(-1913)
Kietrz. Town, southern Poland
: Katscher (-1945), Germany
Kihsien [Chi-hsien]. Town,
northeastern China : Kichow
(-1913)
Kikinda. City, northeastern
Yugoslavia : Velika Kikinda
(-c. 1947)
Kikvidze. Urban settlement,
Volgograd Oblast, RSFSR :
Preobrazhenskaya (-1936)
Kilbourn see Wisconsin Dells
Kilien [Ch'i-lien]. Town, north-
western China : Papao (-1939)
Kiliti see Balatonkiliti
Kilómetro 924 see Angaco
Norte
Kilómetro 1082 see Joaquín
V. González
Kilómetro 1172 see Campo
Quijano
Kim. Village, Leninabad Oblast,
Tadzhik SSR : Santo (-1929)
Kimch'aek. City, northeastern
North Korea : Sŏngjin (-1952)
Kimovsk. Town, Tula Oblast,
RSFSR : Mikhaylovka (-1952)
Kimpersaysky see Batam-
shinsky
Kinchai [Chin-chai]. Town,
eastern China : Kinkiachai
(-1933), Lihwang (1933-49)
Kincheloe Air Force Base.
Michigan, USA : Kinross Air

Force Base (*1941-c. 1959)
Kincheng see Yüchung
Kinchow see Chinhsien
King Chiang Saen see Chiang
Saen
Kingchow see (1) Kiangling
[Chiang-ling]; (2) Kingchwan
[Ching-ch'uan]
Kingchwan [Ching-ch'uan]. Town,
north-central China : Kingchow
(-1913)
Kingfu see Sinhsien [Hsin-
hsien] (1)
King George V National Park
see Taman Negara National
Park
Kingisepp (1). Town, Estonian
SSR : Arensburg (-?),
Kuressaare (?-1952)
Kingisepp (2). Town, Leningrad
Oblast, RSFSR : Yamburg [Jam-
burg] (-1922)
Kingku [Ching-ku]. Town, south-
western China : Weiyüan
(-1914)
King's County see Offaly
Kingstown see Dun Laoghaire
Kingtai [Ching-t'ai]. Town,
north-central China : Talutang
(-1934)
Kingtehchen [Ching-te-chen] see
Fowliang [Fou-liang]
Kingwilliamstown see Ballydes-
mond
Kingyüan [Ching-yüan]. Town,
eastern China : Yenshan (-1949)
Kingyüan see Ishan
Kinho see Kinping [Chin-p'ing]
(1)
Kinhsien see Yüchung
Kinkiachai see Kinchai [Chin-
chai]
Kinping [Chin-p'ing] (1). Town,
southwestern China : Kinho
(-1936)
Kinping [Chin-p'ing] (2). Town,
southern China : Liping (-1913)
Kinross Air Force Base see
Rickenbacker Air Force Base
Kinsha [Chin-sha]. Town, southern
China : Sinchang (-1932)
Kinshasa. Capital of Zaïre,
central Africa : Léopoldville

(-1966)
Kintang [Chin-t'ang]. Village,
southern China : Shangyütung
(-1932)
Kirchdorf am Haunpold see
Bruckmühl
Kirda see Gulbakhor
Kirgiz Autonomous Oblast see
Kirgiz SSR
Kirgiz Autonomous SSR see
(1) Kazakh SSR; (2) Kirgiz
SSR
Kirgiz-Kulak see Chirchik
Kirgiz SSR. USSR : Kara-
Kirgiz Autonomous Oblast
(*1924-25), Kirgiz Autono-
mous Oblast (1925-26), Kirgiz
Autonomous SSR (1926-36)
Kirillovo. Village, Sakhalin
Oblast, RSFSR : Uryu (1905-
45), Japan
Kirin. City, northeastern
China : Yungki (1929-37)
Kirkuk see Al-Tamim
Kirkwood. Town, Cape of
Good Hope, South Africa :
Bayville (-1913)
Kirmasti see Mustafa Kemal
Paşa
Kirov (1). Town, Kaluga Oblast,
RSFSR : Pesochnya (-1936)
Kirov (2). Capital of Kirov
Oblast, RSFSR : Vyatka
(-1934)
Kirova. Bay, Azerbaijan SSR
: Kyzylagach (-c. 1960)
Kirova, imeni see (1) Bank;
(2) Kirovo (1), (2); (3)
Kirovsk (2)
Kirovabad. Town, Azerbaijan
SSR : Gandzha (-1804, 1918-
35), Yelizavetpol (1804-1918)
Kirovabad see Pyandzh
Kirovakan. Town, Armenian
SSR : Karaklis (-1935)
Kirovgrad. Town, Sverdlovsk
Oblast, RSFSR : Kalatinsky
Zavod (-1928), Kalata (1928-
35)
Kirovo (1). Urban settlement,
Fergana Oblast, Uzbek SSR :
Besh-Aryk (-1937), Kirova,
imeni (1937-c. 1940)

Kirovo (2). Urban settlement,
Donetsk Oblast, Ukrainian
SSR : Kirova, imeni (-c. 1960)
Kirovo (3). Village, Kurgan
Oblast, RSFSR : Voskresenskoye
(-1939)
Kirovo see Kirovograd
Kirovo-Chepetsk. Town, Kirov
Oblast, RSFSR : Kirovo-
Chepetsky (-1955)
Kirovo-Chepetsky see Kirovo-
Chepetsk
Kirovograd. Capital of Kirovograd
Oblast, Ukrainian SSR : Yeli-
zavetgrad (-1924), Zinovyevsk
(1924-36), Kirovo (1936-39)
Kirovsk (1). Town, Murmansk
Oblast, RSFSR : Khibinogorsk
(*1929-34)
Kirovsk (2). Urban settlement,
Donetsk Oblast, Ukrainian
SSR : Kirova, imeni (-c. 1960)
Kirovsk (3). Town, Leningrad
Oblast, RSFSR : Nevdubstroy
(-1953)
Kirovsk (4). Urban settlement,
Mogilyov Oblast, Belorussian
SSR : Startsy (-1939)
Kirovskoye (1). Village, Kirgiz
SSR : Aleksandrovskoye (-1937)
Kirovskoye (2). Village, Chim-
kent Oblast, Kazakh SSR :
Bagara (-c. 1960)
Kirovskoye (3). Urban settlement,
Crimean Oblast, Ukrainian
SSR : Islam-Terek (-1944)
Kirovskoye (4). Village, Sakhalin
Oblast, RSFSR : Rykovskoye
(-1937)
Kirovsky (1). Urban settlement,
Astrakhan Oblast, RSFSR :
Nikitinskiye promysly (-1934)
Kirovsky (2). Suburb of Dneprope-
trovsk, Dnepropetrovsk Oblast,
Ukrainian SSR : Obukhovka
(-1938)
Kirovsky (3). Urban settlement,
Primorsky Kray, RSFSR :
Uspenka (-1939)
Kisangani. City, northeastern
Zaïre, central Africa :
Stanleyville (-1966)
Kishinyov. Capital of Moldavian

SSR : Chişinău (1918-40),
Romania
Kishkareny see Lazo
Kishui see Sishui [Hsi-shui]
Kisiaying see Wutung
Kisielice. Town, northeastern
Poland : Freystadt (-1919,
1939-45), Germany
Kíssamos. Town, western
Crete, Greece : Kastéllion
(-1960s)
Kistétény see Budatétény
Kistna see Krishna
Kisumu. City, western Kenya,
East Africa : Port Florence
(-?)
Kisykkamys see Dzhangala
Kita-kozawa see Telnovsky
Kitami. City, eastern Hokkaido,
Japan : Nokkeushi (-1942)
Kitchener. City, Ontario, Cana-
da : Berlin (-1916)
Kitose see Chkalovo (2)
Kiuchüan [Chiu-chüan]. Town,
north-central China : Suchow
(-1913)
Kiungchow see (1) Kiunglai
[Ch'iung-lai]; (2) Kiungshan
[Ch'iung-shan]
Kiunglai [Ch'iung-lai]. Town,
central China : Kiungchow
(-1913)
Kiungshan [Ch'iung-shan]. City,
southeastern China : Kiung-
chow (-1912)
Kiungtung [Ch'iung-tung]. Town,
southeastern China : Hweitung
(-1914)
Kiupu see Chihteh [Chih-te]
Kiutai [Chiu-t'ai]. Town,
northeastern China : Siakiutai
(-1947)
Kivu. Province, eastern Zaïre,
central Africa : Costermans-
ville (1935-47)
Kiya-Shaltyr see Belogorsk (3)
Kizil-agach see Yelkhovo
Klaipeda. Town, Lithuanian
SSR : Memel (1918-23, 1941-
44), Germany
Klausberg see Mikulczyce
Klausenburg see Cluj
Kléber see Sidi Benyekba

Klein-Schlatten see Zlatna
Kleitoría. Village, southern
Greece : Káto Kleitoría
(-1960s)
Klimovsk. Town, Moscow Ob-
last, RSFSR : Klimovsky
(1938-40)
Klimovsky see Klimovsk
Kljajićevo. Village, northeastern
Yugoslavia : Krnjaja (-1948)
Kłodzko. Town, southwestern
Poland : Glatz (-1945), Ger-
many
Kluczbork. Town, southern
Poland : Kreuzburg (in Ober-
schlesien) (-1945), Germany
Klukhori see Karachayevsk
Klyuchevsk. Urban settlement,
Sverdlovsk Oblast, RSFSR :
Tyoply Klyuch (*1930s-33)
Klyuchevsky. Urban settlement,
Chita Oblast, RSFSR : Klyuchi
(-c. 1960)
Klyuchi see Klyuchevsky
Klyuchinsky see Krasnomaysky
Klyundevka see Vishnyovaya (2)
Knight's Enham see Enham
Alamein
Knob Lake see Schefferville
Knox. Borough, Pennsylvania,
USA : Edenburg (-1933)
Knyaginin see Knyaginino
Knyaginino. Urban settlement,
Gorky Oblast, RSFSR :
Knyaginin (-1926)
Knyazhitsa see Slobozhanka
Koartac. Town, Quebec, Canada
: Notre-Dame-de Koartac
(-1965)
Kobarid. Village, northwestern
Yugoslavia : Caporetto (-1947),
Italy
Kobbelbude see Svetloye
Köben (an der Oder) see
Chobienia
Kobylyanka see (1) Rassvetnaya
(1); (2) Znamenka (2)
Kočevje. Village, northwestern
Yugoslavia : Gottschee (-1918),
Germany
Kocgiri see Zara
Kochow [Kaochow] see Mowming
Kochubey. Urban settlement,

Dagestan Autonomous SSR, RSFSR : Chyorny Rynok (-c. 1960)
Kochubeyevskoye. Village, Stavropol Kray, RSFSR : Olginskoye (-c. 1960)
Kodiak. Island, Alaska, USA : Kadiak (-1901)
Kodok. Town, central Sudan : Fashoda (-1905)
Kohlfurt see Węgliniec
Koivisto see (1) Bolshoy Beryozovy; (2) Primorsk (2)
Kokankishlak see Pakhtaabad
Kokloioí see Koukloioí
Koktash see Leninsky (2)
Kok-Tash. Urban settlement, Osh Oblast, Kirgiz SSR : Mayli-Su (-c. 1960)
Koktebel see Planyorskoye
Kolageran see Dzoraget
Kolai see Azovskoye
Kolarov. Mountain, western Bulgaria : Belmeken (-1949)
Kolarovgrad see Shumen [Šumen]
Kolberg see Kołobrzeg
Kolchugino see Leninsk-Kuznetsky
Koleno see Zalesnaya
Kölesd. Town, southwestern Hungary : Tormáskölesd (*1938-39)
Kolkhozabad. Urban settlement, Tadzhik SSR : Tugalan (-?), Kaganovichabad (?-1957)
Kolkhozabad see Vose, imeni
Kolkhoznoye see Ulyanovskoye (2)
Koło. Town, central Poland : Warthbrücken (1939-45), Germany
Kołobrzeg. Town, northwestern Poland : Kolberg (-1945), Germany
Kolosjoki see Nikel
Kolosovka (1). Village, Omsk Oblast, RSFSR : Nizhne-Kolosovskoye (-c. 1940)
Kolosovka (2). Village, Minsk Oblast, Belorussian SSR : Pustoy Ugol (-1964)
Kolosovo (1). Village, Vitebsk

Oblast, Belorussian SSR : Kholopkovichi (-1964)
Kolosovo (2). Village, Grodno Oblast, Belorussian SSR : Suchki (-1964)
Kolpakovskoye see Dzerzhinskoye (1)
Komárom. Town, northwestern Hungary : Komáromújváros (*1919-23)
Komáromújváros see Komárom
Komarovo. Urban settlement, Leningrad Oblast, RSFSR : Kelomyakki [Kellomäki] (-1948), Finland (-1940)
Komavangard see Sobinka
Komi Autonomous Oblast see Komi Autonomous SSR
Komi Autonomous SSR. RSFSR : Komi Autonomous Oblast (*1921-36)
Komintern see (1) Marganets; (2) Novoshakhtinsk
Kominterna, imeni. Village, Novgorod Oblast, RSFSR : Sosninskaya (-c. 1930)
Kominternovskoye. Urban settlement, Odessa Oblast, Ukrainian SSR : Antono-Kodintsevo (-1930s)
Kommunar. Urban settlement, Khakass Autonomous Oblast, Krasnoyarsk Kray, RSFSR : Bogomdarovanny (-1932)
Kommunarka (1). Village, Grodno Oblast, Belorussian SSR : Laptikha (-1964)
Kommunarka (2). Village, Vitebsk Oblast, Belorussian SSR : Skulovichi (-1964)
Kommunarsk. Town, Voroshilovgrad Oblast, Ukrainian SSR : Alchevsk (-1931), Voroshilovsk (1931-61)
Kommunizm, Peak = Communism Peak
Komotau see Chomutov
Komotine. City, northeastern Greece : Gumuljina (-1913), Turkey
Kompegádion see Néon Kompegádion
Kompong Som. Town, southern

Kampuchea : Sihanoukville
(-1970)

Komsomolabad. Village, Tadzhik
SSR : Pombachi (-c. 1935)

Komsomolsk (1). Town, Ivanovo
Oblast, RSFSR : IvGRES
(*1931-50)

Komsomolsk (2). Village,
Kaliningrad Oblast, RSFSR :
Löwenhagen (-1946), Germany
(-1945)

Komsomolsk (3). Urban settlement, Chardzhou Oblast,
Turkmen SSR : Stary Chardzhuy (-1937), Kaganovichevsk
(1937-c. 1957)

Komsomolsk (4). Village,
Samarkand Oblast, Uzbek
SSR : Tailak-Paion (-1939)

Komsomolsk see Komsomolsk-
na-Amure

Komsomolskaya. Village, Minsk
Oblast, Belorussian SSR :
Pukovo (-1964)

Komsomolsk-na-Amure. Town,
Khabarovsk Kray, RSFSR :
Permskoye (-1932), Kom-
somolsk (1932-50)

Komsomolskoye (1). Village,
Chuvash Autonomous SSR,
RSFSR : Bolshoy Kosheley
(-1939)

Komsomolskoye (2). Village,
Saratov Oblast, RSFSR :
Fridenfeld (-1941)

Komsomolskoye (3). Town,
Donetsk Oblast, Ukrainian
SSR : Karakubstroy (-c. 1945)

Komsomolskoye (4). Village,
Vinnitsa Oblast, Ukrainian
SSR : Makhnovka (-c. 1935)

Komsomolsky (1). Urban settlement, Kalmyk Autonomous
SSR, RSFSR : Krasny Kamy-
shanik (-c. 1960)

Komsomolsky (2). Settlement,
Arkhangelsk Oblast, RSFSR :
Oktyabrsky (-c. 1960)

Komsomolsky (3). Urban settlement, Tula Oblast, RSFSR :
Oktyabrsky (-c. 1960)

Komsomolsky (4). Urban settlement, Mordovian Autonomous

SSR, RSFSR : Zavodskoy
(-c. 1960)

Komsomolsky see Chirchik

Konakovo. Town, Kalinin Oblast,
RSFSR : Kuznetsovo (-1930)

Kondinskoye. Urban settlement,
Khanty-Mansi Autonomous
Okrug, Tyumen Oblast, RSFSR
: Nakhrachi (-c. 1960)

Kondinskoye see Oktyabrskoye
(5)

Koneshime see Neshime

Kongmoon see Sunwui

Königgrätz see Hradec Králové

Königinhof (an der Elbe) see
Dvůr Králové (nad Labem)

Königsberg see (1) Chojna;
(2) Kaliningrad (1)

Königsberg Oblast see Kaliningrad Oblast

Königshütte see Chorzów

Koniya. Town, Ryukyu Islands,
Japan : Higashi-kata (-1936)

Konjice. Village, northwestern
Yugoslavia : Gonobitz (-1918)

Konradshof see Skawina

Konstadt see Wołczyn

Konstantinograd see Krasnograd

Konstantinovsk. Town, Rostov
Oblast, RSFSR : Konstantinovskaya (-1941), Konstantinovsky
(1941-67)

Konstantinovskaya see Konstantinovsk

Konstantinovsky see Konstantinovsk

Kontóstablos see Arkhaíai
Kleonaí

Konuma see Novoaleksandrovsk
(1)

Kopeysk. Town, Chelyabinsk
Oblast, RSFSR : Ugolnyye
Kopi (-1917), Goskopi (1917-
28), Chelyabkopi (1928-33)

Kopryu-Koi see Ivanski

Korenica see Titova Korenica

Korenovsk. Town, Krasnodar
Kray, RSFSR : Korenovskaya
(-1961)

Korenovskaya see Korenovsk

Kornevo. Village, Kaliningrad
Oblast, RSFSR : Zinten
(-1945), Germany

Kornilovichi see Udarnaya (1)
Korobkovo see Gubkin
Korostovka see Borovaya (2)
Korovino see Solntsevo
Korsakov. Town, Sakhalin
Oblast, RSFSR : Muravyovsky
(-1905); Otomari (1905-46),
Japan (-1945)
Korsovka see Karsava
Korsun see Korsun-Shevchen-
kovsky
Korsun-Shevchenkovsky. Town,
Cherkassy Oblast, Ukrainian
SSR : Korsun (-1944)
Koryavinets see Podlesskaya
Koryskhádes. Village, central
Greece : Kypséle (-1960s)
Koshan [K'o-shan]. Town,
northeastern China : Sanchan
(-1915)
Koshu-Kavak see Krumovgrad
Košice. City, southeastern
Czechoslovakia : Kaschau
(-1920, 1939-45), Germany;
Kassa (1938-39), Hungary
Kosiorovo see Stanichno-
Luganskoye
Kos-Istek see Leninskoye (4)
Köslin see Koszalin
Kosta-Khetagurovo see Nazran
Kostakoz see Kayrakkum
Kostenets see Dimitrovo
Kostrzyn. City, western Poland
: Küstrin (-1945), Germany
Koszalin. City, northwestern
Poland : Köslin (-1945),
Germany
Kotabaru see Dzhezdy
Kota Kinabalu. Capital of Sabah,
Malaysia : Jesselton (-1968)
Kotelnikovo (1). Town, Volgo-
grad Oblast, RSFSR : Kotel-
nikovskaya (-1929)
Kotelnikovo (2). Village, Lenin-
grad Oblast, RSFSR : Salyuzi
(-1949)
Kotelnikovskaya see Kotel-
nikovo (1)
Kotikovo. Village, Sakhalin
Oblast, RSFSR : Chirie
(1905-45), Japan
Kotor. Village, southwestern
Yugoslavia : Cattaro (1941-44),

Italy
Kotoura. Town, southwestern
Honshu, Japan : Tanokuchi
(-1907)
Kotovsk (1). Town, Odessa
Oblast, Ukrainian SSR :
Birzula (-1935)
Kotovsk (2). Town, Moldavian
SSR : Gancheshty (-1940),
Kotovskoye (1940-65)
Kotovsk (3). Town, Tambov
Oblast, RSFSR : Krasny
Boyevik (1930-40)
Kotovskoye see Kotovsk (2)
Kotsyubinskoye. Urban settle-
ment, Kiev Oblast, Ukrainian
SSR : Berkovets (-1941)
Koty see Sosnovaya (1)
Kotzenau see Chocianów
Koukloioí. Village, western
Greece : Kokloioí (-1960s)
Koúkoura see Hagía Anna
Koúmares see Hellenikón
Kousseri. Town, northern
Cameroon, western Africa :
Fort-Foureau (-1974)
Koutroumpoúkhion see Dáphne
Kovno see Kaunas
Kowary. Town, southwestern
Poland : Schmiedeberg (-1945),
Germany
Koyiu. Town, southeastern
China : Shiuhing (-1912)
Kozhemyaki see Pervomaysky
(2)
Kozhevnikovo. Village, Taymyr
Autonomous Okrug, Krasnoyarsk
Kray, RSFSR : Nordvik (-1943)
Koźle. Town, southern Poland :
Cosel (-1945), Germany
Kozlikha see Sitniki
Kozlov see Michurinsk
Kozodoi see Zaslonovo
Kożuchów. Town, western Po-
land : Freystadt (-1945),
Germany
Kozyol see Mikhaylo-Kotsyubin-
skoye
Krainburg see Kranj
Krakau see Kraków
Kraków. City, southern Poland :
Krakau (-1918), Germany
Kraljevo. Town, east-central

Yugoslavia : Rankovićevo
(1949-c. 1966)
Kranéa Deskátes see Kranéa
Elassónos
Kranéa Elassónos. Village,
eastern Greece : Kranéa
Deskátes (-1960s)
Kranj. Village, northwestern
Yugoslavia : Krainburg
(-1918), Germany
Kranjska Gora. Village, north-
western Yugoslavia : Kronau
(-1918), Germany
Kranz see Zelenogradsk
Krapkowice. Town, southwestern
Poland : Krappitz (-1945),
Germany
Krappitz see Krapkowice
Kraskino. Urban settlement,
Primorsky Kray, RSFSR :
Novokiyevskoye (-?)
Krasnaya Presnya. District of
Moscow, Moscow Oblast,
RSFSR : Presnya (-1918)
Krasnaya Sloboda. Urban settle-
ment, Minsk Oblast, Belo-
russian SSR : Vyzna (-1924)
Krasnaya Sloboda see Kras-
noslobodsk
Krásno. Village, western Czech-
oslovakia : Schönfeld (-1918,
1939-45), Germany
Krasnoarmeysk (1). Town,
Saratov Oblast, RSFSR :
Goly Karamysh (-1926),
Baltser (1926-42)
Krasnoarmeysk (2). Town,
Donetsk Oblast, Ukrainian
SSR : Grishino (-1938)
Krasnoarmeysk (3). Suburb of
Volgograd, Volgograd Oblast,
RSFSR : Sarepta (-1920)
Krasnoarmeysk (4). Town,
Kokchetav Oblast, Kazakh
SSR : Tayncha (-1962)
Krasnoarmeysk (5). Town,
Moscow Oblast, RSFSR :
Voznesenskaya Manufaktura
(-1920s), Fabrika imeni
Krasnoy Armii i Flota (1920s-
28), Krasnoarmeysky (1928-
47)
Krasnoarmeyskaya (1). Village,

Minsk Oblast, Belorussian
SSR : Kabany (-1964)
Krasnoarmeyskaya (2). Village,
Krasnodar Kray, RSFSR :
Poltavskaya (-1930s)
Krasnoarmeyskoye. Village,
Chuvash Autonomous SSR,
RSFSR : Peredniye Traki
(-1939)
Krasnoarmeyskoye see (1) Urus-
Martan; (2) Volnyansk
Krasnoarmeysky. Settlement,
Rostov Oblast, RSFSR :
Kuberle (-c. 1960)
Krasnoarmeysky see Krasnoar-
meysk (5)
Krasnoarmeysky Rudnik see
Dobropolye
Krasnoberezhye. Village, Gomel
Oblast, Belorussian SSR :
Zlodin (-1964)
Krasnodar. Capital of Krasnodar
Kray, RSFSR : Yekaterinodar
(-1920)
Krasnodon. Town, Voroshilovgrad
Oblast, Ukrainian SSR :
Sorokino (*1912-38)
Krasnogorsk (1). Town, Moscow
Oblast, RSFSR : Banki (-1940)
Krasnogorsk (2). Town, Sakhalin
Oblast, RSFSR : Chinnai
(1905-47), Japan (-1945)
Krasnogorskoye (1). Village,
Udmurt Autonomous SSR,
RSFSR : Baryshnikovo (-1938)
Krasnogorskoye (2). Village,
Altay Kray, RSFSR : Staraya
Barda (-c. 1960)
Krasnogorsky. Urban settlement,
Mari Autonomous SSR, RSFSR
: Ilet (-1938)
Krasnograd. Town, Kharkov
Oblast, Ukrainian SSR :
Konstantinograd (-1922)
Krasnogrigoryevka see Cher-
vonogrigorovka
Krasnogvardeysk. Town, Samark-
land Oblast, Uzbek SSR :
Rostovsevo (-1930s)
Krasnogvardeysk see Gatchina
Krasnogvardeyskoye (1). Urban
settlement, Belgorod Oblast,
RSFSR : Biryuch (-early1920s),

Budyonnoye (early1920s-c. 1960) Krasnogvardeyskoye (2). Urban settlement, Crimean Oblast, Ukrainian SSR : Kurman-Kemelchi (-1945)

Krasnogvardeyskoye (3). Village, Stavropol Kray, RSFSR : Medvezhye (-1936), Yevdokimovskoye (1936-39), Molotovskoye (1939-57)

Krasnogvardeyskoye (4). Village, Adygey Autonomous Oblast, Krasnodar Kray, RSFSR : Nikolayevskoye (-c. 1960)

Krasnogvardeysky. Urban settlement, Sverdlovsk Oblast, RSFSR : Irbitsky Zavod (-1938)

Krasnokokshaysk see Yoshhar-Ola

Krasnolesye. Village, Kaliningrad Oblast, RSFSR : Hardteck (-1946), Germany (-1945)

Krasnomaysky. Urban settlement, Kalinin Oblast, RSFSR : Klyuchinsky (-1940)

Krasnooktyabrsky (1). Suburb of Moscow, Moscow Oblast, RSFSR : Khovrino (-1928)

Krasnooktyabrsky (2). Urban settlement, Mari Autonomous SSR, RSFSR : Mitkino (-c. 1960)

Krasnoostrovsky. Village, Leningrad Oblast, RSFSR : Byorkyo [Björkö] (-1940), Finland; Byorksky (1940-48)

Krasnorechenskoye. Urban settlement, Voroshilovgrad Oblast, Ukrainian SSR : Kabanye (-1973)

Krasnoslobodsk. Town, Volgograd Oblast, RSFSR : Krasnaya Sloboda (-1955)

Krasnoturansk. Village, Krasnoyarsk Kray, RSFSR : Abakanskoye (-?)

Krasnoturyinsk. Town, Sverdlovsk Oblast, RSFSR : Turyinskiye Rudniki (-1944)

Krasnouralsk. Town, Sverdlovsk Oblast, RSFSR : Uralmedstroy

(*1925-32)

Krasnouralsky Rudnik see Novoasbest

Krasnovichi. Village, Mogilyov Oblast, Belorussian SSR : Volchyi Yamy (-1964)

Krasnovodsk Nature Reserve : Krasnovodsk Oblast, Turkmen SSR : Gasan-Kuli Nature Reserve (*1932-69)

Krasnoye see (1) Chervonoye (1); (2) Ulan-Erge

Krasnoye Ekho. Urban settlement, Vladimir Oblast, RSFSR : Novogordino (-1925)

Krasnozavodsk. Town, Moscow Oblast, RSFSR : Zagorsky (-1940)

Krasnoznamensk. Town, Kaliningrad Oblast, RSFSR : Lasdehnen (-1938), Germany; Haselberg (1938-46), Germany (-1945)

Krasny see (1) Kyzyl; (2) Mozhga

Krasny Boyevik see Kotovsk (3)

Krasny Kamashanik see Komsomolsky (1)

Krasny Karachay. Village, Karachayevo-Cherkess Autonomous Oblast, Stavropol Kray, RSFSR : Gornoye (-c. 1960)

Krasny Klyuch. Urban settlement, Bashkir Autonomous SSR, RSFSR : Bely Klyuch (-?)

Krasny Liman. Town, Donetsk Oblast, Ukrainian SSR : Liman (-1938)

Krasny Log. Village, Gomel Oblast, Belorussian SSR : Krestovy Log (-1964)

Krasny Luch. Town, Voroshilovgrad Oblast, Ukrainian SSR : Krindachyovka (-1926)

Krasny Mayak. Urban settlement, Vladimir Oblast, RSFSR : Yakunchikov (-1925)

Krasny Oktyabr. Urban settlement, Vladimir Oblast, RSFSR : Voznesensky (-1919)

Krasny Oktyabr see Baran

Krasny Profintern (1). Urban settlement, Donetsk Oblast, Ukrainian SSR : Guzitsino (-1945)

Krasny Profintern (2). Urban settlement, Yaroslavl Oblast, RSFSR : Ponizovkino (-c. 1926)

Krasny Profintern (3). Urban settlement, Donetsk Oblast, Ukrainian SSR : Verovka (-?)

Krasny Steklovar. Urban settlement, Mari Autonomous SSR, RSFSR : Kuzhery (-1939)

Krasny Sulin. Town, Rostov Oblast, RSFSR : Sulin (-1926)

Krasny Tekstilshchik. Urban settlement, Saratov Oblast, RSFSR : Saratovskaya Manufaktura (-1929)

Krasny Tkach. Urban settlement, Moscow Oblast, RSFSR : Shuvoya (-1935)

Krasny Ural see Uralete

Krasny Vostok. Village, Mogilyov Oblast, Belorussian SSR : Shelomy (-1964)

Krasnyye Baki. Urban settlement, Gorky Oblast, RSFSR : Baki (-?)

Krasnyye Okny. Urban settlement, Odessa Oblast, Ukrainian SSR : Okny (-1920)

Krathiás see Kráthion

Kráthion. Village, southern Greece : Paralía Akrátas [Krathiás] (-1960s)

Kratske see Podchinny

Kreiger see Libau

Kremenets. Town, Ternopol Oblast, Ukrainian SSR : Krzemieniec (1921-39), Poland

Kremges see Svetlovodsk

Krenau see Chrzanów

Krestovy Log see Krasny Log

Kreuz see Krzyż

Kreuzberg see Fraserwood

Kreuzburg see (1) Kluczbork; (2) Slavskoye

Kreuzingen see Bolshakovo

Kribi see Ocean

Krindachyovka see Krasny Luch

Krinichnaya. Village, Vitebsk Oblast, Belorussian SSR : Badyaly (-1964)

Krishna. River, southern India : Kistna (-1966)

Kristiania see Oslo

Kristians see Opland

Kristinopol see Chervonograd

Kritsínion see Taziárkhai

Krivaya Kosa see Sedovo

Krk. Island and village, northwestern Yugoslavia : Veglia (1919-47), Italy

Krn. Mountain, northwestern Yugoslavia : Nero (-1947), Italy

Krnjaja see Kljajićevo

Królewska Huta see Chorzów

Kromníkos see Galáne

Kronau see Kranjska Gora

Kronstadt see Brașov

Kropotkin (1). Town, Krasnodar Kray, RSFSR : Romanovsky Khutor (-1921)

Kropotkin (2). Urban settlement, Irkutsk Oblast, RSFSR : Tikhono-Zadonsky (-1930)

Krosno (Ordzańskie). Town, western Poland : Crossen (-1945), Germany

Krško. Village, northwestern Yugoslavia : Gurkfeld (-1918), Germany

Kruger National Park : Transvaal, South Africa : Sabi Game Reserve (-1926)

Kruglyakov see Oktyabrsky (5)

Krummau see Český Krumlov

Krummhübel see Karpacz

Krumovgrad. City, southern Bulgaria : Koshu-Kavak (-1934)

Krylovskaya. Village, Krasnodar Kray, RSFSR : Yekaterinovskaya (-c. 1960)

Krymsk. Town, Krasnodar Kray, RSFSR : Krymskaya (-1958)

Krymskaya see Krymsk

Krynichka. Village, Minsk Oblast, Belorussian SSR : Pupelichi (-1964)

Krzemieniec see Kremenets

Krzyż. Town, west-central Poland : Kreuz (-1945), Germany

Ksar Chellala. Village, northern Algeria, northern Africa : Reïbell (-c. 1962)

Ksar el Boukhari. Town, northern Algeria, northern Africa :

Boghari (-c. 1962)
Kuang-han = Kwanghan
Kuang-hua = Kwanghwa
Kuang-jao = Kwangjao
K'uang-wu = Kwangwu
Kuan-yün = Kwanyün
Kuberle see Krasnoarmeysky
Kuchan see Huma
Kuchang [Ku-ch'ang]. Suburb
of Kunming, southwestern
China : Kwantu (-1945)
Kuchow see Jungkiang [Jung-
chiang]
Kuckerneese see Yasnoye
Kuçovë see Stalin
Kudara see Kudara-Somon
Kudara-Somon. Village, Buryat
Autonomous SSR, RSFSR :
Kudara (-1948)
Kudelka see Asbest
Kudinovo see Elektrougli
Kudowa Zdrój. Town, south-
western Poland : Bad Kudowa
(-1945), Germany
Kuei-ch'ih = Kweichih
Kuei-chu = Kweichu
Kuei-p'ing = Kweiping
Kuei-te = Kweiteh
Kühlungsborn. Town, northern
West Germany : Brunshaupten
(-1938)
Kuhwa see Poshow
Kukarka see Sovetsk (1)
Kukishi see Gvardeyskaya
Kukkus see Privolzhskoye
Kükong. Town, southeastern
China : Shiuchow (-1912)
Kukonosy see Podlesye
Kükoshakia see Kweiteh
[Kuei-te]
Kükow see Kungho
Kukshik see Pervomaysky (3)
Kulakovtsy see Zarechnaya (2)
Kuldiga. Town, Latvian SSR :
Goldingen (-?)
Kulnevo. Village, Vitebsk Ob-
last, Belorussian SSR :
Tserkovishche (-1964)
Kumashkino see Kurchum
Künchow see Künhsien [Chün-
hsien]
Kunersdorf see Kunowice
Kungchang see Lungsi [Lung-hsi]

Kungho. Town, northwestern
China : Kükow (-1931)
Kungrad. Town, Karakalpak
Autonomous SSR, Uzbek SSR :
Zheleznodorozhny (-1969)
Kungshan. Village, southwestern
China : Tala (-1935)
Künhsien [Chün-hsien]. Town,
east-central China : Künchow
(-1912)
Kunice. Town, northwestern
Poland : Kunitz (-1945), Ger-
many
Kunitz see Kunice
Kunming [K'un-ming]. City,
southwestern China : Yunnan
(-1912)
Kunowice. Village, western
Poland : Kunersdorf (-1945),
Germany
Kuokkala see Repino
Kuolayarvi. Village, Murmansk
Oblast, RSFSR : Salla (1937-
40)
Kurakhovo. Town, Donetsk
Oblast, Ukrainian SSR :
Kurakhovstroy (-1956)
Kurakhovstroy see Kurakhovo
Kuratovo. Village, Komi Au-
tonomous SSR, RSFSR :
Kibra (-c. 1940)
Kurbat. Village, northeastern
Bulgaria : Balbunar (-1934)
Kurchaloy. Village, Checheno-
Ingush Autonomous SSR, RSFSR
: Chkalovo (-c. 1960)
Kurchum. Village, East Kazakh-
stan Oblast, Kazakh SSR :
Kumashkino (-c. 1960)
Kuressaare see Kingisepp (1)
Kurgaldzhinsky. Urban settle-
ment, Tselinograd Oblast,
Kazakh SSR : Kazgorodok
(-1937)
Kurganinsk. Town, Krasnodar
Kray, RSFSR : Kurgannaya
(-1961)
Kurgannaya see Kurganinsk
Kurganovka. Suburb of Beryozov-
sky, Kemerovo Oblast, RSFSR
: Zaboyshchik (-1944)
Kurhessen see Hesse-Kassel
Kurilsk. Town, Kuril Islands,

Sakhalin Oblast, RSFSR :
Shana (1905-46), Japan (-1945)
Kurisches Haff see Kursky
Gulf
Kurman-Kemelchi see Kras-
nogvardeyskoye (2)
Kursky Gulf. Inlet of Baltic
Sea, Lithuanian SSR and
Kaliningrad Oblast, RSFSR :
Kurisches Haff (-1946), Ger-
many (-1945)
Kursu see Salla
Küş Gölü. Island, western Tur-
key : Manyas Gölü (-1973)
Kushalnagar. Town, southern
India : Fraserpet (-1950s)
Kushan. Town, northeastern
China : Takushan (-1947)
Kushnarenkovo. Village, Bash-
kir Autonomous SSR, RSFSR
: Topornino (-1930s)
Kushunnai see Ilyinsky
Kusochek see Roshchino (1)
Kussen see Vesnovo
Küstrin see Kostrzyn
Kusye-Aleksandrovsky. Urban
settlement, Perm Oblast,
RSFSR : Kusye-Aleksandrovsky
Zavod (-1946)
Kusye-Aleksandrovsky Zavod
see Kusye-Aleksandrovsky
Kut see Wasit
Kutaradja see Banda Atjeh
Kutuzovka. Village, Minsk
Oblast, Belorussian SSR :
Drekhcha Panenskaya (-1964)
Kutuzovo. Village, Kaliningrad
Oblast, RSFSR : Schirwindt
(-1945), Germany
Kuybyshev (1). Town, Novosi-
birsk Oblast, RSFSR : Kainsk
(-1935)
Kuybyshev (2). Capital of
Kuybyshev Oblast, RSFSR :
Samara (-1935)
Kuybyshev (3). Town, Tatar
Autonomous SSR, RSFSR :
Spassk (-1926), Spassk-
Tatarsky (1926-35)
Kuybyshev Oblast. RSFSR :
Middle Volga Oblast (*1928-
29), Middle Volga Kray (1929-
35), Kuybyshev Kray (1935-36)

Kuybysheva, imeni see Kuyby-
shevo (3)
Kuybyshevabad see Kuybyshevsk
Kuybyshevka-Vostochnaya see
Belogorsk (1)
Kuybyshev Kray see Kuybyshev
Oblast
Kuybyshevo (1). Urban settle-
ment, Crimean Oblast, Ukrain-
ian SSR : Albat (-1944)
Kuybyshevo (2). Village, Rostov
Oblast, RSFSR : Golodayevka
(-c.1936)
Kuybyshevo (3). Urban settlement,
Fergana Oblast, Uzbek SSR :
Rishtan (-1937), Kuybysheva,
imeni (1937-c.1940)
Kuybyshevo (4). Village, Sak-
halin Oblast, RSFSR : Rubetsu
(1905-45), Japan
Kuybyshevo (5). Village, Mary
Oblast, Turkmen SSR : Talk-
hatan-Baba (-c.1940)
Kuybyshevo (6). Urban settle-
ment, Zaporozhye Oblast,
Ukrainian SSR : Tsarekonstan-
tinovka (-c.1935)
Kuybyshevsky (1). Urban settle-
ment, Tadzhik SSR : Aral
(-c.1935), Kuybyshevabad
(c.1935-40)
Kuybyshevsky (2). Urban settle-
ment, Kokchetav Oblast,
Kazakh SSR : Trudovoy (-1969)
Kuybyshevsky Zaton. Urban
settlement, Tatar Autonomous
SSR, RSFSR : Spassky Zaton
(-1935)
Kuyüan see Paoyüan
Kuzhery see Krasny Steklovar
Kuznetsk see Novokuznetsk
Kuznetsovo see Konakovo
Kvirily see Zestafoni
Kwabhaca. Town, northern
Transkei, southern Africa :
Mount Frere (-1976)
Kwaki see Kweichu [Kuei-chu]
Kwangchang see Laiyüan
Kwanghan [Kuang-han]. Town,
central China : Hanchow (-1913)
Kwanghwa [Kuang-hua]. Town
east-central China : Laohokow
[Lao-ho-k'ou] (-1947)

Kwangjao [Kuang-jao]. Town,
  eastern China : Loan (-1914)
Kwangning see Pehchen
Kwangping see Yungnien
Kwangsi see Lusi [Lu-hsi] (1)
Kwangsin see Shangjao
Kwangwu [K'uang-wu]. Town,
  eastern China : Linghsien
  (-1949)
Kwanpao see Hweichwan
  [Hui-chuan]
Kwantu see Kuchang [Ku-ch'ang]
Kwanyün [Kuan-yün]. Town,
  eastern China : Panpu (-1912)
Kweichih [Kuei-ch'ih]. Town,
  eastern China : Chihchow
  (-1912)
Kweichow see (1) Fengkieh
  [Feng-chieh]; (2) Tzekwei
  [Tzu-kuei]
Kweichu [Kuei-chu]. Town,
  southern China : Kwaki
  (-1930)
Kweihwa see (1) Mingki
  [Ming-ch'i]; (2) Tzeyün
  [Tzu-yün]
Kweiping [Kuei-p'ing]. Town,
  southern China : Sünchow
  (-1913)
Kweishun see Tsingsi
  [Ching-hsi]
Kweiteh [Kuei-te]. Town,
  northwestern China : Küko-
  shakia (-1928)
Kweiyang see Jucheng [Ju-
  ch'eng]
Kwidzyń. Town, northern Po-
  land : Marienwerder (-1919,
  1939-45), Germany
Kwilu-Ngongo. Town, western
  Zaïre, central Africa :
  Moerbeke (-1972)
Kyaikkami. Town, southwestern
  Burma : Amherst (-?)
Kyakhta. Town, Buryat Au-
  tonomous SSR, RSFSR :
  Troitskosavsk (-1935)
Kyŏmipo see Songnim
Kypséle (1). Village, western
  Greece : Khósepse (-1960s)
Kypséle (2). Village, northern
  Greece : Neokhórion (-1960s)
Kypséle see (1) Koryskhádes;

(2) Kypséle Methánon
Kypséle Methánon. Village,
  northern Greece : Kypséle
  (-1960s)
Kyzyl. Capital of Tuva Autono-
  mous SSR, RSFSR : Belotsarsk
  (*1914-18), Krasny (1918),
  Khem-Beldyr (1918-26),
  Kyzyl-Khoto (1926-?)
Kyzylagach see Kirova
Kyzylasker. Suburb of Frunze,
  Kirgiz SSR : Chalakazaki
  (-1944)
Kyzyl-Burun see Siazan
Kyzyl-Khoto see Kyzyl
Kzyl-Mazar see Sovetsky (3)
Kzyl-Orda. Capital of Kzyl-
  Orda Oblast, Kazakh SSR :
  Ak-Mechet (*1820-53, c. 1920-
  25), Perovsk (1853-c. 1920)

Laband see Łabędy
Łabędy. Town, southern Poland
  : Laband (-1945), Germany
Labes see Lobez
Labiau see Polessk
Labinsk. Town, Krasnodar Kray,
  RSFSR : Labinskaya (-1947)
Labinskaya see Labinsk
Labrador. Municipality, Pangasi-
  nan, Philippines : San Isidro
  Labrador (-1914)
Labrang see Siaho [Hsia-ho]
La Calle see El Kala
Laccadive, Minicoy and Amindivi
  Islands see Lakshadweep
La Charqueada see General
  Enrique Martínez
Lachine see La Salle
Lackawanna. City, New York,
  USA : Limestone Hill (-1909)
La Concepción see Ri-Aba
La Cordillera. Department,
  central Paraguay, South Amer-
  ica : Caraguatay (-1944)
Lacub see Fabian Marcos
Lada Bay. Inlet, Sunda Strait,
  Java, Indonesia : Peper Bay
  (-1963)
Lądek Zdrój. Town, southwestern

Ladushkin 80

Poland : Bad Landeck (-1945), Germany
Ladushkin. Town, Kaliningrad Oblast, RSFSR : Ludwigsort (-1946), Germany (-1945)
Ladysmith. City, Vancouver Island, British Columbia, Canada : Oyster Harbour (-1901)
La Estrelleta. Province, western Dominican Republic, West Indies : San Rafael (*1942-65)
Lafayette see Bougaâ
Lafayette National Park see Acadia National Park
Laflèche. Suburb of Montreal, Quebec, Canada : Mackayville (-1959)
Lagan see Kaspiysky
Laggan see Lake Louise
Lagiewniki. Town, southwestern Poland : Elvershagen (-1945), Germany
Lagona see Laguna Beach
Lagos Airport see Murtala Muhammed Airport
La Goulette see Halq-el-Oued
Laguna see Padilla
Laguna Beach. City, California, USA : Lagona (-1904)
Lahij. Town, western Yemen [People's Democratic Republic of Yemen] : al-Hawtah (1960s)
Lähn see Wleń
Laibach see Ljubljana
Laichow see Yehsien
Laishev see Laishevo
Laishevo. Urban settlement, Tatar Autonomous SSR, RSFSR : Laishev (-c. 1928)
Laiyüan. Town, northeastern China : Kwangchang (-1914)
Lajeado see Guiratinga
Lajes see Itaretama
Lake Bogoria. Town, west-central Kenya, eastern Africa : Lake Hannington (-1975)
Lake City. Town, Tennessee, USA : Coal Creek (-1939)
Lake Hannington see Lake Bogoria

Lake Lanao see Sultan Alonto
Lake Louise. Village, Alberta, Canada : Laggan (-1914)
Lake Oswego. City, Oregon, USA : Oswego (-1909)
Lake Rudolf see Lake Turkana
Lake Turkana. Town, northern Kenya, eastern Africa : Lake Rudolf (-1975)
Lake Worth. City, Florida, USA : Lucerne (-1913)
Lakiashih see Tungteh [T'ung-te]
Lakinsk. Town, Vladimir Oblast, RSFSR : Lakinsky (-1969)
Lakinsky see Lakinsk
Lakhdaria. Village, northern Algeria, northern Africa : Palestro (-c. 1962)
Lakshadweep. Island territory, southwestern India : Laccadive, Minicoy and Amindivi Islands (*1956-73)
Lambèse see Tazoult
La Mirada. City, California, USA : Mirada Hills (-1960)
Lamoricière see Ouled Mimoun
Landau see Shirokolanovka
Landeck see Lędyczek
Landeshut see Kamienna Góra
Landsberg see (1) Górowo Iławeckie; (2) Gorzów Wielkopolski
Landsberg (an der Warthe) see Gorzów Wielkopolski
Landsberg in Oberschlesien see Gorzów (Śląski)
Landsweiler-Reden. Town, western West Germany : Landsweiler (-1937)
Lang-ang see Santa Theresa
Lang-ch'i = Langki
Langchu see Ninglang
Langchung. Town, central China : Paoning (-1913)
Langenbielau see Bielawa
Langki [Lang-ch'i]. Town, eastern China : Kienping (-1914)
Langkiung see Erhyüan
Langshan. Town, northern China : Yunganpao (-1942)
Lankao. Town, central China : Chwanping (-1913)

Lans see Lans-en-Vercors
Lans-en-Vercors. Village,
southeastern France : Lans
(-1947)
Lansweiler see Lansweiler-
Reden
Lantsang [Lan-ts'ang]. Town,
southwestern China : Chen-
pien (-1914)
Lao-ho-k'ou see Kwanghwa
Laohokow [Lao-ho-k'ou] see
Kwanghwa [Kuang-hua]
Laoighis [Laois, Leix]. County,
central Ireland : Queen's
County (-1920)
Laois = Laoighis
La Olmeda de las Cabolla see
La Olmeda de las Fuentes
La Olmeda de las Fuentes.
Village, central Spain : La
Olmeda de las Cebolla (-c.
1960)
Laoyao see Lienyün
Laoyatan see Yentsing
La Pampa. Province, central
Argentina, South America :
Eva Perón (1952-55)
La Parida see (Cerro) Bolívar
La Park see Huntington Park
La Plata. City, eastern Ar-
gentina, South America : Eva
Perón (1952-55)
Laptevo see Yasnogorsk
Laptev Sea. Arctic Ocean,
northeastern USSR : Norden-
skjöld Sea (-1913)
Lapti see Mayskaya
Laptikha see Kommunarka (1)
La Puebla del Río. Village,
southwestern Spain : Puebla
(-c. 1920)
Laragaran see Plaridel (1)
Laranjal see Laranjal Paulista
Laranjal Paulista. City, south-
eastern Brazil, South Amer-
ica : Laranjal (-1944)
Laranjeiras see (1) Alagoa
Nova; (2) Laranjeiras do Sul
Laranjeiras do Sul. City,
southern Brazil, South Amer-
ica : Laranjeiras (-1944),
Iguaçu (1944-48)
L'Arbaa Naït Irathen. Town,

north-central Algeria, northern
Africa : Fort-National (-c. 1962)
Largeau. Town, northern Chad,
north-central Africa : Faya
(-1913)
L'Argentière see L'Argentière-
la-Bessée
L'Argentière-la-Bessée. Village,
southeastern France :
L'Argentière (-1941)
Larinsky see Never
Larkins see South Miami
La Salle. Suburb of Montreal,
Quebec, Canada : Lachine
(-1912)
Lasdehnen see Krasnoznamensk
Lasko. Village, northwestern
Yugoslavia : Tüffer (-1918),
Germany
Las Palmas. Province, Canary
Islands : Canarias (-1927)
Laspokhórion see Leúke
Las Rosas. Town, southern Mex-
ico, North America : Pinola
(-1934)
Las Torres de Cotillas. Village,
southeastern Spain : Cotillas
(-c. 1920)
Las Villas. Province, central
Cuba : Santa Clara (-1940)
Latakia. Governorate, north-
western Syria : Alawiya (1920-
42)
Latgale see Daugavpils
La Thuile. Village, northwestern
Italy : Porta Littoria (c. 1938-
45)
Latina (1). City, south-central
Italy : Littoria (*1932-47)
Latina (2). Province, south-
central Italy : Littoria (*1934-
47)
La Toma see Cuatro de Junio
La Trinidad see Villa La
Trinidad
La Trinitaria. Town, southern
Mexico, North America :
Zapaluta (-1934)
Lauban see Lubań
Lauenburg see Lębork
La Unión. Town, eastern Gua-
temala, Central America :
Monte Oscuro (-c. 1920)

Laurahütte see Siemianowice
Śląskie
Laurel Hollow. Village, New
York, USA : Laurelton
(-1935)
Laurelton see Laurel Hollow
Laval see Laval-sur-Vologne
Laval-sur-Vologne. Village,
eastern France : Laval (-1937)
La Vereda. Village, central
Spain : El Vado (-c. 1950)
Lavras see (1) Lavras da
Mangabeira; (2) Lavras do
Sul
Lavras da Mangabeira. City,
northeastern Brazil, South
America : Lavras (-1944)
Lavras do Sul. City, southern
Brazil, South America :
Lavras (-1944)
Lavrentiya. Village, Chukot
Autonomous Okrug, Magadan
Oblast, RSFSR : Chukotskaya
Kultbaza (-c. 1960)
Lavumisa. Town, southern
Swaziland, southern Africa :
Gollel (-1970)
Lazarev. Urban settlement,
Khabarovsk Kray, RSFSR :
Mys Lazarev (-c. 1960)
Lazo. Village, Moldavian SSR
: Kishkareny (-c. 1960)
Lazovsk. Urban settlement,
Moldavian SSR : Synzhereya
(-c. 1960)
Lbishchensk see Chapayev
Leaksville see Eden
Lebedevka. Health resort,
Odessa Oblast, Ukrainian
SSR : Burnas (-?)
Lebedinovskoye see Voroshilov-
skoye
Lębork. City, northern Poland
: Lauenburg (-1945), Germany
Le Center. Village, Minnesota,
USA : Le Sueur Center (-1931)
Łęczyca. Town, central Po-
land : Lentschütz (1939-45),
Germany
Ledengskoye see Babushkina,
imeni
Ledo Road see Stilwell Road
Lędyczek. Town, northwestern

Poland : Landeck (-1945),
Germany
Leeudoringstad. Village, Trans-
vaal, South Africa : Leeudorns
Halte (-1906)
Leeudorns Halte see Leeudor-
ingstad
Leeu-Gamka. Town, Cape of
Good Hope, South Africa :
Fraserburg Road (-?)
Legnica. Town, southwestern
Poland : Liegnitz (-1945),
Germany
Leipe see Lipno
Leishan. Town, southern China :
Tankiang (-1943)
Leix = Laoighis
Leksura see Lentekhi
Lemberg see Lvov
Lemeshensky see Orgtrud
Lempira. Department, western
Honduras, Central America :
Gracias (-1943)
Lençóis see Lençóis Paulista
Lençóis Paulista. City, south-
eastern Brazil, South Amer-
ica : Lençóis (-1944), Ubirama
(1944-48)
Lengwethen see Lunino
Lengyeltóti. Town, southwestern
Hungary : Lengyeltótihács
(-1907)
Lengyeltótihács see Lengyeltóti
Lenina, imeni. Suburb of Krivoy
Rog, Dnepropetrovsk Oblast,
Ukrainian SSR : Kalachevsky
rudnik (-1926)
Leninabad. Capital of Leninabad
Oblast, Tadzhik SSR : Khod-
zhent (-1936)
Leninakan. Town, Armenian SSR
: Aleksandropol (-1924)
Lenina V. I., imeni. Urban settle-
ment, Ulyanovsk Oblast, RSFSR
: Rumyantsevo (-1938)
Lenin-Dzhol. Village, Osh Ob-
last, Kirgiz SSR : Massy (-?)
Leningrad. Capital of Leningrad
Oblast, RSFSR [capital of
Russia 1712-28, 1732-1918] :
St. Petersburg (-1914), Petro-
grad (1914-24)
Leningrad Guberniya (1927†).

RSFSR : St. Petersburg Gu-
berniya (-1914), Petrograd
Guberniya (1914-24)
Leningradskaya. Village, Kras-
nodar Kray, RSFSR : Uman-
skaya (-1930s)
Leningradsky. Urban settlement,
Tadzhik SSR : Muminabad
(-1973)
Lenin Hills. Section of right
bank of river Moskva, Moscow,
RSFSR : Sparrow Hills (-1935)
Lenino (1). Suburb of Irkutsk,
Irkutsk Oblast, RSFSR : In-
nokentyevskaya (-1930s)
Lenino (2). Urban settlement,
Crimean Oblast, Ukrainian
SSR : Sem Kolodezey (-1957)
Lenino (3). Suburb of Moscow,
Moscow Oblast, RSFSR :
Tsaritsyno-Dachnoye (-1939),
Lenino-Dachnoye (1939-?)
Lenino see Leninsk-Kuznetsky
Lenino-Dachnoye see Lenino
(3)
Leninogorsk (1). Town, Tatar
Autonomous SSR, RSFSR :
Novaya Pismyanka (-1955)
Leninogorsk (2). Town, East
Kazakhstan Oblast, Kazakh
SSR : Ridder (-1941)
Lenin Peak. Mountain, Kirgiz/
Tadzhik SSR : Kaufman Peak
(-1928)
Leninsk (1). Town, Volgograd
Oblast, RSFSR : Prishib
(-1919)
Leninsk (2). Town, Andizhan
Oblast, Uzbek SSR : Zelensk
(1930s), Assake (-1938)
Leninsk see (1) Petrodvorets;
(2) Yaldom
Leninskaya Sloboda. Urban
settlement, Gorky Oblast,
RSFSR : Kadnitsy (-1935)
Leninsk-Kuznetsky. Town,
Kemerovo Oblast, RSFSR :
Kolchugino (-1922), Lenino
(1922-25)
Leninskoye (1). Village, Chim-
kent Oblast, Kazakh SSR :
Alekseyevskoye (-1924)
Leninskoye (2). Urban settle-

ment, Kirov Oblast, RSFSR :
Bogorodskoye (-1917), Sha-
balino (1917-c. 1940)
Leninskoye (3). Village, Kus-
tanay Oblast, Kazakh SSR :
Demyanovka (-c. 1960)
Leninskoye (4). Village, Aktyu-
binsk Oblast, Kazakh SSR :
Kos-Istek (-c. 1960)
Leninskoye (5). Village, Uralsk
Oblast, Kazakh SSR : Mastek-
say (-c. 1960)
Leninskoye (6). Village, Jewish
Autonomous Oblast, Khabarovsk
Kray, RSFSR : Mikhailovo-
Semyonovskoye (-?), Blyuk-
herovo (?-1939)
Leninskoye (7). Village, Osh
Oblast, Kirgiz SSR : (Novaya)
Pokrovka (-1937)
Leninsk (-Turkmensky) see
Chardzhou
Leninsky (1). Urban settlement,
Tula Oblast, RSFSR : Domman-
Asfaltovy Zavod (-1939)
Leninsky (2). Urban settlement,
Tadzhik SSR : Koktash (-c.
1960), Sardarova Karakhana,
imeni (c. 1960-70)
Leninsky (3). Urban settlement,
Mari Autonomous SSR, RSFSR
: Marino (-1941)
Leninsky (4). Urban settlement,
Yakutsk Autonomous SSR,
RSFSR : Nizhnestalinsk (?-1962)
Leninsky (5). Urban settlement,
Kzyl-Orda Oblast, Kazakh SSR
: Zarya (-c. 1960)
Leninváros. Town, northeastern
Hungary : Tiszaszederkény
(*1950-70)
Leninváros see Pestszenterzsébet
Lensk. Town, Yakutsk Autonomous
SSR, RSFSR : Mukhtuya (-1963)
Lentekhi. Urban settlement,
Georgian SSR : Leksura (-1938)
Lentschütz see Łęczyca
Leobschütz see Głubczyce
León see Cotopaxi
Leonidovo. Urban settlement,
Sakhalin Oblast, RSFSR :
Kami-shikuka (1905-45), Japan
Leopold II, Lake see Mai-

Ndombe, Lake
Leopoldina see (1) Aruaña;
(2) Colônia Leopoldina; (3)
Parnamirim
Léopoldville see Kinshasa
Lepaya = Liepaja
Lermontov. Town, Stavropol
Kray, RSFSR : Lermontovsky
(-1956)
Lermontovo. Village, Penza
Oblast, RSFSR : Tarkhany
(-?)
Lermontovsky see Lermontov
Leschnitz see Leśnica
Leselidze. Health resort,
Abkhazian Autonomous SSR,
Georgian SSR : Yermolovsk
(-1944)
Lesínion. Village, central
Greece : Palaiokatoúna (-1960s)
Leskhimstroy see Severodo-
netsk
Leslau see Włocławek
Leśnica. Town, southern Po-
land : Leschnitz (-1937),
Germany; Bergstadt (1937-
45), Germany
Lesnoy see (1) Seskar; (2)
Umba
Lesogorsk. Town, Sakhalin
Oblast, RSFSR : Nayoshi
(1905-46), Japan (-1945)
Lesogorsky. Urban settlement,
Leningrad Oblast, RSFSR :
Yaski [Jääski] (-1948), Fin-
land (-1940)
Lesotho. Kingdom, southern
Africa : Basutoland (-1966)
Lesovka see Ukrainsk
Lesozavodsky see Novovyatsk
Lesten see Czernina
Lestershire see Johnson City
Les Trembles see Sidi Hama-
douche
Le Sueur Center see Le Center
Leszno. City, west-central
Poland : Lissa (-1919), Ger-
many
Leubus see Lubiąz
Leúke. Village, eastern Greece
: Laspokhórion (-1960s)
Leukothéa. Village, western
Greece : Kephalóvryson (-1960s)

Leuthen see Lutynia
Leutschau see Levoča
Levelland. City, Texas, USA :
Hockley (*1921-24)
Leverburgh. Village, Western
Isles, Scotland, UK : Obbe
(-1920s)
Leverger see Santo Antônio do
Leverger
Leverville see Lusanga
Levittown see Willingboro
Levoča. Town, northeastern
Czechoslovakia : Leutschau
(-1918, 1939-45), Germany
Levski. Mountain, north-central
Bulgaria : Ambarica (-c. 1967)
Levskigrad. Town, central Bul-
garia : Karlovo (-1953)
Lev Tolstoy. Urban settlement,
Lipetsk Oblast, RSFSR :
Astapovo (-1927)
Lewin. Town, southwestern
Poland : Hummelstadt (1938-
45), Germany
Lewin Brzeski. Town, south-
western Poland : Löwen (-1945),
Germany
Lewis. Locality, Manitoba,
Canada : Rateau (-1918)
Lewisporte. Town, Newfound-
land, Canada : Marshallville
(-c. 1900)
Lexington Park. Village, Mary-
land, USA : Jarboesville (-1950)
Lezhni see Bereznitsa (1)
Liangchow see Wuwei
Liaocheng [Liao-ch'eng]. Town,
north-central China : Tung-
chang (-1913)
Liaochow see Tsochüan
Liaohsien see Tsochüan
Liaoning. Province, northeastern
China : Feng-t'ien (1903-28)
Liaoyüan see Schwangliao
[Shuang-liao]
Libagon. Municipality, Leyte,
Philippines : Sugod Sur (-1913)
Libau. Hamlet, Manitoba, Cana-
da : Kreiger (-1906)
Libau see Liepaja
Libava see Liepaja
Liberec. City, northwestern
Czechoslovakia : Reichenberg

(-1918, 1939-45), Germany
Libertad (1). Barrio, Cagayan,
Philippines : Colonia (-1957)
Libertad (2). Barrio, Leyte,
Philippines : Malirong (-1957)
Libertador see Dajabón
Liberty Island. Upper New
York Bay, New York City,
USA : Bedloe's Island (-1956)
Libya see Socialist People's
Libyan Arab Jamahirrya
Libyan Arab Republic see So-
cialist People's Libyan Arab
Jamahirrya
Libyo. Municipality, Surigao
del Norte, Philippines :
Albor (-1967)
Licania. City, northeastern
Brazil, South America :
Santana (-1944)
Licheng [Li-cheng]. Town,
eastern China : Wangshejen-
chwang (-1935)
Lichinga. Town, northwestern
Mozambique, southeastern
Africa : Vila Cabral (-1976)
Lichow see Lihsien (1)
Lichtenstein. City, southeastern
East Germany : Lichtenstein-
Callnberg (-?)
Lichtenstein-Callnberg see
Lichtenstein
Li-ch'uan = Lichwan
Lichwan [Li-ch'uan]. Town,
southeastern China : Sincheng
(-1914)
Lidice. Village, Illinois, USA
: Stern Park Gardens (-1942)
Lidzbark Warmiński. Town,
northeastern Poland : Heilsberg
(-1945), Germany
Liebau see Lubawka
Liebenau bei Schweibus see
Lubrza
Liebenfelde see Zalesye
Liebenthal see Lubomierz
Liegnitz see Legnica
Lienshan. Village, southwestern
China : Chanta (-1935)
Lienshui. Town, eastern China
: Antung (-1914)
Lienyün. Town, eastern China
: Laoyao (-1935)

Liepaja [Lepaya]. Town, Latvian
SSR : Libava (-1917), Russia;
Libau (1917-18, 1941-45),
Germany
Lifan see Lihsien (2)
Lifudzin see Rudny
Ligourión see Lygoúrion
Lihsien (1). Town, south-central
China : Lichow (-1913)
Lihsien (2). Town, central
China : Lifan (-1945)
Lihsien see Hwaning [Hua-ning]
Li-hua = Lihwa
Lihwa [Li-hua]. Town, southern
China : Litang (-1913)
Lihwang see Kinchai [Chin-
chai]
Likasi. City, southeastern Zaïre,
central Africa : Jadotville
(-1966)
Likhachyovo see Pervomaysky
(4)
Likhaya see Likhovskoy
Likhinichi see Rakushevo
Likhovskoy. Urban settlement,
Rostov Oblast, RSFSR : Likhaya
(-1930)
Likhvin see Chekalin
Lillo see Puebla de Lillo
Lillooet Lake see Alouette Lake
Liman. Urban settlement, Astra-
khan Oblast, RSFSR : Dolban
(-1944)
Liman see Krasny Liman
Limanowa. Town, southern Po-
land : Ilmenau (1939-45), Ger-
many
Limbuhan see Pio V. Corpuz
Limchow see Hoppo
Limeira see Joaçaba
Limestone Hill see Lackawanna
Limkong. Town, southeastern
China : Shekshing (-1914)
Limoeiro see (1) Limoeiro de
Anadia; (2) Limoeiro do Norte
Limoeiro de Anadia. City, north-
eastern Brazil, South America
: Limoeiro (-1944)
Limoeiro do Norte. City, north-
eastern Brazil, South America
: Limoeiro (-1944)
Linchow see Linhsien
Linchüan [Lin-ch'uan]. Town,

eastern China : Shenkiu (-1934)
Lincolnwood. Village, Illinois,
USA : Tessville (-1935)
Linden. Town, northeastern
Guyana, South America :
Mackenzie (-1973)
Linden see Gladstone
Linfen. Town, northeastern
China : Pingyang (-1912)
Lingchow see Lingwu
Linghsien see Kwangwu [K'-
uang-wu]
Lingling. Town, south-central
China : Yungchow (-1913)
Lingnan see Tsingping
Lingshan see Sansui
Lingwu. Town, northwestern
China : Lingchow (-1913)
Lingyüan. Town, northeastern
China : Kienchang (-1914),
Takow (1914)
Lingyün. Town, southern
China : Szecheng (-1913)
Linhai. City, eastern China :
Taichow (-1912)
Lin-hsia = Linsia
Linhsien. Town, southeastern
China : Linchow (-1912)
Lini. City, northeastern
China : Ichow [I-chou] (-1911)
Linju. Town, east-central
China : Juchow (-1913)
Linkiang see (1) Tsingkiang
[Chin-chiang]; (2) Tungkiang
[T'ung-chiang]
Linli. Town, south-central
China : Anfu (-1914)
Linlithgow see West Lothian
Linnam. Town, southeastern
China : Chaikang (-1942)
Linsen. Town, southeastern
China : Hungshankiao (-c. 1945)
Linsia [Lin-hsia]. Town, north-
central China : Hochow
(-1913), Taoho (1913-28)
Lintan [Lin-t'an]. Town, north-
central China : Taochow
(-1913)
Lintao [Lin-t'ao]. Town, north-
central China : Titao (-1928)
Lintien. Town, northeastern
China : Tungtsichen (-1917)
Linton see Delray Beach

Lin-tse = Lintseh
Lintseh [Lin-tse]. Town, north-
central China : Fuyi (-1913)
Linugos see Magsaysay
Linyovo. Urban settlement,
Volgograd Oblast, RSFSR :
Gussenbakh (-1941), Medvedit-
skoye (1941-c. 1960)
Linyü. Town, northeastern
China : Haiyang (-1949)
Linyü see Shanhaikwan
Lipiany. Town, northwestern
Poland : Lippehne (-1945),
Germany
Liping see Kinping [Chin-p'ing]
(2)
Lipno. Town, central Poland :
Leipe (1939-45), Germany
Lipová. Village, northwestern
Czechoslovakia : Hanšpach
(-1947)
Lippehne see Lipiany
Lipras see Villa Ramos
Lishih. Town, northeastern
China : Yungning (-1912)
Lishui. Town, eastern China :
Chuchow (-1913)
Liski see Georgiu-Dezh
Lispeszentadorján. Town, western
Hungary : Szentadorján (*1937-
42)
Lissa see Leszno
Lister og Mandals see Vest-
Agder
Litang see Lihwa [Li-hua]
Litsingtien see Nanchao
Little Saskatchewan see Min-
nedosa
Littoria see Latina (1), (2)
Litvino see Sosnovoborsk
Livermore Falls. Town, Maine,
USA : East Livermore (-1930)
Livingstone see Mosi-oa-Toenja
(1)
Livramento see (1) José de
Freitas; (2) Livramento do
Brumado; (3) Nossa Senhora
do Livramento; (4) Oliveira
Fortes
Livramento do Brumado. City,
eastern Brazil, South America
: Livramento (-1944)
Lizuny see Mayskoye (1)

Ljubljana. City, northwestern
Yugoslavia : Laibach (-1918),
Germany

Ljutomer. Village, northwestern
Yugoslavia : Luttenberg
(-1918), Germany

Llano de Bureba. Village,
northern Spain : Solas de
Bureba (-c. 1950)

Llanta Apacheta see Millares

Loan see Kwangjao [Kuang-
jao]

Loben see Lubliniec

Lobethal. Town, South Australia, Australia : Tweedvale (c. 1914-35)

Łobez. Town, northwestern
Poland : Labes (-1945), Germany

Lobovsky No 33/37 Rudnik see
Shakhta No 33/37

Lobva. Urban settlement,
Sverdlovsk Oblast, RSFSR :
Lobvinsky Zavod (-1928)

Lobvinsky Zavod see Lobva

Lochmoor see Grosse Pointe
Woods

Lockbourne Air Force Base
see Rickenbacker Air Force
Base

Locsin see Daraga

Lodi see Draâ Esmar

Loho see Lotien

Loire-Atlantique. Department,
western France : Loire-
Inférieure (-1957)

Loire-Inférieure see Loire-
Atlantique

Lokot, Cape. Komsomolets
Island, Severnaya Zemlya,
Krasnoyarsk Kray, RSFSR :
Rozy Lyuksemburg, Cape
(*c. 1930-c. 1960)

Lomahasha. Town, northeastern
Swaziland, southern Africa :
Nomahasha (-1976)

Lomonosov. Town, Leningrad
Oblast, RSFSR : Oranienbaum
(-1948)

Longonot. Satellite station, south-
central Kenya, eastern Africa :
Mount Margaret (-1971)

Longos see Kalayaan

Loning. Town, east-central
China : Yungning (-1914)

Loos see Loos-en-Gohelle

Loos-en-Gohelle. Town, northern
France : Loos (-1937)

Lopasnya see Chekhov (1)

Lopatino see Volzhsk

López de Filippis see Mariscal
Estigarribia

Lorraine see Baker

Loshan. Town, central China :
Kiating (-1913)

Losino-Ostrovskaya see Babushkin (1)

Losino-Petrovsky. Town, Moscow
Oblast, RSFSR : Petrovskaya
Sloboda (-1928)

Loslau see Wodzisław Śląski

Lotien. Town, southern China :
Loho (-1930)

Lotu. Town, northwestern
China : Ningpo (-1928)

Lötzen see Gizycko

Lough Gowna. Town, County
Cavan, Ireland : Scrabby
(-1950)

Louis Gentil see Youssoufia

Lourenço Marques see Maputo

Loutrópolis Methánon. Town,
northern Greece : Methánon
(-1960s)

Löwen see Lewin Brzeski

Löwenberg see Lwówek Śląski

Löwenhagen see Komsomolsk (2)

Löwenstadt see Brzeziny

Löwentin see Niegocin

Loxton. Town, South Australia,
Australia : Loxton's Hut (-1907)

Loxton's Hut see Loxton

Loya see Loyeh

Loyang. City, east-central
China : Honan (-1913)

Loyeh. Town, southern China :
Loya (-1936)

Lozno-Aleksandrovka. Urban
settlement, Voroshilovgrad
Oblast, Ukrainian SSR : Aleksandrovka (-mid-1930s)

Luan see Changchih [Ch'ang-
chih]

Luau. Town, west-central
Angola, southwestern Africa :
Bailundo (-1930s), Vila Teixeira

da Silva (1930s-c. 1976)
Luba. Municipality, Ilocos Sur,
Philippines : Barrit-Luluno
(-1914)
Lubań. Town, southwestern Po-
land : Lauban (-1945), Ger-
many
Lubawka. Town, southwestern
Poland : Liebau (-1945),
Germany
Lüben see Lubin
Lubiąz. Village, southwestern
Poland : Leubus (-1945),
Germany
Lubin. Town, southwestern
Poland : Lüben (-1945),
Germany
Lubliniec. Town, southern
Poland : Loben (1939-45),
Germany
Lubomierz. Town, southwestern
Poland : Liebenthal (-1945),
Germany
Lubrza. Town, western Po-
land : Liebenau bei
Schwiebus (-1945), Germany
Lubsko. Town, western Po-
land : Sommerfeld (-1945),
Germany
Lubumbashi. City, southeastern
Zaïre, central Africa :
Élisabethville (*1910-1966)
Lucena see New Lucena
Lucerne see Lake Worth
Luchang see Lushui
Lucheng see Tiensi [T'ien-hsi]
Lu-chou. City, south-central
China : Lu-ch'uan (-1912)
Lüchow see (1) Hofei; (2)
Luhsien
Lu-ch'uan see Lu-chou
Lucio Laurel. Barrio, Oriental
Mindoro, Philippines :
Calamunding (-1969)
Luditz see Žlutice
Ludweiler see Ludweiler-
Warndt
Ludweiler-Warndt. Town,
western West Germany :
Ludweiler (-1936)
Ludwigsort see Ladushkin
Lugansk see Voroshilovgrad
Lugansk Oblast see Voroshilov-

grad Oblast
Lugovaya (1). Village, Brest
Oblast, Belorussian SSR :
Durnevichi (-1964)
Lugovaya (2). Village, Vitebsk
Oblast, Belorussian SSR :
Malaya Dyatel (-1964)
Lugovaya (3). Village, Minsk
Oblast, Belorussian SSR :
Svinka (-1964)
Lugovaya Proleyka see Primorsk
(3)
Luho. Town, southern China :
Changku (-1914)
Lu-hsi = Lusi
Luhsien. Town, central China :
Luchow (-1913)
Luichow see Hoihong
Luís Correia. City, northeastern
Brazil, South America : Amar-
ração (-1939)
Luki see Tzeki [Tz'u-ch'i]
Lukov. Urban settlement, Volyn
Oblast, Ukrainian SSR :
Matseyevo (-1946)
Lukowkiao see Wanping
Luling see Kian [Chi-an]
Luluabourg see Kananga
Lulung. Town, northeastern
China : Yungping (-1913)
Lumangbayan. Barrio, Batangas,
Philippines : Sambat (-1947)
Lumba Bayabao. Municipality,
Lanao, Philippines : Maguing
(-1956)
Luna (1). Municipality, Isabela,
Philippines : Antatet (-1951)
Luna (2). Municipality, La
Union, Philippines : Namacpa-
can (-1906)
Lunacharskoye see Ordzhonikidze
(4)
Lundenburg see Břeclav
Lungan see Pingwu [P'ing-wu]
Lung-ch'i = Lungki
Lung-ching = Lungtsin
Lungchow see (1) Lunghsien;
(2) Lungtsin [Lung-ching]
Lungchüan see Suichwan [Sui-
ch'uan]
Lungchüanchen see Ian
Lung-hsi = Lungsi
Lunghsien. Town, central China

: Lungchow (-1913)
Lunghwasze see Muchwan
[Mu-ch'uan]
Lungki [Lung-ch'i]. Town,
southeastern China : Chang-
chow (-1913)
Lungkiang see Tsitsihar
Lung-kuan = Lungkwan
Lungkwan [Lung-kuan]. Town,
northeastern China : Lungmen
(-1914)
Lungmen see Lungkwan
[Lung-kuan]
Lungping see Lungyao
Lungsheng. Town, northern
China : Chotzeshan (-1949)
Lungshih see Ningkang
Lungsi [Lung-hsi]. Town,
north-central China :
Kungchang (-1913)
Lungsinhü see Yungyün
Lungtsin [Lung-ching]. Town,
southern China : Lungchow
(-1937)
Lungwusze see Tungjen
[T'ung-jen]
Lungyang see Hanshow
[Han-shou]
Lungyao. Town, northeastern
China : Lungping (-1949)
Luning. Village, southern
China : Luningying (-1946)
Luningying see Luning
Lunino. Village, Kaliningrad
Oblast, RSFSR : Lengwethen
(-1938), Germany; Hohensalz-
burg (1938-45), Germany
Lunyevka. Urban settlement,
Perm Oblast, RSFSR :
Lunyevskiye Kopi (-c. 1928)
Lunyevskiye Kopi see Lunyevka
Luperón. Town, northern Domin-
ican Republic, West Indies :
Blanco (-1927)
Lupin see Man-chou-li
Lusambo see Kasai
Lusanga. Town, southwestern
Zaïre, central Africa :
Leverville (-1972)
Lusavan see Charentsavan
Lushan. Town, southern China
: Tsingping (-1914)
Lushui. Village, southwestern

China : Luchang (-1935)
Lüshun = Port Arthur
Lusi [Lu-hsi] (1). Town, south-
western China : Kwangsi (-1929)
Lusi [Lu-hsi] (2). Village,
southwestern China : Mengka
(-1935)
Lutgardita see General Peraza
Luting. Town, southern China :
Lutingkiao (-1913)
Lutingkiao see Luting
Luttenberg see Ljutomer
Lutynia. Village, southwestern
Poland : Leuthen (-1945),
Germany
Luzhki see Chervonoye (2)
Luziânia. City, central Brazil,
South America : Santa Luzia
(-1945)
Luzilândia. City, northeastern
Brazil, South America : Pôrto
Alegre (-1944)
Luzurriaga see Valencia
Lvov. Capital of Lvov Oblast,
Ukrainian SSR : Lemberg
(-1919), Germany; Lwów
(1919-44), Poland
Lwów see Lvov
Lwówek. Town, western Poland :
Neustadt (-1945), Germany
Lwówek Śląski. Town, southwest-
ern Poland : Löwenberg (-1945),
Germany
Lyakhovtsy see Belogorye
Lyall see Garson
Lyck see Ełk
Lydía. Village, northern Greece
: Hydrómyloi (-1960s)
Lygoúrion. Village, southern
Greece : Ligourión (-1960s)
Lykoudésion see Khrysikós
Lykóvryse see Lykóvrysis
Lykóvrysis. Village, central
Greece : Lykóvryse (-1960s)
Lyndhurst. Township, New
Jersey, USA : Union (-1917)
Lyttelton see Verwoerdburg
Lyubinsky. Urban settlement,
Omsk Oblast, RSFSR : Novo-
lyubino (-1947)
Lyudvipol see Sosnovoye
Lyuksemburg see (1) Bolnisi;
(2) Rozovka

Lyuksemburgi see Bolnisi
Lyustdorf see Chernomorka

Macario Adriatico. Barrio,
 Oriental Mindoro, Philip-
 pines : Tubig (-1969)
Macarthur. City, Leyte,
 Philippines : Ormoc (-1950)
Macatuba. City, southeastern
 Brazil, South America :
 Bocaiúva (-1944)
Macaubal. Town, southeastern
 Brazil, South America :
 Macaúbas (-1944)
Macaúbas see Macaubal
Ma-chiang = Makiang
Macias. Barrio, Zamboanga,
 Philippines : Dinokot (-1968)
Macias Nguema Bijogo. Island
 territory, Equatorial Guinea,
 western Africa : Fernando
 Po (-1973)
Mackayville see Laflèche
Mackeim see Maków (Mazo-
 wiecki)
Mackenzie see Linden
MacLeod see Fort MacLeod
MacMahon see Aïn Touta
MacPherson see Kapuskasing
Madagascar see Democratic
 Republic of Madagascar
Madhya Pradesh. State, cen-
 tral India : Central Pro-
 vinces (-1947)
Madinat-al-Thawra see
 Tabaqah
Madinat ash-Sha'b. Adminis-
 trative capital of Yemen
 [People's Democratic Re-
 public of Yemen] : Al-
 Ittihad (*1959-67)
Madniskhevi see Uchkulan
Madona. Town, Latvian SSR :
 Birzhi (-1926)
Madras see Tamil Nadu
Macaloge. Town, northwestern
 Mozambique, southeastern
 Africa : Miranda (-1976)
Macapá see Peri Mirim
Madre de Deus see Brejo

da Madre de Deus
Mafuteni see Mafutseni
Mafutseni. Town, central
 Swaziland, southern Africa :
 Mafuteni (-1976)
Magallanes see Punta Arenas
Magallon see Moises Padilla
Maghnia. Town, northwestern
 Algeria, northern Africa :
 Marnia (-c. 1962)
Magoúla. Village, eastern
 Greece : Phanárion Magoúla
 (-1960s)
Magsaysay. Municipality,
 Misamis Oriental, Philippines
 : Linugos (-1957)
Magu. District, northern Tan-
 zania, eastern Africa :
 Mwanza (-1974)
Maguari see Cruz do Espírito
 Santo
Maguing see Lumba Bayabao
Maguntan-hama see Pugachyovo
Maha see Makiang [Ma-chiang]
Mahabad. Town, northwestern
 Iran : Saujbulagh (-1930s)
Mahato. Municipality, Capiz,
 Philippines : Taft (-1917)
Mährisch-Budwitz see Morav-
 ská Budějovice
Mährisch-Kromau see Moravský
 Krumlov
Mährisch-Schönberg see Šum-
 perk
Mährisch-Trubau see Moravská
 Třebová
Mährisch-Weisskirchen see
 Hranice
Mai-Ndombe, Lake. Lake,
 western Zaïre, central Africa
 : Léopold II, Lake (-1972)
Mainfranken see Unterfranken
Mairiporã. City, southeastern
 Brazil, South America :
 Juqueri (-1948)
Maison-Blanche see Dar el
 Beïda
Maison-Carrée see El-Harrach
Major Isidoro. City, northeastern
 Brazil, South America :
 Sertãozinho (-1944)
Makanza. Town, northwestern
 Zaïre, central Africa :

Nouvelle Anvers (-1972)
Makarov. Town, Sakhalin Oblast, RSFSR : Shiritoru (1905-46), Japan (-1945)
Makasar see Ujung Pandang
Makati. Municipality, Rizal, Philippines : San Pedro Macati (-1914)
Makeyevka. Town, Donetsk Oblast, Ukrainian SSR : Dmitriyevsky (-1920), Dmitriyevsk (1920-31)
Makhachkala. Capital of Dagestan Autonomous SSR, RSFSR : Petrovsk-Port (-1922)
Makhambet. Village, Guryev Oblast, Kazakh SSR : Yamankhalinka (-c. 1960)
Makharadze. Town, Georgian SSR : Ozurgety (-1934)
Makhnovka see Komsomolskoye (4)
Makiang [Ma-chiang]. Town, southern China : Maha (-1930)
Makinka see Makinsk
Makinsk. Town, Tselinograd Oblast, Kazakh SSR : Makinka (*1928-44)
Maków (Mazowiecki). Town, east-central Poland : Mackeim (1939-45), Germany
Ma-kuan = Makwan
Makwan [Ma-kuan]. Town, southwestern China : Anping (-1914)
Malabo. Capital of Equatorial Guinea, western Africa : Santa Isabel (-1973)
Malabon see General Trias
Malabrigo see Puerto Chicama
Malafeyevichi see Vishnya (1)
Malagasy Republic see Democratic Republic of Madagascar
Malathriá see Díon
Malawi. Republic, southeastern Africa : British Central Africa (Protectorate) (1891-1907), Nyasaland (1907-64)
Malawi, Lake. Malawi/Mozam-

bique/Tanzania, southeastern Africa : Nyasa, Lake (-1965)
Malaya Dyatel see Lugovaya (2)
Malayan Federation (1963†).
Southeastern Asia [now incorporated in Malaysia] : Malayan Union (*1946-48)
Malayan Union see Malayan Federation
Malbork. Town, northern Poland : Marienburg (-1945), Germany
Malé. City, southern Brazil, South America : São Pedro de Mallet (-1930s)
Malebo Pool [name used in Zaïre]. River Congo, Congo/Zaïre, central Africa : Stanley Pool (-1972)
Malema see Entre-Rios
Mali. Republic, northwestern Africa : French Sudan (-1902, 1920-58), Senegambia and Niger Territories (1902-04), Upper Senegal and Niger (1904-20), Sudanese Republic (1958-60)
Malinovoye Ozero. Urban settlement, Altay Kray, RSFSR : Mikhaylovsky (-c. 1960)
Malirong see Libertad (2)
Mallwen see Mayskoye (2)
Mallwischken see Mayskoye (2)
Malokurilskoye. Village, Kuril Islands, Sakhalin Oblast, RSFSR : Shakotan (1905-45), Japan
Malomalsk see Glubokaya
Maĺujowice. Village, southwestern Poland : Mollwitz (-1945), Germany
Maluko see Manolo Fortich
Malusak see Narra (2)
Maly Taymyr. Island, Laptev Sea, Krasnoyarsk Kray, RSFSR : Tsarevicha Alekseya (*1913-c. 1918)
Mambiliama Falls. Town, northwestern Zambia, south-central Africa : Johnston Falls (-1976)
Mamonovo. Town, Kaliningrad Oblast, RSFSR : Heiligenbeil (-1947), Germany (-1945)

Manawan see Rizal (1)
Man-chou-li. City, northern
China : Lupin (1913-49)
Mandala, Puncak. Mountain,
Irian Jaya, Indonesia :
Juliana Top (-1963)
Mandigos see Manica (1)
Mandrenska see Sredecka
Mangin see El Braya
Mangli see Kiangcheng
[Chiang-ch'eng]
Mangniuyingtze see Tsingping
Mangoche. Town, southern
Malawi, southeastern
Africa : Fort Johnston
(-c. 1966)
Manguaba see Pilar
Mangush see Pershotravnevoye
(1)
Manica (1). City, west-central
Mozambique, southeastern
Africa : Mandigos (-1916),
Vila Pery (1916-76)
Manica (2). Province, south-
western Mozambique, south-
eastern Africa : Vila Pery
(-1976)
Manissobal. City, eastern Bra-
zil, South America : Bel-
monte (-1944)
Mankaiana see Mankayane
Mankayane. Town, western
Swaziland, southern Africa
: Mankaiana (-1976)
Manning. Town, southeastern
China : Wanchow (-1912)
Manolo Fortich. Municipality,
Bukidnon, Philippines :
Maluko (-1957)
Mansa. Town, northern Zam-
bia, south-central Africa :
Fort Rosebery (-1967)
Manta. City, western Ecuador,
northwestern South Amer-
ica : San Pablo de Manta
(-1965)
Manuel Urbano. Town, western
Brazil, South America :
Castelo (-1944)
Manyas Gölü see Kuş Gölü
Manzini. Town, central Swa-
ziland, southeastern Africa
: Bremersdorp (-1960)

Manzovka see Sibirtsevo
Mao. City, northwestern Domini-
can Republic, West Indies :
Valverde (-1959)
Maohsien = Mowhsien
Maoka see Kholmsk
Maomu see Tingsin
Maputo. Capital of Mozambique,
southeastern Africa : Lourenço
Marques (-1976)
Maraak [Meraak, Merok] see
Geiranger
Maraisburg see Hofmeyr
Maranhão see São Luís
Marathonisi see Gýtheion
Marawi. City, Mindanao, Philip-
pines : Dansalan (-?)
Marayskoye see Mostovskoye
Marburg see Maribor
Marchand see Rommani
Marechal Deodoro. City, north-
eastern Brazil, South America
: Alagoas (-1939)
Marechal Floriano see Piranhas
Marele-Voevod-Mihai see
Februarie 16, 1933
Marengo see Hadjout
Marganets. Town, Dnepropetrovsk
Oblast, Ukrainian SSR :
Gorodishche (-c. 1926), Komin-
tern (c. 1926-40)
Marganets see Dzhezdy
Marggrabowa see Olecko
Margilan. Town, Fergana Oblast,
Uzbek SSR : Stary Margilan
(1876-1907)
Mari. Town, northeastern Bra-
zil, South America : Araçá
(-1944)
Mariánské Lázne. Town, western
Czechoslovakia : Marienbad
(-1918, 1939-45), Germany
Maria Pereira see Mombaça
Maria Rast see Ruše
Maria Theresiopel see Subotica
Maribor. City, northwestern
Yugoslavia : Marburg (-1918),
Germany
Maricourt. Town, Quebec,
Canada : Wakeham Bay (-1967)
Marie Byrd Land see Byrd
Land
Marienbad see Mariánské Lázne

Marienburg see Malbork
Marienhof see Nikitovka
Mariental see Sovetskoye (4)
Marienwerder see Kwidzyń
Marihatag. Municipality, Suri-
 gao, Philippines : Oteiza
 (-1955)
Mariinskoye see Maryevka
Mariinsk Water System see
 Volga-Baltic Waterway
Marino see Leninsky (3)
Marino Alejandro Selkirk see
 Robinson Crusoe
Mariscal Estigarribia. Village,
 northern Paraguay, South
 America : López de Filippis
 (-1945)
Mariupol see Zhdanov
Mariyampole see Kapsukas
Markhamat. Town, Andizhan
 Oblast, Uzbek SSR :
 Russkoye Selo (-1974)
Markhlevsk see Dovbysh
Märkisch Buchholz. Town,
 northern East Germany :
 Wendisch Buchholz (-1937)
Märkisch Friedland see
 Mirosławiec
Markovo. Urban settlement,
 Ivanovo Oblast, RSFSR :
 Markovo-Sbornoye (-1940)
Markovo-Sbornoye see Markovo
Marks. Town, Saratov Oblast,
 RSFSR : Yekaterinenshtadt
 [Baronsk] (-1922), Markssh-
 tadt (1922-42)
Marksshtadt see Marks
Marneuli. Town, Georgian
 SSR : Borchalo (-1964)
Marnia see Maghnia
Marquês de Valença. City,
 southeastern Brazil, South
 America : Valença (-1943)
Marruás see Pôrto
Marshallville see Lewisporte
Marshfield see Coos Bay
Martynovka see Bolshaya
 Martynovka
Martynovskoye see Bolshaya
 Martynovka
Martyshki see Beryozy
Marvão see Castelo do Piauí
Mary. Capital of Mary Oblast,

 Turkmen SSR : Merv (-1937)
Maryborough see Port Laoise
Maryevka. Village, North
 Kazakhstan Oblast, Kazakh
 SSR : Mariinskoye (-1939)
Maryino see Pristen
Más Afuera see Alejandro
 Selkirk
Más a Tierra see Robinson
 Crusoe
Masi. Barrio, Cagayan, Philip-
 pines : Zimigui-Ziwanan (-1957)
Masimpur see Arunachal
Massa-Carrara. Province, cen-
 tral Italy : Apuania (*1938-45)
Massawa [Mitsiwa]†. Administra-
 tive division, Eritrea, north-
 eastern Ethiopia, northeastern
 Africa : Bassopiano Orientale
 (-1941)
Massingire see Morrumbala
Massow see Maszewo
Massy see Lenin-Dzhol
Mastanli see Momchilgrad
Masteksay see Leninskoye (5)
Masulipat(n)am. Town, southeast-
 ern India : Bandar (-1949)
Maszewo. Town, northwestern
 Poland : Massow (-1945),
 Germany
Mata Grande. City, northeastern
 Brazil, South America : Paulo
 Affonso (-1939)
Matangala see Augusto Cardosa
Mataripe. Town, eastern Brazil,
 South America : Socorro (-1944)
Mataúna see Palmeiras de Goiás
Mati see President Roxas
Matões see Parnarama
Matola see Salazar
Matrosovo. Village, Kaliningrad
 Oblast, RSFSR : Uggehnen
 (-1946), Germany (-1945)
Matseyevo see Lukov
Matsubara see Takahagi
Mauritius, Cape see Zhelaniya,
 Cape
Mavabo. Village, northwestern
 Mozambique, southeastern
 Africa : Valadim (-1976)
Maxambamba see Nova Iguaçu
Maxesibeni. Town, northern
 Transkei, southern Africa :

Mount Ayliff (-1976)
Mayachnaya. Village, Minsk
Oblast, Belorussian SSR :
Porosyatniki (-1964)
Mayakovsky. Urban settlement,
Georgian SSR : Bagdadi
(-1940)
Mayak-Salyn see Primorskoye
(1)
Mayli-Su see Kok-Tash
Maysan. Province, eastern
Iraq : Amara (-1971)
Maysk (1). Village, Minsk
Oblast, Belorussian SSR :
Panskoye (-1964)
Maysk (2). Village, Mogilyov
Oblast, Belorussian SSR :
Pupsa (-1964)
Mayskaya. Village, Gomel
Oblast, Belorussian SSR :
Lapti (-1964)
Mayskoye (1). Village, Vitebsk
Oblast, Belorussian SSR :
Lizuny (-1964)
Mayskoye (2). Village, Kalinin-
grad Oblast, RSFSR : Mall-
wischken (-1938), Germany;
Mallwen (1938-46), Germany
(-1945)
Mayskoye (3). Village, Gomel
Oblast, Belorussian SSR :
Shapilovo (-1964)
Mazagán see El Jadida
Mazeikiai. Town, Lithuanian
SSR : Muravyevo (-1920)
Mbala. Town, northern Zambia,
south-central Africa : Aber-
corn (-1967)
Mbandaka. Town, northeastern
Zaïre, central Africa :
Coquilhatville (-1966)
Mbanza-Ngungu. Town, western
Zaïre, central Africa :
Thysville (-1966), Songololo
(1966-72)
Mbini. River, Río Muni,
Equatorial Guinea, western
Africa : Río Benito (-1974)
Mbuji-Mayi. City, southern
Zaïre, central Africa :
Bakwanga (-1966)
McHattiesburg see Balfour
Mchinji. Town, west-central

Malawi, southeastern Africa :
Fort Manning (-c. 1966)
McKinley, Mount. Mountain,
Antarctica : Grace McKinley,
Mount (-1967)
Meathas Truim [Mostrim]. Town,
County Longford, Ireland :
Edgeworthstown (-?)
Mechanicsham see Gretna
Mechtal see Miechowice
Mecseknádasd. Town, southern
Hungary : Püspöknadasd
(-1950)
Meddouza. Cape, western Moroc-
co, northwestern Africa :
Cantin, Cap (-1970)
Mednogorsk. Town, Orenburg
Oblast, RSFSR : Medny
(*1938-39)
Medny see Mednogorsk
Medveditskoye see Linyovo
Medvezhye see Krasnogvardey-
skoye (3)
Medvode. Village, northwestern
Yugoslavia : Zwischenwässern
(-1918), Germany
Meftah. Village, northern Al-
geria, northern Africa : Rivet
(-c. 1962)
Mehlauken see Zalesye
Meihsien. Town, southeastern
China : Kaying (-1912)
Mekhomiya see Razlog
Melanie Damishana. Village,
northern Guyana, South Amer-
ica : Elizabeth Hall (-1975)
Meléa see Káto Meléa
Melekess see Dimitrovgrad (2)
Memel see Klaipeda
Mendeleyevsk. Town, Tatar
Autonomous SSR, RSFSR :
Bondyuzhsky Zavod (-c. 1940),
Bondyuzhsky (c. 1940-67)
Ménerville see Thenia
Menghai see Fohai
Mengka see Lusi [Lu-hsi] (2)
Mengkiang see Tsingyü
Mengshan. Town, southern
China : Yungan (-1914)
Mengwang see Ningkiang
[Ning-chiang]
Menthon see Menthon-Saint-
Bernard

Menthon-Saint-Bernard. Village, southeastern France : Menthon (-1943)

Menzeh-Ifrane. Town, north-central Morocco, northwestern Africa : Val d'Ifrane (-1971)

Menzel-Bourguiba. Town, northern Tunisia, northern Africa : Ferryville (-c. 1963)

Meraak see Geiranger

Merchand see Rommani

Meriti see São João de Meriti

Merok see Geiranger

Merouana. Village, northeastern Algeria, northern Africa : Corneille (-c. 1962)

Merritt. Town, British Columbia, Canada : The Forks (*1906-11)

Merv see Mary

Mése. Village, northeastern Greece : Pagoúria (-1960s)

Mesembria see Nesebar

Mesemvriya see Nesebar

Meseritz see Międzyreszcz

Meshkhede-Ser see Babolser

Mestia. Village, Georgian SSR : Seti (-c. 1955)

Mestre Caetano. Town, southeastern Brazil, South America : Cuiabá (-1944)

Metamórphosis. Village, southern Greece : Katavóthra (-1960s)

Methánon see Loutrópolis Methánon

Metlika. Village, northwestern Yugoslavia : Möttling (-1918), Germany

Meyer's Ferry see Surfer's Paradise

Meylieu-Montrond see Montrond-les-Bains

Mezhdurechensk (1). Town, Kemerovo Oblast, RSFSR : Olzheras (-1955)

Mezhdurechensk (2). Urban settlement, Kuybyshev Oblast, RSFSR : Perevoloki (-?)

Mezhdurechye see Shali

Mezhevaya Ukta see Sinegorsky

Mezőfalva. Town, west-central Hungary : Hercegfalva (-1951)

Mezőszilas. Town, west-central Hungary : Szilasbalhás (-1942)

Miami Shores see North Miami

Miami Springs. Town, Florida, USA : Country Club Estates (*1926-30)

Miastko. Town, northwestern Poland : Rummelsburg (-1945), Germany

Michelet see Aïn el Hammam

Miches. Town, east Dominican Republic, West Indies : El Jovero (-1936)

Michurin. Town, southeastern Bulgaria : Vasiliko (-1934), Tsarevo (1934-50)

Michurinsk. Town, Tambov Oblast, RSFSR : Kozlov (-1932)

Middle Congo see People's Republic of the Congo

Middle Volga Kray see Kuybyshev Oblast

Middle Volga Oblast see Kuybyshev Oblast

Mid-Western State. State, southern Nigeria, western Africa : Mid-West Region (*1963-67)

Mid-West Region see Mid-Western State

Miechowice. Town, southern Poland : Mechtal (-1945), Germany

Międzybórz. Town, southwestern Poland : Neumittelwalde (-1945), Germany

Międzylesie. Town, southwestern Poland : Mittelwalde (-1945), Germany

Międzyreszcz. Town, western Poland : Meseritz (-1945), Germany

Międzyzdroje. Town, northwestern Poland : Misdroy (-1945), Germany

Mielau see Mława

Mieroszów. Town, southwestern Poland : Friedland (-1945), Germany

Mies see Stříbro

Miguel Calmon. City, eastern

Brazil, South America :
Djalma Dutra (1939-44)
Mihidjan see Chittaranjan
Mikasa. Town, west-central
Hokkaido, Japan : Mikasay-
ama (-early 1940s)
Mikasayama see Mikasa
Mikhailovgrad. City, northwest-
ern Bulgaria : Ferdinand
(-1945)
Mikhailovo-Semyonovskoye see
Leninskoye (6)
Mikhalpol see Mikhaylovka
Mikha Tskhakaya. Town,
Georgian SSR : Senaki
(-1935)
Mikhaylo-Kotsyubinskoye. Urban
settlement, Chernigov Ob-
last, Ukrainian SSR :
Kozyol (-c. 1935)
Mikhaylovka. Village, Khmel-
nitsky Oblast, Ukrainian
SSR : Mikhalpol (-1946)
Mikhaylovka see Kimovsk
Mikhaylovsk. Town, Sverdlovsk
Oblast, RSFSR : Mikhay-
lovsky Zavod (-1942)
Mikhaylovskoye see Shpakov-
skoye
Mikhaylovsky see Malinovoye
Ozero
Mikhaylovsky Zavod see
Mikhaylovsk
Mikoyan see Yekhegnadzor
Mikoyana, imeni see Kara-
Balty
Mikoyanabad see Tartki
Mikoyanovka see Oktyabrsky
(6)
Mikoyan-Shakhar see
Karachayevsk
Mikulczyce. Town, southern
Poland : Mikultschütz
(-1935), Germany; Klaus-
berg (1935-45), Germany
Mikulov. Town, southern
Czechoslovakia : Nikols-
burg (-1918, 1939-45), Ger-
many
Mikultschütz see Mikulczyce
Mikuriya see Shin-mikuriya
Milenino see Priupsky
Milevsko. Town, southwestern

Czechoslovakia : Mühlhausen
(-1918, 1939-45), Germany
Milicz. Town, southwestern
Poland : Militsch (-1945),
Germany
Militsch see Milicz
Millares. Town, south-central
Bolivia, South America :
Llanta Apacheta (-1900s)
Millersburg see Pierron
Mimoso do Sul. City, southeast-
ern Brazil, South America :
João Pessoa (-1944)
Minami-nayoshi see Shebunino
Minami-oji see Yasaka
Min-ch'in = Mintsin
Minchow see Minhsien
Mindanao and Sulu. Department,
Philippines : Moro (-1913)
Mineiros see Mineiros do Tietê
Mineiros do Tietê. City, south-
eastern Brazil, South America
: Mineiros (-1944)
Ming-ch'i = Mingki
Mingki [Ming-ch'i]. Town,
southeastern China : Kweihwa
(-1933)
Mingshui. Town, northeastern
China : Hinglungchen (-1929)
Mingshui see Changkiu [Chang-
chiu]
Minho. Town, northwestern
China : Chwankow (-1933)
Minhow see Foochow [Fuchow,
Fu-chou]
Minhsien. Town, north-central
China : Minchow (-1913)
Minlo. Town, north-central
China : Hungshui (-1933)
Minnedosa. River, Manitoba,
Canada : Little Saskatchewan
(-1928)
Mintsin [Min-ch'in]. Town,
north-central China : Chenfan
(-1928)
Minyar. Town, Chelyabinsk
Oblast, RSFSR : Minyarsky
Zavod (-c. 1928)
Minyarsky Zavod see Minyar
Mirabeau see Draâ Ben Khedda
Miracatu. City, southeastern
Brazil, South America :
Prainha (-1944)

Miracema see Miracema do
Norte
Miracema do Norte. City,
north-central Brazil, South
America : Miracema (-1944),
Cherente (1944-48)
Mirada Hills see La Mirada
Miraflores see Rovira
Miranda see Macaloge
Mirandópolis. City, southeastern
Brazil, South America :
Comandante Arbues (-1944)
Mir-Bashir. Town, Azerbaijan
SSR : Terter (-1949)
Mirnaya (1). Village, Minsk
Oblast, Belorussian SSR :
Glod (-1964)
Mirnaya (2). Village, Mogilyov
Oblast, Belorussian SSR :
Glupiki (-1964)
Mirnaya (3). Village, Vitebsk
Oblast, Belorussian SSR :
Khudeni (-1964)
Mirnaya (4). Village, Grodno
Oblast, Belorussian SSR :
Trebushki (-1964)
Mirnoye (1). Village, Gomel
Oblast, Belorussian SSR :
Mogilnoye (-1964)
Mirnoye (2). Settlement,
Dnepropetrovsk Oblast,
Ukrainian SSR : Zhyoltyye
Vody (-c. 1960)
Mirny. Village, Magadan Ob-
last, RSFSR : Stakhanovets
(-c. 1960)
Míron. Village, southern
Greece : Moíras (-1960s)
Mirosławiec. Town, northwestern
Poland : Märkisch Friedland
(-1945), Germany
Mirsk. Town, southwestern
Poland : Friedeberg (-1945),
Germany
Mirzachul see Gulistan
Mirzoyan see Dzhambul
Misamis see Ozamis
Misdroy see Międzyzdroje
Misericordia see Itaporanga
Misery, Mount see Rangoon
Heights
Mishih see Ningtung
Mission City. Town, British

Columbia, Canada : Mission
Junction (-1922)
Mission Junction see Mission
City
Mitake see Tsuya
Mitava see Jelgava
Mitkino see Krasnooktyabrsky
(2)
Mitrowitz see Sremska Mitro-
vica
Mitsang [Mi-ts'ang]. Town,
northern China : Santaokiao
(-1942)
Mitsiwa = Massawa
(Mittel) Schreiberhau see
Szklarska Poręba
Mittelwalde see Międzylesie
Mizo Hills see Mizoram
Mizoram. Union territory,
northeastern India : Mizo Hills
(-1972)
Mladá Boleslav. City, northwest-
ern Czechoslovakia : Jungbunz-
lau (-1918, 1939-45), Germany
Mladá Vožice. Town, southwest-
ern Czechoslovakia : Jungwo-
schitz (-1918, 1939-45),
Germany
Mława. Town, northeastern
Poland : Mielau (1939-45),
Germany
Mobayembongo. Town, northern
Zaïre, central Africa :
Banzyville (-1972)
Mobutu Sese Seko, Lake. Zaïre/
Uganda, central Africa :
Albert, Lake (-1973)
Mocha see Chapayevka
Mo-chiang = Mokiang
Mochu see Schwangpo [Shuang-
po]
Modderfontein see Niekerkshoop
Modlin. Village, east-central
Poland : Novogeorgiyevsk
(1815-1919), Russia
Moerbeke see Kwilu-Ngongo
Mogador see Essaouira
Mogilnoye see Mirnoye (1)
Mohammadia. Town, northwestern
Algeria, northern Africa :
Perrégaux (-c. 1962)
Mohammédia. City, northwestern
Morocco, northwestern Africa :

Fédala (-?)

Mohammerah see Khorramshahr

Mohrin see Moryń

Moíras see Míron

Moi's Bridge. Village, western Kenya, eastern Africa : Hoey's Bridge (-1975)

Moises Padilla. Municipality, Negros Occidental, Philippines : Magallon (-1957)

Mokiang [Mo-chiang]. Town, southwestern China : Talang (-1916)

Mokvin see Pershotravnevoye (2)

Moldavian Autonomous SSR see Moldavian SSR

Moldavian SSR. USSR : Moldavian Autonomous SSR (*1924-40)

Mole Hill see Mountain

Molière see Bordj Bounaama

Molles see Carlos Reyles

Mollet see San Juan de Mollet

Mollwitz see Małujowice

Molodechno. Town, Minsk Oblast, Belorussian SSR : Molodeczno (1919-39), Poland

Molodeczno see Molodechno

Molotov see (1) Arktichesky; (2) Perm

Molotovabad see Uchkorgon

Molotova, imeni see Uchkupryuk

Molotova V. M. , imeni see Oktyabrsky (6)

Molotovo see (1) Oktyabrskoye (2); (2) Pristanskoye; (3) Uchkupryuk

Molotov Oblast see Perm Oblast

Molotov, Peak see Moskva, Peak

Molotovsk see (1) Kainda; (2) Nolinsk; (3) Severodvinsk

Molotovskoye see Krasnogvardeyskoye (3)

Molvitino see Susanino

Mombaça. City, northeastern Brazil, South America : Maria Pereira (-1944)

Momchilgrad. City, southern Bulgaria : Mastanli (-1934)

Mona. Locality, Manitoba, Canada : Mulvihill (-1930)

Monastir see Bitola

Monastyr see Sosnovets

Moncha-Guba see Monchegorsk

Monchegorsk. Town, Murmansk Oblast, RSFSR : Moncha-Guba (-1937)

Mönchengladbach. City, western West Germany : München-Gladbach (-1950)

Monda see Agnew

Mondino see Cheryomushki (1)

Moneron. Island, Sea of Japan, Sakhalin Oblast, RSFSR : Kaiba-tu (1905-45), Japan

Monfestino in Serra Mazzoni see Serramazzoni

Mongalla see Equatoria

Monoikon see Hagion Pneuma

Monroeville. Borough, Pennsylvania, USA : Patton (-1951)

Monsanto see Monte Santo de Minas

Monschau. Town, western West Germany : Montjoie (-1920s)

Montagnac see Remchi

Montañana see Puente de Montañana

Monte Alegre see Timbiras

Monte Azul. City, southeastern Brazil, South America : Tremedal (-1939)

Monte Azul see Monte Azul Paulista

Monte Azul do Turvo see Monte Azul Paulista

Monte Azul Paulista. City, southeastern Brazil, South America : Monte Azul (-1944), Monte Azul do Turvo (1944-48)

Montebello. City, California, USA : Newmark (-1916), Monterey Park (1916-20)

Montejo de Liceras see Montejo de Tiermes

Montejo de Tiermes. Village, north-central Spain : Montejo de Liceras (-c. 1950)

Monteleone di Calabria see Vibo Valentia

Montenegro. City, southern
Brazil, South America :
São João de Montenegro
(-1930s)
Montenegro see Camassari
Monte Nevoso see Sneznik
Monte Oscuro see La Unión
Monterey Park see Montebello
Monterrubio de Demanda. Vil-
lage, northern Spain :
Monterrubio de la Sierra
(-c. 1920)
Monterrubio de la Sierra see
Monterrubio de Demanda
Monte San Giuliano see Erice
Monte Santo de Minas. City,
southeastern Brazil, South
America : Monsanto (1944-
48)
Montes de Toledo. Mountain
range, south-central Spain :
Cordillera Oretana (-c. 1960)
Monte Trujillo see Duarte,
Pico
Montferri. Village, eastern
Spain : Puigtiñós (-c. 1920)
Montgolfier see Rahouia
Montgomery see Sahiwal
Montjoie see Monschau
Montrond-les-Bains. Village,
east-central France :
Meylieu-Montrond (-1937)
Moodyville see North Van-
couver
Mook see Vanstadensrus
Mórahalom. Town, southeastern
Hungary : Alsóközpont
(*1950)
Moravská Budějovice. Town,
southern Czechoslovakia :
Mährisch-Budwitz (-1918,
1939-45), Germany
Moravská Ostrava see Ostrava
Moravská Trebová. Town,
west-central Czechoslovakia
: Mährisch-Trubau (-1918,
1939-45), Germany
Moravský Beroun. Town, northern
Czechoslovakia : Bärn
(-1918, 1939-45), Germany
Moravský Krumlov. Town,
southern Czechoslovakia :
Mährisch-Kromau (-1918,

1939-45), Germany
Mordovian Autonomous Oblast
see Mordovian Autonomous
SSR
Mordovian Autonomous SSR
[Mordvinian Autonomous SSR].
RSFSR : Mordovian Okrug
(*1928-30), Mordovian Autono-
mous Oblast (1930-34)
Mordovian Okrug see Mordovian
Autonomous SSR
Mordovskaya Bokla see Sovet-
skoye (5)
Mordvinian Autonomous SSR =
Mordovian Autonomous SSR
More see More og Romsdal
More og Romsdal. County,
western Norway : Romsdal
(-1918), More (1918-35)
Moro see Mindanao and Sulu
Moron see Morong
Morón. City, east-central Ar-
gentina, South America :
Seis de Septiembre (1930-43)
Morong. Municipality, Bataan,
Philippines : Moron (-1955)
Morozov. Mountain, central
Bulgaria : Goljam Bratan
(-1967)
Morozovsk. Town, Rostov Oblast,
RSFSR : Morozovskaya (-1941)
Morozovskaya see Morozovsk
Morro Grande see Barão de
Cocais
Morrumbala. Town, central
Mozambique, southeastern
Africa : Massingire (-1945)
Moryń. Town, northwestern
Poland : Mohrin (-1945), Ger-
many
Moscow Canal. Linking rivers
Moskva and Volga, RSFSR :
Moscow-Volga Canal (*1932-47)
Moscow Oblast. RSFSR : Central
Industrial Oblast (*1929)
Moscow-Volga Canal see Moscow
Canal
Moses Lake. City, Washington,
USA : Neppel (*1910-38)
Mosi-oa-Toenja (1). Town,
southern Zambia, south-central
Africa : Livingstone (-c. 1970)
Mosi-oa-Toenja (2). Province,

southern Zambia, south-central Africa : Victoria Falls (-1970)

Moskovsk. Urban settlement, Chardzhou Oblast, Turkmen SSR : Buyun-Uzun (-c. 1960)

Moskovsky. Urban settlement, Kulyab Oblast, Tadzhik SSR : Chubek (-c. 1960)

Moskovsky see Shakhrikhan

Moskva, Peak. Mountain, northwestern Pamir range, Tadzhik SSR : Molotov, Peak (?-c. 1957), Moskva-Pekin, Peak (c. 1957-?)

Moskva-Pekin, Peak see Moskva, Peak

Mostovskoye. Village, Kurgan Oblast, RSFSR : Maray-skoye (-c. 1960)

Mostrim = Meathas Truim

Mosty Wielkie see Velikiye Mosty

Mosul see Ninawa

Motodomari see Vostochny

Möttling see Metlika

Mountain. Town, Virginia, USA : Mole Hill (-?)

Mount Ayliff see Maxesibeni

Mount Frere see Kwabhaca

Mount Margaret see Longonot

Mount Pearl. Suburb of St. John's, Newfoundland, Canada : Mount Pearl Park-Glendale (1955-58)

Mount Pearl Park-Glendale see Mount Pearl

Mount Shasta (City). Town, California, USA : Sisson (-1925)

Mou-p'ing = Mowping

Mowchow see Mowhsien [Maohsien]

Mowhsien [Maohsien]. Town, central China : Mowchow (-1913)

Mowning. Town, southeastern China : Kochow [Kaochow] (-1912)

Mowping [Mou-p'ing]. Town, eastern China : Ninghai (-1914)

Moyen-Congo see People's

Republic of the Congo

Mozambique. Republic, south-eastern Africa : Portuguese East Africa (-1975)

Mozhaysky. Urban settlement, Leningrad Oblast, RSFSR : Dudergof (-1944), Nagornoye (1944-?)

Mozhga. Town, Udmurt Autonomous SSR, RSFSR : Syuginsky (-c. 1920), Krasny (c. 1920-26)

Mozirje. Village, northwestern Yugoslavia : Prassberg (-1918), Germany

Mpásion see Drosopegé

Mrkonjič Grad. Village, west-central Yugoslavia : Varcar Vukuf (-1930s)

Mu-ch'uan = Muchwan

Muchwan [Mu-ch'uan]. Town, central China : Lunghwasze (-1930)

Muela see Villa Rivero

Muheza. District, northeastern Tanzania, eastern Africa : Tanga (-1974)

Mühlhausen see Milevsko

Muine Bheag. Town, County Carlow, Ireland : Bagenalstown (-?)

Mukden (1). City, northeastern China : Fengtien (1934-46)

Mukden (2). City, northeastern China : Shen-yang (1949-54)

Mukhtuya see Lensk

Mukiaying see Sichi [Hsi-chi]

Muli see Vysokogorny

Mulungu. Town, northeastern Brazil, South America : Camarazal (1944-48)

Mulvihill see Mona

Muminabad see Leningradsky

München-Gladbach see Monchengladbach

Mundelein. Suburb of Chicago, Illinois, USA : Area (*1909-25)

Mundo Novo see Urupés

Munster see Voortrekkerstrand

Münsterberg see Ziębice

Muping see Paohing [Pao-hsing]

Muqui. City, southeastern Brazil, South America : São João do Muqui (-1944)

Muranga. Town, south-central
  Kenya, eastern Africa :
  Fort Hall (-1975)
Murat Bay see Ceduna
Muravyevo see Mazeikiai
Muravyovsky see Korsakov
Murchison Falls see Kabarega
  Falls
Murchison Falls National Park
  see Kabarega National Park
Murgab. Village, Gorno-
  Badakhshan Autonomous
  Oblast, Tadzhik SSR :
  Pamirsky Post (-c. 1929)
Murmansk. Capital of Murmansk
  Oblast, RSFSR : Romanov-
  na-Murmane (-1917)
Murotozaki. Town, southern
  Shikoku, Japan : Tsuro
  (-1929)
Murphy's Station see Sunnyvale
Murtala Muhammed Airport.
  Southwestern Nigeria, west-
  ern Africa : Lagos Airport
  (-1977)
Musala. Mountain, southwestern
  Bulgaria : Stalin, Peak
  (1949-?)
Muscat and Oman see Oman
Mussolinia di Sardegna see
  Arborea
Mustafa Kemal Paşa. Town,
  northwestern Turkey :
  Kirmasti (-?)
Mustayevka see Mustayevo
Mustayevo. Village, Orenburg
  Oblast, RSFSR : Mustayevka
  (-c. 1940)
Mutum. City, southeastern Bra-
  zil, South America : São
  Manuel do Mutum (-1939)
Muyupampa see Vaca Guzmán
Muzhichi see Pervomayskoye
  (6)
Muzhichok see Ozyornaya (1)
Muztor see Toktogul
Mwanza see Magu
My Lai 4 see Tinh Shon
Mýlos see Smértos
Mymensingh. City, central
  Bangladesh : Nasirabad (-?)
Myrtiá. Village, central Crete,
  Greece : Várvaron (-1960s)

Mys Lazarev see Lazarev
Myślibórz. Town, northwestern
  Poland : Soldin (-1945), Ger-
  many
Mysłowice. Town, southern
  Poland : Myslowitz (-1922),
  Germany
Myslowitz see Mysłowice
Mysore see Karnataka
Mysovka. Village, Kaliningrad
  Oblast, RSFSR : Karkeln
  (-1945), Germany
Mysovsk see Babushkin (2)
Mzizima see Dar es Salaam

Naas see Nás na Ríogh
Naberezhnaya. Village, Brest
  Oblast, Belorussian SSR :
  Vonki (-1971)
Naberezhnyye Chelny. Town,
  Tatar Autonomous SSR, RSFSR
  : Chelny (-1930)
Nabresina see Aurisina
Naciria. Village, northern Al-
  geria, northern Africa : Haus-
  sonvillers (-c. 1962)
Nadezhdinsk see Serov
Nadezhdinsky Priisk see Aprelsk
Nadezhdinsky Zavod see Serov
Nadterechnaya. Village, Checheno-
  Ingush Autonomous SSR, RSFSR
  : Nizhny Naur (-1944)
Naga. Municipality, Ambos
  Camarines, Philippines :
  Nueva Caceres (-1914)
Nagaba see Jordan (1)
Nagahama see Ozyorsky
Naga Hills see Nagaland
Nagaland. State, northeastern
  India : Naga Hills (-1963)
Nagibovo. Village, Jewish
  Autonomous Oblast, Khabarovsk
  Kray, RSFSR : Stalinsk (?-1961)
Nagornoye see Mozhaysky
Nagpartian see Burgos (1)
Nagykapos see Velké Kapušany
Nagyszombat see Trnava
Nagyvárad see Oradea
Naibo see Dobroye
Naibuchi see Nayba

Naihoro see Gornozavodsk (1)

Nairo see Gastello

Nakel see Nakło

Nakhodka. Bay, Primorsky Kray, RSFSR : Amerika (-1974)

Nakhrachi see Kondinskoye

Nakło (nad Notecią). Town, north-central Poland : Nakel (1939-45), Germany

Nalasin see General Artemio Ricarte

Naldrug see Osmanabad

Namacpacan see Luna (2)

Namhoi. City, southeastern China : Fatshan (-1912)

Namibia [United Nations designated name]. Territory, southwestern Africa : German Southwest Africa (-1921), South West Africa (1921-68)

Namp'o. City, western North Korea : Chinnamp'o (-1947)

Namslau see Namysłów

Nam Tha see Houa Khong

Namysłów. Town, southwestern Poland : Namslau (-1945), Germany

Nanan see (1) Schwangpo [Shuang-po]; (2) Tayü

Nanchao. Town, east-central China : Litsingtien (-c. 1947)

Nancheng (1). Town, central China : Hanchung (-1913)

Nancheng [Nan-ch'eng] (2). Town, southeastern China : Kienchang (-1912)

Nan-chiao = Nankiao

Nanchow see Nanhsien

Nanchung [Nan-ch'ung]. Town, central China : Shunking (-1913)

Nanhsien. Town, south-central China : Nanchow (-1913)

Nankang see Singtze [Hsing-tzu]

Nankiao [Nan-chiao]. Town, southwestern China : Wufu (-1934)

Nankiao see Fengsien [Fenghsien]

Nanking. City, east-central China : Chiang-ning [Kiangning] (-1911)

Nanlung see Anlung

Nanning. City, southeastern China : Yung-ning (1913-45)

Nanping [Nan-p'ing]. City, southeastern China : Yenping [Yen-p'ing] (-1913)

Nantitien see Ichwan [I-ch'uan]

Napo see Tienyang [T'ien-yang]

Narbada see Narmada

Narimanabad. Urban settlement, Azerbaijan SSR : Sara-Ostrov (-c. 1960)

Narimanova, imeni see Bank

Narmada. River, central India : Narbada (-1966)

Narra (1). Barrio, Oriental Mindoro, Philippines : Batingan (-1969)

Narra (2). Barrio, Oriental Mindoro, Philippines : Malusak (-1969)

Nartkala. Town, Kabardino-Balkarian Autonomous SSR, RSFSR : Dokshukino (-1967)

Nartovskoye. Village, North Ossetian Autonomous SSR, RSFSR : Kantyshevo (-1944)

Naryan-Mar. Capital, Nenets Autonomous Okrug, Arkhangelsk Oblast, RSFSR : Beloshchelye (-1933), Dzerzhinskogo, imeni (1933-35)

Naryn. Village, Andizhan Oblast, Uzbek SSR : Khakulabad (-c. 1935)

Naryn Oblast. Kirgiz SSR : Tyan-Shan Oblast (*1939-62; reformed under present name 1970)

Nasirabad see Mymensingh

Nás na Ríogh. Capital of County Kildare, Ireland : Naas (-c. 1930)

Natividade see (1) Natividade da Serra; (2) Natividade do Carangola

Natividade da Serra. City, southeastern Brazil, South America : Natividade (-1944)

Natividade do Carangola. City, southeastern Brazil, South America : Natividade (-1944)

Naugard see Nowogard

Naumburg am Queis see Nowogrodziec

Navan. Town, County Meath, Ire-
land : An Uaimh (c. 1930-71)
Navangar see Jamnagar
Navarredonda de Gredos. Vil-
lage, east-central Spain :
Navarredonda de la Sierra
(-1969)
Navarredonda de la Sierra see
Navarredonda de Gredos
Navoi. Town, Bukhara Oblast,
Uzbek SSR : Kermine (-1958)
Navozy see Oreshnitsa
Nayarit. State, west-central
Mexico, North America :
Tepic (-1917)
Nayba. River, Sakhalin Oblast,
RSFSR : Naibuchi (1905-45),
Japan
Nayosi see Lesogorsk
Nayung. Town, southern China
: Tatuchang (-1932)
Nazaré see Nazaré da Mata
Nazaré da Mata. City, north-
eastern Brazil, South Amer-
ica : Nazaré (-1944)
Nazimovo see Putyatin
Nazran. Town, Checheno-Ingush
Autonomous SSR, RSFSR :
Georgiye-Osetinskoye (-1944),
Kosta-Khetagurovo (1944-67)
Nazyvayevsk. Town, Omsk
Oblast, RSFSR : Sibirsky
(*1910-c. 1935), Novonazy-
vayevka (c. 1935-56)
Ndjamena. Capital of Chad,
north-central Africa : Fort
Lamy (*1900-73)
Néa Ekklesoúla. Village,
southern Greece : Ekklesoúla
(-1960s)
Néai Vrysoúlai. Village, southern
Greece : Vrysoúlai (-1960s)
Néa Kóme see Pontolívadon
Néa Philadélpheia. Village,
northern Greece : Philadel-
phianá (-1960s)
Nedenes see Aust-Agder
Neftechala see Dvadtsati
Shesti Bakinskikh Komissa-
rov, imeni
Neftegorsk. Urban settlement,
Sakhalin Oblast, RSFSR :
Vostok (-1970)

Neftekamsk. Town, Bashkir
Autonomous SSR, RSFSR :
Kasevo (-1963)
Neidenburg see Nidzica
Neisse see Nysa
Nekrasovo. Village, Mogilyov
Oblast, Belorussian SSR :
Tsarevsk (-1964)
Nekrasovskoye. Urban settlement,
Yaroslavl Oblast, RSFSR :
Bolshiye Soli (-1938)
Neman. Town, Kaliningrad
Oblast, RSFSR : Ragnit
(-1947), Germany (-1945)
Německý Brod see Havlíčkův
Brod
Németbóly see Bóly
Nemours see Ghazaouet
Neokhórion see Kypséle (2)
Néon Kompegádion. Village,
southern Greece : Kompegádion
(-1960s)
Néon Kríkellon. Village, central
Greece : Káto Vardátai (-1960s)
Neppel see Moses Lake
Nero see Krn
Nesebar. City, eastern Bulgaria
: Mesemvriya [Mesembria]
(-1934)
Neshime. Town, southern
Kyushu, Japan : Koneshime
(-1943)
Nesísta Néas Helládos see
Rodaugé
Nesterov (1). Town, Kaliningrad
Oblast, RSFSR : Stallupönen
(-1938), Germany; Ebenrode
(1938-46), Germany (-1945)
Nesterov (2). Town, Lvov Oblast,
Ukrainian SSR : Zholkev
(-1941), Poland; Zholkva
(1941-51)
Nesvetevich see Proletarsk (2)
Netherlands East Indies see
Indonesia
Netherlands Indies see Indonesia
Neu Bentschen see Zbąszynek
Neuenberg (an der Elbe) see
Nymburk
Neuhaus see (1) Dobrna; (2)
Jindřichův Hradec
Neuhäusel see Nové Zámky
Neuhausen see Guryevsk

Neukirch see Timiryazevo
Neukuhren see Pionersky
Neu-Langenburg see Tukuyu
Neumarkt see (1) Nowy Targ;
(2) Środa Śląska
Neumarktl see Tržič
Neu-Mecklenburg see New
Ireland
Neumittelwalde see Międzybórz
Neumyvaki see Orekhovskaya
Neu-Pommern see New Britain
Neusalz (an der Oder) see
Nowa Sól
Neu-Sandec see Nowy Sącz
Neu Sandez see Nowy Sącz
Neusatz see Novi Sad
Neusohl see Banská Bystrica
Neustadt see (1) Lwówek;
(2) Prudnik; (3) Wejherowo
Neustadt an der Hardt see
Neustadt (an der Wein-
strasse)
Neustadt (an der Weinstrasse).
City, western West Germany
: Neustadt an der Hardt
(-1936, 1945-50)
Neustädtel see Nowe Mias-
teczko
Neustädtl see Novo Mesto
Neustettin see Szczecinek
Neutitschein see Nový Jičín
Neuwedell see Drawno
Nevbily see Zaborovtsy
Nevdubstroy see Kirovsk (3)
Nevelsk. Town, Sakhalin
Oblast, RSFSR : Honto
(1905-46), Japan (-1945)
Never. Urban settlement, Amur
Oblast, RSFSR : Larinsky
(-?)
Neves see Neves Paulista
Neves Paulista. City, south-
eastern Brazil, South
America : Neves (-1944),
Iboti (1944-48)
Neviges. Town, northwestern
West Germany : Hardenberg
(-1935)
Nevskoye. Village, Kaliningrad
Oblast, RSFSR : Pillupönen
(-1938), Germany; Schloss-
bach (1938-45), Germany
New Ayuquitan see Amlan

New Barbadoes see Hackensack
New Berlin see North Canton
Newbridge see Droichead Nua
New Brighton see Kaiaua
New Britain. Island, Bismarck
Archipelago, Papua New
Guinea : New Pomerania
[Neu-Pommern] (1884-1920),
Germany
(New) Brookland see West
Colombia
New Butler see Butler
Newcastle. Town, Natal, South
Africa : Viljoensdorp (1899-
1900)
New Guinea. Part of Papua
New Guinea : German New
Guinea (1884-1920), Germany
New Harbour see Keppel
Harbour
New Ireland. Island, Bismarck
Archipelago, Papua New
Guinea : Neu-Mecklenburg
(1884-1920), Germany
New Lucena. Municipality,
Iloilo, Philippines : Lucena
(-1955)
Newmark see Montebello
New Mecklenburg see New
Ireland
New Pomerania see New
Britain
New Smyrna see New Smyrna
Beach
New Smyrna Beach. City,
Florida, USA : New Smyrna
(-1937)
Newtown see Newtownshandrum
Newtownbarry see Bunclody
Newtownshandrum. Town, County
Cork, Ireland : Newtown (-1971)
Ney-Valter see Sverdlovo
Neyvo-Rudyanka. Urban settle-
ment, Sverdlovsk Oblast,
RSFSR : Neyvo-Rudyansky
Zavod (-1928)
Neyvo-Rudyansky Zavod see
Neyvo-Rudyanka
Nezametny see Aldan
Ngaliema, Mount [name used in
Zaïre]. Mountain, Zaïre/
Uganda, east-central Africa :
Stanley, Mount (-1972)

Ngwa. Town, southeastern
  China : Onliu (-1941)
Nhlangano. Town, southwestern
  Swaziland, southern Africa :
  Goedgegun (-c. 1970)
Niangsiang see Chungyang
Niassa. Province, northwestern
  Mozambique, southeastern
  Africa : Vila Cabral (*1945-
  46), Lago (1946-54)
Nicholas II Land see Severnaya
  Zemlya
Nico Pérez see José Batlle y
  Ordóñez
Nidaros see Trondheim
Nidzica. Town, northeastern
  Poland : Neidenburg (-1945),
  Germany
Niegocin. Lake, northeastern
  Poland : Löwentin (-1945),
  Germany
Niekerkshoop. Village, Cape of
  Good Hope, South Africa :
  Modderfontein (-1902)
Niemcza. Town, southwestern
  Poland : Nimptsch (-1945),
  Germany
Niemodlin. Town, southwestern
  Poland : Falkenberg (-1945),
  Germany
Niger (*1908). Province, west-
  central Nigeria, western
  Africa : Nupe (1918-26)
Niger Coast Protectorate†.
  Area, delta of Niger River,
  western Africa : Oil Rivers
  Protectorate (-1900)
Niislel Khureheh see Ulan
  Bator
Niitoi see Novoye (2)
Nikel. Urban settlement, Mur-
  mansk Oblast, RSFSR :
  Kolosjoki (*c. 1935-1944),
  Finland
Nikitinskiye Promysly see
  Kirovsky (1)
Nikitovka. Village, Kaliningrad
  Oblast, RSFSR : Marienhof
  (-1945), Germany
Nikolainkaupunki see Vaasa
Nikolaistad see Vaasa
Nikolayevsk. Town, Volgograd
  Oblast, RSFSR : Nikolayev-

sky (1936-67)
Nikolayevsk see Pugachyov
Nikolayevskoye see Krasnogvar-
  deyskoye (4)
Nikolayevsky see Nikolayevsk
Nikolsburg see Mikulov
Nikolsk. Town, Penza Oblast,
  RSFSR : Nikolskaya Pestravka
  (-1954)
Nikolskaya Pestravka see
  Nikolsk
Nikolskoye see (1) Sheksna;
  (2) Ussuriysk
Nikolsk-Ussuriysky see
  Ussuriysk
Nikolsky Khutor see Sursk
Nikópolis. Village, western
  Greece : Smyrtoúla (-1960s)
Niles Center see Skokie
Nimptsch see Niemcza
Ninawa. Province, northwestern
  Iraq : Mosul (-1971)
Ningcheng [Ning-ch'eng]. Town,
  northeastern China : Siaocheng-
  tze (-1947)
Ning-chiang = Ningkiang
Ningchow see (1) Hwaning
  [Hua-ning]; (2) Ninghsien
Ningerh. Town, southwestern
  China : Puerh (-1914)
Ninghai see Mowping [Mou-p'ing]
Ninghsien. Town, south-central
  China : Ningchow (-1913)
Ninghsien see (1) Hwaning
  [Hua-ning]; (2) Ningpo
Ningkang. Town, southeastern
  China : Lungshih (-1934)
Ningkiang [Ning-chiang]. Village,
  southwestern China : Mengwang
  (-1935)
Ningkwo see Süancheng [Hsüan-
  ch'eng]
Ninglang. Village, southwestern
  China : Langchu (-1936)
Ningnan. Town, southern China :
  Pisha (-1930)
Ningpo. City, eastern China :
  Ninghsien (1911-49)
Ningpo see Lotu
Ningpo = Lotu
Ningshuo see Ningso
Ningsia see Yinchwan [Yin-
  ch'uan]
Ningso [Ningshuo]. Town, north-

western China : Siaopapao
(-1942)

Ningting. Town, north-central
China : Taitsesze (-1919)

Ningtsing see Chenhwa [Chen-
hua]

Ningtung. Village, southern
China : Mishih (-1938)

Ningyüan see (1) Hingcheng
[Hsing-ch'eng]; (2) Sichang
[Hsi-chang]; (3) Wushan

Ninomiya. Town, central
Honshu, Japan : Azuma
(-1935)

Niquelândia. City, east-central
Brazil, South America :
São José do Tocantins
(-1944)

Nishi-ichiki see Ichiki

Nishi-shakutan see Boshnyakovo

Nísia Floresta. City, eastern
Brazil, South America :
Papari (-1948)

Nivenskoye. Village, Kaliningrad Oblast, RSFSR : Wittenberg (-1946), Germany
(-1945)

Nizhegorod Kray see Gorky
Oblast

Nizhegorod Oblast see Gorky
Oblast

Nizhnegniloye see Sosnovka

Nizhnegorsky. Urban settlement,
Crimean Oblast, Ukrainian
SSR : Seitler (-1944)

Nizhne-Kolosovskoye see
Kolosovka (1)

Nizhnesaldinsky Zavod see
Nizhnyaya Salda

Nizhne-Saraninsky see Sarana

Nizhneserginsky Zavod see
Nizhniye Sergi

Nizhnestalinsk see Leninsky
(4)

Nizhnetroitsky. Town, Bashkir
Autonomous SSR, RSFSR :
Nizhnetroitsky Zavod (-1928)

Nizhnetroitsky Zavod see
Nizhnetroitsky

Nizhneturinsky Zavod see
Nizhnyaya Tura

Nizhneufaleysky Zavod see
Nizhny Ufaley

Nizhniye Kresty see Chersky

Nizhniye Sergi. Town, Sverdlovsk
Oblast, RSFSR : Nizhneserginsky Zavod (-c. 1928)

Nizhniye Ustriki see Ustrzyki-
Dolne

Nizhny Agdzhakend see Shaumyanovsk

Nizhnyaya see Ust-Bagaryak

Nizhnyaya Akhtala see Akhtala

Nizhnyaya Dobrinka see Dobrinka

Nizhnyaya Salda. Town, Sverdlovsk Oblast, RSFSR : Nizhnesaldinsky Zavod (-?)

Nizhnyaya Tura. Town, Sverdlovsk Oblast, RSFSR :
Nizhneturinsky Zavod (-1929)

Nizhny Naur see Nadterechnaya

Nizhny Novgorod see Gorky

Nizhny Ufaley. Urban settlement,
Chelyabinsk Oblast, RSFSR :
Nizhneufaleysky Zavod (-1928)

Nizovye. Village, Kaliningrad
Oblast, RSFSR : Waldau
(-1945), Germany

Noda see Chekhov (2)

Nogaysk see Primorskoye (2)

Noginsk. Town, Moscow Oblast,
RSFSR : Bogorodsk (-1930)

Nógrádverőce see Verőce

Nokia. Town, southwestern Finland : Pohjois-Pirkkala (-1938)

Nokkeushi see Kitami

Nolinsk. Town, Kirov Oblast,
RSFSR : Molotovsk (1940-57)

Nomahasha see Lomahasha

Norak see Nurek

Norashen see Ilyichyovsk

Nor-Bayazet see Kamo

Nordenskjöld Sea see Laptev
Sea

Nordre Bergenhus see Sogn og
Fjordane

Nordre Trondhjem see Nord-
Trondelag

Nord-Trondelag. County, central
Norway : Nordre Trondhjem
(-1918)

Nordvik see Kozhevnikovo

Nor-Kharberd. Urban settlement,
Armenian SSR : Nor-Kyank
(-c. 1960)

Nor-Kyank see Nor-Kharberd

Norris Lake = Norris Reservoir
Norris Reservoir [Norris Lake].
Lake, Tennessee, USA :
Clinch-Powell Reservoir
(*1936-?)
North Bedfordshire. Adminis-
trative district, Bedfordshire,
England, UK : Bedford
(*1973-76)
North Borneo see Sabah
North Canton. City, Ohio,
USA : New Berlin (-1918)
North Caucasus Kray see
Stavropol Kray
North East Frontier Agency
see Arunachal Pradesh
North-East New Guinea. Part
of New Guinea, Papua New
Guinea : Kaiser-Wilhelms-
land (1884-1920), Germany
Northern Rhodesia see Zambia
North Greenfield see West
Allis
North Las Vegas. Suburb of
Las Vegas, Nevada, USA :
Vegas Verde (*early 1920s-
1932)
North Little Rock. City, Arkan-
sas, USA : Argenta (-1901)
North Miami. Suburb of Miami,
Florida, USA : Miami
Shores (1926-36)
North Miami Beach. City,
Florida, USA : Fulford
(-1926)
Northon see Fulgencio
North Union see Shaker Heights
North Vancouver. City, British
Columbia, Canada : Moody-
ville (-1907)
North-Western Provinces and
Oudh see Uttar Pradesh
North Yakima see Yakima
Norusovo see Kalinino (1)
Nossa Senhora do Livramento.
City, northeastern Brazil,
South America : Livramento
(-1943), São José dos Cocais
(1944-48)
Notre-Dame-de Koartac see
Koartac
Notre-Dame-d'Ivugivic see
Ivugivic

Nottaway see Senneterre
Nouadhibou. Town, northwestern
Mauritania, western Africa :
Port-Étienne (-c. 1965)
Nouveau Comptoir. Town,
Quebec, Canada : Paint Hills
(-1967)
Nouvelle Anvers see Makanza
Novabad. Urban settlement,
Tadzhik SSR : Shulmak (-1959)
Nova Dantzig see Cambé
Nova Era. City, southeastern
Brazil, South America : São
Jośe da Lagoa (-1930s),
Presidente Vargas (1930s-
1944)
Nova Fontesvila see Vila Machado
Nova-Freixo. City, north-central
Mozambique, southeastern
Africa : Cuamba (-1942)
Nova Goa see Panaji
Nova Iguaçu. Suburb of Rio de
Janeiro, southeastern Brazil,
South America : Maxambamba
(-?)
Nova Lamego. Village, north-
eastern Guinea-Bissau, western
Africa : Gabú (Sara) (-1948)
Nova Lisboa see Huambo
Nova Prata. City, southern
Brazil, South America :
Prata (-1944)
Nova Vicenza see Farroupilha
Novaya see Novokruchininsky
Novaya Aleksandriya see Puławy
Novaya Bukhara see Kagan
Novaya Eushta see Timiryazev-
sky
Novaya Lyala. Town, Sverdlovsk
Oblast, RSFSR : Novolyalinsky
Zavod (-c. 1928)
Novaya Pismyanka see Lenino-
gorsk (1)
(Novaya) Pokrovka see Lenin-
skoye (7)
Novaya Tarya see Rybachy (1)
Novaya Zhizn see Kazinka
Nové Zámky. Town, southeastern
Czechoslovakia : Neuhäusel
(-1918), Germany; Ersekújvár
(1938-45), Hungary
Novgradets see Suvorovo (1)
Novi Becej see Vološinovo

Noviki (1). Village, Vitebsk
Oblast, Belorussian SSR :
Beda (-1964)

Noviki (2). Village, Mogilyov
Oblast, Belorussian SSR :
Bolvanovka (-1964)

Novi Pazar. Town, west-central Yugoslavia : Yeni-Pazar
(-1913), Turkey

Novi Sad. City, northeastern
Yugoslavia : Neusatz (-1918),
Germany

Novoaleksandrovsk (1). Village,
Sakhalin Oblast, RSFSR :
Konuma (1905-45), Japan

Novoaleksandrovsk (2). Town,
Stavropol Kray, RSFSR :
Novoaleksandrovskaya (-1971)

Novoaleksandrovsk see Zarasai

Novoaleksandrovskaya see
Novoaleksandrovsk (2)

Novoaltaysk. Town, Altay
Kray, RSFSR : Chesnokovka
(-1962)

Novoanninskaya see Novoanninsky

Novoanninsky. Town, Volgograd
Oblast, RSFSR : Novoan-
ninskaya (-c. 1939)

Novoasbest. Urban settlement,
Sverdlovsk Oblast, RSFSR :
Krasnouralsky Rudnik
(-1933)

Novoazovsk. Town, Donetsk
Oblast, Ukrainian SSR :
Novonikolayevka (-c. 1935),
Budyonnovka (c. 1935-66)

Novobureysky. Urban settlement, Amur Oblast, RSFSR
: Bureya-Pristan (-c. 1960)

Novocheremshansk. Urban
settlement, Ulyanovsk Ob-
last, RSFSR : Stary Salavan
(-c. 1960)

Novodvinsk. Town, Arkhangelsk
Oblast, RSFSR : Pervomay-
sky (-1977)

Novogeorgiyevsk see Modlin

Novogordino see Krasnoye
Ekho

Novograd-Volynsk see Novograd-Volynsky

Novograd-Volynsky. Town,

Zhitomir Oblast, Ukrainian
SSR : Novograd-Volynsk
(-c. 1928)

Novogroznensky. Urban settlement, Checheno-Ingush Au-
tonomous SSR, RSFSR :
Oisungur (-1944)

Novokashirsk. Suburb of Kashira,
Moscow Oblast, RSFSR :
Ternovsky (-1932), Ternovsk
(1932-c. 1935), Kaganovich
(c. 1935-c. 1957)

Novokiyevskoye see Kraskino

Novokocherdyk see Tselinnoye
(1)

Novokruchininsky. Urban settlement, Chita Oblast, RSFSR :
Novaya (-c. 1960)

Novokubansk. Town, Krasnodar
Kray, RSFSR : Novokubansky
(-1966)

Novokubansky see Novokubansk

Novokuznetsk. Town, Kemerovo
Oblast, RSFSR : Kuznetsk
(-1931); Stalinsk (1932-61)

Novolakskoye. Village, Dagestan
Autonomous SSR, RSFSR :
Yaryksu-Aukh (-1944)

Novolyalinsky Zavod see Novaya
Lyala

Novolyubino see Lyubinsky

Novo-Mariinsk see Anadyr

Novo Mesto. Village, northwestern
Yugoslavia : Neustädtl (-1918),
Germany

Novomoskovsk. Town, Tula
Oblast, RSFSR : Bobriki
(-1934), Stalinogorsk (1934-61)

Novonazyvayevka see Nazyvayevsk

Novonikolayevka see Novoazovsk

Novo-Nikolayevka see Chkalovo
(3)

Novonikolayevsk see Novosibirsk

Novoorsk. Urban settlement,
Orenburg Oblast, RSFSR :
Novoorskaya (-c. 1935)

Novoorskaya see Novoorsk

Novopashiysky see Gornozavodsk
(2)

Novoselskoye see Achkhoy-
Martan

Novoshakhtinsk. Town, Rostov

Oblast, RSFSR : Tretyego Internatsionala, imeni (1920s), Komintern (1929-39)

Novosibirsk. Capital of Novosibirsk Oblast, RSFSR : Gusevka (-1903), Novonikolayevsk (1903-25)

Novosineglazovsky. Urban settlement, Chelyabinsk Oblast, RSFSR : Sineglazovo (-c. 1960)

Novo-Starobinsk see Soligorsk

Novostroyevo. Village, Kaliningrad Oblast, RSFSR : Trempen (-1946), Germany (-1945)

Novosyolovskoye. Urban settlement, Crimean Oblast, Ukrainian SSR : Fraidorf (-1944)

Novo-Troitskoye see (1) Baley; (2) Sokuluk

Novo-Urgench see Urgench

Novovyatsk. Town, Kirov Oblast, RSFSR : Grukhi (-1939), Lesozavodsky (1939-55)

Novoye (1). Village, Vitebsk Oblast, Belorussian SSR : Gryaznoye (-1964)

Novoye (2). Village, Sakhalin Oblast, RSFSR : Niitoi (1905-45), Japan

Novy Afon. Urban settlement, Abkhazian Autonomous SSR, Georgian SSR : Psirtskha (-1948), Akhali-Afoni (1948-c. 1965)

Nový Bor. Town, northwestern Czechoslovakia : Bor u Ceske Lipy (-1946)

Nový Jičín. Town, central Czechoslovakia : Neutitschein (-1918, 1939-45), Germany

Novy Karachay. Urban settlement, Karachayevo-Cherkess Autonomous Oblast, Stavropol Kray, RSFSR : Pravoberezhnoye (-c. 1960)

Novy Margelan see Fergana

Novy Yarychev. Urban settlement, Lvov Oblast, Ukrain-

ian SSR : Jaryczów Nowy (-1940), Poland

Novyye Aldy see Chernorechye

Novyye Petushki see Petushki

Novy Zay see Zainsk

Nowa Sól. Town, western Poland : Neusalz (an der Oder) (-1945), Germany

Nowawes see Babelsberg

Nowe Miasteczko. Town, western Poland : Neustädtel (-1945), Germany

Nowogard. Town, northwestern Poland : Naugard (-1945), Germany

Nowogrodziec. Town, southwestern Poland : Naumburg am Queis (-1945), Germany

Noworadomsk see Radomsko

Nowy Sącz. City, southern Poland : Neu-Sandec (-1919), Germany; Neu Sandez (1939-45), Germany

Nowy Targ. Town, southern Poland : Neumarkt (-1914), Germany

Nsanje. City, southern Malawi, southeastern Africa : Port Herald (-c. 1964)

Nsiom Fumu. Town, western Zaïre, central Africa : Vista (-1972)

Nueva Caceres see Naga

Nueva Valencia see Valencia

Nukha see Sheki

Nukus see Pristansky

Nuling see Sultan Kudarat

Numancia de la Sagra. Village, south-central Spain : Azaña (-c. 1940)

Numancin see del Carmen

Nupe see Niger

Nurek. Town, Tadzhik SSR : Norak (-1937)

Nuristan. District, eastern Afghanistan : Kafiristan (-c. 1900)

Nutley. Town, New Jersey, USA : Franklin (-1902)

Nyahururu. Town, west-central Kenya, eastern Africa : Thomson's Falls (-1975)

Nyando see Roosevelttown

Nyasa, Lake see Malawi,
Lake
Nyasaland see Malawi
Nyírbakta see Baktalóránthaza
Nymburk. Town, western
Czechoslovakia : Neuenberg
(an der Elbe) (-1918, 1939-
45), Germany
Nysa. City, southern Poland :
Neisse (-1945), Germany

Oak Bluffs. Town, Massachu-
setts, USA : Cottage City
(-1907)
Oakville. Village, Manitoba,
Canada : Kawende (-1939)
Oban. Township, Stewart
Island, New Zealand : Half-
Moon Bay (-early 1940s)
Obbe see Leverburgh
Obdorsk see Salekhard
Obedovo see Oktyabrsky (7)
Oberburg see Gornji Grad
Oberdonau see Upper Austria
Oberdorf see Remennikovo
Oberglogau see Głogówek
Oberlaibach see Vrhnika
Obernigk see Oborniki
Sląskie
Oberösterreich = Upper
Austria
Obiralovka see Zheleznodo-
rozhny (2)
Oborniki Sląskie. Town, south-
western Poland : Obernigk
(-1945), Germany
Obruchevo see Ulyanovo (2)
Obukhovka see Kirovsky (2)
Ocean. Administrative division,
western Cameroon, western
Africa : Kribi (-1974)
Ocean Ridge. Town, Florida,
USA : Boynton Beach (*1931-
37)
Ocean View see Albany
Ocheng [O-ch'eng]. Town, east-
central China : Showchang
(-1914)
Ochyor. Town, Perm Oblast,
RSFSR : Ochyorsky Zavod
(-1929)

Ochyorsky Zavod see Ochyor
Oco see San Jose (3)
O'Connor. Province, southern
Bolivia, South America :
Salinas (-1906)
Ödenburg see Sopron
Odesskaya see Rozy Lyuksem-
burg
Oebisfelde. Town, eastern East
Germany : Oebisfelde-Kalten-
dorf (-1938)
Oebisfelde-Kaltendorf see
Oebisfelde
Oeiras see Araticu
Oels (in Schlesien) see Oleśnica
Offaly. County, east-central Ire-
land : King's County (-1920)
Offutt Air Force Base. Nebraska,
USA : Fort Crook (-1946)
Oglethorpe, Mount. Mountain,
Georgia, USA : Grassy Moun-
tain (-1929)
Ogloblya see Slavyanka
Oguni. Town, northern Honshu,
Japan : Oguni-moto (-late 1930s)
Oguni-moto see Oguni
O'Higgins Land see Antarctic
Peninsula
Ohlau see Oława
Oil Rivers Protectorate see
Niger Coast Protectorate
Oisungur see Novogroznensky
Oka see Aiga
Okachi. Town, northern Honshu,
Japan : Jugohama (-late 1930s)
Okny see Krasnyye Okny
Oko see Yasnomorsky
Okonek. Town, northwestern
Poland : Ratzebuhr (-1945),
Germany
Oktemberyan. Town, Armenian
SSR : Sardarabad (-1932)
Oktyabrsk (1). Village, Kulyab
Oblast, Tadzhik SSR : Chichka
(-?)
Oktyabrsk (2). Town, Aktyubinsk
Oblast, Kazakh SSR : Kandagach
(-1967)
Oktyabrskoye (1). Urban settle-
ment, Crimean Oblast, Ukrain-
ian SSR : Biyuk-Onlar (-1944)
Oktyabrskoye (2). Village,
Lipetsk Oblast, RSFSR :
Dryazgi (-1948), Molotovo

(1948-57)
Oktyabrskoye (3). Village,
Orenburg Oblast, RSFSR :
Isayevo-Dedovo (-1923),
Kashirinskoye (1923-37)
Oktyabrskoye (4). Village,
Chuvash Autonomous SSR,
RSFSR : Ismeli (-1939)
Oktyabrskoye (5). Urban settle-
ment, Khanty-Mansi Autono-
mous Okrug, Tyumen Ob-
last, RSFSR : Kondinskoye
(-1963)
Oktyabrskoye (6). Village,
North Ossetian Autonomous
SSR, RSFSR : Sholkhi
(-1944), Kartsa (1944-c.
1960)
Oktyabrskoye see Zhovtnevoye
(1)
Oktyabrskoy Revolyutsii, imeni.
Suburb of Krivoy Rog,
Dnepropetrovsk Oblast,
Ukrainian SSR : Rostkovsky
Rudnik (-c. 1926)
Oktyabrsky (1). Urban settle-
ment, Kostroma Oblast,
RSFSR : Brantovka (-1939)
Oktyabrsky (2). Urban settle-
ment, Perm Oblast, RSFSR
: Chad (-c. 1960)
Oktyabrsky (3). Urban settle-
ment, Gomel Oblast, Belo-
russian SSR : Karpilovka
(-c. 1960)
Oktyabrsky (4). Village, Adygey
Autonomous Oblast, Krasno-
dar Kray, RSFSR : Khaku-
rate (-1938), Takhtamukay
(1938-c. 1960)
Oktyabrsky (5). Urban settle-
ment, Volgograd Oblast,
RSFSR : Kruglyakov
(-c. 1960)
Oktyabrsky (6). Urban settle-
ment, Gorky Oblast, RSFSR
: Molotova V. M. , imeni
(?-1957)
Oktyabrsky (7). Urban settlement, Ivanovo Oblast, RSFSR
: Obedovo (-1941)
Oktyabrsky (8). Urban settlement, Ryazan Oblast, RSFSR
: Sapronovo (-1927)

Oktyabrsky (9). Urban settle-
ment, Belgorod Oblast, RSFSR
: Voskresenovka (-?), Miko-
yanovka (?-1957)
Oktyabrsky see Komsomolsky
(2), (3)
Oława. City, southwestern Po-
land : Ohlau (-1945), Germany
Olbia. Town, northeastern Sar-
dinia, Italy : Terranova
Pausania (-1939)
Old Ayuquitan see Ayuquitan
Old Calabar see Calabar
Old Glory. Town, Texas, USA :
Brandenburg (-1917)
Old Hickory. Village, Tennessee,
USA : Jacksonville (-1923)
Olecko. Town, northeastern
Poland : Marggrabowa (-1928),
Germany; Treuburg (1928-45),
Germany
Olenegorsk. Town, Murmansk
Oblast, RSFSR : Olenya (-1957)
Olenya see Olenegorsk
Oleskow see Tolstoi
Oleśnica. City, southwestern
Poland : Oels (in Schlesien)
(-1945), Germany
Olesno. Town, southern Poland
: Rosenberg (-1945), Germany
Olginskoye see Kochubeyevskoye
Oliveira Fortes. Town, south-
eastern Brazil, South America
: Livramento (-1944)
Olkhovka† [now joined with Us-
penka]. Urban settlement,
Voroshilovgrad Oblast, Ukrain-
ian SSR : Olkhovsky Zavod
(-c. 1940)
Olkhovskaya. Village, Vitebsk
Oblast, Belorussian SSR :
Zabuldychino (-1964)
Olkhovsky see Artyomovsk
Olkhovsky Zavod see Olkhovka
Olkusz. Town, southern Poland :
Ilkenau (1939-45), Germany
Ollila see Solnechnoye
Olmütz see Olomouc
Olomouc. City, northern Czecho-
slovakia : Olmütz (-1918,
1939-45), Germany
Olsztyn. City, northeastern
Poland : Allenstein (-1945),
Germany

Olsztynek. Town, northeastern
Poland : Hohenstein (-1945),
Germany
Oludere see Harmanlijska
Olviopol see Pervomaysk (1)
Olzheras see Mezhdurechensk
(1)
Oma. Town, northern Honshu,
Japan : Ooku (-early 1940s)
Oman. Sultanate, southeastern
Arabian Peninsula : Muscat
and Oman (-1970)
Omchak. Urban settlement,
Magadan Oblast, RSFSR :
Timoshenko, imeni (-c. 1960)
Omortag. City, east-central
Bulgaria : Osman Pazar
(-1934)
Oneşti see Gheorghe Gheorghiu-
Dej
Onjiva. Town, southern Angola,
southwestern Africa : Vila
Pereira de Eça (-c. 1976)
Onliu see Ngwa
Ooku see Oma
Opatija. Town, northwestern
Yugoslavia : Abbazia (1919-
45), Italy
Opava. City, central Czecho-
slovakia : Troppau (-1918,
1939-45), Germany
Ophir, Mount see Talakmau,
Mount
Opland. County, south-central
Norway : Kristians (-1918)
Opole. City, southern Poland :
Oppeln (-1945), Germany
Oppeln see Opole
Oradea. City, northwestern
Romania : Nagyvárad
(-1919, 1940-45), Hungary
Orange Free State. Province,
east-central South Africa :
Orange River Colony (1900-
10)
Orange River Colony see Orange
Free State
Oranienbaum see Lomonosov
Oranje Top see Jayawijaya,
Puncak
Oraşul Stalin see Braşov
Orchard Park. Village, New
York, USA : East Hamburg

(-1934)
Ordzhonikidze (1). Urban settle-
ment, Dnepropetrovsk Oblast,
Ukrainian SSR : Aleksandrovka
(-1939)
Ordzhonikidze (2). Village,
Kustanay Oblast, Kazakh SSR :
Denisovka (-c. 1960)
Ordzhonikidze (3). Urban settle-
ment, Georgian SSR : Khara-
gouli (-1949)
Ordzhonikidze (4). Suburb of
Tashkent, Tashkent Oblast,
Uzbek SSR : Lunacharskoye
(-c. 1935)
Ordzhonikidze (5). Capital of
North Ossetian Autonomous
SSR, RSFSR : Vladikavkaz
(-1931), Dzaudzhikau (1944-54)
Ordzhonikidze see Yenakiyevo
Ordzhonikidzeabad. Town,
Tadzhik SSR : Yangibazar
(-1936)
Ordzhonikidzegrad see Bezhitsa
Ordzhonikidze Kray see Stavro-
pol Kray
Ordzhonikidzevskaya. Village,
Checheno-Ingush Autonomous
SSR, RSFSR : Sleptsovskaya
(-1939)
Orekhi-Vydritsa see Orekhovsk
Orekhovichi. Village, Vitebsk
Oblast, Belorussian SSR :
Khlevishche (-1964)
Orekhovsk. Urban settlement,
Vitebsk Oblast, Belorussian
SSR : Orekhi-Vydritsa (-1946)
Orekhovskaya. Village, Minsk
Oblast, Belorussian SSR :
Neumyvaki (-1964)
Orenburg. Capital of Orenburg
Oblast, RSFSR : Chkalov
(1938-57)
Orenburg Oblast (*1934). RSFSR
: Chkalov Oblast (1938-57)
Oreshenka. Village, Vitebsk
Oblast, Belorussian SSR :
Popovka (-1964)
Oreshnitsa. Village, Minsk
Oblast, Belorussian SSR :
Navozy (-1964)
Orgeyev. Town, Moldavian
SSR : Orhei (1918-40, 1941-44),

Romania
Orgtrud. Urban settlement,
Vladimir Oblast, RSFSR :
Lemeshensky (1927-c. 1940)
Orhei see Orgeyev
Oriente. Province, eastern
Cuba : Santiago (de Cuba)
(-1905)
Orizona. City, east-central
Brazil, South America :
Campo Formoso (-1944)
Orkhaniye see Botevgrad
Orkhomenós. Village, southern
Greece : Kalpákion (-1960s)
Orléansville see El Asnam
Orlov see Khalturin
Orlovo. Village, Sakhalin Ob-
last, RSFSR : Ushiro
(1905-45), Japan
Ormoc see MacArthur
Ormond see Ormond Beach
Ormond Beach. City, Florida,
USA : Ormond (-1949)
Ormoz. Village, northwestern
Yugoslavia : Friedau (-1918),
Germany
Orta-koi see Ivailovgrad
Ortelsburg see Szczytno
Ortona. Town, south-central
Italy : Ortona a Mare
(c. 1938-47)
Ortona a Mare see Ortona
Orzysz. Town, northeastern
Poland : Arys (-1945),
Germany
Oshan. Town, southwestern
China : Siwo (-1929)
Oshmyany. Town, Grodno Ob-
last, Belorussian SSR :
Oszmiana (1921-45), Poland
Osipenko see Berdyansk
Oslo. Capital of Norway :
[Christiania (1624-1877)],
Kristiania (1877-1924)
Osmalenik see Udarnaya (2)
Osmanabad. District, south-
central India : Naldrug (-c.
1920)
Osman-Kasayevo. Village,
Mogilyov Oblast, Belorussian
SSR : Sermyazhenka (-1964)
Osman Pazar see Omortag
Ośno. Town, western Poland :

Drossen (-1945), Germany
Ossersee see Zarasai
Ossining. Village, New York,
USA : Sing Sing (-1901)
Ostenburg see Pułtusk
Osterode (in Ostpreussen) see
Ostróda
Österreich ober der Ems see
Upper Austria
Ostfold. County, southeastern
Norway : Smaalenene (-1918)
Ostrava see Moravská-Ostrava
Ostróda. City, northeastern
Poland : Osterode (in Ostpreus-
sen) (-1945), Germany
Ostrołęka. Town, northeastern
Poland : Scharfenwiese (1939-
45), Germany
Ostrovskoye. Urban settlement,
Kostroma Oblast, RSFSR :
Semyonovskoye (-1956)
Ostrów (Wielkopolski). City,
west-central Poland : Ostrowo
(-1918), Germany
Ostrowo see Ostrów (Wielkopol-
ski)
Ostyako-Vogulsk see Khanty-
Mansiysk
Ostyak-Vogul National Okrug see
Khanty-Mansi Autonomous
Okrug
Oswego see Lake Oswego
Oświęcin. Town, southern Po-
land : Auschwitz (-1918, 1939-
45), Germany
Osy-kolyosy see Slavino
Oszmiana see Oshmyany
Otani see Sokol
Otdykh see Zhukovsky
Oteiza see Marihatag
Otiai see Dolinsk
Otmuchów. Town, southern Po-
land : Ottmachau (-1945),
Germany
Otomari see Korsakov
Otpor see Zabaykalsk
Otradnoye. Health resort, Kalinin-
grad Oblast, RSFSR : Georgen-
swalde (-1945), Germany
Otradnoye see Otradny
Otradny. Town, Kuybyshev Ob-
last, RSFSR : Otradnoye (-1956)
Otrogovo see Stepnoye

Otsu see Izumi-otsu
Ottmachau see Otmuchów
Otvazhnoye see Zhigulyovsk
Otvazhny see Zhigulyovsk
Ouachita National Forest. Ar-
  kansas/Oklahoma, USA :
  Arkansas National Forest
  (*1907-26)
Oued el Abtal. Village, north-
  western Algeria, northern
  Africa : Uzès-le-Duc (-c.
  1962)
Oued Rhiou. Village, northern
  Algeria, northern Africa :
  Inkermann (-c. 1962)
Ouled Mimoun. Village, north-
  western Algeria, northern
  Africa : Lamoricière (-c.
  1962)
Ouled Moussa. Town, northern
  Algeria, northern Africa :
  Saint-Pierre-Saint-Paul
  (-c. 1962)
Oulmes-le-Thermes see
  Tarmilate
Oulx see Ulzio
Ovechki see Sosnovtsy
Owando. Town, central People's
  Republic of the Congo, cen-
  tral Africa : Fort-Rousset
  (-1977)
Oyrat Autonomous Oblast see
  Gorno-Altay Autonomous
  Oblast
Oyrot Autonomous Oblast see
  Gorno-Altay Autonomous
  Oblast
Oyrot-Tura see Gorno-Altaysk
Oyster Harbour see Ladysmith
Ozamis. City, Mindanhao,
  Philippines : Misamis
  (-1940s)
Oznachennoye see Sayanogorsk
Ozurgety see Makharadze
Ozyorki. Village, Kaliningrad
  Oblast, RSFSR : Gross
  Lindenau (-1946), Germany
  (-1945)
Ozyornaya (1). Village, Mogilyov
  Oblast, Belorussian SSR :
  Muzhichok (-1964)
Ozyornaya (2). Village, Vitebsk
  Oblast, Belorussian SSR :

Popova Luka (-1964)
Ozyornoye. Village, Saratov
  Oblast, RSFSR : Durasovka
  (-c. 1960)
Ozyorsk. Town, Kaliningrad
  Oblast, RSFSR : Darkehmen
  (-1938), Germany; Angerapp
  (1938-46), Germany (-1945)
Ozyorsky. Urban settlement,
  Sakhalin Oblast, RSFSR :
  Nagahama (1905-45), Japan

Paan. Town, southern China :
  Batang (-1913)
Pacajús. City, northeastern
  Brazil, South America :
  Guarani (-1944)
Pachai see Tanchai
Pachow see (1) Pachung; (2)
  Pahsien
Pachung. Town, central China :
  Pachow (-1913)
Paciencia. Barrio, Dao, Philip-
  pines : Taguimtim (-1957)
Pacific City see Huntington
  Beach
Pacific Range see Western
  Test Range
Paczków. Town, southwestern
  Poland : Patschkau (-1945),
  Germany
Padali see Amursk
Paderno. Village, northern
  Italy : Paderno Ossolaro
  (-1950)
Paderno Ossolaro see Paderno
Padilla. Town, south-central
  Bolivia, South America :
  Laguna (-1900s)
Padre Las Casas. Town, south-
  western Dominican Republic,
  West Indies : Túbano (-1928)
Padre Miguelinho see Santo
  Antônio (1)
Pagalu. Island, Equatorial
  Guinea, western Africa :
  Annobón (-1973)
Pagayawan. Municipality, Lanao
  del Sur, Philippines : Tatari-
  kan (-1914)

Pagoúria

Pagoúria see Mése
Pahlevi. Town, northwestern
   Iran : Enzeli (-1925)
Pahsien. Town, northeastern
   China : Pachow (-1913)
Paimawan see Kanghsien
   [K'ang-hsien]
Paint Hills see Nouveau
   Comptoir
Paishambe see Payshanba
Paituk see Vose, imeni
Paiyentsing see Yenfeng
Paiyintailai see Tungliao
   [T'ung-liao]
Pakhtaabad. Urban settlement,
   Andizhan Oblast, Uzbek
   SSR : Kokankishlak (-1975)
Pakhtakor. Urban settlement,
   Dzhizak Oblast, Uzbek SSR
   : Ziyautdin (-1937), Binokor
   (1971-74)
Pakiachen see Tsingyüan
Paklay see Sayaboury
Palaiá Halônia see Petrálona
Palaikatoúna see Lesínion
Palandoc see Ramon Magsay-
   say
Palau de Montagut see San
   Jaime de Llierca
Palau de Plegamáns. Village,
   northeastern Spain : Palau-
   solitar (-c. 1940)
Palausolitar see Palau de
   Plegamáns
Palawan. Island, southwestern
   Philippines : Paragua
   (*1902-05)
Paldiski. Town, Estonian SSR
   : Baltiysky (Port) (-1917),
   Russia
Palestina see Jordânia
Palestro see Lakhdaria
Palikao see Tighennif
Palma see (1) Coreaú; (2)
   Paraná
Palmares see Emílio Meyer
Palmeira see Palmeira das
   Missões
Palmeira das Missões. City,
   southern Brazil, South
   America : Palmeira (-1944)
Palmeirais. City, northeastern
   Brazil, South America :

Belém (-1944)
Palmeiras see (1) Palmeiras
   de Goiás; (2) Santa Cruz das
   Palmeiras
Palmeiras de Goiás. City,
   central Brazil, South America
   : Palmeiras (-1944), Mataúna
   (1944-48)
Palmer Peninsula see Antarctic
   Peninsula
Palmerston see Darwin
Palmnicken see Yantarny
Palmyras see Santos Dumont
Palpalicong see Franco
Pama see Wankang
Pamirsky Post see Murgab
Pamyati 13 Bortsov. Urban
   settlement, Krasnoyarsk Kray,
   RSFSR : Znamensky (-?)
Panagía see Askraía
Panaji. Town, western India :
   Nova Goa (-1961)
Panapaan see Pedro Espiritu
Panchow see Panhsien [P'an-
   hsien]
Pandvapura. Town, southern
   India : French Rocks (-1950s)
Panfilov. Town, Taldy-Kurgan
   Oblast, Kazakh SSR : Dzhar-
   kent (-1942)
Panfilovskoye. Village, Kirgiz
   SSR : Staro-Nikolayevskoye
   (-1942)
Panghü see Pingchih [P'ing-
   chih]
Pangi see Gaudencio Antonio (1)
Panhsien [P'an-hsien]. Town,
   southern China : Panchow
   (-1913)
Pannonhalma. Town, northwestern
   Hungary : Györszentmárton
   (-1965)
Panpu see Kwanyün [Kuan-yün]
Panskoye see Maysk (1)
Panteleímon. Village, northern
   Greece : Platamón (-1960s)
Paoan see Chihtan
Pao-ch'ing see Shao-yang
Paofeng see Hweinung [Hui-nung]
Paohing [Pao-hsing]. Town,
   southern China : Muping (-1929)
Pao-hsing = Paohing
Paoning see Langchung

Paoshan. Town, southwestern
China : Yungchang (-1914)
Paosintsi see Sihsien [Hsi-
hsien] (2)
Pao-ting. City, northeastern
China : Tsingyüan [Ch'ing-
yüan] (-1958)
Paoyüan. Town, northeastern
China : Kuyüan (-1950)
Papao see Kilien [Ch'i-lien]
Papari see Nísia Floresta
Papendorp see Woodstock
Paracales see Paracelis
Paracelis. Municipality, Moun-
tain Province, Philippines :
Paracales (-1966)
Paradise Island. Northeast of
New Providence Island, Ba-
hamas, West Indies : Hog
Island (-c. 1960)
Paragua see Palawan
Paraguaçu see Paraguaçu
Paulista
Paraguaçu Paulista. City,
southeastern Brazil, South
America : Paraguaçu
(-1944), Araguaçu (1944-48)
Paraíba see João Pessoa
Paralía Akrátas see Kráthion
Paraná. City, southern Brazil,
South America : Palma
(-1944)
Paranaíba. City, western Bra-
zil, South America : Santana
do Paranaíba (-1939)
Parapitinga. City, northeastern
Brazil, South America :
São Francisco (-1944)
Paraprastáina see Proástion
Parati see Araquari
Paratinga. City, eastern
Brazil, South America :
Rio Branco (-1944)
Parchwitz see Prochowice
Parco see (1) Altofonte;
(2) Sinclair
Pardubice. Town, northwestern
Czechoslovakia : Pardubitz
(-1918, 1939-45), Germany
Pardubitz see Pardubice
Paredon see Anzaldo
Parizhskaya Kommuna. Suburb
of Kommunarsk, Voroshilov-

grad Oblast, Ukrainian SSR :
Seleznevsky Rudnik (-1926)
Parkań see Sturovo
Park City. Town, Kentucky,
USA : Glasgow Junction (-1938)
Parnamirim. City, northeastern
Brazil, South America :
Leopoldina (-1944)
Parnarama. City, northeastern
Brazil, South America : São
José dos Matões (-1944),
Matões (1944-48)
Pärnu. Town, Estonian SSR :
Pernov (-1917), Russia
Parreiras see Caldas
Parroquia de Besalú see San
Ferreol
Parr Siding see Harding
Parshevichi see Berezovichi
Partizanka. Village, Minsk
Oblast, Belorussian SSR :
Zhabovka (-1964)
Partizanovka. Village, Grodno
Oblast, Belorussian SSR :
Pleshki (-1964)
Partizansk. Town, Primorsky
Kray, RSFSR : Suchan (-1972)
Partizanskaya (1). Village,
Gomel Oblast, Belorussian
SSR : Avraamovskaya (-1964)
Partizanskaya (2). Village,
Grodno Oblast, Belorussian
SSR : Puzovichi (-1964)
Partizanskaya (3). Village,
Vitebsk Oblast, Belorussian
SSR : Zhirospyory (-1964)
Partizánske. Town, west-central
Czechoslovakia : Šimonovany
(-1947), Batovany (1947-49)
Partizanskoye. Village, Kras-
noyarsk Kray, RSFSR :
Perovo (-1930s)
Partizanskoye see Prokhladnoye
Partizany (1). Village, Gomel
Oblast, Belorussian SSR :
Siporovka (-1964)
Partizany (2). Village, Vitebsk
Oblast, Belorussian SSR :
Torbinka (-1964)
Pârvomaj. City, south-central
Bulgaria : Borisovgrad (-1944)
Pasarel Dam see Stalin Dam
Pashalu see Azizbekov

Pashiya. Urban settlement,
Perm Oblast, RSFSR :
Arkhangelo-Pashisky Zavod
(-1929)
Pashmakli see Smolyan
Pašićevo see Zmajevo
Pasłęk. Town, northeastern
Poland : Preussisch Holland
(-1945), Germany
Passenheim see Pasym
Pasym. Town, northeastern
Poland : Passenheim
(-1945), Germany
Patos see Patos de Minas
Patos de Minas. City, south-
eastern Brazil, South
America : Patos (-1944)
Patriarsheye see Donskoye
(2)
Patrocínio see (1) Abolição;
(2) Pio Nôno
Patschkau see Paczków
Patton see Monroeville
Pau d'Alho see Ibirarema
Pau Gigante see Ibiraçu
Paulis see Isiro
Paulista see Paulistana
Paulistana. City, northeastern
Brazil, South America :
Paulista (-1944)
Paulo Affonso see Mata Grande
Pavlogradskiye Khutora pervyye
see Vishnyovoye (2)
Pavlovka see Bogatoye
Pavlovo. Village, Grodno
Oblast, Belorussian SSR :
Puzovichi (-1964)
Pavlovsk. Town, Leningrad
Oblast, RSFSR : Slutsk
(c. 1917-44)
Payapa see General Tinio
Payen see Hwalung [Hua-lung]
Payenyungko see Hwalung
[Hua-lung]
Payne Bay see Bellin
Payo. Municipality, Catanduanes,
Philippines : Jose Pangani-
ban (-1957)
Payo Obispo see Chetumal
Payshanba. Village, Samarkand
Oblast, Uzbek SSR : Pai-
shambe (-c. 1935), Kara-
Darya (c. 1935-c. 1960)

Payung see Hwalung [Hua-lung]
Pazardžik. City, southwestern
Bulgaria : Tatar-Pazardžik
(-1934)
Peć. Town, southwestern
Yugoslavia : Ipek (-1913),
Turkey
Pechenga. Urban settlement,
Murmansk Oblast, RSFSR :
Petsamo (1920-44), Finland
Pedra see Delmiro
Pedra Azul. City, southeastern
Brazil, South America :
Fortaleza (-1944)
Pedras Brancas see Guaíba
Pedro Avelino. City, northeastern
Brazil, South America : Epi-
tácio Pessoa (-1948)
Pedro Espiritu. Barrio, Cavite,
Philippines : Panapaan (-1969)
Pehchen. Town, northeastern
China : Kwangning (-1914)
Pehchwan [Pei-ch'uan]. Town,
central China : Shihchwan
(-1914)
Pehtatung see Weiyüan
Peichow see Pihsien [P'ei-hsien]
Pei-ch'uan = Pehchwan
Peifeng see Sian [Hsi-an] (2)
P'ei-hsien = Pihsien
Peiping [Pei-p'ing] see Peking
Peking. Capital of China :
Peiping [Pei-p'ing] (1928-49)
Peklevskaya see Troitsky
Pełczyce. Town, western Poland
: Bernstein (-1945), Germany
Pemba. City, northeastern
Mozambique, southeastern
Africa : Porto Amélia (-1976)
Pemberton Spur see Pritchard
Pendência. Town, northeastern
Brazil, South America : In-
dependência (-1944)
Pengan [P'eng-an]. Town,
central China : Pengchow
(-1913)
Pengchow see Pengan [P'eng-an]
Penglai [P'eng-lai]. Town,
eastern China : Tengchow
(-1913)
Penn see Penn Hills
Penn Hills. Township, Pennsyl-
vania, USA : Penn (-1958)

Penny Hole see Gemswick
Pensky Sakharny Zavod see
    Karl Libknekhta, imeni (1)
Penthièvre see Aïn Berda
Pentyukhi see Vysochany (1)
Peny see Karla Libknekhta,
    imeni (1)
People's Democratic Republic
    of Yemen see Yemen
People's Republic of the Congo.
    Republic, west-central
    Africa : Middle Congo
    [Moyen-Congo] (*1903-58),
    Congo (Brazzaville) (1958-69)
Peper Bay see Lada Bay
Peravia. Province, southern
    Dominican Republic, West
    Indies : Trujillo Valdéz
    (*1944-61)
Perdigão. Town, southeastern
    Brazil, South America :
    Saúde (-1944)
Perdizes see Videira
Peredelki see Borovshchina (1)
Peredniye Traki see Kras-
    noarmeyskoye
Peremozhets. Village, Minsk
    Oblast, Belorussian SSR :
    Smorkovo (-1964)
Peremyshl see Przemyśl
Perevoloki see Mezhdurechensk
    (2)
Perevoz. Urban settlement,
    Gorky Oblast, RSFSR :
    Pyansky Perevoz (-c. 1960)
Pereyaslav see Pereyaslav-
    Khmelnitsky
Pereyaslav-Khmelnitsky. Town,
    Kiev Oblast, Ukrainian SSR
    : Pereyaslav (-1943)
Perigotville see Aïn el Kebira
Peri Mirim. City, northeastern
    Brazil, South America :
    Macapá (-1944)
Perkhayly see Zarechnaya (3)
Perm. Capital of Perm Oblast,
    RSFSR : Molotov (1940-57)
Perm Oblast. RSFSR : Molotov
    Oblast (*1940-57)
Permskoye see Komsomolsk-
    na-Amure
Pernik. Town, western Bul-
    garia : Dimitrovo (1949-63)

Pernov see Pärnu
Perovo see Partizanskoye
Perovsk see Kzyl-Orda
Perparim see Pogradec
Perrégaux see Mohammadia
Pershotravenka see Terny
Pershotravensk. Town, Dneprope-
    trovsk Oblast, Ukrainian SSR
    : Shakhtyorskoye (-c. 1960),
    Pershotravnevoye (c. 1960-66)
Pershotravnevoye (1). Urban
    settlement, Donetsk Oblast,
    Ukrainian SSR : Mangush
    (-1946)
Pershotravnevoye (2). Urban
    settlement, Rovno Oblast,
    Ukrainian SSR : Mokvin
    (-c. 1960)
Pershotravnevoye see Persho-
    travensk
Persia see Iran
Pervomay (1). Village, Gomel
    Oblast, Belorussian SSR :
    Gorovakha (-1964)
Pervomay (2). Village, Minsk
    Oblast, Belorussian SSR :
    Plevaki (-1964)
Pervomaysk (1). Town, Nikolayev
    Oblast, Ukrainian SSR : Olvio-
    pol (-1919)
Pervomaysk (2). Town, Voro-
    shilovgrad Oblast, Ukrainian
    SSR : Petromaryevka (-1938)
Pervomaysk (3). Village, Vitebsk
    Oblast, Belorussian SSR :
    Svinoye (-1964)
Pervomaysk (4). Town, Gorky
    Oblast, RSFSR : Tashino
    (-1951)
Pervomaysk (5). Village, Minsk
    Oblast, Belorussian SSR :
    Zhivoglodovichi (-1964)
Pervomayskoye (1). Village,
    Brest Oblast, Belorussian
    SSR : Bluden (-1964)
Pervomayskoye (2). Village,
    Chuvash Autonomous SSR,
    RSFSR : Bolshiye Arabuzy
    (-1939)
Pervomayskoye (3). Urban
    settlement, Crimean Oblast,
    Ukrainian SSR : Dzurchi
    (-1944)

Pervomayskoye (4). Village, Saratov Oblast, RSFSR : Gnadenflyur (-1941)

Pervomayskoye (5). Village, Rostov Oblast, RSFSR : Golodayevka (-1940)

Pervomayskoye (6). Village, Checheno-Ingush Autonomous SSR, RSFSR : Muzhichi (-1944)

Pervomayskoye (7). Village, Tomsk Oblast, RSFSR : Pyshkino-Troitskoye (-c. 1960)

Pervomayskoye (8). Village, Altay Kray, RSFSR : Srednekrayushkino (-c. 1960)

Pervomaysky (1). Urban settlement, Tambov Oblast, RSFSR : Bogoyavlenskoye (-c. 1960)

Pervomaysky (2). Urban settlement, Kuybyshev Oblast, RSFSR : Kozhemyaki (-c. 1960)

Pervomaysky (3). Urban settlement, Bashkir Autonomous SSR, RSFSR : Kukshik (-1943)

Pervomaysky (4). Urban settlement, Kharkov Oblast, Ukrainian SSR : Likhachyovo (-c. 1960)

Pervomaysky (5). Suburb of Slobodskoy, Kirov Oblast, RSFSR : Spas (-1938)

Pervomaysky see (1) Novodvinsk; (2) Podlesny

Pervouralsk. Town, Sverdlov Oblast, RSFSR : Shaytansky Zavod (-1928), Pervouralsky (1928-33)

Pervouralsky see Pervouralsk

Pervy Severny see Severny

Pescado see Villa Serrano

Peschanoye see Yashkul

Pesochnya see Kirov (1)

Pesterszébet see Pestszenterzsébet

Pestovo see Zavolzhye

Pestszenterzsébet. Suburb of Budapest, Hungary : Erzsébetfalva (-1919), Leninváros (1919-24), Pesterzsébet (1924-32)

Pestszentimre. Suburb of Budapest, Hungary : Soroksárpéteri (*1930-31)

Pestújhely. Suburb of Budapest, Hungary : Széchenyitelep (*1909-10)

Peterborough. Town, South Australia, Australia : Petersburg (-c. 1915)

Peterborough see Wilmer

Petergof see Petrodvorets

Peterhof see Petrodvorets

Petersburg see Peterborough

Petitjean see Sidi Kacem

Petrálona. Village, western Greece : Palaiá Halónia (-1960s)

Petra Stuchki, imeni see Stuchka

Petroaleksandrovsk see Turtkul

Petrodvorets. Town, Leningrad Oblast, RSFSR : Leninsk (1930s), Petergof [Peterhof] (-1944)

Petro-Golenishchevo see Dolinovskoye

Petrograd see Leningrad

Petrograd Guberniya see Leningrad Guberniya

Petrokrepost. Town, Leningrad Oblast, RSFSR : Shlisselburg [Schlüsselburg] (-1944)

Petrolândia. City, northeastern Brazil, South America : Jatobá (-1939), Itaparica (1939-43)

Petromaryevka see Pervomaysk (2)

Petropavlovsk-Kamchatsky. Capital of Kamchatka Oblast, RSFSR : Petropavlovsky port (-1924)

Petropavlovsky see Severouralsk

Petropavlovsky port see Petropavlovsk-Kamchatsky

Petroverovka see Zhovten (1)

Petrovgrad see Zrenjanin

Petrovskaya Sloboda see Losino-Petrovsky

Petrovskogo G. I., imeni see Gorodishche

Petrovskoye. Town, Voroshilovgrad Oblast, Ukrainian SSR :

Shterovskogo zavoda imeni
Petrovskogo (-1963)
Petrovskoye see Svetlograd
Petrovsk-Port see Makhach-
kala
Petrovsky Zavod see Petrovsk-
Zabaykalsky
Petrovsk-Zabaykalsky. Town,
Chita Oblast, RSFSR :
Petrovsky Zavod (-1926)
Petrozavodsk. Capital of
Karelian Autonomous SSR,
RSFSR : Kalininsk (1930s)
Petsamo see Pechenga
Petukhovo. Town, Kurgan
Oblast, RSFSR : Yudino
(-1944)
Petuna see Fuyü
Petushki. Town, Vladimir
Oblast, RSFSR : Novyye
Petushki (-1965)
Phanárion Magoúla see
Magoúla
Philadelphianá see Néa
Philadélpheia
Philippeville see Skikda
Philippopolis see Plovdiv
Philipstown see Daingean
Phou-Khao-Khuai. Mountain
resort, eastern Laos :
Ritaville (-1967)
Piatã. City, eastern Brazil,
South America : Anchieta
(-1944)
Pi-chiang [Pikiang]
Picos see Colinas
Piedras Negras. City, northern
Mexico, North America :
Ciudad Porfirio Díaz
(1888-c. 1911)
Piekar see Piekary (Śląskie)
Piekary (Śląskie). City, southern
Poland : Piekar (-1945)
Pierrefonds. City, Quebec,
Canada : Sainte-Geneviève
(-1958)
Pierron. Village, Illinois,
USA : Millersburg (-1939)
Pietole see Virgilio
Pihsien [P'ei-hsien]. Town,
eastern China : Peichow
(-1912)
Pikiang [Pi-chiang]. Village,

southwestern China : Yingpankai
(-1934)
Piła. Town, northwestern Po-
land : Schneidemühl (-1945),
Germany
Pilar. City, northeastern Brazil,
South America : Manguaba
(1944-48)
Pilar see (1) Itacê; (2) Pilar
do Sul
Pilar do Sul. City, southeastern
Brazil, South America : Pilar
(-1944)
Pilawa. Town, southwestern
Poland : Beilau (-1945), Ger-
many
Pilimsit, Puncak. Mountain,
Irian Jaya, Indonesia : Iden-
burg Top (-1963)
Piliscsév. Town, northern
Hungary : Csév (-1954)
Pillau see Baltiysk
Pillkallen see Dobrovolsk
Pillupönen see Nevskoye
Piloto Juan Fernandez see
Alejandro Selkirk
Pilsen see (1) Pilzno; (2)
Plzeň
Pilzno. Town, southeastern
Poland : Pilsen (1939-45),
Germany
Pinchow see (1) Pinhsien (1),
(2); (2) Pinyang
Pinellas see Pinellas Park
Pinellas Park. City, Florida,
USA : Pinellas (-1911)
Pingchang [P'ing-ch'ang]. Town,
central China : Kiangkow
(-1944)
Pingchih [P'ing-chih]. Town,
southern China : Panghü (-1936)
Pingfan see Yungteng
Pingmei see Tsungkiang [Ts'ung-
chiang]
Pingpien [P'ing-pien]. Town,
southwestern China : Tsingpien
(-1933)
Pingtang [P'ing-t'ang]. Town,
southern China : Tungchow
(-1942)
Pingtichüan see Tsining
Pingtung [P'ing-tung]. Town,
southern Taiwan : Akow (-1920)

Pingwu [P'ing-wu]. Town,
central China : Lungan
(-1913)
Pingyang see Linfen
Pingyüan see Chihkin [Chih-
chin]
Pinheiro see Icoraci
Pinhsien (1). Town, central
China : Pinchow (-1913)
Pinhsien (2). Town, eastern
China : Pinchow (-1913)
Pinkiang see Harbin
Pinola see Las Rosas
Pinyang. Town, southern
China : Pinchow (-1912)
Pioner. Suburb of Kemerovo,
Kemerovo Oblast, RSFSR :
Ishanovo (-1936)
Pionersky. Town, Kaliningrad
Oblast, RSFSR : Neukuhren
(-1947), Germany (-1945)
Pio Nôno. City, northeastern
Brazil, South America :
Patrocínio (-1944)
Pio V. Corpuz. Municipality,
Masbate, Philippines :
Limbuhan (-1954)
Piperno see Priverno
Piracanjuba. City, central Bra-
zil, South America : Pouso
Alto (-1944)
Piraí see Piraí do Sul
Piraí do Sul. City, southern
Brazil, South America :
Piraí (-1944), Piraí Mirim
(1944-48)
Piraí Mirim see Piraí do Sul
Pirajaí see Cabrália Paulista
Piranhas. City, northeastern
Brazil, South America :
Marechal Floriano (1939-48)
Pirapora see Pirapora do
Bom Jesus
Pirapora do Bom Jesus. Town,
southeastern Brazil, South
America : Pirapora (-1944)
Piraquara. City, southern
Brazil, South America :
Deodoro (-c.1935)
Pirchivan see Zangelan
Pirogovsky. Urban settlement,
Moscow Oblast, RSFSR :
Proletarskaya Pobeda

(c.1918-28)
Pisha see Ningnan
Pishpek see Frunze (2)
Pistianá. Village, western
Greece : Pistianá Néas
Helládos (-1960s)
Pistianá Néas Helládos see
Pistianá
Pisyuta see Zalesskaya
Pisz. Town, northeastern Po-
land : Johannisburg (-1945),
Germany
Pitschen see Byczyna
Pittsburg. City, California,
USA : Black Diamond (-1911)
Pittsworth. Town, Queensland,
Australia : Beauaraba (-1915)
Pitzewo see Sinkin [Hsin-chin]
Pitzthal see Sankt Leonard im
Pitzdal
Piyüan see Tangho [T'ang-ho]
Plagiá see Kephalokhórion
Planyorskoye. Urban settlement,
Crimean Oblast, Ukrainian
SSR : Koktebel (-1944)
Plaridel (1). Municipality,
Misamis, Philippines :
Laragaran (-1914)
Plaridel (2). Municipality,
Bulacan, Philippines : Quingua
(-1936)
Plaridel see Calamba
Platamón. Village, northern
Greece : Stathmós (-1960s)
Platamón see Pantaleímon
Platána. Village, Euboea,
eastern Greece : Káto Potamiá
(-1960s)
Platános. Village, western
Greece : Akhoúria Vavouríou
(-1960s)
Plathe see Płoty
Platt National Park. Oklahoma,
USA : Sulphur Springs National
Reservation (*1902-06)
Playa de Cabra see Playa de
Santa María
Playa de Santa María. Village,
eastern Spain : Playa de
Cabra (-c.1960)
Plazigaz see Yasen
Pleasureville see South Plea-
sureville

Plekhovo see Zalesovtsy
Pleshivtsy see Zelyonaya (1)
Pleshki see Partizanovka
Pleskau see Pskov
Plevaki see Pervomay (2)
Ploče see Kardeljevo
Plock. City, central Poland :
  Plotsk (-1921), USSR;
  Schröttersburg (1939-45),
  Germany
Plöhnen see Płonsk
Plokhino see Ulyanovo (3)
Płonsk. Town, east-central
  Poland : Plöhnen (1939-45),
  Germany
Plotsk see Plock
Płoty. Town, northwestern Po-
  land : Plathe (-1945), Ger-
  many
Plovdiv. City, southern Bulgaria
  : Philippopolis (-c. 1918)
Plzeň. City, western Czecho-
  slovakia : Pilsen (-1918,
  1939-45), Germany
Poai. Town, north-central
  China : Tsinghwa (-1929)
Pobedinsky see Zarechny
Pobednaya (1). Village, Mogil-
  yov Oblast, Belorussian
  SSR : Polzukhi (-1964)
Pobednaya (2). Village, Minsk
  Oblast, Belorussian SSR :
  Rakoyedovshchina (-1964)
Pobednaya (3). Village, Gomel
  Oblast, Belorussian SSR :
  Stary Folvarok (-1964)
Pochow see Pohsien
Poções. City, eastern Brazil,
  South America : Djalma
  Dutra (1944-48)
Podchinny. Settlement, Volgo-
  grad Oblast, RSFSR :
  Kratske (-1941)
Poddannyye see Cheryomushki
  (2)
Podgorica see Titograd
Podgornaya (1). Village, Grodno
  Oblast, Belorussian SSR :
  Bloshno (-1964)
Podgornaya (2). Village, Brest
  Oblast, Belorussian SSR :
  Gavinovichi (-1964)
Podlesnaya. Village, Minsk

Oblast, Belorussian SSR :
  Telyatki (-1964)
Podlesnoye. Village, Saratov
  Oblast, RSFSR : Untervalden
  (-1941)
Podlesny. Urban settlement,
  Tula Oblast, RSFSR : Pervo-
  maysky (-c. 1960)
Podlesskaya. Village, Mogilyov
  Oblast, Belorussian SSR :
  Koryavinets (-1964)
Podlesye. Village, Vitebsk
  Oblast, Belorussian SSR :
  Kukonosy (-1964)
Podlipki see Kaliningrad (2)
Podmokly. Town, northwestern
  Czechoslovakia : Bodenbach
  (-1918, 1939-45), Germany
Podonki see Znamenka (3)
Podrassolay see Vishnya (2)
Pogradec. Town, southeastern
  Albania : Perparim (1939-43),
  Italy
Pogranichny (1). Urban settle-
  ment, Grodno Oblast, Belorus-
  sian SSR : Berestovitsa (-1978)
Pogranichny (2). Urban settle-
  ment, Primorsky Kray, RSFSR
  : Grodekovo (-1958)
Pohjois-Pirkkala see Nokia
Pohsien. Town, eastern China :
  Pochow (-1912)
Pokrovka see (1) Leninskoye
  (3); (2) Priamursky
Pokrovsk see Engels
Pokrovskoye see (1) Priazov-
  skoye; (2) Velikooktyabrsky
Pola see Istria
Polanice Zdrój. Town, south-
  western Poland : Bad Altheide
  (-1945), Germany
Polanów. Town, northwestern
  Poland : Pollnow (-1945),
  Germany
Połczyn Zdrój. Town, northwest-
  ern Poland : Bad Polzin
  (-1945), Germany
Polessk. Town, Kaliningrad
  Oblast, RSFSR : Labiau
  (-1946), Germany (-1945)
Polesskoye. Urban settlement,
  Kiev Oblast, Ukrainian SSR :
  Khabno(ye) (-c. 1935), Kagano-

vich (c. 1935-c. 1940), Kag-
anovichi pervyye (c. 1940-57)
Polevskoy. Town, Sverdlovsk
Oblast, RSFSR : Polevskoy
Zavod (-1928)
Polevskoy Zavod see Polevskoy
Police. Suburb of Szczecin,
northwestern Poland : Pölitz
(-1945), Germany
Poliny Osipenko, imeni. Village,
Khabarovsk Kray, RSFSR :
Kerbi (-1939)
Pölitz see Police
Polkowice. Town, western Po-
land : Polkwitz (-1938),
Germany; Heerwegen (1938-
45), Germany
Polkwitz see Polkowice
Pollnow see Polanów
Pologi. Town, Zaporozhye
Oblast, Ukrainian SSR :
Chubarovka (c. 1928-39)
Polonia. Settlement, Manitoba,
Canada : Huns Valley
(-1921)
Polovinka see (1) Ugleuralsky;
(2) Umaltinsky
Poltavka see Bashtanka
Poltavskaya see Krasnoarmey-
skaya (2)
Poltoratsk see Ashkhabad
Poludeno see Poludino
Poludino. Village, North
Kazakhstan Oblast, Kazakh
SSR : Poludeno (-1937)
Polyarny. Town, Murmansk
Oblast, RSFSR : Aleksan-
drovsk (-1930s)
Polzukhi see Pobednaya (1)
Pomabamba see Azurduy
Pomba see Rio Pomba
Pombachi see Komsomolabad
Pomoriye. City, eastern
Bulgaria : Ankhialo (-1934)
Pompei. Town, southern Italy
: Valle di Pompei (-1928)
Ponizovkino see Krasny
Profintern (2)
Ponoka. Town, Alberta, Cana-
da : Siding No. 14 (-1904)
Pont-du-Chéliff see Sidi Bel
Atar
Ponthierville see Ubundi

Pontolívadon. Village, northern
Greece : Néa Kóme (-1960s)
Poona Bayabao. Municipality,
Lanao, Philippines : Gata
(-1956)
Popasnaya. Town, Voroshilovgrad
Oblast, Ukrainian SSR : Kaga-
novicha L. M., imeni (1938-43)
Poplar Head see Dothan
Popova Luka see Ozyornaya (2)
Popovichskaya see Kalininskaya
Popovka see Oreshenka
Porechye see Demidov
Poronaysk. Town, Sakhalin
Oblast, RSFSR : Shikuka
(1905-46), Japan (-1945)
Porosyatniki see Mayachnaya
Porozhsky. Urban settlement,
Irkutsk Oblast, RSFSR :
Bratsk (-c. 1960)
Porrette Terme. Town, north-
central Italy : Bagni della
Porretta (-c. 1931)
Porsy see Kalinin (1)
Porta Littoria see La Thuile
Port Arthur [Lüshun]. City,
northeastern China : Ryojun
(1905-45), Japan
Port-Cartier. Town, Quebec,
Canada : Shelter Bay (*1918-
1950s)
Port Durnford see Bur Gavo
Port Étienne see Nouadhibou
Port Florence see Kisumu
Port Francqui see Ilebo
Port Gueydon see Azetfoun
Port Harrison see Inoucdjouac
Port Herald see Nsanje
Port Hueneme. City, California,
USA : Hueneme (-1940)
Port Kelang. Town, southwestern
Malaya, Malaysia : Port Swet-
tenham (1971)
Port-Khorly see Khorly
Port Laoise. Town, County
Laois, Ireland : Maryborough
(-?)
Port Lyautey see Kenitra
Port Nouveau-Québec. Town,
Quebec, Canada : George
River (-1967)
Pôrto. City, northeastern Bra-
zil, South America : Marruás

(-1930s), João Pessoa
(1930s-44)
Pôrto Alegre see Luzilândia
Porto Amélia see Pemba
Porto Azzurro. Town, Elba,
central Italy : Porto
Longone (-1949)
Porto Longone see Porto
Azzurro
Porto Maurizio see Imperia
Pôrto Real see Iguatama
Porto Rico see Puerto Rico
Pôrto Seguro see Guadalupe
Porto Valter. Town, western
Brazil, South America :
Humaitá (-1944)
Port Radium. Village, North-
west Territories, Canada :
Eldorado (*1929-44)
Port St. Johns see Umzimvuba
Port Swettenham see Port
Kelang
Portuguese East Africa see
Mozambique
Portuguese Guinea see Guinea-
Bissau
Portuguese Timor see Timor
Timur
Portuguese West Africa see
Angola
Posen see Poznań
Poshow. Town, southern China
: Yungning (-1915), Kuhwa
(1915-33)
Posmahlen see Pushkino (1)
Possedimenti Italiani dell' Egeo
see Dodecanese
Poste de la Baleine. Town,
Quebec, Canada : Great
Whale River (-1967)
Postojna. Town, northwestern
Yugoslavia : Postumia
(-1947), Italy
Postumia see Postojna
Pouso Alto see Piracanjuba
Powell. City, Wyoming, USA
: Camp Coulter (*1906-09)
Power House see Drayton
Valley
Poyang [P'o-yang]. Town,
southeastern China : Jaochow
(-1912)
Poyo del Cid. Village, eastern

Spain : El Poyo (-1962)
Pozharskoye. Village, Primorsky
Kray, RSFSR : Tikhonovka
(-1939)
Poznań. City, western Poland :
Posen (-1919, 1939-45), Ger-
many
Prabuty. Town, northeastern
Poland : Riesenburg (-1919,
1919-45), Germany
Praia da Condúcia. Village,
eastern Mozambique, south-
eastern Africa : Choca (-1971)
Prainha see Miracatu
Prassberg see Mozirje
Prata see Nova Prata
Prausnitz see Prusice
Praust see Pruszcz (Gdański)
Pravda. Urban settlement,
Sakhalin Oblast, RSFSR :
Hirochi (1905-46), Japan
(-1945)
Pravdino. Village, Kaliningrad
Oblast, RSFSR : Grumbkow-
felde (-c. 1930), Germany;
Grumbkowkeiten (c. 1930-45),
Germany
Pravdinsk. Town, Kaliningrad
Oblast, RSFSR : Friedland
(-1946), Germany (-1945)
Pravoberezhnoye see Novy
Karachay
Predgornoye. Village, Checheno-
Ingush Autonomous SSR, RSFSR
: Staryye Atagi (-1944)
Preobrazhenskaya see Kikvidze
Presidencia de la Plaza. Town,
northern Argentina, South
America : Presidente de la
Plaza (-early 1940s)
Presidente de la Plaza see
Presidencia de la Plaza
Presidente Dutra. City, north-
eastern Brazil, South America
: Curador (-1948)
Presidente Juán Perón see
Chaco
Presidente Vargas see (1) Ita-
bira; (2) Nova Era
President González Videla see
Greenwich Island
President Roxas. Barrio, Leyte,
Philippines : Mati (-1957)

Presnya see Krasnaya
Presnya
Pressburg see Bratislava
Preussisch Eylau see Bagrationovsk
Preussisch Friedland see Debrzno
Preussisch Holland see Pasłęk
Preussisch Stargard see Starogard (Gdański)
Priamursky. Urban settlement, Jewish Autonomous Oblast, Khabarovsk Kray, RSFSR : Pokrovka (-c. 1960)
Priargunsk. Urban settlement, Chita Oblast, RSFSR : Tsurukhaytuy (-1962)
Priazovskoye. Urban settlement, Zaporozhye Oblast, Ukrainian SSR : Pokrovskoye (-c. 1935)
Pribalkhash see Balkhash
Příbor. Town, north-central Czechoslovakia : Freiberg (-1919, 1939-45), Germany
Pridnestrovskoye. Village, Moldavian SSR : Vertyuzhany (-c. 1960)
Pridorozhnoye see Khulkhuta
Prikumsk see Budyonnovsk
Primkenau see Przemków
Primorsk (1). Town, Kaliningrad Oblast, RSFSR : Fischhausen (-1946), Germany (-1945)
Primorsk (2). Town, Leningrad Oblast, RSFSR : Koivisto (-1949), Finland (-1940)
Primorsk (3). Urban settlement, Volgograd Oblast, RSFSR : Lugovaya Proleyka (-c. 1960)
Primorskoye (1). Village, Crimean Oblast, Ukrainian SSR : Mayak-Salyn (-1944)
Primorskoye (2). Urban settlement, Zaporozhye Oblast, Ukrainian SSR : Nogaysk (-c. 1960)
Primorskoye (3). Urban settlement, Donetsk Oblast, Ukrainian SSR : Sartana (-1946)
Primorsky. Urban settlement,

Primorsky Kray, RSFSR : Ust-Mongugay (-c. 1960)
Primorye. Village, Minsk Oblast, Belorussian SSR : Skulovka (-1964)
Prince George. City, British Columbia, Canada : Fort George (-1915)
Principele-Nicolae see Decemvrie 30, 1947
Prinkipo see Büyükada
Prins Hendrik Top see Yamin, Puncak
Priozyorsk. Town, Leningrad Oblast, RSFSR : Keksgolm [Kexholm, Käkisalmi] (-1948), Finland (-1940)
Prishib see Leninsk (1)
Pristanskoye. Village, Omsk Oblast, RSFSR : Izylbash (-?), Molotovo (?-1957)
Pristansky. Urban settlement, Karakalpak Autonomous SSR, Uzbek SSR : Nukus (-c. 1960)
Pristen. Urban settlement, Kursk Oblast, RSFSR : Maryino (-c. 1960)
Pritchard. Town, British Columbia, Canada : Pemberton Spur (-1911)
Priupsky. Urban settlement, Tula Oblast, RSFSR : Milenino (-c. 1960)
Priverno. Town, south-central Italy : Piperno (-1928)
Privolzhsk. Town, Ivanovo Oblast, RSFSR : Yakovlevskoye (-1941)
Privolzhskoye. Village, Saratov Oblast, RSFSR : Kukkus (-1941)
Privolzhsky. Suburb of Astrakhan, Astrakhan Oblast, RSFSR : Kalmytsky Bazar (-1936), Kanukov (1936-44)
Proástion. Village, eastern Greece : Paraprástaina (-1960s)
Prochowice. Town, southwestern Poland : Parchwitz (-1945), Germany
Proctor. Village, Minnesota, USA : Proctorknott (-1939)
Proctorknott see Proctor

Prokhladnoye. Village, Crimean Oblast, Ukrainian SSR : Partizanskoye (-c. 1960)

Proletarsk (1). Urban settlement, Leninabad Oblast, Tadzhik SSR : Dragomirovo (-?)

Proletarsk (2). Suburb of Lisichansk, Voroshilovgrad Oblast, Ukrainian SSR : Nesvetevich (-?)

Proletarsk (3). Town, Rostov Oblast, RSFSR : Proletarskaya (-1970)

Proletarskaya see Proletarsk (3)

Proletarskaya Pobeda see Pirogovsky

Proletarsky (1). Urban settlement, Belgorod Oblast, RSFSR : Gotnya (-?)

Proletarsky (2). Urban settlement, Moscow Oblast, RSFSR : Proletary (-1928)

Proletary see Proletarsky (2)

Promyshlennovsky. Urban settlement, Kemerovo Oblast, RSFSR : Bolshaya Promyshlenka (-c. 1960)

Promzino see Surskoye

Propoysk see Slavgorod

Proskurov see Khmelnitsky

Prossnitz see Prostějov

Prostějov. City, central Czechoslovakia : Prossnitz (-1918, 1939-45), Germany

Prudnik. City, southwestern Poland : Neustadt (-1945), Germany

Prusice. Town, southwestern Poland : Prausnitz (-1945), Germany

Pruszcz (Gdański). Town, northern Poland : Praust (-1945), Germany

Przemków. Town, western Poland : Primkenau (-1945), Germany

Przemyśl. Town, southeastern Poland : [right bank of River San] Peremyshl (1939-40), USSR; [left bank] Deutsch Przemysl (1939-40), Germany

Przhevalsk. Capital of Issyk-Kul Oblast, Kirgiz SSR : Karakol (1869-89, 1921-39)

Przhevalskoye. Village, Smolensk Oblast, RSFSR : Sloboda (-c. 1960)

Psedakh see Alanskoye

Psirtskha see Novy Afon

Pskov. Capital of Pskov Oblast, RSFSR : Pleskau (1941-44), Germany

Psyché see Hagíos Nikólaos

Puchow see (1) Puhsien [P'u-hsien]; (2) Yüngtsi [Yüng-chi]

Pudjut Point. Cape, northwestern Java, Indonesia : Saint Nicholas Point (-1963)

Puebla see La Puebla del Río

Puebla de D. Fadrique see Villa de D. Fadrique

Puebla de la Mujer Muerta see Puebla de la Serra

Puebla de la Serra. Village, central Spain : Puebla de la Mujer Muerta (-c. 1940)

Puebla de Lillo. Village, northwestern Spain : Lillo (-c. 1920)

Pueblo de la Capilla see Sauce del Yí

Pueblo Viejo see Villa Canales

Puente de Montañana. Village, northeastern Spain : Montañana (-c. 1960)

Puerh see Ningerh

Puerto Acosta. Town, western Bolivia, South America : Huaicho (-1908)

Puerto Aguirre see Puerto Iguazú

Puerto Chicama. Town, northwestern Peru, South America : Malabrigo (-1920)

Puerto de Cabras see Puerto del Rosario

Puerto de Castilla. Village, east-central Spain : Casas del Puerto de Tornavacas (-c. 1940)

Puerto del Rosario. Village, Gran Canaria, Canary Islands : Puerto de Cabras (-c. 1960)

Puerto de San Juan see Puerto Lápice

Puerto de Son. Village, northwestern Spain : Son (-c. 1950)

Puerto Iguazú. Village, northeastern Argentina, South America : Puerto Aguirre (-1940s)

Puerto Lápice. Village, south-central Spain : Puerto de San Juan (-c. 1930)

Puerto México see Coatzacoalcos

Puerto Pérez. Town, western Bolivia, South America : Chililaya (-1900)

Puerto Rico. Island commonwealth, West Indies : Porto Rico (-1932)

Puerto-Seguro. Village, western Spain : Barba de Puerco (-c. 1960)

Pugachyov. Town, Saratov Oblast, RSFSR : Nikolayevsk (-1918)

Pugachyovo. Village, Sakhalin Oblast, RSFSR : Maguntanhama (1905-45), Japan

Puhsien [P'u-hsien]. Town, north-central China : Puchow (-1913)

Puigtiñós see Montferri

Pukova see Komsomolskaya

Pulau Blakang Mati see Sentosa

Puławy. Town, eastern Poland : Novaya Aleksandriya (-c. 1914), Russia

Pulgan see Frunzenskoye

Pulin see Chervonoarmeysk (1)

Pułtusk. Town, east-central Poland : Ostenburg (1939-45), Germany

Pungarabato see Altamirano

Punta Arenas. City, southern Chile, South America : Magallanes (1927-37)

Punyü. Town, southeastern China : Shikiu (-1946)

Punyü see Canton

Pupelichi see Krynichka

Pupsa see Maysk (2)

Pushkin. Town, Leningrad Oblast, RSFSR : Tsarskoye Selo (-1918), Detskoye Selo

(1918-37)

Pushkino (1). Village, Kaliningrad Oblast, RSFSR : Dosmahlen (-1946), Germany (-1945)

Pushkino (2). Urban settlement, Saratov Oblast, RSFSR : Urbakh (-1941)

Püspöknádasd see Mecseknádasd

Pustoy Ugol see Kolosovka (2)

Pustynka see Svetlaya Roshcha

Putao. Government post, northern Burma : Fort Hertz (-?)

Putien [P'u-t'ien]. Town, southeastern China : Hinghwa (-1913)

Putyatin. Urban settlement, Putyatin island, Primorsky Kray, RSFSR : Nazimovo (c. 1947-c. 1960)

Puyang [P'u-yang]. Town, north-central China : Kaichow (-1913)

Puziki see (1) Borovshchina (2); (2) Safonovo

Puzol see Tugaoen

Puzovichi see (1) Partizanskaya (2); (2) Pavlovo

Pwani. Administrative region, eastern Tanzania, eastern Africa : Coast (-1976)

Pyandzh. Town, Kulyab Oblast, Tadzhik SSR : Saray Komar (-1931), Baumanabad (1931-36), Kirovabad (1936-63)

Pyandzh see Dusti

Pyansky Perevoz see Perevoz

Pyany Les see Sosnovaya (2)

Pyarnu = Pärnu

Pyatikhatika see Pyatikhatki

Pyatikhatki. Town, Dnepropetrovsk Oblast, Ukrainian SSR : Pyatikhatka (-1944)

Pyrénées-Atlantiques. Department, southwestern France : Basses-Pyrénées (-1969)

Pyshkino-Troitskoye see Pervomayskoye (7)

Pyshma see Verkhnyaya Pyshma

Pyshminsky Zavod see Staropyshminsk

Quebec West see Vanier (2)

Queen Elizabeth National Park
see Ruwenzori National
Park
Queen's County see Laois
Queenstown see Cóbh
Quezon. Province, Luzon,
Philippines : Tayabas
(-1946)
Quingua see Plaridel (2)
Quintanilla de Abajo see
Quintanilla de Onésimo
Quintanilla de Onésimo. Village,
north-central Spain : Quin-
tanilla de Abajo (-c. 1950)
Qytet Stalin = Stalin

Rača. Town, west-central
Czechoslovakia : Račisdorf
(-1946)
Racibórz. Town, south-central
Poland : Ratibor (-1945),
Germany
Račisdorf see Rača
Radeče. Village, northwestern
Yugoslavia : Ratschach
(-1918), Germany
Radishchevo (1). Village,
Ulyanovsk Oblast, RSFSR :
Dvoryanskaya Tereshka
(-1918)
Radishchevo (2). Village, Penza
Oblast, RSFSR : Verkhneye
Ablyazovo (-?)
Radków. Town, southwestern
Poland : Wünschelburg
(-1945), Germany
Radmannsdorf see Radovljica
Radomir. Mountain, southwest-
ern Bulgaria : Kalabak
(-1967)
Radomsko. Town, south-central
Poland : Noworadomsk
(-1914)
Radovitsky. Urban settlement,
Moscow Oblast, RSFSR :
Tsentralny (-c. 1960)
Radovljica. Village, northwest-
ern Yugoslavia : Radmanns-
dorf (-1918), Germany
Radzivilov see Chervonoar-

meysk (2)
Radzivilovichi see Dzerzhinsk
(3)
Ragnit see Neman
Ragusa see Dubrovnik
Rahouia. Village, northern
Algeria, northern Africa :
Montgolfier (-c. 1962)
Rainbow City. Town, Panama
Canal Zone, Central America
: Silver City (-?)
Raivola see Roshchino (2)
Rajaori. District, northern
India : Riasi (-c. 1948)
Rajasthan. State, northwestern
India : Rajputana (1818-1950)
Rajhenburg. Village, northwestern
Yugoslavia : Reichenburg
(-1918), Germany
Rajputana see Rajasthan
Rakhmanovka. Urban settlement,
Dnepropetrovsk Oblast,
Ukrainian SSR : Aleksandrov
Dar (-c. 1960)
Rakoyedovshchina see Pobednaya
(2)
Rakushevo. Village, Mogilyov
Oblast, Belorussian SSR :
Likhinichi (-1967)
Ramat Gan. City, west-central
Israel : En Gannim (*1920-c.
1921)
Ramit. Village, Tadzhik SSR :
Uramir (-c. 1935)
Ramon Magsaysay. Barrio,
Zamboanga del Norte, Philip-
pines : Palandoc (-1968)
Randolph see Brea
Ranenburg see Chaplygin
Rangoon Heights. Mountain,
North Island, New Zealand :
Misery, Mount (-1966)
Rankovićevo. Village, northeast-
ern Yugoslavia : Karlovac
(-1947)
Rankovićevo see Kraljevo
Rantomari see Yablochny
Raritan see (1) Edison; (2)
Highland Park
Ras Asir. Cape, northeastern
Somalia, eastern Africa :
Guardafui (-?)
Ras el Ma. Town, northwestern

Algeria, northern Africa :
Bedeau (-c. 1962)
Ras el Oued. Village, north-
eastern Algeria, northern
Africa : Tocqueville (-c.
1962)
Rassvet. Village, Vitebsk
Oblast, Belorussian SSR :
Chertovshchina (-1964)
Rassvetnaya (1). Village, Gomel
Oblast, Belorussian SSR :
Kobylyanka (-1964)
Rassvetnaya (2). Village, Minsk
Oblast, Belorussian SSR :
Tsitskovichi (-1964)
Rastenburg see Kętrzyn
Rastorguyevo see Vidnoye
Rastyapino see Dzerzhinsk (1)
Rateau see Lewis
Rathluirc. Town, County Cork,
Ireland : Charleville (-1939)
Ratibor see Racibórz
Ratschach see Radeče
Ratzebuhr see Okonek
Rauschen see Svetlogorsk (1)
Rautenberg see Uzlovoye
Rautu see Sosnovo
Rawicz. Town, west-central
Poland : Rawitsch (1939-45),
Germany
Rawitsch see Rawicz
Razdan (1). Town, Armenian
SSR : Akhta (-1959)
Razdan (2). Settlement, Armen-
ian SSR : Ulukhanlu (-?),
Zangibasar (?-1964)
Razdolnaya. Village, Vitebsk
Oblast, Belorussian SSR :
Bezdelichi (-1964)
Razdolnoye. Urban settlement,
Crimean Oblast, Ukrainian
SSR : Ak-Sheikh (-1944)
Razino. Village, Kaliningrad
Oblast, RSFSR : Doristhal
(-1945), Germany
Razlog. City, southwestern
Bulgaria : Mekhomiya (-1925),
Turkey
Recz. Town, northwestern
Poland : Reetz (-1945), Ger-
many
Redcliff see Ikawai
Redencão see Redenção da

Serra
Redenção da Serra. City, south-
eastern Brazil, South America
: Redenção (-1944)
Red Jacket see Calumet
Red Oak. City, Iowa, USA :
Red Oak Junction (-1901)
Red Oak Junction see Red Oak
Reetz see Recz
Regar see Tursunzade
Regele Carol II see Suvorovo
(2)
Regele Mihai I see Suvorovo
(2)
Regenwalde see Resko
Reïbell see Ksar Chellala
Reichenau see (1) Bogatynia;
(2) Rychnov nad Kněžnou
Reichenau (bei Gablonz) see
Rychnov
Reichenbach see Dzerżoniów
Reichenberg see Liberec
Reichenburg see Rajhenburg
Reichenstein see Złoty Stok
Reichshof see Rzeszow
Reichstadt see Zákupy
Reifnig see Ribnica (na
Pohorju)
Relizane see Ighil Izane
Remate de Males. Town, north-
western Brazil, South Amer-
ica : Benjamin Constant (-1939)
Remchi. Village, northwestern
Algeria, northern Africa :
Montagnac (-c. 1962)
Remennikovo. Village, Volgograd
Oblast, RSFSR : Oberdorf
(-1941)
Renault see Sidi M'Hamed Ben
Ali
Repelen-Baerl see Rheinkamp
Repino. Urban settlement,
Leningrad Oblast, RSFSR :
Kuokkala (-1948), Finland
(-1940)
Reppen see Rzepin
Republic of Ireland = Ireland
Republic of South Africa =
South Africa
Rerik. Town, northeastern East
Germany : Alt Gaarz (-1938)
Reriutaba. City, northeastern
Brazil, South America :

Santa Cruz (-1944)
Residensia. Township, Trans-
vaal, South Africa : Evaton
(*1904-62)
Resko. Town, northwestern
Poland : Regenwalde (-1945),
Germany
Resulayn see Ceylanpinar
Reszel. Town, northeastern
Poland : Rössel (-1945),
Germany
Reutov. Town, Moscow Oblast,
RSFSR : Reutovo (-1940)
Reutovo see Reutov
Revel see Tallinn
Reza'iyeh [Rizaiyeh]. City and
lake, northwestern Iran :
Urmia (-1926)
Rezekne. Town, Latvian SSR :
Rezhitsa (-1920)
Rezhitsa see Rezekne
Rheinkamp. City, western West
Germany : Repelen-Baerl
(-?)
Rhodesia. Republic, southeastern
Africa : Southern Rhodesia
(*1923-65)
Ri-Aba. Town, Macias Nguema
Biyogo Island, Equatorial
Guinea, western Africa :
La Concepción (-1974)
Riachão see Riachão do Dantas
Riachao do Dantas. City,
northeastern Brazil, South
America : Riachão (-1944)
Riasi see Rajaori
Ribas do Rio Pardo. City,
western Brazil, South
America : Rio Pardo (-1944)
Ribeirão see Guapó
Ribnica (na Pohorju). Village,
northwestern Yugoslavia :
Reifnig (-1918), Germany
Rickenbacker Air Force Base.
Ohio, USA : Lockbourne
Air Force Base (*1942-74)
Ridder see Leninogorsk (2)
Riesenburg see Prabuty
Rigglådes see Áno Leukímme
Rijeka. City, northwestern
Yugoslavia : Fiume (1924-
45), Italy
Rimske Toplice. Village, north-

western Yugoslavia : Römerbad
(-1918), Germany
Río Benito see Mbini
Rio Bonito see (1) Caiapônia;
(2) Tangará
Rio Branco see (1) Arcoverde;
(2) Paratinga; (3) Roraima;
(4) Visconde do Rio Branco
Río Branco. Town, northeastern
Uruguay, South America :
Artigas (-1909)
Rio Brilhante. City, western
Brazil, South America : Entre
Rios (-1943), Caiuás (1944-48)
Rio Claro see Itaverá
Rio da Dúvida see Roosevelt,
Rio
Rio das Flores. City, south-
eastern Brazil, South America
: Santa Teresa (-1943)
Rio do Sul. City, southern
Brazil, South America : Bela
Aliança (*1903-?), Itajahy do
Sul (?-?)
Rio Novo see (1) Ipiaú; (2)
Itapoama
Rio Pardo see (1) Iúna; (2)
Ribas do Rio Pardo; (3) Rio
Pardo de Minas
Rio Pardo de Minas. City,
southeastern Brazil, South
America : Rio Pardo (-1944)
Rio Pomba. City, southeastern
Brazil, South America : Pomba
(-1948)
Rio Prêto see (1) Ibipetuba;
(2) São José do Rio Prêto
Río Seco see Villa de María
Rippin see Rypin
Rishabhatírtha. Town, central
India : Gunji (-1950s)
Rishtan see Kuybyshevo (3)
Ritaville see Phou-Khao-Khuai
Ritlyab see Sayasan
Riva see Riva-del-Garda
Riva-del-Garda. Town, north-
eastern Italy : Riva (-1971)
Riversdale see Albertinia
Rivet see Meftah
Riviera see Riviera Beach
Riviera Beach. City, Florida,
USA : Riviera (-1940)
Rivière-du-Loup. City, Quebec,

Canada : Fraserville (-1919)
Rivoli see Hasei Nameche
Rizaiyeh = Reza'iyeh
Rizal (1). Municipality, Cagayan,
Philippines : Manawan
(-1914)
Rizal (2). Barrio, Sorsogon,
Philippines : Tublijon (-1914)
Robertshoogte see Voortrek-
kerhoogte
Robinson Crusoe. Island, Juan
Fernandez group, Chile :
Más a Tierro (-1962),
Marino Alejandro Selkirk
(1962-66)
Rock Springs. Village, Wiscon-
sin, USA : Ableman (-1947)
Roda see Stadtroda
Rodaugé. Village, western
Greece : Nesísta Néas
Helládos (-1960s)
Rodó = (José Enrique) Rodó
Rogaland. County, southwestern
Norway : Stavanger (-1918)
Rogaška Slatina. Village,
northwestern Yugoslavia :
Rohitsch-Sauerbrunn (-1918),
Germany
Rohitsch-Sauerbrunn see
Rogaška-Slatina
Rolândia. City, southern Brazil,
South America : Caviúna
(1944-48)
Romanov see Dzerzhinsk (4)
Romanov-Borisoglebsk see
Tutayev
Romanovka see Bessarabka
Romanov-na-Murmane see
Murmansk
Romanovsky Khutor see
Kropotkin (1)
Römerbad see Rimske Toplice
Rommani. Town, northwestern
Morocco, northwestern
Africa : Marchand (-1971)
Romsdal see More og Romsdal
Rondônia. Territory, western
Brazil, South America :
Guaporé (*1943-56)
Ronne Land. Territory, Antarc-
tica : Edith Ronne Land
(*1948-?)
Roosevelt. Borough, New Jersey,

USA : Jersey Homesteads
(*1933-c. 1940)
Roosevelt see Carteret
Roosevelt, Rio. River, west-
central Brazil, South America
: Rio da Dúvida (-1914)
Roosevelttown. Town, New York,
USA : Nyando (-1934)
Roraima. Territory, northern
Brazil, South America : Rio
Branco (*1943-62)
Rosário see (1) Rosário do
Catete; (2) Rosário do Sul
Rosário do Catete. City, north-
eastern Brazil, South America
: Rosário (-1944)
Rosário do Sul. City, southern
Brazil, South America :
Rosário (-1944)
Rosenberg see (1) Olesno;
(2) Susz
Roshcha. Village, Vitebsk Oblast,
Belorussian SSR : Gnilyaki
(-1964)
Roshchino (1). Village, Gomel
Oblast, Belorussian SSR :
Kusochek (-1964)
Roshchino (2). Urban settlement,
Leningrad Oblast, RSFSR :
Raivola (-1948), Finland (-1940)
Roshchino (3). Village, Vitebsk
Oblast, Belorussian SSR :
Zvyagi (-1964)
Rössel see Reszel
Rossitten see Rybachy (2)
Rossman Lake. Lake, Manitoba,
Canada : Fishing Lake (-1967)
Rossony. Urban settlement,
Vitebsk Oblast, Belorussian
SSR : Stanislavovo (-c. 1940)
Rostkovsky Rudnik see Oktya-
brskoy Revolyutsii, imeni
Rostovtsevo see Krasnogvardeysk
Rot-Front see Dobropolye
Rouffach see Ebn Ziad
Rovigno (d'Istria) see Rovinj
Rovinj. Town, northwestern
Yugoslavia : Rovigno (d'Istria)
(-?), Italy
Rovira. Town, west-central
Colombia, South America :
Miraflores (-1930)
Rovnoye. Urban settlement,

Saratov Oblast, RSFSR :
Zelman (-1941)
Równe see Złoty Stok
Roxas. City, Capiz, Philip-
pines : Capiz (-?)
Rozenburg see Rozovka
Rozhdestvenskaya see (1)
Dzerzhinskoye (2); (2)
Sivashskoye
Rozovka. Urban settlement,
Zaporozhye Oblast, Ukrain-
ian SSR : Rozenburg (-c.
1935), Lyuksemburg (c.
1935-41)
Rozy Lyuksemburg. Village,
Gomel Oblast, Belorussian
SSR : Odesskaya (-1919)
Rozy Lyuksemburg, Cape see
Lokot, Cape
Ruanda see Rwanda
Rubetsu see Kyubushevo (4)
Rubezhnaya see Rubezhnoye
Rubezhnoye. Town, Voroshilov-
grad Oblast, Ukrainian SSR
: Rubezhnaya (-c. 1940)
Ruby Beach see Jacksonville
Beach
Rudaka see Aniva
Rudnaya Pristan. Urban settle-
ment, Primorsky Kray,
RSFSR : Tetyukhe-Pristan
(-1972)
Rudnichny. Urban settlement,
Sverdlovsk Oblast, RSFSR :
Auerbakhovsky Rudnik (-1933)
Rudnik imeni Shvartsa see
Zhyoltyye Vody
Rudnik Ingichka see Ingichka
Rudny. Urban settlement,
Primorsky Kray, RSFSR :
Lifudzin (-1972)
Rukhlovo see Skovorodino
Rummelsburg see Miastko
Rumyantsevo see Lenina V.I.,
imeni
Rupert House. Village, Quebec,
Canada : Fort-Rupert (-?)
Ruše. Village, northwestern
Yugoslavia : Maria Rast
(-1918), Germany
Rushan. Village, Gorno-Badakh-
shan Autonomous Oblast,
Tadzhik SSR : Kalai-Vamar

(-c. 1935)
Russkoye Selo see Markhamat
Rust see El Cerrito
Ruth. Town, North Carolina,
USA : Hampton (-1939)
Ruth, Mount. Mountain, Antarc-
tica : Ruth Black, Mount
(?-1967)
Ruth Black, Mount see Ruth,
Mount
Ruthenia see Transcarpathian
Oblast
Rutland Water. Reservoir,
Leicestershire, England, UK :
Empingham Reservoir (*1971-
76)
Rutten. Lake, Manitoba, Canada :
Karsakuwigamak (-1972)
Ruwenzori National Park. South-
western Uganda, eastern Africa
: Queen Elizabeth National
Park (*1952-?)
Rwanda. Republic, east-central
Africa : Ruanda (-1962)
Rybachy (1). Urban settlement,
Kamchatka Oblast, RSFSR :
Novaya Tarya (-c. 1960)
Rybachy (2). Urban settlement,
Kaliningrad Oblast, RSFSR :
Rossitten (-1946), Germany
(-1945)
Rybalskaya see Karlo-Marksovo
Rybinsk. Town, Yaroslavl Oblast,
RSFSR : Shcherbakov (1946-57)
Rychnov. Village, northwestern
Czechoslovakia : Reichenau
(bei Gablonz) (-1918, 1939-45),
Germany
Rychnov nad Knežnou. Town,
east-central Czechoslovakia :
Reichenau (-1918, 1939-45),
Germany
Rykovo see Yenakiyevo
Rykovskoye see Kirovskoye (4)
Ryojun see Port Arthur
Rypin. Town, north-central
Poland : Rippin (1939-45),
Germany
Rzepin. Town, western Poland :
Reppen (-1945), Germany
Rzeszow. City, southeastern
Poland : Reichshof (1939-45),
Germany

Saar (in Mähren) see Zdar
Saarlautern see Saarlouis
Saarlouis. City, western West
    Germany : Saarlautern
    (1936-45)
Saaz see Zatec
Sabah. State, eastern Malaysia
    : North Borneo (-1963)
Sabaneta see Santiago Rodríguez
Sabani see Gabaldon
Sabi Game Reserve see Kruger
    National Park
Sablino see Ulyanovka
Sabra. Village, northwestern
    Algeria, northern Africa :
    Turenne (-c. 1962)
Saby see Bogatyye Saby
Sacramento see Itatupã
Sadovoye. Village, Astrakhan
    Oblast, RSFSR : Kegulta
    (-1944)
Šafárikovo. Town, southwestern
    Czechoslovakia : Tornala
    (-1949)
Safonovo. Village, Mogilyov
    Oblast, Belorussian SSR :
    Puziki (-1964)
Sagan see Żagań
Sagbayan. Municipality, Bohol,
    Philippines : Borja (-1957)
Saglouc. Village, Quebec,
    Canada : Sugluk (-1975)
Sahiwal. City, northeastern
    Pakistan : Montgomery (-?)
Saigon see Ho Chi Minh (City)
Saint-Aimé see Jdiouia
Saint-Alban see Saint-Alban-
    Leysse
Saint-Alban-Leysse. Commune,
    southeastern France : Saint-
    Alban (-1946)
Saint-Arnaud see El Eulma
Saint-Barthélemy-le-Plain. Vil-
    lage, southern France :
    Saint-Barthélemy-le-Plein
    (-1939)
Saint-Barthélemy-le-Plein see
    Saint-Barthélemy-le-Plain
Saint-Bon see Saint-Bon-Taren-
    taise
Saint-Bon-Tarentaise. Village,
    southeastern France : Saint-
    Bon (-1941)

Saint Briac see Saint-Briac-
    sur-Mer
Saint-Briac-sur-Mer. Village,
    western France : Saint-Briac
    (-1939)
Saint-Cloud see Gdyel
Saint-Dalmas-de-Tende. Village,
    southeastern France : San
    Dalmazzo di Tenda (-1947),
    Italy
Saint-Denis (-du-Sig) see Sig
Sainte-Geneviève see Pierrefonds
Saint-Étienne see Saint-Étienne-
    lès-Remiremont
Saint-Étienne-lès-Remiremont.
    Village, southeastern France :
    Saint-Étienne (-1937)
Saint-Eugène see Bologhine
St. Ferdinand see Florissant
Saint-Joseph-d'Alma see Alma
Saint-Leu see Bettioua
Saint-Louis see Boufatis
Saint-Lucien see Zahana
Saint-Macaire see Saint-Macaire-
    en-Mauges
Saint-Macaire-en-Mauges. Town,
    western France : Saint-Macaire
    (-1939)
St. Marks see Cofimvaba
Saint Nicholas Point see Pudjut,
    Point
Saint Paul. Town, Alberta,
    Canada : Saint Paul de Métis
    (*1912-19)
Saint Paul de Métis see Saint
    Paul
St. Petersburg see Leningrad
St. Petersburg Guberniya see
    Leningrad Guberniya
Saint-Pierre-de-la-Point-aux-
    Esquimaux see Havre-Saint-
    Pierre
Saint-Pierre-Saint-Paul see
    Ouled Moussa
St. Thomas see Charlotte
    Amalie
Sakaehama see Starodubskoye
Sakiz-Adasi see Chios
Salazar. City, southern Mozam-
    bique, southeastern Africa :
    Matola (-1972)
Salcedo. Municipality, Ilocos
    Sur, Philippines : Bauguen

(-1957)
Salegard see Salekhard
Salekhard. Capital of Yamalo-
Nenets Autonomous Okrug,
Tyumen Oblast, RSFSR :
Obdorsk (-1933), Salegard
(1933-38)
Salinas see (1) O'Connor;
(2) Salinópolis
Salinópolis. City, northern
Brazil, South America :
Salinas (-1944)
Salla. Commune, northeastern
Finland : Kursu (-1940)
Salla see Kuolayarvi
Salonika see Thessaloniki
Salop. County, west-central
England, UK : Shropshire
(-1974)
Salsk. Town, Rostov Oblast,
RSFSR : Torgovaya (-1926)
Salvacion (1). Barrio, Leyte,
Philippines : Cogon-Bingkay
(-1957)
Salvacion (2). Barrio, Palawan,
Philippines : Tapul (-1957)
Salyuzi see Kotelnikovo (2)
Salzburgen see Château-Salins
Salzgitter. City, northeastern
West Germany : Watenstadt-
Salzgitter (-1951)
Sama. Settlement, Sverdlovsk
Oblast, RSFSR : Severnaya
Sama (-c. 1960)
Samar. Province, Philippines :
Western Samar (-1969)
Samara see Kuybyshev (2)
Samarkandsky see Temirtau
Sambat see Lumangbayan
Samos. Island, Aegean Sea,
Greece : Susam-Adasi (-1913),
Turkey
Samothrace. Island, Aegean
Sea, Greece : Semadrek
(-1913), Turkey
Samsonovo see Amudarya
Samtredi see Samtredia
Samtredia. Town, Georgian
SSR : Samtredi (-1936)
San Angel see Silvestre
Domingo
San Antonio. Barrio, Oriental
Mindoro, Philippines :

Dalagan (-1969)
San Antonio (de Cortés). Town,
west-central Honduras, Cen-
tral America : Talpetate
(-early 1930s)
San Bartolomé see Venustiano
Carranza
San-Beyse see Choybalsan
San Carlos see Butuka-Luba
Sanchan see Koshan [K'o-shan]
San-chou see Hsin-yang
Sanchursk. Urban settlement,
Kirov Oblast, RSFSR :
Tsaryovo-Sanchursk (-1918)
San Cristóbal. Province, south-
central Dominican Republic,
West Indies : Trujillo (*1935-
61)
San Cristobal de Trabancos.
Village, east-central Spain :
Cebolla de Trabancos (-c. 1960)
San Dalmazzo di Tenda see
Saint-Dalmas-de-Tende
San Daniele del Carso see
Štanjel na Krasu
Sandanski. City, southwestern
Bulgaria : Sveti Vrach (-1949)
San Eugenio see Artigas
San Ferreol. Village, northeastern
Spain : Parroguia de Besalú
(-c. 1930)
Sanford see Guyman
San Francesco de Malabon see
General Trias
San Francisco (1). Municipality,
Surigao del Norte, Philippines
: Anao-aon (-1911)
San Francisco (2). Municipality,
Quezon, Philippines : Aurora
(-1967)
San Gabriel. Barrio, Quezon,
Philippines : Tubog (-1957)
San Giuliano Terme. Town,
central Italy : Bagni San
Giuliano (-1935)
Sangorodok see Ust-Vorkuta
Sangpiling see Tingsiang
Sanho see Santu
San Isidoro see Torrecilla sobre
Alesanco
San Isidro. Barrio, Ilocos Norte,
Philippines : Batuli (-1969)
San Isidro see Ureña

San Isidro de Potot see Burgos (2)

San Isidro Labrador see Labrador

Sanitary and Ship Canal. Linking southern branch of Chicago and Des Plaines Rivers, Illinois, USA : Chicago Drainage Canal (-1930)

San Jacinto see Catigbian

San Jaime de Llierca. Village, northeastern Spain : Palau de Montagut (-c. 1930)

San Jose (1). Municipality, Romblon, Philippines : Carabao Island (-1905)

San Jose (2). Barrio, La Union, Philippines : Garampang (-1957)

San Jose (3). Barrio, Catanduanes, Philippines : Oco (-1969)

San Jose Sur see Santo Niño (3)

San Juan. Province, west-central Dominican Republic, West Indies : Benefactor (*1938-61)

San Juan Bautista see Villahermosa

San Juan de Bocboc see Juan de Bolbok

San Juan de Bolbok. Municipality, Batangas, Philippines : San Juan de Bocboc (-1914)

San Juan de Guimba see Guimba

San Juan del Olmo. Village, east-central Spain : Grajos (-c. 1960)

San Juan de Mollet. Village, northeastern Spain : Mollet (-c. 1920)

San Juan de Villa Hermosa see Villahermosa

San Julián de Vallfogona. Village, northeastern Spain : Vallfogona (-1961)

Sankieh see Kiashan [Chiashan]

Sankiocheng see Haiyen

Sankioh see Santu

Sankt Leonard im Pitzdal. Village, western Austria : Pitzthal (-1935)

Sankt Leonhard see Bad Sankt Leonhard im Lavanttale

Sankt Marein see Šmarje (pri Jelšah)

San Luis see (1) Entre Ríos; (2) Sevilla

San Magro see Santiago (1)

San Manuel. Municipality, Isabela, Philippines : Callang (-1905)

San Martín see Tarapoto

San Martín de Tous. Village, northeastern Spain : Tous (-c. 1920)

San Martín Land see Antarctic Peninsula

San Miguel see (1) Diez y Ocho de Julio; (2) Sarrat

San Nicolás de Buenos Aires. Town, central Mexico, North America : (San Nicolás) Malpaís (-1941)

(San Nicolas) Malpaís see San Nicolás de Buenos Aires

San Pablo del Monte see Villa (General) Vicente Guerrero

San Pablo de Manta see Manta

San Pedro. Municipality, Laguna, Philippines : San Pedro Tunasan (-1914)

San Pedro Macati see Makati

San Pedro Remate see Bella Vista

San Pedro Tunasan see San Pedro

San Rafael see La Estrelleta

San Rogue. Barrio, Leyte, Philippines : Curba (-1957)

San Sadurní de Noya. Village, northeastern Spain : San Saturnino de Noya (-c. 1960)

San Saturnino de Noya see San Sadurní de Noya

Sanshui see Sünyi [Hsün-i]

Sansui. Town, southern China : Angshui (-1913), Lingshan (1926-31)

Santa Bárbara see Santa Bárbara d'Oeste

Santa Bárbara d'Oeste. City, southeastern Brazil, South

America : Santa Bárbara
(-1944)
Santa Clara see Las Villas
Santa Cruz see (1) Aracruz;
(2) Reriutaba; (3) Santa
Cruz do Sul
Santa Cruz das Palmeiras.
City, southeastern Brazil,
South America : Palmeiras
(-1944)
Santa Cruz de Bravo see
Felipe Carrillo Puerto
Santa Cruz (de Galeana) see
Juventino Rosas
Santa Cruz de Malabon see
Tanza
Santa Cruz de Tenerife. Pro-
vince, Canary Islands :
Canarias (-1927)
Santa Cruz do Sul. City,
southern Brazil, South
America : Santa Cruz
(-1944)
Santa Isabel see (1) João
Coelho; (2) Malabo;
(3) Tapuruquá
Santa Luzia see Luziânia
Santa Maria. Barrio, Occidental
Mindoro, Philippines :
Bulbugan (-1969)
Santa María de Barbará. Vil-
lage, northeastern Spain :
Barbará (-c. 1920)
Santa María del Tiétar. Vil-
lage, east-central Spain :
Escarabajosa (-c. 1960)
Santa Maria do Araguaia see
Araguacema
Santa Monica. Municipality,
Surigao del Norte, Philip-
pines : Sapao (-1967)
Santana see (1) Licania;
(2) Uruaçu
Santana de Tinonganine. Vil-
lage, southern Mozambique,
southeastern Africa : Tinon-
ganine (-1963)
Santana do Paranaíba see
Paranaíba
Santaokiao see Mitsang [Mi-
ts'ang]
Santarém see Ituberá
Santa Rita do Araguaia see

Guiratinga
Santa Rita (do Paranaíba) see
Itumbiara
Santa Rosa see (1) Bella
Unión; (2) Santa Rosa de
Viterbo; (3) Santo Thomas
Santa Rosa de Viterbo. City,
southeastern Brazil, South
America : Santa Rosa (-1944),
Icaturama (1944-48)
Santa Teresa see Rio das Flores
Santa Theresa. Barrio, Oriental
Mindoro, Philippines : Lang-
ang (-1969)
Santiago (1). Barrio, Ilocos
Norte, Philippines : San
Magro (-1968)
Santiago (2). City, southern
Brazil, South America :
Santiago do Boqueirão (-1938)
Santiago de Alcántara. Village,
western Spain : Santiago de
Carbajo (-c. 1960)
Santiago de Carbajo see Santiago
de Alcántara
Santiago (de Cuba) see Oriente
Santiago do Boqueirão see
Santiago (2)
Santiago Rodríguez. Town,
northwestern Dominican Re-
public, West Indies : Sabaneta
(-1936)
Santiváñez. Town, central Bo-
livia, South America : Caraza
(-1900s)
Santo see Kim
Santo Amaro see (1) General
Câmara; (2) Santo Amaro da
Imperatriz; (3) Santo Amaro
das Brotas
Santo Amaro da Imperatriz. Town,
southern Brazil, South Amer-
ica : Santo Amaro (-1944),
Cambirela (1944-48)
Santo Amaro das Brotas. City,
northeastern Brazil, South
America : Santo Amaro (-1944)
Santo Antônio (1). City, north-
eastern Brazil, South America : Padre Miguelinho (1944-
48)
Santo Antônio (2). City, southern
Brazil, South America : Santo

Antônio da Patrulha (-1938)
Santo Antônio see Santo
Antônio do Leverger
Santo Antônio da Cachoeira see
Itaguatins
Santo Antônio da Patrulha see
Santo Antonio (2)
Santo Antônio de Balsas see
Balsas
Santo Antônio do Leverger.
City, western Brazil, South
America : Santo Antônio do
Rio Abaixo (-1939), Santo
Antônio (1939-43), Leverger
(1944-48)
Santo Antônio do Rio Abaixo
see Santo Antônio do Lever-
ger
Santo Domingo. Capital of Do-
minican Republic, West
Indies : Ciudad Trujillo
(1936-61)
Santo Inácio. City, eastern
Brazil, South America :
Gamelleira do Assuruá
(-?), Assuruá (?-1939)
Santomischel see Zaniemyśl
Santo Niño (1). Municipality,
Cagayan, Philippines :
Faire (1914-69)
Santo Niño (2). Barrio, Leyte,
Philippines : Haclagan
(-1950)
Santo Niño (3). Barrio, Bohol,
Philippines : San Jose Sur
(-1968)
Santos Dumont. City, south-
eastern Brazil, South Amer-
ica : Palmyras (-1930s)
Santo Tomas. Barrio, Iloilo,
Philippines : Santa Rosa
(-1957)
Santo Tomas see Arcangel
Santu. Town, southern China :
Sankioh (-?), Sanho (?-
1942)
Sanyen see Wucheng [Wu-ch'eng]
São Benedito see (1) Benedi-
tinos; (2) Curuzu
São Bento see (1) São Bento
do Sul; (2) São Bento do
Una
São Bento do Sul. City,

southern Brazil, South Amer-
ica : São Bento (-1944), Serra
Alta (1944-48)
São Benta do Una. City, north-
eastern Brazil, South America
: São Bento (-1944)
São Domingos da Boa Vista see
Capim
São Domingos do Capim see
Capim
São Felipe see Içana
São Felippe see Eirunepé
São Francisco see (1) Francisco
do Maranhão; (2) Itapagé;
(3) Parapitinga; (4) São
Francisco do Conde; (5) São
Francisco do Sul
São Francisco do Conde. City,
eastern Brazil, South America
: São Francisco (-1944)
São Francisco do Maranhão.
City, northeastern Brazil,
South America : São Francisco
(-1944), Iguaratinga (1944-48)
São Francisco do Sul. City,
southern Brazil, South America
: São Francisco (-1944)
São Gabriel see Uaupés
São Gonçalo see (1) Anacetaba;
(2) Araripina; (3) Felipe
Camarão; (4) São Gonçalo dos
Campos
São Gonçalo dos Campos. City,
eastern Brazil, South America
: São Gonçalo (-1944)
São Jerônimo see Araíporanga
São João da Bocâina see Bocâina
São João de Camaquã see
Camaquã
São João de Meriti. Suburb of
Rio de Janeiro, southeastern
Brazil, South America :
Meriti (-1944)
São João de Montenegro see
Montenegro
São João do Muqui see Muqui
São Joaquim see (1) São
Joaquim da Barra; (2) São
Joaquim do Monte
São Joaquim da Barra. City,
southeastern Brazil, South
America : São Joaquim (-1944)
São Joaquim do Monte. City,

northeastern Brazil, South America : São Joaquim (-1944), Camaratuba (1944-48)

São José da Lagoa see Nova Era

São José do Campestre. City, northeastern Brazil, South America : Campestre (-1944)

São José do Rio Prêto. City, southeastern Brazil, South America : Rio Prêto (-1944)

São José dos Cocais see Nossa Senhora do Livramento

São José dos Matões see Parnarama

São José do Tocantins see Niquelândia

São Lourenço see São Lourenço da Mata

São Lourenço da Mata. City, northeastern Brazil, South America : São Lourenço (-1944)

São Luís. City, northeastern Brazil, South America : São Luíz do Maranhão [Maranhão] (-?)

São Luís Gonzaga see Ipixuna

São Luíz de Cáceres see Cáceres

São Luíz do Maranhão see São Luís

São Manuel see Eugenópolis

São Manuel do Mutum see Mutum

São Mateus see (1) Jucás; (2) São Mateus do Sul

São Mateus do Sul. City, southern Brazil, South America : São Mateus (-1943)

São Miguel see São Miguel das Matas

São Miguel das Matas. City, eastern Brazil, South America : São Miguel (-1944)

São Miguel do Guamá see Guamá

São Paulo see Frei Paulo

São Pedro see São Pedro do Sul

São Pedro de Mallet see Malé

São Pedro (do Cariry) see Caririaçu

São Pedro do Sul. City, southern Brazil, South America : São Pedro (-1944)

São Roque see São Roque do Paraguaçu

São Roque do Paraguaçu. Town, eastern Brazil, South America : São Roque (-1944)

São Salvador do Congo see Banza Congo

São Sebastião see (1) São Sebastião do Passé; (2) Sebastianópolis

São Sebastião da Grama. City, southeastern Brazil, South America : Grama (-1948)

São Sebastião do Caí see Caí

São Sebastião do Passé. City, eastern Brazil, South America : São Sebastião (-1944)

São Vicente see (1) Araguatins; (2) General Vargas

Sapao see Santa Monica

Sapé see Sapeaçu

Sapeaçu. Town, eastern Brazil, South America : Sapé (-1944)

Sapronovo see Oktyabrsky (8)

Sarana. Urban settlement, Sverdlovsk Oblast, RSFSR : Nizhne-Saraninsky (-1933)

Saranovo see Septemvri

Sara-Ostrov see Narimanabad

Saratovskaya Manufaktura see Krasny Tekstilshchik

Saravia see Enrique B. Magalona

Saray Komar see Pyandzh

Sarbinowo. Village, western Poland : Zorndorf (-1945), Germany

Sardarabad see Oktemberyan

Sardarova Karakhana, imeni see Leninsky (2)

Sarepta see Krasnoarmeysk (3)

Sarera Bay. Bay, northern Irian Jaya, Indonesia : Geelvink Bay (-1963)

Sarh. Town, southern Chad, central Africa : Fort-Archambault (-1974)

Sarrat. Municipality, Ilocos Norte, Philippines : San Miguel (-1914)

Sars. Urban settlement, Perm Oblast, RSFSR : Sarsinsky Zavod (-1939)

Sarsinsky Zavod see Sars

Sartana see Primorskoye (3)

Sauce see Juan Lacaze

Sauce del Yí. Town, south-central Uruguay, South America : Pueblo de la Capilla (-1924)

Saúde see Perdigão

Saujbulagh see Mahabad

Sawmill see Concepcion

Sayaboury. Town, northwestern Laos : Paklay (-1946), Thailand (1941-46)

Sayanogorsk. Town, Khakass Autonomous Oblast, Krasnoyarsk Kray, RSFSR : Oznachennoye (-1975)

Sayasan. Village, Checheno-Ingush Autonomous SSR, RSFSR : Ritlyab (1944-c. 1960)

Saybrook see Deep River

Saybusch see Żywiec

Sazanovka see Ananyevo

Sazonovo. Urban settlement, Vologda Oblast, RSFSR : Belyye Kresty (-1947)

Scarpanto see Karpathos

Schaaksvitte see Kashirskoye

Scharfenwiese see Ostrołęka

Schässburg see Sighişoara

Schatzlar see Žaclér

Schefferville. Town, Quebec, Canada : Knob Lake (*c. 1950-55)

Schemnitz see Banská Stiavnica

Schieratz see Sieradz

Schippenbeil see Sępopol

Schirwindt see Kutuzovo

Schivelbein see Świdwin

Schlawa see Sława

Schlesiersee see Sława

Schlettstadt see Sélestat

Schlichtingsheim see Szlichtyngowa

Schlochau see Człuchów

Schloppe see Człopa

Schlossbach see Nevskoye

Schlossberg see Dobrovolsk

Schlüsselburg see Petrokrepost

Schmiedeberg see Kowary

Schneidemühl see Piła

Schömberg see Chełmsko Śląskie

Schönau see Świerzawa

Schönberg see Sulików

Schöneck see Skarszewy

Schönfeld see Krásno

Schönlanke see Trzcianka

Schonstein see Šoštanj

Schreckenstein see Střekov

Schreiberhau see Szklarska Poręba

Schröttersburg see Plock

Schwangliao [Shuang-liao]. Town, northeastern China : Liaoyüan (-1949)

Schwangpo [Shuang-po]. Town, southwestern China : Nanan (-1913), Mochu (1913-29)

Schwarzheide. Town, eastern East Germany : Zschornegosda (-1936)

Schweidnitz see Świdnica

Schwerin see Skwierzyna

Schwiebus see Świebodzin

Scottsdale. Town, Tasmania, Australia : Ellesmere (-1906)

Scrabby see Lough Gowna

Seabra see Tarauacá

Seawell Airport see (Sir) Grantley Adams Airport

Sebastianópolis. Town, northeastern Brazil, South America : São Sebastião (-1944)

Sechenovo. Village, Gorky Oblast, RSFSR : Tyoply Stan (-1945)

Seckenburg see Zapovednoye

Sedova G. Ya., imeni see Sedovo

Sedovo. Urban settlement, Donetsk Oblast, Ukrainian SSR : Krivaya Kosa (-1941), Sedova G. Ya., imeni (1941-c. 1960)

Seeburg see Jeziorany

Seelowitz see Ždrlochovice

Segaon see Sevagram

Segeberg see Bad Segeberg

Segewold see Sigulda

Seidemenukha see Kalininskoye
(2)
Seine-Inférieure see Seine-
Maritime
Seine-Maritime. Department,
northern France : Seine-
Inférieure (-1955)
Seis de Septiembre see Morón
Seitler see Nizhnegorsky
Sélestat. Town, northeastern
France : Schlettstadt (1870-
1918), Germany
Seleznevsky Rudnik see Parizh-
skaya Kommuna
Semadrek see Samothrace
Semibratovo. Urban settlement,
Yaroslavl Oblast, RSFSR :
Isady (-1948)
Seminole. City, Oklahoma,
USA : Tidmore (-1906)
Semirechensk Guberniya see
Dzhetysuy Guberniya
Sem Kolodezey see Lenino (2)
Semyonovka see Arsenyev
Semyonovskoye see (1) Berez-
nik; (2) Ostrovsky
Senaki see Mikha Tskhakaya
Senegambia and Niger Territories
see Mali
Senftenberg see Žamberk
Senhor do Bonfim. City, eastern
Brazil, South America :
Bonfim (-1944)
Senneterre. Town, Quebec,
Canada : Nottaway (*1914-
18)
Sentosa. Island, south of Singa-
pore Island, southeastern
Asia : Pulau Blakang Mati
(-1970)
Sępolno (Kraiński). Town,
northwestern Poland : Zem-
pelburg (-1945), Germany
Sępopol. Village, northeastern
Poland : Schippenbeil (-1945),
Germany
Septemvri. Village, west-cen-
tral Bulgaria : Saranovo
(-1950)
Sept-Îles. City, Quebec, Canada
: Seven Islands (-1951)
Serafimovich. Town, Volgograd
Oblast, RSFSR : Ust-Med-

veditskaya (-1933)
Serangoon see Coney
Serdán see (Ciudad) Serdán
Serdobol see Sortavala
Serebrovsky. Urban settlement,
Azerbaijan SSR : Karachukhur
(-c. 1960)
Serebryanyye Prudy. Urban
settlement, Moscow Oblast,
RSFSR : Sergiyevy Prudy
(-c. 1928)
Sereda see Furmanov
Sergiopol see Ayaguz
Sergiyev see Zagorsk
Sergiyevsky see Fakel
Sergiyevy Prudy see Serebryanyye
Prudy
Sergo see Stakhanov
Sergunia [Szirguni]. Urban settle-
ment, northeastern Israel :
Hazorim (*1939-48)
Sermyazhenka see Osman-
Karayevo
Serov. Town, Sverdlovsk Oblast,
RSFSR : Nadezhdinsky Zavod
(-1926), Nadezhdinsk (1926-35,
1938-39), Kabakovsk (1935-38)
Serra Alta see São Bento do
Sul
Serra Branca. City, eastern
Brazil, South America : Ita-
morotinga (1944-48)
Sérrai. City, northern Greece :
Siroz (-1913), Turkey
Serramazzoni. Village, north-
central Italy : Monfestino in
Serra Mazzoni (-1948)
Serra Negra see Serra Negra
do Norte
Serra Negra do Norte. City,
northeastern Brazil, South
America : Serra Negra (-1944)
Serra Talhada. City, northeastern
Brazil, South America : Villa
Bella (-1939)
Serravalle Libarna. Village,
northern Italy : Serravalle
Scrivia (-early 1930s)
Serravalle Scrivia see Serravalle
Libarna
Serrinha see Juripiranga
Sertânia. City, northeastern
Brazil, South America : Alagoa

de Baixo (-1944)
Sertãozinho see Major Isidoro
Seskar. Island, Gulf of Finland,
Baltic Sea, Leningrad Ob-
last, RSFSR : Lesnoy
(-c. 1960)
Seto(-kanayama) see Shirahama
Sevagram. Village, central
India : Segaon (*1936-40)
Sevan (1). Lake, Armenian
SSR : Gökçe (-?), Turkey
Sevan (2). Town, Armenian
SSR : Yelenovka (-c. 1935)
Seven Islands see Sept-Îles
Severnaya Sama see Sama
Severnaya Zemlya. Archipelago,
Arctic Ocean, Taymyr
Autonomous Okrug, Kras-
noyarsk Kray, RSFSR :
Zemlya Imperatora Nikolaya
II [Nicholas II Land] (*1913-
26)
Severnoye. Village, Orenburg
Oblast, RSFSR : Sok-Karmala
(-c. 1960)
Severny. Urban settlement,
Sverdlovsk Oblast, RSFSR :
Pervy Severny (-c. 1960)
Severny Suchan see Uglekamensk
Severodonetsk. Town, Voro-
shilovgrad Oblast, Ukrainian
SSR : Leskhimstroy (*1934-
58)
Severodvinsk. Town, Arkhangelsk
Oblast, RSFSR : Sudostroy
(*c. 1918-38), Molotovsk
(1938-57)
Severokavkazsky Kray see
Stavropol Kray
Severo-Kurilsk. Town, Kuril
Islands, Sakhalin Oblast,
RSFSR : Kashiwabara
(1905-45), Japan
Severomorsk. Town, Murmansk
Oblast, RSFSR : Vayenga
(-1951)
Severouralsk. Town, Sverdlovsk
Oblast, RSFSR : Petropav-
lovsky (-1944)
Seversk. Town, Donetsk Oblast,
Ukrainian SSR : Yama (-1973)
Sevilla. City, western Colombia,
South America : San Luis

(*1903-14)
Sevlyush see Vinogradov
Sewell see Camp Hughes
Shaarikhan see Shakhrikhan
Shaba. Province, southern
Zaïre, central Africa :
Élisabethville (1935-47),
Katanga (1947-72)
Shabalino see Leninskoye (2)
Shabbaz see Biruni
Shafirkan. Village, Bukhara
Oblast, Uzbek SSR : Khodzha-
Arif (-c. 1935), Bauman
(c. 1935-37)
Shagali see Vaagni
Shahi. Town, northern Iran :
Aliabad (-mid-1930s)
Shahpur. Town, northwestern
Iran : Dilman (-1930)
Shaker Heights. Suburb of
Cleveland, Ohio, USA : North
Union (-1900s)
Shakhimardan see Khamza
Shakhrikhan. Urban settlement,
Andizhan Oblast, Uzbek SSR :
Shaarikhan (-1937), Stalina,
imeni (1937-c. 1940), Stalino
(c. 1940-61), Moskovsky (1961-
70)
Shakhta No 7/8. Town, Voro-
shilovgrad Oblast, Ukrainian
SSR : Karlomarksovsky No
7/8 Rudnik (-?)
Shakhta No 33/37. Town, Voro-
shilovgrad Oblast, Ukrainian
SSR : Lobovsky No 33/37
Rudnik (-?)
Shakhty. Town, Rostov Oblast,
RSFSR : Aleksandrovsk-
Grushevsky (-1920)
Shakhty imeni Engelsa see
Engelsovo
Shakhtyorsk (1). Town, Sakhalin
Oblast, RSFSR : Toro (1905-
47), Japan (-1945)
Shakhtyorsk (2). Town, Donetsk
Oblast, Ukrainian SSR :
Zapadno-Gruppsky (-1945),
Katyk (1945-53)
Shakhtyorskoye see Pershotra-
vensk
Shakotan see Malokurilskoye
Shali. Village, Checheno-Ingush

Autonomous SSR, RSFSR :
Mezhdurechye (1944-c. 1960)
Shamkhor. Town, Azerbaijan
SSR : Annenfeld [Annino]
(c. 1928-37)
Shana see Kurilsk
Shangchih. Town, northeastern
China : Wuchuho (-1927),
Chuho (1927-49)
Shangchow see Shanghsien
Shanghsien. Town, central
China : Shangchow (-1913)
Shangi. Town, northeastern
China : Tatsingkow (-1935)
Shangjao. Town, southeastern
China : Kwangsin (-1912)
Shangpo see Fukung
Shangri-La see Camp David
Shangtsichang see Suileng
Shangyütung see Kintang
[Chin-t'ang]
Shanhaikwan. City, northeastern
China : Linyü (1912-49)
Shani see Taosha [T'ao-sha]
Shan-yang see Huai-an
Shao-yang. City, southeastern
China : Pao-ch'ing (-1912)
Shapilovo see Mayskoye (3)
Shargun. Town, Surkhandarya
Oblast, Uzbek SSR :
Takchiyan (-1973)
Sharlak see Druzhba (3)
Shatilki see Svetlogorsk (2)
Shatoy see Sovetskoye (6)
Shatura. Town, Moscow
Oblast, RSFSR : Shaturtorf
(-1928)
Shaturtorf see Shatura
Shaumyan see Shaumyani
Shaumyani. Urban settlement,
Georgian SSR : Shulavery
(-1925), Shaumyan (1925-36)
Shaumyanovsk. Urban settle-
ment, Azerbaijan SSR :
Nizhny Agdzhakend (-1938)
Shavli see Siauliai
Shaydan see Asht
Shaygino. Urban settlement,
Gorky Oblast, RSFSR :
Tonshayevo (-c. 1960)
Shaytansky Zavod see Pervou-
ralsk
Shcheglovsk see Kemerovo

Shcherbakov see Rybinsk
Shcherbinovka see Dzerzhinsk
(5)
Shchors. Town, Chernigov
Oblast, Ukrainian SSR : Snovsk
(-1935)
Shchorsk. Urban settlement,
Dnepropetrovsk Oblast, Ukrain-
ian SSR : Bozhedarovka (-c.
1940)
Shchuchinsk. Town, Kokchetav
Oblast, Kazakh SSR : Shchuchye
(-1939)
Shchuchye see Shchuchinsk
Shebunino. Urban settlement,
Sakhalin Oblast, RSFSR :
Minami-nayoshi (1905-46),
Japan (-1945)
She-hsien. City, eastern China
: Hui-chou (-1912)
Sheki. Town, Azerbaijan SSR :
Nukha (-1968)
Shekshing see Limkong
Sheksna. Urban settlement,
Vologda Oblast, RSFSR :
Nikolskoye (-c. 1960)
Shelekhovo. Village, Kuril
Islands, Sakhalin Oblast,
RSFSR : Kakumabetsu (1905-
46), Japan (-1945)
Shell Beach see Huntington
Beach
Shelomy see Krasny Vostok
Shelter Bay see Port-Cartier
Shelton. City, Connecticut,
USA : Huntington (-1919)
Shelyakino see Sovetskoye (7)
Shenchow see (1) Shenhsien;
(2) Yüanling
Shenhsien. Town, northeastern
China : Shenchow (-1913)
Shenkiu see Linchüan [Lin-
ch'üan]
Shen-yang see Mukden (2)
Shestakovo. Urban settlement,
Irkutsk Oblast, RSFSR : Ilim
(-c. 1960)
Shevchenko. Capital of Mangysh-
lak Oblast, Kazakh SSR :
Aktau (-1964)
Shevchenko see Vita
Shevchenkovo see Dolinskaya
Shibetoro see Slavnoye

Shichijo see Ichijo
Shih-chia-chuang = Shihkiach-
wang
Shihchü [Shih-ch'ü]. Town,
southern China : Shihshu
(-1912)
Shihchwan see Pehchwan
[Pei-ch'uan]
Shihkiachwang [Shih-chia-
chuang]. City, northeastern
China : Shihmen (1947-49)
Shihmen see (1) Shihkiachwang
[Shih-chia-chuang]; (2)
Tsungteh
Shihnan see Enshih
Shihpu see Hwanglung [Huang-
lung]
Shihshu see Shihchü [Shih-
ch'ü]
Shihwei. Town, northeastern
China : Chilalin (-1920)
Shikhirdany see Chkalovskoye
(1)
Shikhrany see Kanash
Shikirlikitai see Suvorovo (2)
Shikiu see Punyü
Shikuka see Poronaysk
Shimba see Dachnoye
Shimotsu. Town, southern
Honshu, Japan : Hamanaka
(-1938)
Shimo-yoshida. Town, southern
Honshu, Japan : Yoshida
(-1928)
Shin-mikuriya. Town, western
Kyushu, Japan : Mikuriya
(-1943)
Shirahama. Town, southern
Honshu, Japan : Seto
(-kanayama) (-early 1940s)
Shiraura see Vzmorye (2)
Shiritoru see Makarov
Shirley City see Woodburn
(City)
Shirokolanovka. Village,
Nikolayev Oblast, Ukrainian
SSR : Landau (-c. 1935),
Karla Libknekhta, imeni
(c. 1935-45)
Shiuchow see Kükong
Shiuhing see Koyiu
Shlisselburg see Petrokrepost
Shmakovsky Rudnik see Karla

Libknekhta, imeni (2)
Shokalsky. Island, Kara Sea,
Tyumen Oblast, RSFSR :
Agnessa (-1926)
Sholkhi see Oktyabrskoye (6)
Shopa see Vysochany (2)
Shoping see Yuyü
Shorewood. Village, Wisconsin,
USA : East Milwaukee (-1917)
Shovgenovsky. Village, Adygey
Autonomous Oblast, Krasnodar
Kray, RSFSR : Khakurinokhabl
(-c. 1960)
Showchang see Ocheng [O-ch'eng]
Showchow see Showhsien
Showhsien. Town, eastern China
: Showchow (-1912)
Shpakovskoye. Village, Stavropol
Kray, RSFSR : Mikhaylovskoye
(-c. 1960)
Shropshire see Salop
Shterovskogo Zavoda imeni
Petrovskogo see Petrovskoye
Shuang-liao = Schwangliao
Shuang-po = Schwangpo
Shulan. Town, northeastern
China : Chaoyangchwan (-1910)
Shulavery see Shaumyani
Shulmak see Novabad
Shumanay. Village, Karakalpak
Autonomous SSR, Uzbek SSR :
Taza-Bazar (-1950)
Shumatovo see Sovetskoye (8)
Shumen [Šumen]. Province and
its capital (*1949), northeastern
Bulgaria : Kolarovgrad (1950-
65)
Shumikhinsky. Urban settlement,
Perm Oblast, RSFSR : Gore-
loye (-c. 1960)
Shunking see Nanchung [Nan-
ch'ung]
Shunteh see Singtai [Hsing-t'ai]
Shuragat. Village, Dagestan
Autonomous SSR, RSFSR :
Alleroi (-1944)
Shurala. Village, Sverdlovsk
Oblast, RSFSR : Shuralinsky
Zavod (-c. 1930)
Shuralinsky Zavod see Shurala
Shuvoya see Krasny Tkach
Shwangliuchen see Taonan
[T'ao-nan]

Siaho [Hsia-ho]. Town, north-
central China : Labrang
(-1928)

Siakiutai see Kiutai [Chiu-t'ai]

Siali see Tingnan

Siam see Thailand

Sian [Hsi-an] (1). City, northwestern China : Changan
(1913-32), Siking (1932-43)

Sian [Hsi-an] (2). City, northeastern China : Peifeng (1947-
49)

Sianghsien [Hsiang-hsien]. Town,
southern China : Hsiang-
ch'ou (-1912)

Siangkow see Wulung

Siangyün [Hsiang-yün]. Town,
southwestern China : Yunnan
(-1929)

Sianów. Town, northwestern
Poland : Zanow (-1945),
Germany

Siaochengtze see Ningcheng
[Ning-ch'eng]

Siaopapao see Ningso
[Ningshuo]

Siaoyi see Tsoshui

Siapu [Hsia-p'u]. Town,
southeastern China : Funing
(-1913)

Šiauliai. Town, Lithuanian
SSR : Shavli (-1920), Russia

Siazan. Town, Azerbaijan
SSR : Kyzyl-Burun (-1954)

Sibirsky see Nazyvayevsk

Sibirtsevo. Urban settlement,
Primorsky Kray, RSFSR :
Manzovka (-1972)

Sibiu. City, central Romania
: Hermannstadt (-1918),
Germany

Sichang [Hsi-chang]. Town,
southern China : Ningyüan
(-1913)

Sichelberg see Sierpc

Sichi [Hsi-chi]. Town, north-
central China : Mukiaying
(-1941)

Sichow [Hsi-ch'ou]. Town,
southwestern China : Sisakai
(-1929)

Sichow see Sihsien [Hsi-hsien]
(3)

Sidi Ali. Village, northwestern
Algeria : Cassaigne (-c. 1962)

Sidi Bel Atar. Village, northwestern Algeria, northern
Africa : Pont-du-Chéliff
(-c. 1962)

Sidi Benyekba. Village, northwestern Algeria, northern
Africa : Kléber (-c. 1962)

Sidi Hamadouche. Village,
northwestern Algeria, northern
Africa : Les Trembles
(-c. 1962)

Sidi Kacem. Town, northwestern
Morocco, northwestern Africa
: Petitjean (-1971)

Sidi M'Hamed Ben Ali. Village,
northern Algeria, northern
Africa : Renault (-c. 1962)

Siding No. 14 see Ponoka

Siehkangpao see Holan

Siemianowice Śląskie. City,
south-central Poland : Laurahütte (1939-45), Germany

Sieradz. Town, central Poland :
Schieratz (1939-45), Germany

Sieraków. Town, central Poland
: Zirke (1939-45), Germany

Sierpc. Town, north-central
Poland : Sichelberg (1939-45),
Germany

Sierra Morena. Mountain range,
southern Spain : Cordillera
Mariánica (-c. 1960)

Sieur de Monts National Monument
see Acadia National Park

Sig. Town, northwestern Algeria,
northern Africa : Saint-Denis
(-du-Sig) (-c. 1962)

Sighişoara. City, central Romania : Schässburg (-c. 1918),
Germany

Signakh see Signakhi

Signakhi. Town, Georgian SSR
: Signakh (-1936)

Sigulda. Town, Latvian SSR :
Segewold (-early 1920s)

Sihanoukville see Kompong Som

Sihsien [Hsi-hsien] (1). Town,
eastern China : Hweichow
(-1912)

Sihsien [Hsi-hsien] (2). Town,
east-central China : Paosintsi

(-1935)
Sihsien [Hsi-hsien] (3). Town,
    northeastern China : Sichow
    (-1912)
Siking see Sian [Hsi-an] (1)
Silberberg see Srebrna Góra
Silikow see Tulan
Sillein see Žilina
Silva Jardim. City, southeastern
    Brazil, South America :
    Capivari (-1943)
Silvânia. City, central Brazil,
    South America : Bonfim
    (-1944)
Silva Porto see Bié
Silver City see Rainbow City
Silvestre Domingo. Barrio,
    Pangasinan, Philippines :
    San Angel (-1972)
Sim. Town, Chelyabinsk Ob-
    last, RSFSR : Simsky Zavod
    (-c. 1928)
Simão Dias. City, northeastern
    Brazil, South America :
    Anápolis (-1944)
Simbirsk see Ulyanovsk
Simbirsk Guberniya see
    Ulyanovsk Guberniya
Šimonovany see Partizánske
Simsky Zavod see Sim
Sinancha see Cheremshan
Sinchang see (1) Ifeng; (2)
    Kinsha [Chin-sha]
Sincheng see (1) Hingjen
    [Hsing-jen]; (2) Hwantai
    [Huan-t'ai]; (3) Lichwan
    [Li-ch'uan]
Sinchow see Sinhsien [Hsin-
    hsien] (2)
Sinchu see Taoyüan [T'ao-
    yüan]
Sinclair. Town, Wyoming,
    USA : Parco (-1943)
Sinebryukhi see Bereznyaki
Sinegorsk. Urban settlement,
    Sakhalin Oblast, RSFSR :
    Kawakami(-tanzan) (1905-
    45), Japan
Sinegorsky. Urban settlement,
    Sverdlovsk Oblast, RSFSR :
    Mezhevaya Utka (-1963)
Sinelnikovo. Town, Dneprope-
    trovsk Oblast, Ukrainian

SSR : Tovarishcha Khatayevicha,
    imeni (mid-1930s)
Sing Sing see Ossining
Singtai [Hsing-t'ai]. Town,
    northeastern China : Shunteh
    (-1912)
Singtze [Hsing-tzu]. Town,
    southeastern China : Nankang
    (-1912)
Sinhai [Hsin-hai]. City, eastern
    China : Haichow (-1912),
    Tunghai (1912-49)
Sinhai see Hwanghwa [Huang-
    hua]
Sinho see Changpeh
Sinhsien [Hsin-hsien] (1). Town,
    east-central China : Kingfu
    (-1949)
Sinhsien [Hsin-hsien] (2). Town,
    northeastern China : Sinchow
    (-1912)
Sining see Yangyuan
Sinkin [Hsin-chin]. Town,
    northeastern China : Pitzewo
    (-1949)
Sinning see (1) Funan; (2)
    Kaikiang [K'ai-chiang]
Sinpin [Hsin-pin]. Town, north-
    eastern China : Hingking
    (-1929)
Sinsing see Yüki
Sintsi see Kanglo [K'ang-lo]
Siphaqeni. Town, northeastern
    Transkei, southern Africa :
    Flagstaff (-1976)
Sipon(d)zh see Bartang
Siporovka see Partizany (1)
Siqueira Campos see Guaçuí
(Sir) Grantley Adams Airport.
    Barbados, West Indies :
    Seawell Airport (-1976)
Siroz see Serrai
Sisakai see Sichow [Hsi-ch'ou]
Sishui [Hsi-shui]. Town, east-
    central China : Kishui (-1933)
Sisqueira Campos. City, southern
    Brazil, South America : Co-
    lonia Mineira (-c. 1935)
Sisson see Mount Shasta (City)
Sistema Central. Mountain
    range, west-central Spain :
    Cordillera Capetónica (-c.
    1960)

Siteki. Town, eastern Swaziland, southern Africa : Stegi (-1976)

Sitio Rawrawang see Don Mariano

Sitniki. Urban settlement, Gorky Oblast, RSFSR : Kozlikha (-1946)

Siuna see Yüki

Siushui [Hsiu-shui]. Town, southeastern China : Ining (-1912)

Sivashskoye. Urban settlement, Kherson Oblast, Ukrainian SSR : Rozhdestvenskoye (-c. 1935)

Siwo see Oshan

Siyen see Tzeyüan [Tzu-yüan]

Siying [Hsi-ying]. Town, southeastern China : Fort-Bayard (1898-1945)

Skała (nad Zbruczem) see Skala-Podolskaya

Skala-Podolskaya. Urban settlement, Ternopol Oblast, Ukrainian SSR : Skała (nad Zbruczem) (-1940), Poland

Skawina. Town, southern Poland : Konradshof (1939-45), Germany

Skhematárion. Village, central Greece : Skhimatárion (-1960s)

Skhimatárion see Skhematárion

Skikda. City, northeastern Algeria, northern Africa : Philippeville (-c. 1962)

Skit see Divnogorsk

Skobelev see Fergana

Skofja Loka. Village, northwestern Yugoslavia : Bischoflack (-1918), Germany

Skokie. Suburb of Chicago, Illinois, USA : Niles Center (-1940)

Skopje = Skoplje

Skoplje [Skopje]. City, southern Yugoslavia : Üsküb (-1913), Turkey

Skotovataya see Verkhnetoretskoye

Skoúliare see Hagía Kyriaké

Skoúpa see Karudéa

Skovorodino. Town, Amur Oblast, RSFSR : Rukhlovo (-1948)

Skulovichi see Kommunarka (2)

Skulovka see Primorye

Skuratovsky. Urban settlement, Tula Oblast, RSFSR : Yuzhny (-1948)

Skwierzyna. Town, western Poland : Schwerin (-1945), Germany

Slatina Radenci. Village, northwestern Yugoslavia : Bad Radein (-1918), Germany

Slavgorod. Town, Mogilyov Oblast, Belorussian SSR : Propoysk (-1945)

Slavino. Village, Mogilyov Oblast, Belorussian SSR : Osy-Kolyosy (-1964)

Slavjanka. Mountain, southwestern Bulgaria : Ali Butus (-1967)

Slavkov. Town, west-central Czechoslovakia : Austerlitz (-1918, 1939-45), Germany

Slavnoye. Village, Kuril Islands, Sakhalin Oblast, RSFSR : Shibetoro (1905-45), Japan

Slavsk. Town, Kaliningrad Oblast, RSFSR : Heinrichswalde (-1946), Germany (-1945)

Slavskoye. Village, Kaliningrad Oblast, RSFSR : Kreuzburg (-1945), Germany

Slavyanka. Village, Mogilyov Oblast, Belorussian SSR : Ogloblya (-1964)

Slavyanogorsk. Town, Donetsk Oblast, Ukrainian SSR : Bannovsky (-1964)

Slavyanskaya see Slavyansk-na-Kubani

Slavyansk-na-Kubani. Town, Krasnodar Kray, RSFSR : Slavyanskaya (-1958)

Sława. Town, western Poland : Schlawa (-1937), Germany; Schlesiersee (1937-45), Germany

Slawentzitz see Sławięcice

Sławięcice. Village, southern Poland : Slawentzitz (-c. 1935), Germany; Ehrenforst (c. 1935-

45), Germany
Sleptsovskaya see Ordzhoni-
kidzevskaya
Sleptsy see Znamenka (4)
Sloboda see (1) Ezhva; (2)
Przhevalskoye
Slobozhanka. Village, Gomel
Oblast, Belorussian SSR :
Knyazhitsa (-1964)
Slobozhany. Village, Brest
Oblast, Belorussian SSR :
Bovdilovtsy (-1964)
Slomikhino see Furmanovo
Slovenjgradec. Village, north-
western Yugoslavia : Win-
dischgraz (-1918), Germany
(Slovenska) Bistrica. Village,
northwestern Yugoslavia :
Windisch-Feistritz (-1918),
Germany
Słupsk. Town, northwestern
Poland : Stolp (-1945),
Germany
Slutsk see Pavlovsk
Smaalenene see Ostfold
Smaldeel see Theunissen
Šmarje (pri Jelšah). Village,
northwestern Yugoslavia :
Sankt Marein (-1918), Ger-
many
Smértos. Village, western
Greece : Mýlos (-1960s)
Smirnovo. Urban settlement,
North Kazakhstan Oblast,
Kazakh SSR : Smirnovsky
(-1973)
Smirnovsky see Smirnovo
Smolyan. City, southern Bul-
garia : Pashmakli (-1934)
Smorkovo see Peremozhets
Smychka. Suburb of Moscow,
Moscow Oblast, RSFSR :
Ivanovskoye (-1929)
Smyrtóula see Nikópolis
Snegurovka see Tetiyev
Sneznik. Mountain, northwestern
Yugoslavia : Monte Nevoso
(-1947), Italy
Śniardwy. Lake, northeastern
Poland : Spirding (-1945),
Germany
Snovsk see Shchors
Sobięcin. Town, southwestern

Poland : Hermsdorf (-1945),
Germany
Sobinka. Town, Vladimir Oblast,
RSFSR : Komavangard (early
1920s)
Sobótka. Town, southwestern
Poland : Zobten (-1945),
Germany
Sobradinho. City, southern
Brazil, South America : Jacuí
(-1938)
Socialist People's Libyan Arab
Jamahirrya. State, northern
Africa : Libya (-1969), Libyan
Arab Republic (1969-77)
Socorro see (1) Cotinguiba;
(2) Fronteiras; (3) Mataripe
Sofala. Province, southeastern
Mozambique, southeastern
Africa : Beira (-1976)
Sofiyevka see Volnyansk
Sofiyevsky Rudnik see Karla
Marksa, imeni
Sogn og Fjordane. County,
southwestern Norway : Nordre
Bergenhus (-1918)
Sohrau see Zory
Sok-Karmala see Severnoye
Sokol. Urban settlement,
Sakhalin Oblast, RSFSR :
Otani (1905-45), Japan
Sokolov. Town, western Czecho-
slovakia : Falknov (nad Ohří)
(-1948)
Sokuluk. Village, Kirgiz SSR :
Novo-Troitskoye (-1937),
Kaganovich (1937-57)
Solas de Bureba see Llano de
Bureba
Solbad Hall in Tirol. City,
western Austria : Hall (-1938)
Soldatskoye see Soldatsky
Soldatsky. Urban settlement,
Tashkent Oblast, Uzbek SSR :
Yangi-Bazar (-c. 1930),
Soldatskoye (c. 1930-c. 1960)
Soldin see Myślibórz
Soledade. City, northeastern
Brazil, South America :
Ibiapinópolis (1944-48)
Soledade see Soledade de Minas
Soledade de Minas. City, south-
eastern Brazil, South America

: Soledade (-1944), Ibatuba
(1944-48)
Soligorsk. Town, Minsk Oblast,
Belorussian SSR : Novo-
Starobinsk (*1958-59)
Sol-Iletsk. Town, Orenburg
Oblast, RSFSR : Iletskaya
Zashchita (-1945)
Solnechnoye. Urban settlement,
Leningrad Oblast, RSFSR :
Ollila (-1948), Finland
(-1940)
Solnechny see Gorny
Solntsevo. Urban settlement,
Kursk Oblast, RSFSR :
Korovino (-c. 1960)
Solomon Islands : British
Solomon Islands Protectorate
(1893-1975)
Solonópole. City, northeastern
Brazil, South America :
Cachoeira (-1944)
Solun. Town, northeastern
China : Solunshan (-1917)
Solunshan see Solun
Solzavod. Village, Evenki
Autonomous Okrug, Kras-
noyarsk Kray, RSFSR :
Bachinsky (-?), Stalino
(?-c. 1961)
Someitsun see Tehjung
Sommerfeld see Lubsko
Son see (1) Puerto de Son;
(2) Sonsky
Sondre Bergenhus see Horda-
land
Søndre Trondhjem see Sør-
Trøndelag
Songjin see Kimch'aek
Songnim. City, western North
Korea : Kyŏmipo (1910-45),
Japan
Songololo see Mbanza-Ngungu
Sonsky. Urban settlement,
Khakass Autonomous Oblast,
Krasnoyarsk Kray, RSFSR :
Son (-1940)
Soochow [Su-chou]. City, eastern
China : Wuhsien (1912-49)
Sopot see Vazovgrad
Sopron. City, western Hungary
: Ödenburg (-1921), Germany
Soroca see Soroki

Sorochinsk. Town, Orenburg
Oblast, RSFSR : Sorochinskoye
(-c. 1935)
Sorochinskoye see Sorochinsk
Soroka see Belomorsk
Soroki. Town, Moldavian SSR :
Soroca (1918-40, 1941-44),
Romania
Sorokino see Krasnodon
Soroksárpéteri see Pestszen-
timre
Sorsk. Town, Khakass Autonomous
Oblast, Krasnoyarsk Kray,
RSFSR : Dzerzhinsky (-c. 1960)
Sortavala. Town, Karelian
Autonomous SSR, RSFSR :
Serdobol (-1918)
Sør-Trøndelag. County, central
Norway : Søndre Trondhjem
(-1918)
Sosninskaya see Kominterna,
imeni
Sosnogorsk. Town, Komi
Autonomous SSR, RSFSR :
Izhma (-1957)
Sosnovaya (1). Village, Mogilyov
Oblast, Belorussian SSR :
Koty (-1964)
Sosnovaya (2). Village, Vitebsk
Oblast, Belorussian SSR :
Pyany Les (-1964)
Sosnovaya (3). Village, Brest
Oblast, Belorussian SSR :
Zherebilovichi (-1964)
Sosnovets. Village, Gomel
Oblast, Belorussian SSR :
Monastyr (-1964)
Sosnovichi. Village, Brest
Oblast, Belorussian SSR :
Beskhlebichi (-1964)
Sosnovka. Village, Kursk Oblast,
RSFSR : Nizhnegniloye (-c.
1960)
Sosnovo. Settlement, Leningrad
Oblast, RSFSR : Rautu (-1948),
Finland (-1940)
Sosnovoborsk. Urban settlement,
Penza Oblast, RSFSR : Litvino
(-1940)
Sosnovoye. Urban settlement,
Rovno Oblast, Ukrainian SSR :
Lyudvipol (-1946)
Sosnovtsy. Village, Grodno

Oblast, Belorussian SSR :
Ovechki (-1964)
Sosnovy Bor. Village, Vitebsk
Oblast, Belorussian SSR :
Golyashi (-1964)
Sosnowiec. City, southern
Poland : Sosnowitz (1939-45),
Germany
Sosnowitz see Sosnowiec
Šoštanj. Village, northwestern
Yugoslavia : Schönstein
(-1918), Germany
Sosva. Urban settlement,
Sverdlovsk Oblast, RSFSR :
Sosvinsky Zavod (-1938)
Sosvinsky Zavod see Sosva
Soto del Real. Village, central
Spain : Chozas de la Sierra
(-c. 1950)
Sotsgorodok see Gornyak (1)
Soure see Caucaia
Sour el Ghozlane. Town,
northern Algeria, northern
Africa : Aumale (-c. 1962)
South Africa : Union of South
, Africa (1910-61)
South African Republic see
Transvaal
South Auckland see Churchill
South-Eastern Oblast see
Stavropol Kray
Southern Rhodesia see Rhodesia
Southern Yemen (People's Re-
public) see Yemen
South Floral Park. Village,
New York, USA : Jamaica
Square (-1931)
South Kazakhstan Oblast see
Chimkent Oblast
South Miami. Suburb of Miami,
Florida, USA : Larkins
(-1926)
South Newburgh see Garfield
Heights
South Pleasureville. Town,
Kentucky, USA : Pleasure-
ville (-after 1930)
Southport. Town, Queensland,
Australia : Gold Coast (-1959)
South West Africa see Namibia
Sovetabad. Town, Andizhan
Oblast, Uzbek SSR : Kara-
bagish (-1972)

Sovetabad see Gafurov
Sovetsk (1). Town, Kirov Oblast,
RSFSR : Kukarka (-1937)
Sovetsk (2). Town, Kaliningrad
Oblast, RSFSR : Tilsit (-1946),
Germany (-1945)
Sovetskaya (1). Village, Gomel
Oblast, Belorussian SSR :
Amerika (-1964)
Sovetskaya (2). Village, Rostov
Oblast, RSFSR : Chernyshev-
skaya (-c. 1960)
Sovetskaya (3). Village, Mogilyov
Oblast, Belorussian SSR :
Gorevatka (-1964)
Sovetskaya (4). Village, Krasno-
dar Kray, RSFSR : Urupskaya
(-?)
Sovetskaya (5). Village, Vitebsk
Oblast, Belorussian SSR :
Yudenichi (-1964)
Sovetskaya Gavan. Town, Kha-
barovsk Kray, RSFSR :
Imperatorskaya Gavan (-c.
1918)
Sovetskoye (1). Village, Altay
Kray, RSFSR : Gryaznukha
(-c. 1960)
Sovetskoye (2). Urban settlement,
Kabardino-Balkar Autonomous
SSR, RSFSR : Kashkatau
(-1944)
Sovetskoye (3). Village, Dagestan
Autonomous SSR, RSFSR :
Khebda (-c. 1960)
Sovetskoye (4). Village, Saratov
Oblast, RSFSR : Mariental
(-1941)
Sovetskoye (5). Village, Oren-
burg Oblast, RSFSR : Mordov-
skaya Bokla (-c. 1960)
Sovetskoye (6). Village, Checheno-
Ingush Autonomous SSR, RSFSR
: Shatoy (-1944)
Sovetskoye (7). Village, Belgorod
Oblast, RSFSR : Shelyakino
(-c. 1960)
Sovetskoye (8). Village, Chuvash
Autonomous SSR, RSFSR :
Shumatovo (-1939)
Sovetskoye (9). Urban settlement,
Kalmyk Autonomous SSR, RSFSR
: Sukhotinskaya (-c. 1960)

Sovetskoye see Zelenokumsk
Sovetsky (1). Urban settlement,
Crimean Oblast, Ukrainian
SSR : Ichki(-Grammatikovo)
(-1944)
Sovetsky (2). Urban settlement,
Leningrad Oblast, RSFSR :
Johannes (-1948), Finland
(-1940)
Sovetsky (3). Urban settlement,
Kulyab Oblast, Tadzhik SSR
: Kzyl-Mazar (-c. 1960)
Soylan see Azizbekov
Spaccaforno see Ispica
Spadafora. Village, northeastern
Sicily, Italy : Spadafora San
Martino (-1937)
Spadafora San Martino see
Spadafora
Spanish Guinea see Equatorial
Guinea
Sparling see Camrose
Sparrow Hills see Lenin Hills
Spartináiika see Geliniátika
Spas see Pervomaysky (5)
Spassk see (1) Bednodemyan-
ovsk; (2) Kuybyshev (3);
(3) Spassk-Dalny
Spassk-Dalny. Town, Primorsky
Kray, RSFSR : Spassk
(-c. 1930)
Spassk-Tatarsky see Kuybyshev
(3)
Spassky Zaton see Kuybyshevsky
Zaton
Spáta see Spáta-Loútsa
Spáta-Loútsa. Town, central
Greece : Spáta (-1960s)
Spirding see Śniardwy
Spitak. Town, Armenian SSR
: Amamlu (-1948)
Spitsevka. Village, Stavropol
Kray, RSFSR : Spitsevskoye
(-c. 1940)
Spitsevskoye see Spitsevka
Spokane. City, Washington, USA
: Spokane Falls (-1900)
Spokane Falls see Spokane
Spring Forest see Willow
Springs
Sprottau see Szprotawa
Sproule see Ebor
Spyaglitsa see Svetilovichi

Srebrna Góra. Town, southwest-
ern Poland : Silberberg (-1945),
Germany
Sredecka. River, southeastern
Bulgaria : Mandrenska (-1967)
Sredets. Village, southeastern
Bulgaria : Karabunar (-1934)
Srednekrayushkino see Pervo-
mayskoye (8)
Srednyaya Nyukzha. Village,
Amur Oblast, RSFSR : Blyuk-
herovsk (late 1930s)
Sremska Mitrovica. Town,
north-central Yugoslavia :
Mitrowitz (-1918), Germany
Sremski Karlovci. Town,
northeastern Yugoslavia :
Karlowitz (-1918), Germany
Srikakulam. Town, southeastern
India : Chicacole (-1950s)
Sri Lanka. Island state, Indian
Ocean : Ceylon (-1972)
Środa Śląska. Town, southwestern
Poland : Neumarkt (-1945),
Germany
Srpski Itebej see Itebej
Ssu-hai = Szehai
Ssu-hsien = Szehsien
Ssu-yang = Szeyang
Stadtroda. Town, western East
Germany : Roda (-1922)
Stakhanov. Town, Voroshilovgrad
Oblast, Ukrainian SSR : Sergo
(1935-43), Kadiyevka (1943-78)
Stakhanovets see Mirny
Stakhanovo see (1) Zhovten (2);
(2) Zhukovsky
Stalin [Qytet Stalin]. City, south-
central Albania : Kuçovë
(-1950)
Stalin see (1) Braşov; (2)
Donetsk (2); (3) Varna
Stalina, imeni see Shakhrikhan
Stalinabad see Dushanbe
Stalin Dam. On river Iskar,
western Bulgaria : Pasarel
Dam (-1951)
Stalindorf see Zhovtnevoye (2)
Stalingrad see Volgograd
Stalingrad Guberniya (1928†).
USSR : Tsaritsyn Guberniya
(*1919-25)
Stalingrad Kray see Volgograd

Oblast
Stalingrad Oblast see Volgograd
Oblast
Staliniri see Tskhinvali
Stalino see (1) Donetsk (2);
(2) Shakhrikhan; (3) Solzavod
Stalinogorsk see Novomoskovsk
Stalinogród see Katowice
Stalino Oblast see Donetsk
Oblast
Stalin Peak see (1) Commu-
nism Peak; (2) Gerlachovka;
(3) Musala
Stalinsk see (1) Nagibovo;
(2) Novokuznetsk
Stalinskoye see (1) Belovod-
skoye; (2) Zhovtnevoye (2)
Stalinsky see Bolshevo
Stallupönen see Nesterov (1)
Stanichno-Luganskoye. Urban
settlement, Voroshilovgrad
Oblast, Ukrainian SSR :
Kosiorovo (mid-1930s)
Stanimaka see Asenovgrad
Stanislau see Ivano-Frankovsk
Stanislav see Ivano-Frankovsk
Stanislav Oblast see Ivano-
Frankovsk Oblast
Stanislavovo see Rossony
Stanisławow see Ivano-Fran-
kovsk
Štanjel na Krasu. Village,
southwestern Yugoslavia :
San Daniele del Carso
(-1947), Italy
Stanke Dimitrov. Town, south-
western Bulgaria : Dupnitsa
(-1949), Marek (1949-c. 1960)
Stanley, Mount see Ngaliema,
Mount
Stanley Falls see Boyoma
Falls
Stanley Pool see Malebo
Pool
Stanleyville see (1) Eastern
Province; (2) Kisangani
Stannum see Stanthorpe
Stanthorpe. Town, Queensland,
Australia : Stannum (-1902)
Stantsiya-Leninabad see
Gafurov
Stantsiya-Regar see Tursunzade
Stará Ďala see Hurbanovo

Staraya Barda see Krasnogor-
skoye (2)
Staraya Bukhara see Bukhara
Starčevo see Kalipetrovo
Stargard (in Pommern) see
Stargard Szczeciński
Stargard Szczeciński. City,
northwestern Poland : Stargard
(in Pommern) (-1945), Germany
Stari Bečej see Bečej
Starobachaty. Urban settlement,
Kemerovo Oblast, RSFSR :
Bachaty (-c. 1960)
Starodubskoye. Village, Sakhalin
Oblast, RSFSR : Sakaehama
(1905-45), Japan
Starogard (Gdański). Town,
northern Poland : Preussisch-
Stargard (-1945), Germany
Staro-Izobilnoye. Village,
Stavropol Kray, RSFSR :
Izobilnoye (-1930s)
Staromaryevka. Village, Stavro-
pol Kray, RSFSR : Staromaryev-
skoye (-c. 1940)
Staromaryevskoye see Staromar-
yevka
Staromlinovka. Village, Donetsk
Oblast, Ukrainian SSR : Stary
Kermenchik (-1946)
Staro-Nikolayevskoye see Panfil-
ovskoye
Staropyshminsk. Urban settlement,
Sverdlovsk Oblast, RSFSR :
Pyshminsky Zavod (-1943)
Staroutkinsk. Urban settlement,
Sverdlovsk Oblast, RSFSR :
Utkinsky Zavod (-1933)
(Staroye) Drozhzhanoye. Village,
Tatar Autonomous SSR, RSFSR
: Drozhzhanovo (-c. 1940)
Startsevichi see Znamya
Startsy see Kirovsk (4)
Stary Chardzhuy see Komsomolsk
(3)
Stary Dashev see Dashev
Stary Folvarok see Pobednaya
(3)
Stary Kermenchik see Starom-
linovka
Stary Margilan see Margilan
Stary Salavan see Novocherem-
shansk

Su-chou = Soochow
Süchow [Hsü-chou]. City,
    eastern China : Tungshan
    (1912-45)
Suchow see (1) Ipin; (2) Kiu-
    chüan [Chiu-chüan]; (3)
    Suhsien
Sucre. City, northwestern
    Peru, South America :
    Huauco (-1940)
Suçuapara. City, central Brazil,
    South America : Bela Vista
    (-1944)
Sudan. Republic, northeastern
    Africa : Anglo-Egyptian
    Sudan (1899-1956)
Sudanese Republic see Mali
Sudauen see Suwałki
Sudostroy see Severodvinsk
Sufikishlak see Akhunbabayev
Sug-Aksy see Sut-Khol
Sugluk see Saglouc
Sugod. Municipality, Leyte,
    Philippines : Sugod Norte
    (-1913)
Sugod Norte see Sugod
Sugod Sur see Libagon
Suhaile Arabi. Barrio, Zambo-
    anga del Norte, Philippines
    : Bucana (-1969)
Suhsien. Town, eastern China :
    Suchow (-1912)
Sui-chiang = Suikiang
Suichow see Suihsien (1), (2)
Sui-ch'uan = Suichwan
Suichwan [Sui-ch'uan]. Town,
    southeastern China :
    Lungchüan (-1914)
Suifu see Ipin
Suihsien (1). Town, east-central
    China : Suichow (-1913)
Suihsien (2). Town, east-central
    China : Suichow (-1912)
Suikiang [Sui-chiang]. Town,
    southwestern China :
    Tsingkiang (-1914)
Suileng. Town, northeastern
    China : Shangtsichang
    (-1915)
Suiting see Tahsien
Suiyüan see Fuyüan
Sukarnapura see Jayapura
Sukarno, Puntjak see Jaya,

Puncak
Sukhotinskaya see Sovetskoye (9)
Sukhum see Sukhumi
Sukhumi. Capital of Abkhazian
    Autonomous SSR, Georgian
    SSR : Sukhum (-1935)
Sulawesi. Island, Greater Sundas,
    Indonesia : Celebes (-1945)
Sulechów. Town, western Poland
    : Züllichau (-1945), Germany
Sulęcin. Town, western Poland :
    Zielenzig (-1945), Germany
Sulików. Town, southwestern
    Poland : Schönberg (-1945),
    Germany
Sulimov see Cherkessk
Sulin see Krasny Sulin
Sulphur Springs National Reserva-
    tion see Platt National Park
Sultanabad see Arak
Sultan Alonto. Municipality,
    Lanao del Sur, Philippines :
    Lake Lanao (-1905)
Sultan Kudarat. Municipality,
    Cotabato, Philippines : Nuling
    (-1969)
Sumbawanga. District, Tanzania,
    eastern Africa : Ufipa (-1974)
Šumen = Shumen
Šumperk. Town, central Czecho-
    slovakia : Mährisch-Schönberg
    (-1918, 1939-45), Germany
Sünchow see Kweiping [Kuei-
    p'ing]
Sunfung. Town, southeastern
    China : Chongning (-1914)
Sung-chiang. City, eastern
    China : Hua-t'ing (1912-13)
Sünko [Hsün-k'o]. Town, north-
    eastern China : Chike (-1949)
Sunning see Toishan
Sunnyvale. City, California,
    USA : Murphy's Station (-?),
    Encinal (?-1912)
Sunwui. Town, southeastern
    China : Kongmoon (-1931)
Sünyi [Hsün-i]. Town, central
    China : Sanshui (-1914)
Suram see Surami
Surami. Urban settlement,
    Georgian SSR : Suram (-1936)
Surendranagar. Town, western
    India : Wadhwan (-1950s)

Surfer's Paradise. Beach,
Southport, Queensland,
Australia : Meyer's Ferry
(-1920s)

Surinam. Autonomous territory
of the Netherlands, northeastern South America : Dutch
Guiana (-1954)

Sursk. Town, Penza Oblast,
RSFSR : Nikolsky Khutor
(-1953)

Surskoye. Urban settlement,
Ulyanovsk Oblast, RSFSR :
Promzino (-c. 1930)

Surveyors Bay see Whalers Bay

Surville Cliffs. Cape, North
Island, New Zealand :
Kerr Point (-1966)

Susam-Adasi see Samos

Susanino. Urban settlement,
Kostroma Oblast, RSFSR :
Molvitino (-1938)

Süshui [Hsü-shui]. Town,
northeastern China : Ansu
(-1914)

Susz. Town, northeastern Poland : Rosenberg (-1919),
Germany

Sut-Khol. Village, Tuva
Autonomous SSR, RSFSR :
Sug-Aksy (-c. 1960)

Suvorovo (1). Village, eastern
Bulgaria : Novgradets
(-1950)

Suvorovo (2). Urban settlement,
Odessa Oblast, Ukrainian
SSR : Shikirlikitai (-c. 1930);
Regele Carol II (c. 1930-40),
Romania; Regele Mihai I
(1941-44), Romania

Suwałki. Town, northeastern
Poland : Sudauen (1941-45),
Germany

Suyetikha see Biryusinsk

Süyung [Hsü-yung]. Town,
central China : Yungning
(-1913)

Svárov. Town, northwestern
Czechoslovakia : Tanvald
(-1949)

Sverdlova, imeni see Sverdlovsk
(2)

Sverdlovo. Village, Saratov

Oblast, RSFSR : Ney-Valter
(-1941)

Sverdlovo see Sverdlovsky

Sverdlovsk (1). Village, Bukhara
Oblast, Uzbek SSR : Dzhandar
(-c. 1935), Faizully Khodzhayeva,
imeni (c. 1935-37)

Sverdlovsk (2). Town, Voroshilovgrad Oblast, Ukrainian SSR :
Sverdlova, imeni (*1930s-1938)

Sverdlovsk (3). Capital of
Sverdlovsk Oblast, RSFSR :
Yekaterinburg (-1924)

Sverdlovsky. Urban settlement,
Moscow Oblast, RSFSR :
Sverdlovo (-1928)

Sverdlovsky Priisk see Is

Sveti Ivan Zelina see Zelina

Svetilovichi. Village, Grodno
Oblast, Belorussian SSR :
Spyaglitsa (-1964)

Sveti Vrach see Sandanski

Svetlaya Roshcha. Village,
Gomel Oblast, Belorussian
SSR : Pustynka (-1964)

Svetlogorsk (1). Town, Kaliningrad Oblast, RSFSR : Rauschen
(-1947), Germany (-1945)

Svetlogorsk (2). Town, Gomel
Oblast, Belorussian SSR :
Shatilki (-1961)

Svetlograd. Town, Stavropol
Kray, RSFSR : Petrovskoye
(-1965)

Svetlovodsk. Town, Kirovograd
Oblast, Ukrainian SSR :
Khrushchyov (?-1961), Kremges
(1961-70)

Svetloye. Village, Kaliningrad
Oblast, RSFSR : Kobbelbude
(-1945), Germany

Svetogorsk. Town, Leningrad
Oblast, RSFSR : Enso (-1948),
Finland (-1940)

Svetozarevo. Town, east-central
Yugoslavia : Jagodina (-1946)

Svinka see Lugovaya (3)

Svinoye see Pervomaysk (3)

Svitavy. Town, central Czechoslovakia : Zwittau (-1918,
1939-45), Germany

Svoboda. Village, Kaliningrad
Oblast, RSFSR : Janichen

(-1944)
T'ang-chia-kuan = Tangkiakwan
Tangho [T'ang-ho]. Town,
    east-central China : Tangh-
    sien (-1914), Piyüan (1914-
    23)
Tanghsien see Tangho [T'ang-
    ho]
Tangkiakwan [T'ang-chia-kuan].
    Town, southeastern China :
    Chungshan (1930-34)
Tanhsien. Town, southeastern
    China : Tanchow (-1912)
Taning see Wuki [Wu-ch'i]
Tankiang see Leishan
Tannenberg see Stębark
Tannu-Tuva see Tuva
    Autonomous SSR
Tanokuchi see Kotoura
Tan-t'u see Chen-chiang
Tantura see Dor
Tanvald see Svárov
Tanza. Municipality, Cavite,
    Philippines : Santa Cruz de
    Malabon (-1914)
Taoan [T'ao-an]. Town, north-
    eastern China : Tsingan
    (-1914)
Taochen. Town, southern
    China : Tukichang (-1932)
Taochow see (1) Lintan [Lin-
    t'an]; (2) Taohsien
Taofu. Town, southern China :
    Taowu (-1913)
Taoho see Linsia [Lin-hsia]
Taohsien. Town, south-central
    China : Taochow (-1913)
Taonan [T'ao-nan]. Town,
    northeastern China : Shwang-
    liuchen (-1905)
Taosha [T'ao-sha]. Town,
    north-central China : Shani
    (-1914)
Taowu see Taofu
Taoyüan [T'ao-yüan]. Town,
    northern Taiwan : Sinchu
    (1945-50)
Taoyüan see Szeyang [Ssu-yang]
Taperoá. City, northeastern
    Brazil, South America :
    Batalhão (1944-48)
Tapiau see Gvardeysk
Taplacken see Talpaki

Tapul see Salvacion (2)
Tapuruquá. Town, northwestern
    Brazil, South America : Santa
    Isabel (-1944)
Taquari see Taquarituba
Taquarituba. Town, southeastern
    Brazil, South America :
    Taquari (-1944)
Taraka see Tayozhny
Taranovskoye. Village, Kustanay
    Oblast, Kazakh SSR : Viktorovka
    (-c. 1960)
Taranto (*1923). Province,
    southern Italy : Ionio (c. 1937-
    51)
Tarapoto. City, north-central
    Peru, South America : San
    Martín (1940-47)
Tarauacá. City, western Brazil,
    South America : Seabra (-1944)
Tarfaya. Town, southwestern
    Morocco, northwestern Africa :
    Cabo Yubi [Villa Bens] (1950-
    58)
Targoviste. City, eastern Bul-
    garia : Yeski Dzhumaya (-1909)
Tarkhany see Lermontovo
Tarmilate. Town, northwestern
    Morocco, northwestern Africa :
    Oulmes-le-Thermes (-1971)
Târnăveni. Town, central Ro-
    mania : Diciosânmartin (-1930)
Tarnopol see Ternopol
Tarnopol Oblast see Ternopol
    Oblast
Tarnovo see Veliko Tarnovo
Tarnowitz see Tarnowskie Góry
Tarnowskie Góry. Town, southern
    Poland : Tarnowitz (-1921),
    Germany
Tarquinia. Town, central Italy :
    Corneto (Tarquinia) (-1922)
Tarta. Village, Krasnovodsk
    Oblast, Turkmen SSR : Kianly
    (Tarta) (c. 1945-c. 1960)
Tartki. Village, Tadzhik SSR :
    Kabadian (-c. 1935), Mikoyan-
    abad (c. 1935-57)
Tartu. Town, Estonian SSR :
    Yuryev (-1918)
Tashetai see Anpeh
Tashino see Pervomaysk (4)
Tata. Town, northern Hungary :

Tatatóváros (*1938-39)
Tatarikan see Pagayawan
Tatar Pazardžik see Pazardžik
Tatatóváros see Tata
Tatsienlu see Kangting [K'ang-ting]
Tatsingkow see Shangi
Tatuchang see Nayung
Tatung see Tungho [T'ung-ho]
Taus see Domažlice
Tayabas see Quezon
Tay Bac. Region, northeastern Vietnam : Thai Meo (*1955-62)
Tayncha see Krasnoarmeysk (4)
Tayozhny. Urban settlement, Krasnoyarsk Kray, RSFSR : Taraka (-c. 1960)
Tayü. Town, southeastern China : Nanan (-1912)
Tayung. Town, south-central China : Yungting (-1914)
Taza-Bazar see Shumanay
Taza-Kala see Telmansk
Taziárkhai. Village, eastern Greece : Kritsínion (-1960s)
Tazoult. Town, northeastern Algeria, northern Africa : Lambèse (-c. 1962)
Tazovskoye see Khalmer-Sede
Tazuruhuma. Town, central Honshu, Japan : Wakura (-1934)
Tbilisi. Capital of Georgian SSR : Tiflis (-1935)
Tbilisskaya. Village, Krasnodar Kray, RSFSR : Tiflisskaya (-1936)
Tczew. City, northern Poland : Dirschau (-1919), Germany
Te-chiang = Tehkiang
Te-ch'in = Tehtsin
Te-chou = Tehchow
Tegucigalpa see Francisco Morazán
Tehchow [Te-chou]. City, eastern China : Tehsien (1913-49)
Tehhwei [Te-hui]. Town, northeastern China : Tafangshen (-1910)
Tehjung [Te-jung]. Town, southern China : Someitsun

(-1913)
Tehkiang [Te-chiang]. Town, southern China : Anhwa (-1914)
Tehko [Te-ko]. Town, southern China : Tehwa (-1914)
Tehsien see Tehchow [Te-chou]
Tehtsin [Te-ch'in]. Village, southwestern China : Atentze (-1935)
Te-hui = Tehhwei
Tehwa see Tehko
Teian see Anlu
Teixeira Pinto. Village, western Guinea-Bissau, western Africa : Canchungo (-1948)
Te-jung = Tehjung
Te-ko = Tehko
Telanaipura. Town, southeastern Sumatra, Indonesia : Jambi (-c. 1966)
Telemark. County, southeastern Norway : Bratsberg (-1918)
Telford. New town, Salop, England, UK : Dawley (*1963-68)
Telmansk. Urban settlement, Tashauz Oblast, Turkmen SSR : Taza-Kala (-1938)
Telnovsky. Urban settlement, Sakhalin Oblast, RSFSR : Kita-kozawa (1905-47), Japan (-1945)
Telukbajur. Town, western Sumatra, Indonesia : Emma-haven (-c. 1966)
Telyatki see Podlesnaya
Temir-Khan-Shura see Buynaksk
Temirtau. Town, Karaganda Oblast, Kazakh SSR : Samarkandsky (*1934-45)
Tempelburg see Czaplinek
Tenda see Tende
Tende. Village, southeastern France : Tenda (-1947), Italy
Tengchow see (1) Penglai [P'eng-lai]; (2) Tenghsien
Tengchung [T'eng-ch'ung]. Town, southwestern China : Tengyüeh (-1913)
Tenge. Urban settlement, Mangyshlak Oblast, Kazakh SSR : Uzen (-1977)
Tengelic. Town, west-central

Hungary : Gindlicsalád
(-1931)
Tenghsien. Town, east-central
China : Tengchow (-1913)
Tengi-Kharam see Dekhkanabad
Tengyüeh see Tengchung
[T'eng-ch'ung]
T'en-hsi = Tiensi
Teniente Bullaín. Town,
western Bolivia, South
America : Dalence (-early
1940s)
Tepic see Nayarit
Teplice nad Metují. Town,
western Czechoslovakia :
Wekelsdorf (-1918, 1939-
45), Germany
Teplice (-Šanov). City, western
Czechoslovakia : Teplitz
(-Schönau) (-1918, 1939-45),
Germany
Teplitz (-Schönau) see Teplice
(-Šanov)
Teploozyorsk. Urban settlement,
Jewish Autonomous Oblast,
Khabarovsk Kray, RSFSR :
Tyoploye Ozero (-c. 1960)
Terebovlya. Town, Ternopol
Oblast, Ukrainian SSR :
Trembowla (-1945),
Poland
Terezín. Town, western
Czechoslovakia : Theresien-
stadt (-1918, 1939-45),
Germany
Terijoki see Zelenogorsk
Ternopol. Capital of Ternopol
Oblast, Ukrainian SSR :
Tarnopol (1919-44), Poland
Ternopol Oblast. Ukrainian
SSR : Tarnopol Oblast
(*1939-44)
Ternovsk see Novokashirsk
Ternovskoye see Trunovskoye
Ternovsky see Novokashirsk
Terny. Town, Dnepropetrovsk
Oblast, Ukrainian SSR :
Pershotravenka (-c. 1960)
Terpilovichi see Zelenets (1)
Terranova di Sicilia see Gela
Terranova Pausania see Olbia
Terter see Mir-Bashir
Tervel. Village, northeastern

Bulgaria : Curt-Bunar (1913-
40), Romania
Teschen see Český Těšín
Tessville see Lincolnwood
Teterboro. Borough, New Jersey,
USA : Bendiz (1937-43)
Tetiyev. Town, Kiev Oblast,
Ukrainian SSR : Snegurovka
(-c. 1960)
Tetri-Tskaro. Town, Georgian
SSR : Agbulakh (-c. 1945)
Tetschen see Děčín
Tetyukhe see Dalnegorsk
Tetyukhe-Pristan see Rudnaya
Pristan
Teuchezhsk. Town, Krasnodar
Kray, RSFSR : Adygeysk
(-1976)
Tezebazar. Urban settlement,
Tashauz Oblast, Turkmen SSR
: Andreyevsk (-c. 1960)
Thailand. Kingdom, southeastern
Asia : Siam (-1939)
Thai Meo see Tay Bac
The Dalles see City of The
Dalles
The Forks see Merritt
Thenia. Town, northern Algeria,
northern Africa : Ménerville
(-c. 1962)
Theodore Roosevelt Island.
Island, Potomac River, District
of Columbia, USA : Analostan
Island (-?)
Theresienstadt see Terezín
Therma see Eagle Nest
Thessaloníki. City, northern
Greece : Salonika (-1912),
Turkey
Theunissen. Town, Orange
Free State, South Africa :
Smaldeel (-1909)
Thiersville see Ghriss
Thionville. Town, northeastern
France : Diedenhofen (1870-
1919), Germany
Thomson's Falls see Nyahururu
Thorens see Thorens Glières
Thorens-Glières. Village,
southeastern France : Thorens
(-1947)
Thorn see Toruń
Thurston Island. Island, Antarc-

tica : Thurston Peninsula
(?-1961)

Thurston Peninsula see
Thurston Island

Thysville see Mbanza-Ngungu

Tiaret see Tagdempt

Tidmore see Seminole

Tiehli [T'ieh-li]. Town, northeastern China : Tiehshanpao
(-1915)

Tiehshanpao see Tiehli
[T'ieh-li]

T'ien-hsi = Tiensi

Tienpao [T'ien-pao]. Town,
southern China : Chenan
(-1913)

T'ien-shui. City, north-central
China : Ch'in-chou (-1912)

Tiensi [T'ien-hsi]. Town,
southern China : Lucheng
(-1936)

Tientung [T'ien-tung]. Town,
southern China : Enlung
(-1936)

Tienyang [T'ien-yang]. Town,
southern China : Napo
(-1936)

Tiflis see Tbilisi

Tiflisskaya see Tbilisskaya

Tighennif. Town, northwestern
Algeria, northern Africa :
Palikao (-c. 1962)

Tighina see Bendery

Tikhonkaya see Birobidzhan

Tikhonovka see Pozharskoye

Tikhono-Zadonsky see Kropotkin (2)

Tikitki. Town, North Island,
New Zealand : Kahukura
(-1940)

Tiligulo-Berezanka see
Berezanka

Tilsit see Sovetsk (2)

Tiltonsville. Village, Ohio,
USA : Grover (-1930)

Timashyovsk. Town, Krasnodar
Kray, RSFSR : Timashyov-
skaya (-1966)

Timashyovskaya see Timashyovsk

Timbiras. City, northeastern
Brazil, South America :
Monte Alegre (-1944)

Timerhi. Settlement, northern

Guyana, South America :
Atkinson Field (-1968)

Timiryazevo. Village, Kaliningrad Oblast, RSFSR : Neukirch
(-1945), Germany

Timiryazevsky. Town, Tomsk
Oblast, RSFSR : Novaya
Eushta (-1940)

Timon. City, northeastern
Brazil, South America :
Flores (-1944)

Timor Timur. Eastern half of
Timor, Indonesia : Portuguese
Timor (-1976)

Timoshenko, imeni see Omchak

Tinalunan see Gaudencio
Antonio (2)

Tingchow see (1) Changting
[Ch'ang-t'ing]; (2) Tinghsien

Tingfan see Hweishui [Hui-shui]

Ting-hsi = Tingsi

Ting-hsiang = Tingsiang

Tinghsien. Town, northeastern
China : Tingchow (-1913)

Ting-hsin = Tingsin

Tingnan. Town, southeastern
China : Siali (-1928)

Tingsi [Ting-hsi]. Town, north-
central China : Anting (-1914)

Tingsiang [Ting-hsiang]. Town,
southern China : Sangpiling
(-1913)

Tingsin [Ting-hsin]. Town,
north-central China : Maomu
(-1928)

Tingyüan see (1) Chenpa; (2)
Wusheng

Tinh Shon. Village, southern
Vietnam : My Lai 4 (-1976)

Tinonganine see Santana de
Tinonganine

Tirschtiegel see Trzciel

Tissemsilt. Town, northern
Algeria, northern Africa :
Vialar (-c. 1962)

Tiszaszederkény see Leninváros

Tiszaszentimre. Town, east-
central Hungary : Szentimre
(-1902)

Tiszavasvári. Town, northeastern
Hungary : Büdszentmihály
(1941-46, 1950-52)

Titao see Lintao [Lin-t'ao]

Titograd. City, southern Yugoslavia : Podgorica (-1946)

Titova Korenica. Village, northwestern Yugoslavia : Korenica (-c. 1945)

Titovo Užice. Town, central Yugoslavia : Užice (-1946)

Titov Veles. Town, southern Yugoslavia : Veles (-c. 1945)

Tľuste see Tolstoye

Tobias Barreto. City, northeastern Brazil, South America : Campos (-1944)

Tobolsk Guberniya see Tyumensk Guberniya

Tocantinópolis. City, north-central Brazil, South America : Boa Vista (-1944)

Tocqueville see Ras el Oued

Togo. Republic, western Africa : French Togoland (*1920-60)

Toishan. Town, southeastern China : Sunning (-1914)

Tokmak (1). Town, Kirgiz SSR : Bolshoy Tokmak (-1927)

Tokmak (2). Town, Zaporozhye Oblast, Ukrainian SSR : Bolshoy Tokmak (-1963)

Toktogul. Urban settlement, Osh Oblast, Kirgiz SSR : Akchi-Karasu (-1940), Muztor (1944-c. 1960)

Tolbukhin. Town, northeastern Bulgaria : Bazarjik (-1913), Bazargic (1913-40), Romania; Dobrich (1940-49)

Tolbukhino. Village, Yaroslavl Oblast, RSFSR : Davydkovo (-1950)

Tolkemit see Tolmicko

Tolmicko. Town, northern Poland : Tolkemit (-1945), Germany

Tolochin. Town, Vitebsk Oblast, Belorussian SSR : Tolochino (-c. 1940)

Tolochino see Tolochin

Tolstoi. Hamlet, Manitoba, Canada : Oleskow (-1905)

Tolstoye. Urban settlement, Ternopol Oblast, Ukrainian

SSR : Tľuste (-1944), Poland

Tolyatti. Town, Kuybyshev Oblast, RSFSR : Stavropol (-1964)

Tomaniivi, Mount. Mountain, Viti Levu, Fiji : Victoria, Mount (-?)

Tomari. Town, Sakhalin Oblast, RSFSR : Tomarioru (1905-47), Japan (-1945)

Tomari see Golovnino

Tomarikishi see Vakhrushev

Tomarioru see Tomari

Tomás Barrón. Village, western Bolivia, South America : Eucaliptus (-early 1940s)

Tomislavgrad see Duvno

Tonder. City, southern Denmark : Tondern (-1920), Germany

Tondern see Tonder

Tongyŏng see Ch'ungmu

Tonshayevo see Shaygino

Topolovgrad. City, southeastern Bulgaria : Kavaklii (-1934)

Topornino see Kushnarenkovo

Torbinka see Partizany (2)

Torez. Town, Donetsk Oblast, Ukrainian SSR : Chistyakovo (-1964)

Torfelt. Oilfield, North Sea, Norway : Ergfisk (-1971)

Torgovaya see Salsk

Tormáskölesd see Kölesd

Tornala see Šafárikovo

Toro see Shakhtyorsk (1)

Torrecilla sobre Alesanco. Village, northern Spain : San Isidoro (-c. 1950)

Toruń. City, north-central Poland : Thorn (1793-1807, 1815-1918, 1939-45), Germany

Toscanella see Tuscania

Tourane see Da Nang

Tous see San Martín de Tous

Tovarishcha Khatayevicha, imeni see Sinelnikovo

Tovarkovsky. Urban settlement, Tula Oblast, RSFSR : Kaganovich (?-1957)

Toyohara see Yuzhno-Sakhalinsk

Trachenberg see Żmigród

Transcarpathian Oblast [Zakarpat-

skaya Oblast]. Ukrainian
SSR : Ruthenia (1920-46)
Transcaspian Oblast see
Turkmen Oblast
Transjordan(ia) see Jordan (2)
Transvaal. Province, northern
South Africa : South African
Republic (1856-77, 1881-
1900)
Transylvania. Region, north-
western Romania : Erdély
(1867-1918), Hungary
Třebechovice pod Orebem.
Town, east-central Czecho-
slovakia : Hohenbruck
(-1918, 1939-45), Germany
Třebíč. Town, west-central
Czechoslovakia : Trebitsch
(-1918, 1939-45), Germany
Trebitsch see Třebíč
Trebnitz see Trzebnica
Třeboň. Town, southwestern
Czechoslovakia : Wittingau
(-1918, 1939-45), Germany
Trebukhi see Kalinovaya (2)
Trebushki see Mirnaya (4)
Tremblowla see Terebovlya
Tremedal see Monte Azul
Trempen see Novostroyevo
Trentino-Alto Adige. Region,
northern Italy : Venezia
Tridentina (1919-47)
Treptow (an der Rega) see
Trzebiatów
Treptow (an der Tollense) see
Altentreptow
Treputikha see Bereznitsa (2)
Três Rios. City, southeastern
Brazil, South America :
Entre Rios (-1943)
Tretyego Internatsionala, imeni
see Novoshakhtinsk
Treuburg see Olecko
Triaucourt see Triaucourt-
en-Argonne
Triaucourt-en-Argonne. Village,
northeastern France :
Triaucourt (-1947)
Triglav. Mountain, central
Bulgaria : Kademlija (-1967)
Trigo de Morais. City, southern
Mozambique, southeastern
Africa : Guijá (-1960), Vila

Alferes Chamusca (1960-64),
Vila Trigo de Morais (1964-
71)
Trikora, Puncak. Mountain,
Irian Jaya, Indonesia :
Wilhelmina Top (-1963)
Trinidad see Jose Abad Santos
Triumpho see Bom Jesus do
Triunfo
Triunpho see Bom Jesus do
Triunfo
Trnava. City, west-central
Czechoslovakia : Nagyszombat
(-1920), Hungary
Troitsk. Town, Moscow Oblast,
RSFSR : Troitsky (-1977)
Troitskosavsk see Kyakhta
Troitsky. Urban settlement,
Sverdlovsk Oblast, RSFSR :
Peklevskaya (-1928)
Troitsky see Troitsk
Trompsburg. Town, Orange Free
State, South Africa : Hamilton
(-1902)
Trondheim. City, central Norway
: Trondhjem (-1930), Nidaros
(1930-31)
Trondhjem see Trondheim
Troppau see Opava
Trotsk see (1) Chapayevsk;
(2) Gatchina
Trucial States see United Arab
Emirates
Trudovaya Kommuna imeni
Dzerzhinskogo see Dzerzhinsky
Trudovoy see (1) Kuybyshevsky
(2); (2) Yusta
Trujillo see San Cristóbal
Trujillo Valdéz see Peravia
Trukhanovichi see Zarechnaya
(4)
Trunovskoye. Village, Stavropol
Kray, RSFSR : Ternovskoye
(-1936)
Truth or Consequences. Town,
New Mexico, USA : Hot Springs
(-1950)
Trzcianka. Town, northwestern
Poland : Schönlanke (-1938,
1939-45), Germany
Trzciel. Town, western Poland :
Tirschtiegel (-1939, 1939-45),
Germany

Trzcińsko Zdrój. Town, north-
western Poland : Bad
Schönfliess in Neumark
(-1945), Germany
Trzebiatów. Town, northwestern
Poland : Treptow (an der
Rega) (-1945), Germany
Trzebnica. Town, southwestern
Poland : Trebnitz (-1945),
Germany
Tržič. Village, northwestern
Yugoslavia : Neumarktl
(-1918), Germany
Tsagan-Aman. Settlement,
Kalmyk Autonomous SSR,
RSFSR : Burunny (-c. 1960)
Tsangchow see Tsanghsien
[Ts'ang-hsien]
Tsanghsien [Ts'ang-hsien].
Town, northeastern China
: Tsangchow (-1913)
Ts'ang-wu see Wuchow
Tsarekonstantinovka see
Kuybyshevo (6)
Tsarevicha Alekseya see
Maly Taymyr
Tsarevo see Michurin
Tsarevsk see Nekrasovo
Tsaribrod see Dimitrovgrad
(1)
Tsaritsyn see Volgograd
Tsaritsyn Guberniya see
Stalingrad Guberniya
Tsaritsyno-Dachnoye see
Lenino
Tsarskoye Selo see Pushkin
Tsaryovokokshaysk see
Yoshkar-Ola
Tsaryovo-Sanchursk see
Sanchursk
Tschirnau see Czernina
Tsechow see Tsincheng
Tselinnoye (1). Village, Kurgan
Oblast, RSFSR : Novoko-
cherdyk (-c. 1960)
Tselinnoye (2). Village, Altay
Kray, RSFSR : Yaminskoye
(-c. 1960)
Tselinograd. Capital of Tselino-
grad Oblast, Kazakh SSR :
Akmolinsk (-1961)
Tselinograd Oblast (*1961).
Kazakh SSR : Akmolinsk

Oblast (*1939-60)
Tsenkung [Ts'en-kung]. Town,
southern China : Szechow
(-1913), Szehsien (1913-30)
Tsentralnopromyshlennaya Oblast
see Moscow Oblast
Tserkovishche see Kulnevo
Tsetsen Khan see Undur Khan
Tsincheng [Chin-ch'eng]. Town,
northeastern China : Tsechow
(-1912)
Tsinchow see (1) Tsinhsien
[Chin-hsien] (1); (2) Tsinhien
[Ch'in-hsien] (2)
Tsingan see Taoan [T'ao-an]
Tsingchow see Yitu
Tsinghsien [Ching-hsien]. Town,
south-central China : Tsing-
chow (-1913)
Tsinghwa see Poai
Tsingki see Hanyüan
Tsingkiang [Chin-chiang]. Town,
southeastern China : Linkiang
(-1912)
Tsingkiang see (1) Kienho
[Chien-ho]; (2) Suikiang
[Sui-chiang]
Tsingkiang(pu) [Ch'ing-chiang(-pu)].
City, eastern China : Hwaiyin
[Huai-yin] (1911-49)
Tsinglung [Ch'ing-lung]. Town,
northeastern China : Tachangtze
(-1933), Tushan (1933-49)
Tsingpien see Pingpien [P'ing-
pien]
Tsingping [Ch'ing-p'ing]. Town,
northeastern China : Mangniuyingtze (-1947), Lingnan
(1947-49)
Tsingping see Lushan
Tsingsi [Ching-hsi]. Town,
southern China : Kweishun
(-1913)
Tsingyü [Ching-yü]. Town,
northeastern China : Mengkiang
(-1949)
Tsingyüan [Ch'ing-yüan]. Town,
northeastern China : Pakiachen
(-1929)
Tsingyuän see Paoting
Tsinhsien [Chin-hsien] (1). Town,
northeastern China : Tsinchow
(-1913)

Tsinhsien [Ch'in-hsien] (2).
Town, northeastern China :
Tsinchow (-1912)
Tsining [Chi-ning]. City,
northern China : Pingtichüan
[P'ing-ti-ch'üan] (-1922)
Tsinkiang [Chin-chiang]. Town,
southeastern China :
Chüanchow (-1913)
Tsinyang [Ch'in-yang]. Town,
north-central China :
Hwaiking (-1913)
Tsitsihar. City, northeastern
China : Lungkiang (1913-
47)
Tsitskovichi see Rassvetnaya
(2)
Tskhinvali. Capital of South
Ossetian Autonomous Oblast,
Georgian SSR : Staliniri
(1934-61)
Tsochow see Tsohsien
Tsochüan [Tso-ch'üan]. Town,
northeastern China :
Liaochow (-1912), Liaohsien
(1912-49)
Tsohsien. Town, southern
China : Tsochow (-1912)
Tsoshui. Town, central China
: Siaoyi (-1914)
Tsuchizawa. Town, northern
Honshu, Japan : Junikabura
(-early 1940s)
Tsuge. Town, southern Honshu,
Japan : Higashitsuge (-early
1940s)
Tsu-hing = Tzehing
Tsulukidze. Town, Georgian
SSR : Khoni (-1936)
Ts'ung-chiang = Tsungkiang
Tsungkiang [Ts'ung-chiang].
Town, southern China :
Pingmei (-1941)
Tsungshan [Ch'ung-shan].
Town, southern China :
Taiping (-1913)
Tsungteh [Ch'ung-te]. Town,
eastern China : Shihmen
(-1914)
Tsuro see Murotozaki
Tsurukhaytuy see Priargunsk
Tsutski see Vostochnaya (1)
Tsuya. Town, northern Honshu,

Japan : Mitake (-late 1930s)
Tsvetnogorsk. Urban settlement,
Khakass Autonomous Oblast,
Krasnoyarsk Kray, RSFSR :
Yuliya (- c. 1960)
Tsyurupinsk. Town, Kherson
Oblast, Ukrainian SSR :
Alyoshki (-1928)
Tsyurupy, imeni. Urban settle-
ment, Moscow Oblast, RSFSR
: Vanilovo (-1935)
Túbano see Padre Las Casas
Tubig see Macario Adriatico
Tublijon see Rizal (2)
Tubog see San Gabriel
Tucurúi. City, northeastern
Brazil, South America :
Alcobaça (-1944)
Tuczno. Town, northwestern
Poland : Tütz (-1938, 1939-
45), Germany
Tudela see Calandagan
Tüffer see Lasko
Tugalan see Kolkhozabad
Tugaoen. Barrio, Ilocos Norte,
Philippines : Puzol (-1971)
Tukichang see Taochen
Tukuyu. Town, southwestern
Tanzania, southeastern Africa
: Neu-Langenburg (-?)
Tulan. Town, west-central
China : Silikow (-1931)
Tulatovo see Iriston
Tumanyan. Urban settlement,
Armenian SSR : Dzagidzor
(-1951)
Tun see Firdaus
Tungan see (1) Antze [An-tz'u];
(2) Tungnan [T'ung-nan]
Tungchang see Liaocheng
[Liao-ch'eng]
Tungcheng [T'ung-cheng]. Town,
southern China : Yungkang
(-1914)
T'ung-chiang = Tungkiang
Tungchow see (1) Pingtang
[P'ing-t'ang]; (2) Tunghsien
[T'ung-hsien]
T'ung-ch'uan = Tungchwan
Tungchwan [T'ung-ch'uan]. Town,
central China : Tungkwan
(-1946)
Tungchwan see Hweitseh [Hui-tse]

Tungfeng. Town, northeastern
China : Tungpin (-1914)
Tunghai see Sinhai [Hsin-hai]
Tungho [T'ung-ho]. Town,
northeastern China :
Tatung (-1914)
Tunghsien [T'ung-hsien]. Town,
northeastern China :
Tungchow (-1913)
Tungjen [T'ung-jen]. Town,
northwestern China :
Lungwusze (-1934)
Tungjen see Kiangkow
[Chiang-k'ou]
Tungkiang [T'ung-chiang].
Town, northeastern China :
Linkiang (-1913)
Tungkwan see Tungchwan
[T'ung-ch'uan]
Tungliao [T'ung-liao]. Town,
northeastern China :
Paiyintailai (-1908)
Tungnan [T'ung-nan]. Town,
central China : Tungan
(-1914)
Tungon see Wanfow
Tungpin see (1) Tungfeng;
(2) Yenshow [Yen-shou]
Tungshan see (1) Kiangning
[Chiang-ning]; (2) Süchow
[Hsü-chou]
Tungsiang see Süanhan
[Hsüan-han]
T'ung-te = Tungteh
Tungteh [T'ung-te]. Town,
northwestern China :
Lakiashih (-1913)
Tungtsichen see Lintien
Tupacereta see Tupancireta
Tupancireta. City, southern
Brazil, South America :
Tupacereta (-1938)
Tura. Capital of Evenki
Autonomous Okrug, Kras-
noyarsk Kray, RSFSR :
Turinskaya Kultbaza
(c. 1920-1938)
Turcianske Teplice. Town,
southeastern Czechoslovakia :
Štubnianske Teplice (-1945)
Turenne see Sabra
Turinskaya Kultbaza see Tura
Türkeh. Island, Sea of Mar-

mara, Turkey : Avşar (-1973)
Turkmen Oblast (1924†). Turkmen
Autonomous SSR : Transcaspian
[Zakaspiyskaya] Oblast (-1921)
Turnovo see Veliko-Turnovo
Tursunzade. Town, Tadzhik
SSR : Stantsiya Regar (-1952),
Regar (1952-78)
Turtkul. Town, Karakalpak
Autonomous SSR (of which
capital to 1939), Uzbek SSR :
Petroaleksandrovsk (-c. 1920)
Turtucaia see Tutrakan
Turyinskiye Rudniki see Kras-
noturyinsk
Tuscania. Town, central Italy :
Toscanella (-1911)
Tushan see Tsinglung
Tusket Wedge see Wedgeport
Tutayev. Town, Yaroslavl
Oblast, RSFSR : Romanov-
Borisoglebsk (-1918)
Tutrakan. City, northeastern
Bulgaria : Turtucaia (1913-
40), Romania
Tütz see Tuczno
Tuva Autonomous Oblast see
Tuva Autonomous SSR
Tuva Autonomous SSR. USSR :
Uryankhai (-1921), Outer
Mongolia; Tannu-Tuva (1921-
44), Tuva Autonomous Oblast,
(1944-61)
Tuvalu. Island group, western
Pacific Ocean : Ellice Islands
(-1975)
Tver see Kalinin (2)
Twardogóra. Town, southwestern
Poland : Festenberg (-1945),
Germany
Tweedvale see Lobethal
Tyan-Shan Oblast see Naryn
Oblast
Tyatino. Village, Kuril Islands,
Sakhalin Oblast, RSFSR :
Chinomiji (1905-46), Japan
(-1945)
Tyazhin see Tyazhinsky
Tyazhinsky. Urban settlement,
Kemerovo Oblast, RSFSR :
Tyazhin (-c. 1960)
Tymovskoye. Urban settlement,
Sakhalin Oblast, RSFSR :

Derbinskoye (-1949)
Tynda. Town, Amur Oblast,
RSFSR : Tyndinsky (-1975)
Tyndinsky see Tynda
Tyoploye Ozero see Tep-
loozyorsk
Tyoply Klyuch see Klyuchevsk
Tyoply Stan see Sechenovo
Typhloséllion see Drosok-
horíon
Tyumensk Guberniya (1923†).
USSR : Tobolsk Guberniya
(-1919)
Tyuriseva see Ushkovo
Tzechow see (1) Tzechung
[Tsu-chung]; (2) Tzehsien
[Tz'u-hsien]
Tzechung [Tzu-chung]. Town,
central China : Tzechow
(-1913)
Tzehing [Tzu-hsing]. Town,
south-central China :
Hingning (-1914)
Tzehsien [Tz'u-hsien]. Town,
northeastern China : Tzechow
(-1913)
Tzekam. Town, southeastern
China : Wingon (-1914)
Tzeki [Tz'u-ch'i]. Town,
southeastern China : Luki
(-1914)
Tzekiang see Kaiyang [K'ai-
yang]
Tzekwei [Tzu-kuei]. Town,
east-central China : Kwei-
chow (-1912)
Tzeyang [Tzu-yang]. Town,
eastern China : Yenchow
(-1913)
Tzeyuan [Tzu-yuan]. Town,
southern China : Siyen (-1936)
Tzeyun [Tzu-yun]. Town,
southern China : Kweihwa
(-1913)
Tz'u-ch'i = Tzeki
Tzu-chung = Tzechung
Tz'u-hsien = Tzehsien
Tzu-hsing = Tzehing
Tzu-kuei = Tzekwei
Tzu-yang = Tzeyang
Tzu-yuan = Tzeyuan
Tzu-yun = Tzeyun

Uaupés. City, northwestern
Brazil, South America : São
Gabriel (-1944)
Ubaíra. City, eastern Brazil,
South America : Areia (-1944)
Ubaitaba. City, eastern Brazil,
South America : Itapira (-1944)
Ubanghi Shari see Central
African Empire
Ubirama see Lençóis Paulista
Ubundi. Town, northeastern
Zaïre, central Africa :
Ponthierville (-1966)
Uchkorgon. Village, Osh Oblast,
Kirgiz SSR : Molotovabad
(1938-57)
Uchkulan. Village, Karachaevo-
Cherkess Autonomous Oblast,
Stavropol Kray, RSFSR :
Madniskhevi (-c. 1960)
Uchkupryuk. Village, Fergana
Oblast, Uzbek SSR : Molotova,
imeni (1937-40), Molotovo
(1940-57)
Udarnaya (1). Village, Vitebsk
Oblast, Belorussian SSR :
Kornilovichi (-1964)
Udarnaya (2). Village, Gomel
Oblast, Belorussian SSR :
Osmalenik (-1964)
Udarny. Town, Sakhalin Oblast,
RSFSR : Taihei (1905-45),
Japan
Udd see Chkalov
Udine. Province, northeastern
Italy : Friuli (1923-c. 1945)
Udmurt Autonomous Oblast see
Udmurt Autonomous SSR
Udmurt Autonomous SSR. RSFSR
: Votyak Autonomous Oblast
(*1920-32), Udmurt Autonomous
Oblast (1932-34)
Ufipa see Sumbawanga
Uggehnen see Matrosovo
Uglegorsk (1). Town, Sakhalin
Oblast, RSFSR : Esutoru
(1905-47), Japan (-1945)
Uglegorsk (2). Town, Donetsk
Oblast, Ukrainian SSR :
Khatsapetrovka (-c. 1960)
Uglekamensk. Urban settlement,
Primorsky Kray, RSFSR :

Severny Suchan (-1972)
Ugleuralsky. Urban settlement,
Perm Oblast, RSFSR :
Polovinka (*1928-51)
Uglezavodsk. Urban settle-
ment, Sakhalin Oblast,
RSFSR : Higashi-naibuchi
(1905-45), Japan
Ugodsky Zavod see Zhukovo
Ugolny. Urban settlement,
Sakhalin Oblast, RSFSR :
Taiei (1905-45), Japan
Ugolny see (1) Beringovsky;
(2) Karpinsk
Ugolnyye Kopi see Kopeysk
Uherské Hradiště. Town,
central Czechoslovakia :
Ungarisch-Hradisch (-1918,
1939-45), Germany
Uherský Brod. Town, central
Czechoslovakia : Ungarisch
Brod (-1918, 1939-45),
Germany
Uherský Ostroh. Town, central
Czechoslovakia : Ungarisch-
Ostra (-1918, 1939-45),
Germany
Ujazd. Town, southern Poland
: Bischofstal (-1945), Ger-
many
Uji see Higashi-uji
Ujiyamada see Ise
Ujung Pandang. City, south-
western Sulawesi, Indonesia
: Makasar (-c. 1970)
Ukhta. Town, Komi Autonomous
SSR, RSFSR : Chibyu (*1931-
43)
Ukhta see Kalevala
Ukmerge. Town, Lithuanian
SSR : Vilkomir (-1920),
Russia
Ukrainsk. Town, Donetsk
Oblast, Ukrainian SSR :
Lesovka (-1963)
Ukrepleniye Kommunizma see
Ivanishchi
Ulaanbaatar = Ulan Bator
Ulala see Gorno-Altaysk
Ulan Bator [Ulaanbaatar]. Capi-
tal of Mongolian People's
Republic : Urga (-1911),

Niislel Khureheh (1911-24)
Ulan-Erge. Settlement, Kalmyk
Autonomous SSR, RSFSR :
Krasnoye (1944-57)
Ulan Hoto. City, northeastern
China : Wangyehmiao (-1949)
Ulanovka see Ulanovsky
Ulanovsky. Urban settlement,
Tula Oblast, RSFSR : Ulanovka
(-1948)
Ulan-Ude. Capital of Buryat
Autonomous SSR, RSFSR :
Verkhneudinsk (-1934)
Ulugbek. Village, Samarkand
Oblast, Uzbek SSR : Khodzhaak-
hrar (-c. 1960)
Ulukhanlu see Razdan (2)
Ulyanovka. Urban settlement,
Leningrad Oblast, RSFSR :
Sablino (-1922)
Ulyanovo (1). Village, Kaliningrad
Oblast, RSFSR : Breitenstein
(-1946), Germany (-1945)
Ulyanovo (2). Town, Dzhizak
Oblast, Uzbek SSR : Obruchevo
(-1974)
Ulyanovo (3). Village, Kaluga
Oblast, RSFSR : Plokhino
(-1938)
Ulyanovsk. Capital of Ulyanovsk
Oblast, RSFSR : Simbirsk
(-1924)
Ulyanovsk Guberniya (1928†).
USSR : Simbirsk Guberniya
(-1924)
Ulyanovskoye (1). Village,
Sakhalin Oblast, RSFSR :
Dorokawa (1905-45), Japan
Ulyanovskoye (2). Village,
Karaganda Oblast, Kazakh
SSR : Kolkhoznoye (-c. 1960)
Ulzio. Village, northwestern
Italy : Oulx (-1937)
Umaltinsky. Village, Khabarovsk
Kray, RSFSR : Polovinka
(-1942)
Umanskaya see Leningradskaya
Umba. Urban settlement,
Murmansk Oblast, RSFSR :
Lesnoy (-c. 1960)
Umupuia. Settlement, North
Island, New Zealand : Duders

Beach (-1971)
Umzimvubu. Town, eastern
Transkei, southern Africa
: Port St. Johns (-1976)
Una see Ibiúna
Undur Khan. Town, east-
central Mongolian People's
Republic : Tsetsen Khan
(-1931)
Ungarisch Brod see Uherský
Brod
Ungarisch-Hradisch see
Uherské Hradiště
Ungarisch-Ostra see Uherský
Ostroh
Ungvár see Uzhgorod
União see (1) Jaguaruna;
(2) União dos Palmares
União dos Palmares. City,
northeastern Brazil, South
America : União (-1944)
Union see Lyndhurst
Union of South Africa see
South Africa
United Arab Emirates. Federal
state, Arabian Peninsula :
Trucial States (-1971)
United Arab Republic see Arab
Republic of Egypt
United Provinces (of Agra and
Oudh) see Uttar Pradesh
United States of Brazil see
Brazil
United States of Indonesia see
Indonesia
University Heights. Suburb of
Cleveland, Ohio, USA :
Idlewood (*1908-25)
Unruhstadt see Kargowa
Unterdrauburg see Dravograd
Unterfranken. Administrative
district, southern West
Germany : Mainfranken
(1938-45)
Untervalden see Podlesnoye
Upper Austria [Oberösterreich].
State, northeastern Austria
: Österreich ober der Ems
(-1918), Oberdonau (1938-45)
Upper Senegal and Niger see
Mali
Upper Sind Frontier see
Jacobabad

Upper Tallassee Dam see
Yates Dam
Uralets. Urban settlement,
Sverdlovsk Oblast, RSFSR :
Krasny Ural (-1933)
Uralmedstroy see Krasnouralsk
Uralsk Oblast. Kazakh SSR :
West Kazakhstan [Zapadno-
Kazakhstanskaya] Oblast
(*1932-62)
Uramir see Ramit
Urbakh see Pushkino (2)
Ureña. Town, south-central
Costa Rica, Central America :
San Isidro (-1931)
Urga see Ulan Bator
Urgench. Capital of Khorezm
Oblast, Uzbek SSR : Novo-
Urgench (-1929)
Uritskoye (1). Village, Gomel
Oblast, Belorussian SSR :
Volovitsky Krupets (-1929)
Uritskoye (2). Village, Kustanay
Oblast, Kazakh SSR : Vsekh-
svyatskoye (-1923)
Urmia see Reza'iyeh
Urozhaynaya (1). Village, Minsk
Oblast, Belorussian SSR :
Bobovozovshchina (-1964)
Urozhaynaya (2). Village, Brest
Oblast, Belorussian SSR :
Voshkovtsy (-1971)
Urozhaynaya (3). Village, Vitebsk
Oblast, Belorussian SSR :
Zashchesle (-1964)
Ursatyevskaya see Khavast
Uruaçu. City, central Brazil,
South America : Santana
(-1944)
Urundi see Burundi
Urupés. City, southeastern
Brazil, South America : Mundo
Novo (-1944)
Urupskaya see Sovetskaya (4)
Urus-Martan. Village, Checheno-
Ingush Autonomous SSR, RSFSR
: Krasnoarmeyskoye (1944-57)
Uryankhai see Tuva Autonomous
SSR
Uryu see Kirillovo
Ushiro see Orlovo
Ushkovo. Village, Leningrad
Oblast, RSFSR : Tyuriseva

(-1948), Finland (-1940)
Usküb see Skoplje
Usolye see Usolye-Sibirskoye
Usolye-Sibirskoye. Town,
  Irkutsk Oblast, RSFSR :
  Usolye (-1940)
Usolye-Solikamskoye see
  Berezniki
Uspenka see Kirovsky (3)
Ussuriysk. Town, Primorsky
  Kray, RSFSR : Nikolskoye
  (-1926), Nikolsk-Ussuriysky
  (1926-35), Voroshilov (1935-
  57)
Ust-Abakanskoye see Abakan
Ust-Bagaryak. Village, Chelya-
  binsk Oblast, RSFSR :
  Nizhnyaya (-c. 1960)
Ust-Belokalitvenskaya see
  Belaya Kalitva
Ust-Borovaya see Borovsk
Ust-Dvinsk see Daugavgriva
Ust-Dzheguta. Town, Stavropol
  Kray, RSFSR : Ust-Dzhe-
  gutinskaya (-1975)
Ust-Dzhegutinskaya see Ust-
  Dzheguta
Ústí nad Labem. City, north-
  western Czechoslovakia :
  Aussig (-1918, 1939-45),
  Germany
Ústí nad Orlicí. Town,
  northern Czechoslovakia :
  Wildenschwert (-1918,
  1939-45), Germany
Ustka. Town, northwestern
  Poland : Stolpmünde
  (-1945), Germany
Ust-Katav. Town, Chelyabinsk
  Oblast, RSFSR : Ust-
  Katavsky Zavod (-1948)
Ust-Katavsky Zavod see Ust-
  Katav
Ust-Medveditskaya see
  Serafimovich
Ust-Orda see Ust-Ordinsky
Ust-Ordinsky. Capital of Ust-
  Ordinsky Buryat Autonomous
  Okrug, Irkutsk Oblast, RSFSR
  : Ust-Orda (-1941)
Ustrzyki Dolne. City, south-
  eastern Poland : Nizhniye
  Ustriki (1939-51), USSR

Ust-Sysolsk see Syktyvkar
Ust-Vorkuta. Settlement, Komi
  Autonomous SSR, RSFSR :
  Sangorodok (c. 1945-c. 1952)
Ust-Zhuya see Chara
Usumbura see Bujumbura
Utkinsky Zavod see Staroutkinsk
Uttar Pradesh. State, northern
  India : North-Western Provinces
  and Oudh (-1902), United Pro-
  vinces (of Agra and Oudh)
  (1902-50)
Uuras see Vysotsk
Uzen see Tenge
Uzhgorod. Capital of Transcar-
  pathian Oblast, Ukrainian SSR
  : Uzhorod (1919-38), Czecho-
  slovakia; Ungvár (1938-45),
  Hungary
Uzhorod see Uzhgorod
Uzice see Titovo Uzice
Uzlovoye. Village, Kaliningrad
  Oblast, RSFSR : Rautenberg
  (-1945), Germany

Vaagni. Village, Armenian SSR
  : Shagali (-c. 1960)
Vaasa. City, western Finland :
  Nikolainkaupunki [Nikolaistad]
  (c. 1860-1917)
Vác. City, north-central Hungary
  : Waitzen (-?), Germany
Vaca Guzmán. Town, southeastern
  Bolivia, South America :
  Muyupampa (-c. 1945)
Vadinsk. Village, Penza Oblast,
  RSFSR : Kerensk (-c. 1940)
Vagarshapat see Echmiadzin
Vaila Voe Bay. Stewart Island,
  New Zealand : Avelavo Bay
  (-1965)
Vakhan. Village, Gorno-Badakhshan
  Autonomous Oblast, Tadzhik
  SSR : Zung (-c. 1935)
Vakhrushev. Urban settlement,
  Sakhalin Oblast, RSFSR :
  Tomarikishi (1905-45), Japan
Vakhsh. Urban settlement,
  Tadzhik SSR : Vakhshstroy
  (?-c. 1960)

Vakhshstroy see Vakhsh
Valadim see Mavabo
Valdgeym see Dobropolye
Val d'Ifrane see Menzeh-
Ifrane
Valegotsulovo see Dolinskoye
Valença see (1) Marquês de
Valença; (2) Valença do
Piauí
Valenca do Piauí. City, north-
eastern Brazil, South
America : Valença (-1944),
Berlengas (1944-48)
Valencia. Municipality, Negros
Oriental, Philippines :
Nueva Valencia (-1905),
Luzurriaga (1905-48)
Valera. Village, east-central
Spain : Valera de Arriba
(-c. 1960)
Valera de Arriba see Valera
Valinhos see Guaraúna
Valkatlen see Alkatvaam
Valle di Pompei see Pompei
Valley Junction see West
Des Moines
Vallfogona see San Julián
de Vallfogona
Valmiera. Town, Latvian
SSR : Wolmar (-1918),
Germany
Valparaíba see Cachoeira
Paulista
Valverde see Mao
Valverde de la Virgen. Village,
northeastern Spain : Val-
verde del Camino (-c. 1920)
Valverde del Camino see
Valverde de la Virgen
Van Buren see Kettering
Vandenberg Air Force Base.
California, USA : Camp
Cooke (*1941-57)
Vandsburg see Więcbork
Vanier (1). City, Ontario,
Canada : Cummings' Island
(-1900), Eastview (1909-69)
Vanier (2). Suburb of Quebec,
Quebec, Canada : Quebec
West (-1966)
Vanilovo, imeni see Tsyurupy
Vannovsky see Khamza
Vanstadensrus. Town, Orange

Free State, South Africa :
Mook (-1925)
Varcar Vukuf see Mrkonjić
Grad
Várdas. Village, southern
Greece : Vouprásion (-1960s)
Vardenis. Urban settlement,
Armenian SSR : Basargechar
(-1969)
Varna. City, eastern Bulgaria :
Stalin (1949-56)
Várnakas see Georgouláiika
Varttirayiruppu see Watrap
Várvaron see Myrtiá
Vasiliko see Michurin
Vasilkov pervy see Kalinovka
(2)
Vasilyova Sloboda see Chkalovsk
Vasilyovo see Chkalovsk
Vaucluse see Fontaine-de-
Vaucluse
Vaudrevange. Town, eastern
France : Wallerfangen (-1945)
Vayenga see Severomorsk
Vazovgrad. City, central Bul-
garia : Sopot (-1950)
Vedi. Urban settlement, Ar-
menian SSR : Beyuk-Vedi
(-c. 1935)
Vegadea. Village, northwestern
Spain : Vega de Ribadeo
(-c. 1920)
Vega de Ribadeo see Vegadea
Vegas Verde see North Las
Vegas
Veglia see Krk
Veles see Titov Veles
Velika Kikinda see Kikinda
Velikaya Mikhaylovka. Urban
settlement, Odessa Oblast,
Ukrainian SSR : Grosulovo
(-1945)
Velikaya Novosyolka. Urban
settlement, Donetsk Oblast,
Ukrainian SSR : Bolshoy
Yanisol (-1946), Bolshaya
Novosyolka (1946-c. 1960)
Veliki Bečkerek see Zrenjanin
Velikiye Borki. Village, Ternopol
Oblast, Ukrainian SSR : Borki
Wielkie (-1944), Poland
Velikiye Mosty. Town, Lvov
Oblast, Ukrainian SSR : Mosty

Wielkie (-1941), Poland
Velikoalekseyevsky see Bakht
Velikooktyabrsky. Urban
settlement, Kalinin Oblast,
RSFSR : Pokrovskoye
(-1941)
Veliko-Tŭrnovo. Town, north-
central Bulgaria : Tŭrnovo
(-1965)
Veliky Glubochek. Village,
Ternopol Oblast, Ukrainian
SSR : Hŀuboczek Wielki
(-1944), Poland
Velilla de Guardo see Velilla
del Rio Carrión
Velilla del Rio Carrión. Village,
northern Spain : Velilla de
Guardo (-1960)
Velká Bíteš. Town, west-cen-
tral Czechoslovakia : Gross-
Bitesch (-1918, 1939-45),
Germany
Velká Destná. Mountain,
Czechoslovakia/Poland :
Deschnaer Kuppe (-1918,
1939-45), Germany
Velké Kapusany. Town, eastern
Czechoslovakia : Nagykapos
(1938-45), Hungary
Velké Karlovice. Village,
west-central Czechoslovakia
: Karlowitz (-1918, 1939-
45), Germany
Velké Meziříčí. Town, west-
central Czechoslovakia :
Gross-Meseritsch (-1918,
1939-45), Germany
Venezia Tridentina see Tren-
tino-Alto Adige
Ventersburgweg see Hennenman
Ventspils. Town, Latvian SSR
: Vindava (-1917), Russia
Venustiano Carranza. City,
southern Mexico, North
America : San Bartolomé
(-1934)
Veranopolis. City, southern
Brazil, South America :
Alfredo Chaves (-1944)
Vergel see Bom Jardim
Verin-Gusakyan see Gusakyan
Verin-Talin see Talin
Verkhne-Avzyano-Petrovsk see

Verkhny Avzyan
Verkhnedvinsk. Town, Vitebsk
Oblast, Belorussian SSR :
Drissa (-1962)
Verkhne-Saldinsky Zavod see
Verkhnyaya Salda
Verkhnetoretskoye. Urban settle-
ment, Donetsk Oblast, Ukrain-
ian SSR : Skotovataya (-1978)
Verkhneudinsk see Ulan-Ude
Verkhneufaleysky Zavod see
Verkhny Ufaley
Verkhneye Ablyazovo see Radi-
shchevo (2)
Verkhny Avzyan. Urban settle-
ment, Bashkir Autonomous
SSR, RSFSR : Verkhne-
Avzyano-Petrovsk (-1942)
Verkhnyaya Khortitsa. Urban
settlement, Zaporozhye Oblast,
Ukrainian SSR : Khortitsa
(-1930s)
Verkhnyaya Pyshma. Town,
Sverdlovsk Oblast, RSFSR :
Pyshma (-1946)
Verkhnyaya Salda. Town,
Sverdlovsk Oblast, RSFSR :
Verkhne-Saldinsky Zavod
(-1938)
Verkhny Dashkesan see Dash-
kesan
Verkhny Ufaley. Town, Chelya-
binsk Oblast, RSFSR :
Verkhneufaleysky Zavod
(*1933-40)
Verkhovina. Urban settlement,
Ivano-Frankovsk Oblast,
Ukrainian SSR : Zhabye
(-c. 1960)
Verny see Alma-Ata
Vero see Vero Beach
Vero Beach. City, Florida,
USA : Vero (-1925)
Verőce. Town, northern Hun-
gary : Nógrádverőce (-1965)
Verona see Cedar Grove
Verovka see Krasny Profintern
(3)
Vershino-Darasunsky. Urban
settlement, Chita Oblast,
RSFSR : Darasun (-c. 1960)
Vertyuzhany see Pridnestrov-
skoye

Verwoerdburg. Town, Transvaal,
South Africa : Lyttelton
(*1906-67)
Veselí nad Lužnicí. Town,
western Czechoslovakia :
Frohenbruck (-1918, 1939-
45), Germany
Veselí nad Moravou. Town,
central Czechoslovakia :
Wesseli (-1918, 1939-45),
Germany
Vesnovo. Village, Kaliningrad
Oblast, RSFSR : Kussen
(-1946), Germany (-1945)
Vest-Agder. County, southern
Norway : Lister og Mandals
(-1918)
Vestfold. County, southeastern
Norway : Jarlsberg og
Larvik (-1918)
Vetluzhsky. Urban settlement,
Kostroma Oblast, RSFSR :
Golyshi (-c. 1960)
Veznikon see Hagion Pneuma
Vialar see Tissemsilt
Vibo Valentia. Town, southern
Italy : Monteleone di Cala-
bria (-1928)
Vicente Noble. Town, south-
western Dominican Republic,
West Indies : Alpargatal
(-1943)
Victor Hugo see Hamadia
Victoria, Mount see Tomaniivi,
Mount
Victoria Falls see Mosi-oa-
Toenja (2)
Victoria, West Road see
Hutchinson
Victory see Doña Rosario
Videira. City, southern Brazil,
South America : Perdizes
(-1944)
Vidin. Mountain, northwestern
Bulgaria : Acul (-1967)
Vidnoye. Town, Moscow
Oblast, RSFSR : Rastor-
guyevo (-1965)
Vietz see Witnica
Vigia see Almenara
Viipuri see Vyborg
Vijayavada. Town, southeastern
India : Bezwada (-1949)

Viktorovka see Taranovskoye
Vila Alferes Chamusca. Town,
southern Mozambique, south-
eastern Africa : Caniçado
(-1964)
Vila Alferes Chamusca see
Trigo de Morais
Vila António Enes see Angoche
Vila Cabral see Lichinga
Vila da Maganja da Costa. Town,
eastern Mozambique, south-
eastern Africa : Vila João
Coutinho (-1969)
Vila Gouveia see Catambia
Vila João Coutinho see Vila da
Maganja da Costa
Vila Machado. Village, south-
central Mozambique, south-
eastern Africa : Nova Fontes-
vila (-1909)
Vila Nova de Gaza see Xai-Xai
Vila Pereira de Eça see Onjiva
Vila Pery see Manica (1), (2)
Vila Salazar see Dalatando
Vila Teixeira da Silva see
Luau
Vila Trigo de Morais see Trigo
de Morais
Vila Vasco da Gama. Village,
western Mozambique, south-
eastern Africa : Chiputo
(-1924)
Vila-Vila see Villa Viscarra
Viljoensdorp see Newcastle
Vilkomir see Ukmerge
Villa Abecia. Town, southern
Bolivia, South America :
Camataquí (-c. 1945), Villa
General Germán Busch (c. 1945-
c. 1948)
Villa Americana see Americana
Villa Bella see Serra Talhada
Villa Bens see Tarfaya
Villa Canales. Town, south-
central Guatemala, South
America : Pueblo Viejo
(-1921)
Villa Cecilia see Ciudad
Madero
Villa Cisneros see Dakhla
Villa de D. Fadrique. Village,
south-central Spain : Puebla
de D. Fadrique (-c. 1920)

Villa del Nevoso see (Ilirska)
  Bistrica
Villa de María. Town, central
  Argentina, South America :
  Río Seco (-c. 1945)
Villa di Briano. Town, southern
  Italy : Frignano (-1950)
Villafranca de Ordizia. Village,
  northern Spain : Villafranca
  de Oria (-c. 1970)
Villafranca de Oria see
  Villafranca de Ordizia
Villafranca Piemonte. Village,
  northwestern Italy : Villa-
  franca Sabauda (1934-50)
Villafranca Sabauda see Villa-
  franca Piemonte
Villa General Germán Busch
  see Villa Abecia
Villa (General) Pérez. Town,
  western Bolivia, South
  America : Charazani
  (-1930s)
Villa (General) Vicente Guerrero.
  Town, central Mexico,
  North America : San Pablo
  del Monte (-1940)
Villaggio Mussolini see Arborea
Villahermosa. City, south-
  eastern Mexico, North Amer-
  ica : San Juan Bautista
  [San Juan de Villa Hermosa]
  (-1915)
Villa Isabel. Town, northwest-
  ern Dominican Republic,
  West Indies : Villa
  Vásquez (-1938)
Villa la Trinidad. Town,
  northwestern Argentina,
  South America : La Trinidad
  (-c. 1945)
Villaluenga de la Vega. Village,
  northern Spain : Villanueva
  y Gaviños (-1920)
Villanueva de Alpicat see
  Alpicat
Villanueva del Conde see
  Villanueva de Teba
Villanueva de los Infantes.
  Village, south-central
  Spain : Infantes (-c. 1960)
Villanueva de Teba. Village,
  northern Spain : Villanueva

  del Conde (-c. 1920)
Villanueva y Gaviños see Villa-
  luenga de la Vega
Villa Ramos. Barrio, Zamboanga
  del Norte, Philippines :
  Lipras (-1957)
Villar de Argañán. Village,
  western Spain : Villar de
  Puerco (-c. 1960)
Villar de Ciervos see Villar de
  Samaniego
Villar de Puerco see Villar de
  Argañán
Villar de Samaniego. Village,
  western Spain : Villar de
  Ciervos (-c. 1920)
Villa Rivero. Town, central
  Bolivia, South America :
  Muela (-1900s)
Villarreal see Villarreal de
  los Infantes
Villarreal de los Infantes. Vil-
  lage, eastern Spain : Villar-
  real (-c. 1960)
Villa Sanjurjo see Al Hoceima
Villa Serrano. Town, southern
  Bolivia, South America :
  Pescado (-1940s)
Villa Vásquez see Villa Isabel
Villa Viscarra. Town, central
  Bolivia, South America :
  Vila-Vila (-c. 1940)
Vilnius. Capital of Lithuanian
  SSR : Wilno (1920-39), Poland
Vindava see Ventspils
Vinodelnoye see Ipatovo
Vinogradnoye. Village, North
  Ossetian Autonomous SSR,
  RSFSR : Gnadenburg (-1944)
Vinogradov. Town, Transcarpa-
  thian Oblast, Ukrainian SSR :
  Sevlyush (-1946)
Vins see Vins-sur-Calamy
Vins-sur-Calamy. Village,
  southeastern France : Vins
  (-1937)
Vintar. Barrio, Bukidnon,
  Philippines : Cawayanon
  (-1968)
Vipacco see Vipava
Vipava. Village, northwestern
  Yugoslavia : Vipacco (-1947),
  Italy

Virgilio. Village, northern
Italy : Pietole (-?)
Virgin Islands (of the United
States). Island group,
West Indies : Danish West
Indies (-1917)
Virunga National Park. North-
eastern Zaïre, central
Africa : Albert National
Park (*1925-72)
Virungu. Town, southeastern
Zaïre, central Africa :
Baudouinville (-1966)
Visconde do Rio Branco. City,
southeastern Brazil, South
America : Rio Branco
(-1944)
Vishnevets (1). Village,
Grodno Oblast, Belorussian
SSR : Gnoynitsa (-1964)
Vishnevets (2). Village, Vitebsk
Oblast, Belorussian SSR :
Zherebtsy (-1964)
Vishnya (1). Village, Minsk
Oblast, Belorussian SSR :
Malafeyevichi (-1964)
Vishnya (2). Village, Vitebsk
Oblast, Belorussian SSR :
Podrassolay (-1964)
Vishnyovaya (1). Village,
Vitebsk Oblast, Belorussian
SSR : Cherepni (-1964)
Vishnyovaya (2). Village,
Minsk Oblast, Belorussian
SSR : Klyundevka (-1964)
Vishnyovoye (1). Urban settle-
ment, Dnepropetrovsk Oblast
Ukrainian SSR : Erastovka
(-c. 1960)
Vishnyovoye (2). Suburb of
Pavlograd, Dnepropetrovsk
Oblast, Ukrainian SSR :
Pavlogradskiye Khutora
pervyye (-c. 1960)
Visim. Urban settlement,
Sverdlovsk Oblast, RSFSR
: Visimo-Shaytansky Zavod
(-1933)
Visimo-Shaytansky Zavod see
Visim
Visimo-Utkinsk. Urban settle-
ment, Sverdlovsk Oblast,
RSFSR : Visimo-Utkinsky

Zavod (-1946)
Visimo-Utkinsky Zavod see
Visimo Utkinsk
Vislinsky Zaliv = Vistula
Lagoon
Vista see Nsiom Fumu
Vistula Lagoon [Zalew Wiślany,
Vizlinsky Zaliv]. Lagoon,
southwestern coast of Baltic
Sea, Poland/USSR : Frisches
Haff (-1946), Germany (-1945)
Vit. Village, Gomel Oblast,
Belorussian SSR : Gnoyev
(-1964)
Vita. Village, Manitoba, Cana-
da : Szewczenko [Shevchenko]
(-1908)
Vitória see Vitória de Santo
Antão
Vitória da Conquista. City,
eastern Brazil, South America
: Conquista (-1944)
Vitória de Santo Antão. City,
northeastern Brazil, South
America : Vitória (-1944)
Vitória do Alto Parnaíba see
Alto Parnaíba
Vitória do Baixo Mearim see
Vitória do Mearim
Vitória do Mearim. City,
northeastern Brazil, South
America : Vitória do Baixo
Mearim (-1944), Baixo
Mearim (1944-48)
Vittorio see Vittorio Veneto
Vittorio Veneto. Town, north-
eastern Italy : Vittorio (-1923)
Vladikavkaz see Ordzhonikidze
(5)
Vladimirovka see Yuzhno-
Sakhalinsk
Vlakháta see Karavómylos
Vlasova-Ayuta see Ayutinsky
Vlorë. City, southwestern Al-
bania : Avlona (-1912)
Vodopyanovo see Donskoye (2)
Vogelkop see Doberai
Volchyi Yamy see Krasnovichi
Volga-Baltic Waterway. Linking
Volga River and Baltic Sea,
RSFSR : Mariinsk Water
System (-1960)
Volgograd. Capital of Volgograd

Oblast, RSFSR : Tsaritsyn (-1925), Stalingrad (1925-61)
Volgograd Oblast. RSFSR : Stalingrad Kray (*1934-36), Stalingrad Oblast (1936-61)
Volkhov. Town, Leningrad Oblast, RSFSR : Gostinopolye (-1923), Zvanka (1927-36), Volkhovstroy (1936-40)
Volkhovstroy see Volkhov
Volnyansk. Town, Zaporozhye Oblast, Ukrainian SSR : Sofiyevka (-c. 1935), Krasnoarmeyskoye (c. 1935-44), Chervonoarmeyskoye (1944-66)
Volosinovo. Town, southeastern Yugoslavia : Novi Becej (-c. 1947)
Volovitsky Krupets see Uritskoye (1)
Volzhsk. Town, Mari Autonomous SSR, RSFSR : Lopatino (*c. 1935-40)
Volzhsky. Urban settlement, Kuybyshev Oblast, RSFSR : Bolshaya Tsaryovshchina (-c. 1960)
Vonki see Naberezhnaya
Voortrekkerhoogte. Cantonments, Transvaal, South Africa : Robertshoogte (*c. 1902-38)
Voortrekkerstrand. Town, Natal, South Africa : Munster (-1959)
Vorontsovka see Kalinino (2)
Vorontsovo-Aleksandrovskoye see Zelenokumsk
Voroshilov see Ussuriysk
Voroshilova, imeni see Voroshilovo
Voroshilovgrad. Capital of Voroshilovgrad Oblast, Ukrainian SSR : Lugansk (-1935, 1958-70)
Voroshilovgrad Oblast (*1938). Ukrainian SSR : Lugansk Oblast (1958-70)
Voroshilovo. Village, Andizhan Oblast, Uzbek SSR : Karasu (-1937), Voroshilova, imeni

(1937-c. 1940)
Voroshilovsk see (1) Kommunarsk; (2) Stavropol
Voroshilovskoye. Village, Kirgiz SSR : Lebedinovskoye (-1937)
Voroyskogo, imeni. Urban settlement, Moscow Oblast, RSFSR : Khrapunovo (-1941)
Vose, imeni. Urban settlement, Kulyab Oblast, Tadzhik SSR : Paituk (-c. 1935), Kolkhozabad (c. 1935-c. 1960)
Voshkovtsy see Urozhaynaya (2)
Voskresenovka see Oktyabrsky (9)
Voskresensk see Istra
Voskresenskoye see Kirovo (3)
Vostochnaya (1). Village, Vitebsk Oblast, Belorussian SSR : Tsutski (-1964)
Vostochnaya (2). Village, Mogilyov Oblast, Belorussian SSR : Yazvy (-1964)
Vostochny. Urban settlement, Sakhalin Oblast, RSFSR : Motodomari (1905-45), Japan
Vostok see Neftegorsk
Votyak Autonomous Oblast see Udmurt Autonomous SSR
Vouprásion see Várdas
Voznesenskaya Manufaktura see Krasnoarmeysk (5)
Voznesensky see Krasny Oktyabr
Vrbno. Village, north-central Czechoslovakia : Würbenthal (-1918, 1939-45), Germany
Vrchlabí. Town, northwestern Czechoslovakia : Hohenelbe (-1918, 1939-45), Germany
Vrevsky see Almazar
Vrhnika. Village, northwestern Yugoslavia : Oberlaibach (-1918), Germany
Vršac. City, northeastern Yugoslavia : Werschetz (-1918), Germany
Vrysoúlai see Néai Vrysoúlai
Vsekhsvyatskoye see Uritskoye (2)
Vyatka see Kirov (2)
Vyborg. Town, Leningrad Oblast, RSFSR : Viipuri (1919-40),

Finland
Vysochany (1). Village, Vitebsk
Oblast, Belorussian SSR :
Pentyukhi (-1964)
Vysochany (2). Village, Minsk
Oblast, Belorussian SSR :
Shopa (-1964)
Vysoké Mýto. Town, west-
central Czechoslovakia :
Hohenmauth (-1918, 1939-
45), Germany
Vysoké nad Jizerou. Town,
western Czechoslovakia :
Hochstadt (-1918, 1939-
45), Germany
Vysokogorny. Urban settle-
ment, Khabarovsk Kray,
RSFSR : Muli (-c. 1960)
Vysoko-Litovsk see Vysokoye
Vysokoye. Town, Brest
Oblast, Belorussian SSR :
Vysoko-Litovsk (-1939)
Vysotsk. Town, Vysotsky
Island, Leningrad Oblast,
RSFSR : Uuras (-1948),
Finland (-1940)
Vyšší Brod. Settlement,
western Czechoslovakia :
Hohenfurth (-1918, 1939-
45), Germany
Vyzna see Krasnaya Sloboda
Vzmorye (1). Village, Kalinin-
grad Oblast, RSFSR :
Grossheidekrug (-1946),
Germany (-1945)
Vzmorye (2). Urban settlement,
Sakhalin Oblast, RSFSR :
Shiraura (1905-45), Japan

Wadhwan see Surendranagar
Wadowice. Town, southern
Poland : Frauenstadt (1939-
45), Germany
Wafangtien see Fuhsien
Wagstadt see Bílovec
Wainwright. Town, Alberta,
Canada : Denwood (*c. 1905-
09)
Waitzen see Vác
Wakeham Bay see Maricourt

Wakura see Tazuruhuma
Wałbrzych. City, southwestern
Poland : Waldenburg (-1945),
Germany
Wałcz. Town, northwestern
Poland : Deutsch Krone (-1945),
Germany
Waldau see Nizovye
Waldenburg see Wałbrzych
Wallerfangen see Vaudrevange
Wanchow see Manning
Wan-ch'üan see Chang-chia-k'ou
Wanfow. Town, southeastern
China : Tungon (-1914)
Wangerin see Węgorzyno
Wangkü see Changan [Ch'ang-an]
Wangshejenchwang see Lichen
[Li-cheng]
Wangyehmiao see Ulan Hoto
Wankang. Town, southern
China : Pama (-1936)
Wanping [Wan-p'ing]. Town,
northeastern China : Lukowkiao
(-1928)
Wansen see Wiązów
Wanyüan. Town, central China :
Taiping (-1914)
Warmbad. Town, Transvaal,
South Africa : Hartingsburg
(-1903, 1905-20), Warm
Baths (1903-05)
Warm Baths see Warmbad
Warmbrunn see Cieplice
Śląskie Zdrój
Warner Robins. City, Georgia,
USA : Wellston (-c. 1940)
Wartenburg see Barczewo
Wartha see Bardo
Warthbrücken see Koło
Warthenau see Zawiercie
Wasit. Province, eastern Iraq :
Kut (-1971)
Wąsosz. Town, western Poland
: Herrnstadt (-1945), Germany
Watenstadt-Salzgitter see
Salzgitter
Water see Balindong
Waterville see Cypress
Watkins see Watkins Glen
Watkins Glen. Village, New
York, USA : Watkins (-1926)
Watrap. Town, southeastern
India : Varttirayiruppu (-1920s)

Wawa. Village, Ontario,
   Canada : Jamestown
   (c. 1947-60)
Wayaopu see Changtze
   [Ch'ang-tzu]
Wayne. Village, Ohio, USA :
   Freeport (-1931)
Webuye. Town, southern
   Kenya, eastern Africa :
   Broderick Falls (-1973)
Wedgeport. Town, Nova
   Scotia, Canada : Tusket
   Wedge (-1909)
Węgliniec. Town, southwestern
   Poland : Kohlfurt (-1945),
   Germany
Węgorzewo. Town, northeastern
   Poland : Angerburg (-1945),
   Germany
Węgorzyno. Town, northwestern
   Poland : Wangerin (-1945),
   Germany
Węgrów. Town, eastern Po-
   land : Bingerau (-1945),
   Germany
Wehlau see Znamensk
Weichang [Wei-ch'ang]. Town,
   northeastern China :
   Chutzeshan (-1931)
Weifang. City, eastern China :
   Weihsien (-1949)
Weihai. City, eastern China :
   Weihaiwei (-1949)
Weihaiwei see Weihai
Weihsien see Weifang
Weissenburg see Alba Iulia
Weiss-stein see Biały Kamień
Weisswasser see Belá pod
   Bezdězem
Weistritz see Bystrzyca
Weiyüan. Town, eastern
   China : Pehtatung (-1931)
Weiyüan see Kingku [Ching-ku]
Weiyüanpu see Huchu
Wejherowo. Town, northern
   Poland : Neustadt (-1945),
   Germany
Wekelsdorf see Teplice
   nad Metují
Welfare Island see Franklin D.
   Roosevelt Island
Wellston see Warner Robins
Welungen see Wieluń

Welwitschia see Khorixas
Wendisch Buchholz see Märkisch
   Buchholz
Wenling. Town, eastern China :
   Taiping (-1914)
Wenshan. Town, southwestern
   China : Kaihwa (-1914)
Werschetz see Vršac
Weseritz see Bezdružice
Wesermünde see Bremerhaven
Wesseli see Veselí nad Moravou
West Allis. Suburb of Milwaukee,
   Wisconsin, USA : North Green-
   field (-1902)
West Bengal see Bengal
West Columbia. Town, South
   Carolina, USA : (New) Brook-
   land (-1938)
West Des Moines. Suburb of
   Des Moines, Iowa, USA :
   Valley Junction (-1938)
Western. Province, west Zam-
   bia, south-central Africa :
   Barotse (-1971)
Western see Copperbelt
Western Samar see Samar
Western Test Range. Cosmo-
   drome, Point Mugu, north of
   Los Angeles, California, USA
   : Pacific Range (*1957-65)
West Hammond see Calumet
   City
West Irian see Irian Jaya
West Kazakhstan Oblast see
   Uralsk Oblast
Westlake. City, Ohio, USA :
   Dover (-1911)
West Lake see Ziwa Magharibi
West Lothian (1975†). County,
   southeastern Scotland, UK :
   Linlithgow (-?)
West Memphis. City, Arkansas,
   USA : Bragg's Spur (*1910-29)
Westminster. City, Colorado,
   USA : Harris (-1911)
West New Guinea see Irian
   Jaya
West Nimar see Khargone
Westwold. Town, British
   Columbia, Canada : Grande
   Prairie (-1900), Adelphi
   (1900-26)
Whalers Bay. Stewart Island,

New Zealand : Surveyors
Bay (-1965)
Wharemoa. Town, South
Island, New Zealand :
Karoro (-1963)
Whatcom see Bellingham
Whyalla. City, South Australia,
Australia : Hummock Hill
(*1900-20)
Wiązów. Town, southwestern
Poland : Wansen (-1945),
Germany
Wielbark. Town, northeastern
Poland : Willenberg (-1945),
Germany
Wieluń. Town, south-central
Poland : Welungen (1939-
45), Germany
Wiesengrund see Dobřany
Wildenschwert see Ústí nad
Orlicí
Wilhelmina Top see Trikora,
Puncak
Wilhelm-Pieck-Stadt Guben.
City, eastern East Germany
: Guben (-1961)
Willemsdal see Greylingstad
Willenberg see Wielbark
Willingboro. Township, New
Jersey, USA : Levittown
(1959-63)
Willow Springs. Village,
Illinois, USA : Spring
Forest (-1937)
Willowvale see Gatyana
Wilmer. Settlement, British
Columbia, Canada :
Peterborough (-1902)
Wilno see Vilnius
Winam. Town, southwestern
Kenya, eastern Africa :
Kavirondo Gulf (-1975)
Windisch-Feistritz see
(Slovenska) Bistrica
Windischgraz see Slovenjgradec
Wingon see Tzekam
Wińsko. Town, southwestern
Poland : Winzig (-1945),
Germany
Winzig see Wińsko
Wirbeln see Zhavoronkovo
Wisconsin Dells. City, Wiscon-
sin, USA : Kilbourn (-1931)

Wisconsin Rapids. City, Wiscon-
sin, USA : Grand Rapids
(-1920)
Wise. Town, Virginia, USA :
Gladeville (-1924)
Witnica. Town, western Poland
: Vietz (-1945), Germany
Wittenberg see Nivenskoye
Wittenoom see Wittenoom Gorge
Wittenoom Gorge. Town, Western
Australia, Australia : Wittenoom
(-1951)
Wittingau see Třeboň
Wleń. Town, southwestern
Poland : Lähn (-1945), Germany
Włocławek. City, central Poland
: Leslau (1939-45), Germany
Wohlau see Wołów
Wołczyn. Town, southern Poland
: Konstadt (-1945), Germany
Woldenberg see Dobiegniew
Wolframs-Eschenbach. Town,
southern West Germany :
Eschenbach (-1917)
Wolin. Town and island, north-
western Poland : Wollin
(-1945), Germany
Wollin see Wolin
Wolmar see Valmiera
Wołów. Town, southwestern
Poland : Wohlau (-1945),
Germany
Woodburn (City). Town, Indiana,
USA : Shirley City (-1936)
Woodland Hills. Suburb of Los
Angeles, California, USA :
Girard (-1941)
Woodstock. Town, Cape of Good
Hope, South Africa : Papendorp
(-?)
Wrocław. City, southwestern
Poland : Breslau (-1945),
Germany
Wschowa. Town, western
Poland : Fraustadt (-1945),
Germany
Wuchan see Wusi [Wu-hsi]
Wucheng [Wu-ch'eng]. Town,
eastern Tibet : Sanyen (-1913)
Wu-ch'i = Wuki
Wuchow. City, southeastern
China : Ts'ang-wu (1913-46)
Wuchuho see Shangchih

Wufeng. Town, east-central
   China : Changlo (-1914)
Wufu see Nankiao [Nan-chiao]
Wu-hsi = Wusi
Wuhsien see Soochow [Su-
   chou]
Wu-hsing. City, eastern
   China : Hu-chou (-1911)
Wuki [Wu-ch'i]. Town, central
   China : Taning (-1914)
Wulung. Town, central China
   : Siangkow (-1941)
Wuming. Town, southern
   China : Wuyüan (-1913)
Wünschelburg see Radków
Würbenthal see Vrbno
Wushan. Town, north-central
   China : Ningyüan (-1914)
Wusheng. Town, central
   China : Tingyüan (-1914)
Wusi [Wu-hsi]. Town,
   northern China : Wuchan
   (-1950)
Wutan. Town, northeastern
   China : Wutancheng (-1949)
Wutancheng see Wutan
Wuti. Town, eastern China :
   Haifeng (-1914)
Wuting see Hweimin [Hui-
   min]
Wutsin see Changchow [Ch'ang-
   chou]
Wutu. Town, north-central
   China : Kiechow (-1913)
Wutung. Town, northern China
   : Kisiaying (-1949)
Wuwei. City, north-central
   China : Liangchow (-1913)
Wuyüan see Wuming

Xai-Xai. Town, southern
   Mozambique, southeastern
   Africa : Vila Nova de Gaza
   (1922-28), João Belo (1928-
   76)
Xanthe. City, northeastern
   Greece : Eskije (-1912),
   Turkey
Xenía see Kalyvákia
Xerokhórion see Staurodrómion

Xhora. Town, southern Transkei,
   southern Africa : Elliotdale
   (-1976)
Xiririca see Eldorado
Xonrupt see Xonrupt-Longemer
Xonrupt-Longemer. Village,
   eastern France : Xonrupt
   (-1938)

Ya-an. Town, southern China :
   Ya-chou (-1913)
Yabalkovo. Village, south-central
   Bulgaria : Almalii (-c. 1945)
Yablochny. Urban settlement,
   Sakhalin Oblast, RSFSR :
   Rantomari (1905-45), Japan
Yabu. Town, southern Honshu,
   Japan : Yabuichiba (-early
   1940s)
Yabuichiba see Yabu
Ya-chiang = Yakiang
Ya-chou see Ya-an
Yaichow see Aihsien
Yakiang [Ya-chiang]. Town,
   southern China : Hokow (-1913)
Yakima. City, Washington,
   USA : North Yakima (-1918)
Yakovlevskoye see Privolzhsk
Yakunchikov see Krasny Mayak
Yalu. Town, northeastern China
   : Chalantun (-1925, 1932-45)
Yama see Seversk
Yamankhalinka see Makhambet
Yamato. Town, west-central
   Honshu, Japan : Takaki
   (-1930s)
Yamburg see Kingisepp (2)
Yamchow see Yamhsien
Yamhsien. Town, southeastern
   China : Yamchow (-1912)
Yamin, Puncak. Mountain,
   Irian Jaya, Indonesia : Prins
   Hendrik Top (-1963)
Yaminskoye see Tselinnoye (2)
Yamrukchal see Botev
Yang-chou. City, eastern China
   : Kiangtu (1912-49)
Yang-ch'u = Yangku
Yangchung. Town, eastern China
   : Taiping (-1914)

Yanghopao see Yungning
Yang-hsin = Yangsin
Yangibazar see Ordzhonikid-
zeabad
Yangi-Bazar see Soldatsky
Yangiyer. Town, Syrdarya
Oblast, Uzbek SSR :
Chernyayevo (-c. 1917)
Yangiyul. Town, Tashkent
Oblast, Uzbek SSR :
Kaunchi (-c. 1935)
Yangku [Yang-ch'u] see
Taiyuan
Yangsin [Yang-hsin]. Town,
east-central China : Hingkwo
(-1912)
Yangyuan. Town, northeastern
China : Sining (-1914)
Yanov see (1) Ivano-Frankovo;
(2) Ivanovo (2)
Yanovka see Ivanovka
Yantak see Buston
Yantarny. Urban settlement,
Kaliningrad Oblast, RSFSR
: Palmnicken (-1947),
Germany (-1945)
Yanushpol see Ivanopol
Yaoan. Town, southwestern
China : Yaochow (-1913)
Yaochow see (1) Yaoan;
(2) Yaohsien
Yaohsien. Town, central China
: Yaochow (-1913)
Yaonan. Town, eastern China :
Changshan (-1949)
Yarowie see Appila
Yaryksu-Aukh see Novolak-
skoye
Yasaka. Town, southern
Honshu, Japan : Minami-
oji (-early 1940s)
Yasen. Village, northern
Bulgaria : Plazigaz (-c. 1945)
Yashalta. Village, Rostov
Oblast, RSFSR : Esto-
Khaginka (-1944), Stepnoye
(1944-58)
Yashkul. Urban settlement,
Kalmyk Autonomous SSR,
RSFSR : Peschanoye (1944-
c. 1960)
Yaski see Lesogorsky
Yasnogorsk. Town, Tula Oblast,

RSFSR : Laptevo (-1965)
Yasnomorsky. Urban settlement,
Sakhalin Oblast, RSFSR : Oko
(1905-45), Japan
Yasnoye. Village, Kaliningrad
Oblast, RSFSR : Kaukehmen
(-1938), Germany; Kuckerneese
(1938-45), Germany
Yass-Canberra see Australian
Capital Territory
Yates Dam. Dam, Alabama,
USA : Upper Tallassee Dam
(*1928-?)
Yavoshikha see Zalesovshchina
Yaypan see Bazar-Yaypan
Yazvy see Vostochnaya (2)
Yebije-i-Vardar see Giannitsa
Yegorshino see Artyomovsky
Yegri-Dere see Ardino
Yeh-hsien = Yehsien
Yehsien [Yeh-hsien]. Town,
eastern China : Laichow (-1913)
Yekaterinburg see Sverdlovsk
(3)
Yekaterinenshtadt see Marks
Yekaterinodar see Krasnodar
Yekaterinofeld see Bolnisi
Yekaterinoslav see Dneprope-
trovsk
Yekaterinovskaya see Krylov-
skaya
Yekhegnadzor. Urban settlement,
Armenian SSR : Keshishkend
(-c. 1935), Mikoyan (c. 1935-57)
Yelenendorf see Khanlar
Yelenovka see (1) Sevan (2);
(2) Zorinsk
Yelenovskiye Karyery see
Dokuchayevsk
Yelgava = Jelgava
Yelizavetgrad see Kirovograd
Yelizavetpol see Kirovabad
Yelizavetpol Guberniya see
Gandizhan Guberniya
Yelizovo. Urban settlement,
Kamchatka Oblast, RSFSR :
Zavoyko (-1924)
Yelkhovo. City, southeastern
Bulgaria : Kizil-agach (-1925)
Yemen [People's Democratic
Republic of Yemen]. Arabian
Peninsula : Southern Yemen
(People's Republic) (*1967-70)

Yenakiyevo. Town, Donetsk
   Oblast, Ukrainian SSR :
   Rykovo (c. 1928-35),
   Ordzhonikidze (1935-43)
Yenan. Town, central China :
   Fuhsih (1913-48)
Yen-chiang = Yenkiang
Yen-ching = Yentsing
Yenchow see (1) Kienteh
   [Chien-te]; (2) Tzeyang
   [Tzu-yang]
Yenfeng. Town, southwestern
   China : Paiyentsing (-1913)
Yenije-i-Vardar see Giannitsa
Yeni-Pazar see Novi Pazar
Yenkiang [Yen-chiang]. Town,
   northern China : Taerhhu
   (-1942)
Yen-p'ing see Nanping
   [Nan-p'ing]
Yenshan. Town, southwestern
   China : Kiangna (-1933)
Yenshan see Kingyüan
   [Ching-yüan]
Yen-shou = Yenshow
Yenshow [Yen-shou]. Town,
   northeastern China :
   Changshow (-1914), Tungpin
   (1914-29)
Yentsing [Yen-ching]. Town,
   southwestern China :
   Laoyatan (-1917)
Yenukidze see Ambrolauri
Yerevan. Capital of Armenian
   SSR : Erivan (-1936)
Yermolovsk see Leselidze
Yertarskoye see Yertarsky
Yertarsky. Urban settlement,
   Sverdlovsk Oblast, RSFSR
   : Yertarsky Zavod (-c.
   1928), Yertarskoye (1928-40)
Yertarsky Zavod see Yertarsky
Yerzhar see Gagarin (2)
Yeski Dzhumaya see Targo-
   vište
Yevdokimovskoye see
   Krasnogvardeyskoye (3)
Yezhovo-Cherkessk see
   Cherkessk
Yezupol see Zhovten (2)
Yichow see Yihsien
Yihsien [Ihsien]. Town, north-
   eastern China : Yichow

(-1913)
Yin-ch'uan = Yinchwan
Yinchwan [Yin-ch'uan]. City,
   northwestern China : Ningsia
   (-1945)
Ying-chiang = Yingkiang
Yingchow see (1) Fowyang
   [Fou-yang]; (2) Yinghsien
Yinghsien. Town, northeastern
   China : Yingchow (-1912)
Yingkiang [Ying-chiang]. Village,
   southwestern China : Kanai
   (-1935)
Yingpankai see Pikiang [Pi-
   chiang]
Yirga-Alam. Town, southern
   Ethiopia, northeastern Africa :
   Dalle (1936-41)
Yitu [Itu]. Town, eastern China
   : Tsingchow (-1913)
Yiwu see Chenyüeh
Yochow see Yoyang
Yoshida see Shimo-yoshida
Yoshkar-Ola. Capital of Mari
   Autonomous SSR, RSFSR :
   Tsaryovokokshaysk (-1919),
   Krasnokokshaysk (1919-27)
Youssoufia. Town, western
   Morocco, northwestern Africa
   : Louis-Gentil (-c. 1960)
Yoyang. Town, south-central
   China : Yochow (-1913)
Yoyang see Antseh
Yüanchow see (1) Chihkiang
   [Chih-chiang]; (2) Ichun
   [I-ch'un]
Yüanling. Town, south-central
   China : Shenchow (-1913)
Yü-ch'i = Yüki
Yü-chiang = Yükiang
Yü-ch'ien = Yütsien
Yuchow see Fangcheng [Fang-
   ch'eng]
Yüchow see Yütsien
Yuchung. Town, north-central
   China : Kinhsien (-1912),
   Kincheng (1912-19)
Yudenichi see Sovetskaya (5)
Yudino see Petukhovo
Yüeh-chou see Yüeh-yang
Yüeh-yang. Town, southeastern
   China : Yüeh-chou (-1911)
Yug. Urban settlement, Perm

Oblast, RSFSR : Yugovskoy
Zavod (-1943)
Yugo-Kamsky. Urban settle-
ment, Perm Oblast, RSFSR
: Yugokamsky Zavod (-1929)
Yugokamsky Zavod see
Yugo-Kamsky
Yugo-Vostochnaya Oblast see
Stavropol Kray
Yugovskoy Zavod see Yug
Yüki [Yü-ch'i]. Town, south-
western China : Sinsing
(-1913), Siuna (1913-16)
Yükiang [Yü-chiang]. Town,
southeastern China :
Anjen (-1914)
Yuliya see Tsvetnogorsk
Yünchow see Yünhsien (1)
Yungan see Mengshan
Yunganpao see Langshan
Yungchang see Paoshan
Yüng-chi = Yüngtsi
Yungchow see Lingling
Yungkang see Tungcheng
[T'ung-cheng]
Yungki see Kirin
Yungnien. Town, northeastern
China : Kwangping (-1913)
Yungning. Town, northwestern
China : Yanghopao (-1942)
Yungning see (1) Lishih;
(2) Loning; (3) Nanning;
(4) Poshow; (5) Süyung
[Hsü-yung]
Yungpeh see Yungsheng
Yungping see Lulung
Yungsheng. Town, southwestern
China : Yungpeh (-1913)
Yung-shou = Yungshow
Yungshow [Yung-shou]. Town,
central China : Kienkünchen
(-c. 1940)
Yungtai [Yung-t'ai]. Town,
southeastern China : Inghok
(-1941)
Yungteng. Town, north-central
China : Pingfan (-1928)
Yungting see Tayung
Yüngtsi [Yüng-chi]. Town,
northeastern China : Puchow
(-1912)
Yungyün. Town, southeastern
China : Lungsinhü (-1947)

Yünhsien (1). Town, southwestern
China : Yünchow (-1913)
Yünhsien (2). Town, east-central
China : Yünyang (-1912)
Yunnan see (1) Kunming [K'un-
ming]; (2) Siangyün [Hsiang-
yün]
Yunokommunarovsk. Town,
Donetsk Oblast, Ukrainian
SSR : Bunge Rudnik (-?),
Yunykh Kommunarov, imeni
(?-?)
Yünyang see Yünhsien (2)
Yunykh Kommunarov, imeni see
Yunokommunarovsk
Yuryev see Tartu
Yurzdyka see Zelenets (2)
Yusta. Settlement, Kalmyk
Autonomous SSR, RSFSR :
Trudovoy (-c. 1960)
Yutien see Changning [Ch'ang-
ning]
Yütsien [Yü-ch'ien]. Town,
eastern China : Yüchow (-1912)
Yuyü. Town, northeastern
China : Shoping (-1911)
Yuzhno-Kazakhstanskaya Oblast
see Chimkent Oblast
Yuzhno-Kurilsk. Urban settle-
ment, Kuril Islands, Sakhalin
Oblast, RSFSR : Furukamappu
(1905-45), Japan
Yuzhno-Sakhalinsk. Capital of
Sakhalin Oblast, RSFSR :
Vladimirovka (-1905), Toyohara
(1905-45), Japan
Yuzhny see (1) Adyk; (2)
Dostluk; (3) Skuratovsky
Yuzovka see Donetsk (2)

Zabaykalsk. Urban settlement,
Chita Oblast, RSFSR : Otpor
(-c. 1960)
Ząbkowice Śląskie. Town,
southwestern Poland : Franken-
stein (-1945), Germany
Zabłotye see Zabolotye
Zabolotye. Urban settlement,
Volyn Oblast, Ukrainian
SSR : Zabłotye (-1944)

Zaborovtsy. Village, Vitebsk
Oblast, Belorussian SSR :
Nevbily (-1964)
Zaboyshchik see Kurganovka
Zábreh. Town, northern
Czechoslovakia : Hohen-
stadt (-1918, 1939-45),
Germany
Zabrze. City, southern
Poland : Hindenburg
(1915-45), Germany
Zabuldychino see Olkhovskaya
Zachan see Suchan
Žaclér. Village, western
Czechoslovakia : Schatzlar
(-1918, 1939-45), Germany
Zafarabad. Urban settlement,
Leninabad Oblast, Tadzhik
SSR : Ayni (-c. 1960)
Żagań. Town, western Poland
: Sagan (-1945), Germany
Zagornaya. Village, Minsk
Oblast, Belorussian SSR :
Bolvan (-1964)
Zagorodnaya. Village, Brest
Oblast, Belorussian SSR :
Zlomyshle (-1964)
Zagorsk. Town, Moscow
Oblast, RSFSR : Sergiyev
(-1930)
Zagorsky see Krasnozavodsk
Zagreb. City, northwestern
Yugoslavia : Agram (1526-
1918), Germany
Zagryazye see Bereznyanka
Zahana. Village, northwestern
Algeria, northern Africa :
Saint-Lucien (-c. 1962)
Zahirabad. Town, south-central
India : Ekeli (-?)
Zainsk. Town, Tatar Autonomous
SSR, RSFSR : Novy Zay
(-1978)
Zaïre. Republic, central
Africa : Congo Free State
(-1908), Belgian Congo
[Congo Belge] (1908-60),
Democratic Republic of the
Congo [Congo (Kinshasa)],
(1960-71)
Zakamensk. Town, Buryat
Autonomous SSR, RSFSR :
Gorodok (-1959)

Zakarpatskaya Oblast =
Transcarpathian Oblast
Zakaspiyskaya Oblast see
Turkmen Oblast
Zakharovka see Frunzovka
Zakhedan. Town, eastern Iran
: Dozdab (-?)
Zakhmatabad see Ayni
Zákupy. Town, western Czecho-
slovakia : Reichstadt (-1918,
1939-45), Germany
Zaldíbar. Village, northern
Spain : Zaldúa (-c. 1940)
Zaldúa see Zaldíbar
Zaleshany. Village, Vitebsk
Oblast, Belorussian SSR :
Bardily (-1964)
Zalesino. Village, Vitebsk
Oblast, Belorussian SSR :
Glistenets (-1964)
Zalesnaya. Village, Vitebsk
Oblast, Belorussian SSR :
Koleno (-1964)
Zalesovshchina. Village, Grodno
Oblast, Belorussian SSR :
Yavoshikha (-1964)
Zalesovtsy. Village, Grodno
Oblast, Belorussian SSR :
Plekhovo (-1964)
Zalesskaya. Village, Minsk
Oblast, Belorussian SSR :
Pisyuta (-1964)
Zalesye. Village, Kaliningrad
Oblast, RSFSR : Mehlauken
(-1938), Germany; Lieben-
felde (1938-45), Germany
Zalew Wiślany = Vistula
Lagoon
Záloggon. Village, western
Greece : Kamarína (-1960s)
Žamberk. Town, northern
Czechoslovakia : Senftenberg
(-1918, 1939-45), Germany
Zambia. Republic, south-central
Africa : Northern Rhodesia
(*1911-64)
Zangelan. Town, Azerbaijan
SSR : Pirchivan (-1967)
Zangibasar see Razdan (2)
Zanow see Sianów
Zaouet el-Kahla. Town, east-
central Algeria, northern
Africa : Fort Flatters (-c. 1962)

Zapadno-Gruppsky see
Shakhtyorsk (2)
Zapadno-Kazakhstanskaya Oblast
see Uralsk Oblast
Zapaluta see La Trinitaria
Zaporozhye. Capital of
Zaporozhye Oblast, Ukrain-
ian SSR : Aleksandrovsk
(-1921)
Zaporozhye Guberniya (1922†).
Ukrainian SSR : Aleksan-
drovsk Guberniya (*1920-
21)
Zapovednoye. Village, Kalinin-
grad Oblast, RSFSR :
Seckenburg (-1945), Ger-
many
Zara. Town, central Turkey :
Kocgiri (-?)
Zarasai. Town, Lithuanian
SSR : Novoaleksandrovsk
(-1920), Ossersee (1941-
44), Germany
Zárate. City, southeastern
Argentina, South America :
General Uriburu (1932-46)
Zarechnaya (1). Village, Minsk
Oblast, Belorussian SSR :
Boldyuki (-1964)
Zarechnaya (2). Village, Minsk
Oblast, Belorussian SSR :
Kulakovtsy (-1964)
Zarechnaya (3). Village, Grodno
Oblast, Belorussian SSR :
Perkhayly (-1964)
Zarechnaya (4). Village, Vitebsk
Oblast, Belorussian SSR :
Trukhanovichi (-1964)
Zarechny. Urban settlement,
Ryazan Oblast, RSFSR :
Pobedinsky (-c. 1960)
Zaritap. Village, Armenian
SSR : Azizbekov (-c. 1960)
Zarkhanádes see Dasokhórion
Zarya see Leninsky (5)
Zashchesle see Urozhaynaya
(3)
Zaslav see Zaslavl
Zaslavl. Urban settlement,
Minsk Oblast, Belorussian
SSR : Izyaslavl (1920s),
Zaslav (1920s-c. 1935)
Zaslonovo. Village, Vitebsk

Oblast, Belorussian SSR :
Kozodoi (-1945)
Žatec. Town, western Czecho-
slovakia : Saaz (-1918, 1939-
45), Germany
Zatishye see Elektrostal
Zatoka. Urban settlement,
Odessa Oblast, Ukrainian SSR
: Bugaz (-c. 1960)
Zatychina see Cheryomukha
Zavitaya see Zavitinsk
Zavitinsk. Town, Amur Oblast,
RSFSR : Zavitaya (-1954)
Zavodoukovsk. Town, Tyumen
Oblast, RSFSR : Zavodoukovsky
(-1960)
Zavodoukovsky see Zavodoukovsk
Zavodskoy see Komsomolsky
(4)
Zavolzhsk. Town, Ivanovo
Oblast, RSFSR : Zavolzhye
(-1954)
Zavolzhye. Town, Gorky Oblast,
RSFSR : Pestovo (-1964)
Zavolzhye see Zavolzhsk
Zavoyko see Yelizovo
Zawiercie. City, southern
Poland : Warthenau (1939-45),
Germany
Zbąszynek. Town, western
Poland : Neu-Bentschen
(-1945), Germany
Žd'ár. Town, west-central
Czechoslovakia : Saar (in
Mähren) (-1918, 1939-45),
Germany
Zehden see Cedynia
Zelaya. Department, eastern
Nicaragua, Central America :
Bluefields (-c. 1919)
Zelenets (1). Village, Brest
Oblast, Belorussian SSR :
Terpilovichi (-1964)
Zelenets (2). Village, Grodno
Oblast, Belorussian SSR :
Yurzdyka (-1964)
Zelenodolsk. City, Tatar
Autonomous SSR, RSFSR :
Kabachishche (-1932), Zelyony
Dol (1932-c. 1940)
Zelenogorsk. Town, Leningrad
Oblast, RSFSR : Terijoki
(-1948), Finland (-1940)

Zelenogradsk. Town, Kaliningrad Oblast, RSFSR : Kranz (-1947), Germany (-1945)

Zelenokumsk. Town, Stavropol Kray, RSFSR : Vorontsovo-Aleksandrovskoye (-1963), Sovetskoye (1963-5)

Zelensk see Leninsk (2)

Železná Ruda. Village, western Czechoslovakia : Eisenstein (-1918, 1939-45), Germany

Železný Brod. Town, western Czechoslovakia : Eisenbrod (-1918, 1939-45), Germany

Zelina. Village, northwestern Yugoslavia : Sveti Ivan Zelina (-1948)

Zelman see Rovnoye

Zelyonaya (1). Village, Vitebsk Oblast, Belorussian SSR : Pleshivtsy (-1964)

Zelyonaya (2). Village, Gomel Oblast, Belorussian SSR : Zhezlenka (-1964)

Zelyony Bor. Village, Minsk Oblast, Belorussian SSR : Gaden (-1964)

Zelyony Dol see Zelenodolsk

Zelyony Log. Village, Vitebsk Oblast, Belorussian SSR : Khokhulki (-1964)

Zemen. Village, western Bulgaria : Belovo (-c. 1945)

Zemgale see Jelgava

Zemlya Imperatora Nikolaya II see Severnaya Zemlya

Zempelburg see Sępolno (Kraińskie)

Zenkovka see Chkalovskoye (2)

Zernograd. Town, Rostov Oblast, RSFSR : Zernovoy (-1960)

Zernovoy see Zernograd

Zestafoni. Town, Georgian SSR : Kvirily (-1921)

Zhabovka see Partizanka

Zhabye see Verkhovina

Zhavoronkovo. Village, Kaliningrad Oblast, RSFSR : Wirbeln (-1945), Germany

Zhdanov. Town, Donetsk Oblast, Ukrainian SSR : Mariupol (-1948)

Zhelaniya, Cape. Northern Novaya Zemlya, Arctic Ocean, Nenets Autonomous Okrug, Arkhangelsk Oblast, RSFSR : Mauritius, Cape (-c. 1918)

Zheleznodorozhny (1). Urban settlement, Kaliningrad Oblast, RSFSR : Gerdauen (-1946), Germany (-1945)

Zheleznodorozhny (2). Town, Moscow Oblast, RSFSR : Obiralovka (-1939)

Zheleznodorozhny see Kungrad

Zheleznogorsk see Zheleznogorsk-Ilimsky

Zheleznogorsk-Ilimsky. Town, Irkutsk Oblast, RSFSR : Zheleznogorsk (-1965)

Zherdevka. Town, Tambov Oblast, RSFSR : Chibizovka (-1954)

Zherebilovichi see Sosnovaya (3)

Zherebtsy see Vishnevets (2)

Zhezlenka see Zelyonaya (2)

Zhigulyovsk. Town, Kuybyshev Oblast, RSFSR : Otvazhnoye (1946-49), Otvazhny (1949-52)

Zhilyanka see Kargalinskoye

Zhirnovsk. Town, Volgograd Oblast, RSFSR : Zhirnoye (-1954), Zhirnovsky (1954-58)

Zhirnovsky see Zhirnovsk

Zhirnoye see Zhirnovsk

Zhirospyory see Partizanskaya (3)

Zhivkovo. Village, west-central Bulgaria : Avli-koi (-c. 1945)

Zhivoglodovichi see Pervomaysk (5)

Zhob. Town, northeastern Pakistan : Fort Sandeman (-?)

Zholkev see Nesterov (2)

Zholkva see Nesterov (2)

Zhovten (1). Village, Odessa Oblast, Ukrainian SSR : Petroverovka (-c. 1928)

Zhovten (2). Urban settlement, Ivano-Frankovsk Oblast, Ukrainian SSR : Yezupol (-1940), Stakhanovo (1938-47)

Zhovtnevoye (1). Town, Nikolayev

Oblast, Ukrainian SSR :
Bogoyavlensk (-1938), Oktyabr-
skoye (1938-61)
Zhovtnevoye (2). Village,
Dnepropetrovsk Oblast,
Ukrainian SSR : Izluchistaya
(-c. 1928), Stalindorf (c.
1928-44), Stalinskoye (1944-
61)
Zhukovo. Village, Kaluga
Oblast, RSFSR : Ugodsky
Zavod (-1974)
Zhukovsky. Town, Moscow
Oblast, RSFSR : Otdykh
(-1938), Stakhanovo (1938-
47)
Zhyoltaya Reka see Zhyoltyye
Vody
Zhyoltyye Vody. Town, Dnepro-
petrovsk Oblast, Ukrainian
SSR : Rudnik imeni Shvartsa
(-1939), Zhyoltaya Reka
(1939-57)
Zhyoltyye Vody see Mirnoye
(2)
Židlochovice. Town, western
Czechoslovakia : Seelowitz
(-1918, 1939-45), Germany
Ziębice. Town, southwestern
Poland : Münsterberg
(-1945), Germany
Ziebingen see Cybinka
Ziegenhals see Głuchołazy
Zielenzig see Sulęcin
Zielona Góra. Town, west-
central Poland : Grünberg
(in Schlesien) (-1945),
Germany
Zighout Youcef. Village, north-
eastern Algeria, northern
Africa : Condé-Smendou
(-c. 1962)
Žilina. Town, east-central
Czechoslovakia : Sillein
(-1918, 1939-45), Germany
Zimigui-Ziwanan see Masi
Zimnitsa. Village, eastern
Bulgaria : Kashla-koi
(-1906)
Zimogorye. Town, Voroshilov-
grad Oblast, Ukrainian SSR
: Cherkasskoye (-1961)
Zinovyevsk see Kirovograd

Zinten see Kornevo
Zirke see Sieraków
Zirknitz see Cerknica
Ziwa Magharibi. Administrative
region, northwestern Tanzania,
eastern Africa : West Lake
(-1976)
Ziyautdin see Pakhtakor
Zlaté Hory. Village, north-central
Czechoslovakia : Zuckmantel
(-1919, 1939-45), Germany
Zlatna. Village, central Romania
: Klein-Schlatten (-1920),
Germany
Zlatograd. City, southern
Bulgaria : Dara Dere (-1934)
Zlín see Gottwaldov
Zlodin see Krasnoberezhye
Zlokuchen see Ivanski
Zlomyshle see Zagorodnaya
Złotoryja. Town, southwestern
Poland : Goldberg (-1945),
Germany
Złotów. Town, northwestern
Poland : Flatow (-1945),
Germany
Złoty Stok. Town, southwestern
Poland : Reichenstein (-1945),
Germany
Žlutice. Town, western Czecho-
slovakia : Luditz (-1918, 1939-
45), Germany
Zmajevo. Village, northeastern
Yugoslavia : Pašićevo (-1947)
Żmigród. Town, southwestern
Poland : Trachenberg (-1945),
Germany
Zmiyov see Gotwald
Znamenka (1). Village, Brest
Oblast, Belorussian SSR :
Durichi (-1964)
Znamenka (2). Village, Mogilyov
Oblast, Belorussian SSR :
Kobylyanka (-1964)
Znamenka (3). Village, Minsk
Oblast, Belorussian SSR :
Podonki (-1969)
Znamenka (4). Village, Gomel
Oblast, Belorussian SSR :
Sleptsy (-1958)
Znamensk. Urban settlement,
Kaliningrad Oblast, RSFSR :
Wehlau (-1946), Germany (-1945)

Znamensky see Pamyati 13
 Bortsov
Znamya. Village, Minsk Oblast,
 Belorussian SSR : Start-
 sevichi (-1964)
Znauri. Village, South Ossetian
 Autonomous Oblast, Georgian
 SSR : Znaur-Kau (-c. 1945)
Znaur-Kau see Znauri
Zobten see Sobótka
Zolotushing see Gornyak (2)
Zomba. Town, southwestern
 Hungary : Döryzomba
 (*1940-41)
Zongo Rapids. River, north-
 western Zaïre, central
 Africa : Grenfell Rapids
 (-?)
Zorinsk. Town, Voroshilovgrad
 Oblast, Ukrainian SSR :
 Yelenovka (-1963)
Zorndorf see Sarbinowo
Zrenjanin. City, eastern
 Yugoslavia : Veliki

Bečkerek (-1930s), Petrov-
 grad (1930s-c. 1947)
Zschornegosda see Schwarz-
 heide
Zuckmantel see Zlaté Hory
Zudañez. Town, south-central
 Bolivia, South America :
 Tacopaya (-1900s)
Züllichau see Sulechów
Zülz see Biała
Zung see Vakhan
Zvanka see Volkhov
Zvenigovo. Urban settlement,
 Mari Autonomous SSR,
 RSFSR : Zvenigovsky Zaton
 (-c. 1940)
Zvenigovsky Zaton see
 Zvenigovo
Zvolen. Town, southeastern
 Czechoslovakia : Altsohl
 (-1918, 1939-45), Germany
Zvyagi see Roshchino (3)
Zwischenwässern see Medvode
Zwittau see Svitavy

Appendix 1

OFFICIAL NAMES OF COUNTRIES[1]
(as of 1 November 1978)

Afghanistan	Democratic Republic of Afghanistan
Albania	Socialist People's Republic of Albania
Algeria	Democratic and Popular Republic of Algeria
Angola	People's Republic of Angola
Argentina	Argentine Republic
Australia	Commonwealth of Australia
Bahamas, The	Commonwealth of the Bahamas
Bahrain	State of Bahrain
Bangladesh	People's Republic of Bangladesh
Barbados	Barbados
Belgium	Kingdom of Belgium
Belize	Colony of Belize
Benin	People's Republic of Benin
Bhutan	Kingdom of Bhutan
Bolivia	Republic of Bolivia
Botswana	Republic of Botswana
Brazil	Federative Republic of Brazil
Britain	see United Kingdom
Brunei	State of Brunei
Bulgaria	People's Republic of Bulgaria
Burma	Socialist Republic of the Union of Burma
Burundi	Republic of Burundi

---

[1]No dependent states are given except Namibia (South West Africa), Belize, Brunei, Puerto Rico, and the constituents of the United Kingdom.

Cambodia	see Kampuchea
Cameroon	United Republic of Cameroon
Canada	Canada
Cape Verde Islands	Republic of Cape Verde
Central African Empire	Central African Empire
Chad	Republic of Chad
Chile	Republic of Chile
China	People's Republic of China
Colombia	Republic of Colombia
Congo, The	People's Republic of the Congo
Costa Rica	Republic of Costa Rica
Cuba	Republic of Cuba
Cyprus	Republic of Cyprus
Czechoslovakia	Czechoslovak Socialist Republic
Denmark	Kingdom of Denmark
Djibouti	Republic of Djibouti
Dominican Republic	Dominican Republic
East Germany	German Democratic Republic
Ecuador	Republic of Ecuador
Egypt	Arab Republic of Egypt
El Salvador	Republic of El Salvador
England	see United Kingdom
Equatorial Guinea	Republic of Equatorial Guinea
Ethiopia	Ethiopia
Fiji	Fiji
Finland	Republic of Finland
France	French Republic
Gabon	Gabon Republic
Gambia, The	Republic of the Gambia
Ghana	Republic of Ghana
Great Britain	see United Kingdom
Greece	Greek Republic
Grenada	State of Grenada
Guatemala	Republic of Guatemala
Guinea	Republic of Guinea

Guinea-Bissau	Republic of Guinea-Bissau
Guyana	Co-operative Republic of Guyana
Haïti	Republic of Haïti
Holland	see Netherlands, The
Honduras	Republic of Honduras
Hungary	Hungarian People's Republic
Iceland	Republic of Iceland
India	Republic of India
Indonesia	Republic of Indonesia
Iran	Iran
Iraq	Republic of Iraq
Ireland	Republic of Ireland (Irish Republic)
Ireland, Northern	see United Kingdom
Israel	State of Israel
Italy	Italian Republic
Ivory Coast	Republic of Ivory Coast
Jamaica	Jamaica
Japan	Japan
Jordan	Hashemite Kingdom of Jordan
Kampuchea	Democratic Kampuchea
Kenya	Republic of Kenya
Kuwait	State of Kuwait
Laos	People's Democratic Republic of Laos
Lebanon	Republic of Lebanon
Lesotho	Kingdom of Lesotho
Liberia	Republic of Liberia
Libya	Socialist People's Libyan Arab Jamahirrya
Luxembourg	Grand Duchy of Luxembourg
Malawi	Republic of Malawi
Malaysia	Federation of Malaysia
Maldives	Republic of Maldives
Mali	Republic of Mali
Malta	Republic of Malta
Mauritania	Islamic Republic of Mauritania

Mauritius	Mauritius
Mexico	United Mexican States
Monaco	Principality of Monaco
Mongolia	Mongolian People's Republic
Morocco	Kingdom of Morocco
Mozambique	People's Republic of Mozambique
Namibia	see South West Africa
Nepal	Kingdom of Nepal
Netherlands, The	Kingdom of the Netherlands
New Zealand	New Zealand
Nicaragua	Republic of Nicaragua
Niger	Republic of Niger
Nigeria	Republic of Nigeria
North Korea	Democratic People's Republic of Korea
Norway	Kingdom of Norway
Oman	Sultanate of Oman
Pakistan	Islamic Republic of Pakistan
Panama	Republic of Panama
Papua New Guinea	Papua New Guinea
Paraguay	Republic of Paraguay
Peru	Republic of Peru
Philippines, The	Republic of the Philippines
Poland	Polish People's Republic
Portugal	Portuguese Republic
Puerto Rico	Commonwealth of Puerto Rico
Qatar	State of Qatar
Rhodesia	Republic of Rhodesia
Romania	Socialist Republic of Romania
Rwanda	Republic of Rwanda
San Marino	Republic of San Marino
São Tomé and Príncipe	Democratic Republic of São Tomé and Príncipe
Saudi Arabia	Kingdom of Saudi Arabia
Scotland	see United Kingdom
Senegal	Republic of Senegal

Seychelles	Republic of Seychelles
Sierra Leone	Republic of Sierra Leone
Singapore	Republic of Singapore
Somalia	Somali Democratic Republic
South Africa	Republic of South Africa
South Korea	Republic of South Korea
South West Africa	South West Africa (Namibia)[1]
Soviet Union	Union of Soviet Socialist Republics
Spain	Spain
Sri Lanka	Democratic Socialist Republic of Sri Lanka
Sudan, The	Democratic Republic of the Sudan
Surinam	Republic of Surinam
Swaziland	Kingdom of Swaziland
Sweden	Kingdom of Sweden
Switzerland	Swiss Confederation
Syria	Syrian Arab Republic
Taiwan	Republic of China
Tanzania	United Republic of Tanzania
Thailand	Kingdom of Thailand
Tibet	Tibetan Autonomous Region[2]
Togo	Republic of Togo
Tonga	Kingdom of Tonga
Transkei	Republic of Transkei
Trinidad and Tobago	Republic of Trinidad and Tobago
Tunisia	Republic of Tunisia
Turkey	Republic of Turkey
Uganda	Republic of Uganda
United Arab Emirates	United Arab Emirates
United Kingdom	United Kingdom of Great Britain and Northern Ireland

---

[1]United Nations designated name is Namibia, a name not recognized by South Africa, whose presence in the country was declared illegal by the International Court of Justice in June 1971. On 18 August 1976 it was announced that Namibia would become independent from South Africa on 31 December 1978.

[2]Part of the People's Republic of China

United States	United States of America
Upper Volta	Republic of Upper Volta
Uruguay	Oriental [Eastern] Republic of Uruguay
Vatican, The	Vatican City State
Venezuela	Republic of Venezuela
Vietnam	Socialist Republic of Vietnam
Wales	see United Kingdom
Western Samoa	Independent State of Western Samoa
West Germany	Federal Republic of Germany
Yemen (Aden)	People's Democratic Republic of Yemen
Yemen Arab Republic	Yemen Arab Republic
Yugoslavia	Socialist Federal Republic of Yugoslavia
Zaïre	Republic of Zaïre
Zambia	Republic of Zambia

ADMINISTRATIVE AND TERRITORIAL
DIVISIONS OF THE USSR

There are five different kinds of administrative regions in the USSR that are of sufficient size or importance to be used as territorial units for the purposes of locating places in the Gazetteer. In descending order they are the autonomous soviet socialist republic (ASSR), the autonomous oblast (AOb), the autonomous okrug (AOk), the kray and the oblast. (Until 1977 the ten autonomous okrugs were designated national okrugs.)

The number and area of these regions has varied several times since the 1917 Revolution, but at present (November 1978) the distribution over the 15 soviet socialist republics may be presented in tabular form as follows:

	ASSRs	AObs	AOks	Krays	Oblasts
RSFSR	16	5	10	6	49
Armenian SSR	-	-	-	-	-
Azerbaijan SSR	1	1	-	-	-
Belorussian SSR	-	-	-	-	6
Estonian SSR	-	-	-	-	-
Georgian SSR	2	1	-	-	2
Kazakh SSR	-	-	-	-	19
Kirgiz SSR	-	-	-	-	3
Latvian SSR	-	-	-	-	-
Lithuanian SSR	-	-	-	-	-
Moldavian SSR	-	-	-	-	-
Tadzhik SSR	-	1	-	-	3
Turkmen SSR	-	-	-	-	5
Ukrainian SSR	-	-	-	-	25
Uzbek SSR	1	-	-	-	11
USSR	20	8	10	6	117

From this table it will be seen that five republics contain

none of the five major regions.   For this reason places in these
five republics will not be given a precise location in the Gazetteer.
It will also be seen that all the autonomous okrugs and krays are
in the largest republic of all, the RSFSR.

The distribution of the five major regions over the territory
of the USSR is as follows:

RUSSIAN SOVIET FEDERATED SOCIALIST REPUBLIC (RSFSR)
(The five autonomous oblasts [AObs] and ten autonomous okrugs
[AOks] are located within the territory of individual krays and
oblasts.)

ASSRs: Bashkir, Buryat, Checheno-Ingush, Chuvash, Dagestan,
Kabardino-Balkarian, Kalmyk, Karelian, Komi, Mari, Mordovian,
North Ossetian, Tatar, Tuva, Udmurt, and Yakutsk.

Krays: Altay (containing Gorno-Altay AOb), Khabarovsk
(containing Jewish AOb), Krasnodar (containing Adygey AOb),
Krasnoyarsk (containing Khakass AOb and Taymyr and Evenki AOks),
Primorsky, and Stavropol (containing Karachayevo-Cherkess AOb).

Oblasts: Amur, Arkhangelsk (containing Nenets AOk), Astrak-
han, Belgorod, Bryansk, Chelyabinsk, Chita (containing Aginsk-
Buryat AOk), Gorky, Irkutsk (containing Ust-Ordinsky Buryat AOk),
Ivanovo, Kalinin, Kaliningrad, Kaluga, Kamchatka (containing Koryak
AOk), Kenerovo, Kirov, Kostroma, Kurgan, Kursk, Kuybyshev,
Leningrad, Lipetsk, Magadan (containing Chukot AOk), Moscow,
Murmansk, Novgorod, Novosibirsk, Omsk, Orenburg, Orlov, Penza,
Perm (containing Komi-Permyak AOk), Pskov, Rostov, Ryazan,
Sakhalin, Saratov, Smolensk, Sverdlovsk, Tambov, Tomsk, Tula,
Tyumen (containing Khanty-Mansi and Yamalo-Nenets AOks), Ulya-
novsk, Vladimir, Volgograd, Vologda, Voronezh, and Yaroslavl.

AZERBAIJAN SOVIET SOCIALIST REPUBLIC

The republic comprises the Nakhichevan ASSR, the Nagorno-
Karabakh AOb and territory outside these regions.

BELORUSSIAN SOVIET SOCIALIST REPUBLIC

The republic comprises the six oblasts Brest, Gomel, Grodno,
Minsk, Mogilyov, and Vitebsk.

GEORGIAN SOVIET SOCIALIST REPUBLIC

The republic comprises the Abkhazian and Adzhar ASSRs, the
South Ossetian AOb, and territory located outside these regions.

KAZAKH SOVIET SOCIALIST REPUBLIC

The republic comprises the 19 oblasts Aktyubinsk, Alma-Ata,
Chimkent, Dzhambul, Dzhezkazgan, East Kazakhstan, Guryev, Karaganda, Kokchetav, Kustanay, Kzyl-Orda, Mangyshlak, North Kazakhstan, Pavlodar, Semipalatinsk, Taldy-Kurgan, Tselinograd, Turgay,
and Uralsk.

KIRGIZ SOVIET SOCIALIST REPUBLIC

The republic comprises the three oblasts Issyk-Kul, Naryn, and Osh, and territory located outside these regions.

TADZHIK SOVIET SOCIALIST REPUBLIC

The republic comprises the Gorno-Badakhshan AOb, the three oblasts Kulyab, Kurgan-Tyube, and Leninabad, and territory located outside these regions.

TURKMEN SOVIET SOCIALIST REPUBLIC

The republic comprises the five oblasts Ashkhabad, Chardzhou, Krasnovodsk, Mary, and Tashauz.

UKRAINIAN SOVIET SOCIALIST REPUBLIC

The republic comprises the 25 oblasts Cherkassy, Chernigov, Chernovtsy, Crimean, Dnepropetrovsk, Donetsk, Ivano-Frankovsk, Kharkov, Kherson, Khmelnitsky, Kiev, Kirovograd, Lvov, Nikolayev, Odessa, Poltava, Rovno, Sumy, Ternopol, Transcarpathian, Vinnitsa, Volyn, Voroshilovgrad, Zaporozhye, and Zhitomir.

UZBEK SOVIET SOCIALIST REPUBLIC

The republic comprises the Karakalpak ASSR and the 11 oblasts Andizhan, Bukhara, Dzhizak, Fergana, Kashka-Darya, Khorezm, Namangan, Samarkand, Surkhandarya, Syrdarya, and Tashkent.

Appendix 3

TRANSLITERATION OF RUSSIAN NAMES

Apart from conventional spellings of a very few well-known places--Kiev, not "Kiyev"; Azerbaijan, not "Azerbaydzhan"--Russian names in the Gazetteer are transliterated according to the following system:

Russian	English	Russian	English
а	a	р	r
б	b	с	s
в	v	т	t
г	g	у	u
д	d	ф	f
е	e[1]	х	kh
ё	yo	ц	ts
ж	zh	ч	ch
з	z	ш	sh
и	i	щ	shch
й	y[2]	ъ	(none)[3]
к	k	ы	y
л	l	ь	(none)[3]
м	m	э	e
н	n	ю	yu
о	o	я	ya
п	p		

[1]Transliterated "ye" after a vowel or soft sign (ь), e. g. Andreyev not "Andreev"; Kabanye, not "Kabane." (In some systems the soft sign is represented by an apostrophe: "Kaban'ye.")

[2]English letter "y" is used to transliterate the Russian adjectival endings -ый and -ий, which in other systems are sometimes rendered respectively "-yy" and "-iy."

[3]In Russian, these characters do not represent sounds, but serve to indicate value of letters to which they are adjoined. They are, respectively, the soft sign and hard sign.

BIBLIOGRAPHY

Administrativní lexicon obcí republiky Československé (Administrative register of communes of the Czechoslovak republic). Prague, 1955.

Akrigg, G. P. V. , and Helen B. Akrigg. 1001 British Columbia Place Names, 3rd ed. Vancouver, 1973.

Armstrong, G. H. The Origin and Meaning of Place Names in Canada. Toronto, 1930.

Atlas SSSR (Atlas of the USSR), 2d ed. Moscow, 1969.

Bartholomew Gazetteer of Britain, Oliver Mason (comp.). Edinburgh, 1977.

Bolshaya Sovetskaya Entsiklopediya (Great Soviet Encyclopedia). 3d ed. Moscow, 1970- , vols. 1-29.

Cabral, Antonio. Dicionário de nomes geográficos de Moçambique: sua origem (Dictionary of geographical names of Mozambique: their origin). Lourenço Marques, 1975.

Columbia-Lippincott Gazetteer of the World. New York, 1952; with 1961 supplement.

Encyclopaedia Britannica, 15th ed. Chicago, 1974; with revisions, 1976.

Encyclopaedia of Southern Africa, Eric Rosenthal (comp.), 6th rev. ed. London, 1973.

Entsiklopedicheskiy slovar' geograficheskikh nazvaniy (Encyclopedic dictionary of geographical names), S. V. Kalesnik (chief ed.). Moscow, 1973.

Everyman's Encyclopaedia World Atlas, rev. ed. London, 1940.

Gazetteer of Official Standard Names approved by the United States Board on Geographic Names, Washington D. C. , 2d ed. 1970. (No. 42: USSR.)

Geographical Digest, Harold Fullard (ed.). London, 1971-78.

Gorvachevich, K. S. Russkiye geograficheskiye nazvaniya (Russian geographical names). Moscow, 1965.

"Guide to USAF bases at home and abroad," Airforce Magazine (Washington, D. C.), vol. 60, no. 5 (May 1977).

Kniga o Donbasse: priroda, lyudi, dela (Book about the Donbass: landscape, people, business). Donetsk, 1972.

Lexicon ton Dēmon, Koinotēton kai Oikismon tēs Hellados (Register of the boroughs, communities and settlements of Greece). Athens, 1974.

The Library Atlas, 11th ed. London, 1975.

McGraw-Hill Encyclopedia of Russia and the Soviet Union, Michael T. Florinsky (ed.). New York, 1962.

A Magyar Nepköztársaság Helységnévtáta (The place-names register of the Hungarian People's Republic). Budapest, 1973.

Malyy Atlas SSSR (Small Atlas of the USSR), L. N. Mesyatseva (ed.). Moscow 1972; with corrections, 1975.

Manych Jumsai, M. L. "Siam or Thailand, Which Is Right?," Sammaggi Sara (Bangkok), February 1970.

Moore, W. G. Penguin Encyclopedia of Places, 2d ed. London, 1978.

Muir's Historical Atlas, Medieval and Modern, R. F. Treharne and Harold Fullard (eds), 11th ed. London, 1969.

Nazvaniya SSSR, soyuznikh respublik i zarubezhnykh stran na 20 yazykakh (Names of the USSR, union republics and foreign countries in 20 languages), A. M. Kozlov, L. S. Kuznetsova, G. M. Gaydukova, Ye. N. Pokidova (comps), Moscow 1974.

Nienaber, P. J. Suid-Afrikaanse Pleknaamwoordeboek (Dictionary of South African place names), 2d rev. ed. Capetown, 1972.

Nikonov, V. A. Kratkiy toponimichesky slovar' (Concise toponymical dictionary). Moscow, 1966.

Peterson, Charles B. "The Nature of Soviet Place-Names," Names: Journal of the American Name Society, vol. 25, no. 1 (March 1977).

Philips' Concorde World Atlas, Harold Fullard (ed.). London, 1972.

Philips' Record Atlas, Harold Fullard (ed.), 26th rev. ed.   London, 1965.

Post Office Guide, London 1972-77.

Pudnyckyj, J. B.   Manitoba Mosaic of Place Names.   Winnipeg, 1970.

Reed, A. W.   Place Names of Australia.   Sydney, 1973.

Room, Adrian.   Place Names of the World.   Newton Abbot, England, 1974.

Slovar' geograficheskikh nazvaniy SSSR (Dictionary of geographical names of the USSR), M. B. Volostnova (ed.).   Moscow, 1968.

Sovremennaya karta zarubezhnogo mira (Contemporary map of the foreign world), A. G. Shiger (comp.).   Moscow, 1971.

Spaull, Hebe.   New Place Names of the World.   London, 1970.

Statesman's Year Book, J. Paxton (ed.).   London, 1977-78.

Stewart, George R.   American Place-Names.   New York, 1970.

Stieler's Atlas of Modern Geography, H. Haack (ed.), 10th ed.   Gotha, 1930.

Thakore, M. P.   "Changes in Place-Names in India," The Indian Geographer, vol. 1, no. 1 (August 1956).

The Times Atlas of the World, H. A. C. Lewis (ed.).   London, 1972.

Vedemosti Verkhovnogo Soveta SSSR (Journal of the Supreme Soviet of the USSR), Moscow, 1973-78.

Webster's New Geographical Dictionary.   Springfield, Mass., 1972.

Where's Where: A Descriptive Gazetteer.   London, 1974.

Whitaker's Almanack.   London, 1970-78.

Wise's New Zealand Guide: A Gazetteer of New Zealand, 5th ed.   Auckland, 1972.

Yerofeyev, I. A.   Imya Lenina na karte rodiny [The name of Lenin on the map of the motherland].   Moscow, 1977.

Zhuchkevich, V. A.   Kratkiy toponimicheskiy slovar' Belorussii (Concise toponymical dictionary of Belorussia).   Minsk, 1974.

Also consulted, especially for their maps, were the following Special
Reports published by The Times of London (on date given): ASEAN
(2 Aug. 77), Bahrain (16 Dec. 76, 16 Dec. 77), Botswana (21 Sept.
76), Ghana (12 Jan. 74), Hongkong (29 Sept. 76), Ivory Coast (25
March 77), Kenya (14 Dec. 76), Lesotho (27 Nov. 76), Malaysia
(31 Aug. 77), Mauritius (8 March 78), Nigeria (22 July 76, 1 Dec.
77), South Korea (4 Feb. 77, 7 Sept. 77), Sudan (26 Feb. 77),
Swaziland (14 Oct. 76), Uganda [not a Special Report but an adver-
tiser's announcement] (14 Sept. 73), Yugoslavia (23 March 77),
Zaïre (11 Dec. 73)